DirectX 7 Interfaces

INTERFACE	REQUIRED HEADER	REQUIRED LIBRARY	METHOD
IDirectDraw7	ddraw.h	ddraw.lib	DirectDrawCreateEX
IDirectDrawSurface7	"	"	IDirectDraw7::CreateSurface
IDirectDrawClipper	"	"	IDirectDraw7::CreateClipper
IDirectDrawPalette	"	"	IDirectDraw7::CreatePalette
IDirectDrawColorControl	"	"	IDirectDrawSurface7:: QueryInterface
IDirectDrawGamaControl	"	"	IDirectDrawSurface7:: QueryInterface
IDirectDrawVideoPort	dvp.h	ddraw.lib	CreateVideoPort
IDirectDrawVideoPort Container	"	"	IDirectDraw7::QueryInterface
IDirect3D7	d3d.h	d3dim.lib	IDirectDraw7::QueryInterface
IDirect3DDevice7	"	"	IDirect3D7::CreateDevice
IDirectVertexBuffer7	"	"	IDirect3D7::CreateVertexBuffer
IDirectSound	dsound.h	dsound.lib	DirectSoundCreate
IDirectSoundBuffer	"	"	IDirectSound::CreateSoundBuffer
IDirectSound3DBuffer	"	"	IDirectSoundBuffer:: QueryInterface
IDirectSound3DListener	"	"	IDirectSoundBuffer:: QueryInterface
IDirectSoundCapture	"	"	DirectSoundCaptureCreate
IDirectSoundCaptureBuffer	"	"	IDirectSoundCapture:: CreateCaptureBuffer
IDirectSoundNotify	"	"	IDirectSoundBuffer:: QueryInterface
IDirectInput7	dinput.h	dinput.lib	CreateDirectInputEx
IDirectInputDevice7	"	"	IDirectInput7::CreateDeviceEx
IDirectInputEffect	"	"	IDirectInputDevice7::CreateEffect
IDirectPlay4	dplay.h	dplay.h	CoCreateInstance
IDirectPlayLobby3	dplay.h	dplay.h	CoCreateInstance

Teach Yourself DirectX 7 in 24 Hours

Direct Animation

Initializing DirectAnimation

DirectAnimation library file: danim.dll

DirectAnimation Control

CLSID: {B6FFC24C-7E13-11D0-9B47-00C04FC2F51D}

ProgID: DirectAnimation.DirectAnimationIntegratedMediaControl.1

DirectAnimation Windowed Control

CLSID:{69AD90EF-1C20-11D1-8801-00C04FC29D46}

ProgID:
DirectAnimation.DirectAnimationWindowedIntegratedMediaControl.1

Basic DirectAnimation Programming Process

1. Create DirectAnimation control.
2. Obtain IDAViewerControl interface.
3. Obtain IDAStatics interface.
4. Use IDAStatics to create and initialize DABehavior objects.
5. Assign the Image and Sound properties of the IDAViewerControl interface.
6. Call IDAViewerControl->Start() to start the model running.

Default DirectAnimation Units

Distance/Size = meters

Angles = radians (degrees = 180/PI * radians)

Origin: Center of control

DirectX Media Web Site

http://www.microsoft.com/DirectX/dxm/

Robert Dunlop
with Dale Shepherd,
Mark Martin, et al

SAMS
Teach Yourself

DirectX® 7

in **24** Hours

SAMS

A Division of Macmillan USA
201 West 103rd St., Indianapolis, Indiana, 46290

Sams Teach Yourself DirectX® 7 in 24 Hours

Copyright © 2000 by Sams Publishing

International Standard Book Number: 0-672-31634-x

Library of Congress Catalog Card Number: 98-83220

Printed in the United States of America

First Printing: December, 1999

01 00 99   4 3 2 1

Trademarks

Warning and Disclaimer

ASSOCIATE PUBLISHER
Bradley Jones

ACQUISITIONS EDITOR
Chris Webb

DEVELOPMENT EDITOR
Matt Purcell

MANAGING EDITOR
Lisa Wilson

PROJECT EDITOR
Tonya Simpson

COPY EDITOR
Rhonda Tinch-Mize

INDEXER
Eric Schroeder

PROOFREADER
Jill Mazurczyk

TECHNICAL EDITOR
Dale Shepherd

TEAM COORDINATOR
Meggo Barthlow

MEDIA DEVELOPER
Dan Scherf

INTERIOR DESIGNER
Gary Adair

COVER DESIGNER
Aren Howell

COPY WRITER
Eric Borgert

PRODUCTION
Brad Lenser

Contents at a Glance

Contents

About the Authors

Robert Dunlop is Microsoft's first and only MVP (Most Valuable Professional) for DirectX in recognition of his assistance to the game developer community. Robert is a veteran game developer with more than 10 years of programming experience, and a principal of Monarch Interactive, Inc. (www.monarch-interactive.com), a company devoted to creating new entertainment titles for the PC. Robert works very closely with the DirectX team at Microsoft and has been on the DirectX Beta Team since 1994.

Mark Martin is a technical analyst for a business service–oriented company, where he works with a variety of systems and languages specializing in network programming and distributed computing systems. Additionally, he is a partner in an upstart gaming company, where he is completing a large multiplayer game using DirectX, playable over the Internet.

Michael Morrison is a writer, developer, toy inventor, and author of a variety of books, including *Sams Teach Yourself Internet Game Programming with Java in 21 Days* and *Windows 95 Game Developer's Guide*. Michael is the creative lead at Gas Hound Games, a toy company located on the Web at http://www.gashound.com.

Sam Christiansen is a tools and technology programmer at Human Code, an Austin-based video game company, where he has contributed to several commercial games. In addition, Sam performs research for the University of Texas Center for Computer Visualization.

Odin Jensen is a game programmer for Denmark's largest game developer, where he works on popular 3D game titles for the Sony Playstation. He provides DirectX wrappers for beginning game developers at www.nukesoftware.dk.

Josh Martin is a software developer/technical consultant for a custom software firm in Palatine, Illinois. While his workdays are spent developing business applications, he spends many hours after work developing multiplayer games for a new gaming company.

Brian Noyes is a software consultant, developer, and technical writer with DomeWorks Software (http://domeworks.com). A Microsoft Certified Professional, he has developed Windows modeling and simulation applications and multimedia utilities for government and commercial projects.

Kenn Scribner's multimedia experience began in writing flight simulators for the United States Air Force using OpenGL. Kenn began to explore alternatives to OpenGL with the advent of DirectDraw and has continued to use both technologies in his component development.

Recognition from the Publisher

Sams Publishing would like to give a special thanks to **Dale Shepherd**. His timely and accurate assistance on this project helped ensure its completion with true coverage of Microsoft's newest version of Microsoft's DirectX—DirectX 7. By helping on this project, Dale has created this, the best book available, for the new user of DirectX 7.

Tell Us What You Think!

As the reader of this book, *you* are our most important critic and commentator. We value your opinion and want to know what we're doing right, what we could do better, what areas you'd like to see us publish in, and any other words of wisdom you're willing to pass our way.

As an Associate Publisher for Sams, I welcome your comments. You can fax, email, or write me directly to let me know what you did or didn't like about this book—as well as what we can do to make our books stronger.

Please note that I cannot help you with technical problems related to the topic of this book, and that due to the high volume of mail I receive, I might not be able to reply to every message.

When you write, please be sure to include this book's title and author as well as your name and phone or fax number. I will carefully review your comments and share them with the author and editors who worked on the book.

Fax: 317-581-4770

Email: adv_prog@mcp.com

Mail: Associate Publisher
            Sams Publishing
            201 West 103rd Street
            Indianapolis, IN 46290 USA

Introduction

What an exciting time to be involved in game design and multimedia driven application development! Computer hardware continues to evolve and increase in speed in shorter and shorter cycles. And no segment of computer hardware has seen more growth in recent years than the video card market.

Of course, there's more to multimedia than video. There's sound, user input, and music to produce. The Web has created wonderful opportunities to present video and animations.

Of course, our jobs as multimedia application developers haven't gotten easier. With all this new technology comes complexity and learning. And with this new technology, the tools available to us to use it effectively also evolve. Microsoft's DirectX platform has grown up quite nicely for us.

Many tools and SDKS are in the market to handle the myriad of different aspects involved in developing multimedia applications. None are as robust and well rounded as DirectX. With DirectX, you get a very complete set of APIs to use to write next generation apps and games—rich with multimedia. There's the Direct3D portion for creating the (now standard) 3D world for users. DirectMusic and DirectSound cover all your musical requirements. DirectInput takes care of any user-input requirements. For multiplayer capability, we've got the easy-to-use DirectPlay portion.

There are of course many parts to DirectX. And not many books have covered all of them together, or presented them in an easy-to-use fashion. That's why you're reading this book. For the first time, you'll be introduced to the whole of DirectX 7 in a practical way. We've covered version 7 from top to bottom. And we've presented real-world samples to give you hands on experience in using DirectX effectively.

You should come away from reading this book with a working knowledge of DirectX 7, in all of its aspects. And DirectX is a large topic, to be sure. Microsoft has bundled a lot of functionality in their latest release, and they've made it easier than ever for you, as programmer and designer, to use it.

So sit back, grab a can of pop, and enjoy our fun and fast ride. We've got a lot of ground to cover, and only 24 hours to cover it in. You'll enjoy every minute of it, as we've enjoyed writing it. You're well on your way to writing the next blockbuster fully immersive and multiplayer 3D game. And we're exited to see what will be new in DirectX 8.

PART I

Introduction to DirectX

Hour

HOUR 1

About DirectX—The Pieces That Make It Happen

This hour will prepare you for the first steps in learning to program with DirectX by providing a general overview of DirectX and what you will need to begin programming in DirectX.

In this hour, you will

- Learn just what DirectX is
- Learn the components of DirectX
- Learn how to use DirectX
- Be introduced to COM

What Is DirectX?

DirectX is a multimedia development library, created by Microsoft and provided for royalty-free use in the creation of entertainment titles and other Windows-based applications.

Because Microsoft Windows is the predominant operating system on home computers, a huge market exists for entertainment products supporting the Windows operating system. However, although most PCs might share a common operating system, the success of the PC has led to a vast proliferation of available hardware. A multitude of vendors offer products with varying capabilities, and they often lack a reliable standard that we can develop against.

So, how to make the most of our products, while providing support for all popular hardware devices? DirectX tries to bridge the gap by providing a standard software interface, making these issues transparent to the developer in most cases. You aren't fully relieved of the need to test your product with a wide range of hardware, but in many cases, DirectX meets the need.

All major hardware vendors currently supply device drivers for DirectX, which should provide a high-performance interface to their hardware. You also can be confident the drivers you install to support your product are compatible with new hardware in the future.

DirectX Components

The DirectX SDK is comprised of a wide array of components, allowing you to select only the functionality you need for your application. This includes interfaces that will cover all your needs for creating multimedia and entertainment titles. DirectX is actually contained in two separate packages: the DirectX SDK and the DirectX Media SDK. The following two sections are overviews of the interfaces offered in these packages.

The DirectX SDK

The DirectX SDK contains the classes that are the foundation of DirectX. These will provide for the majority of multimedia development requirements.

The following interfaces are included within the DirectX SDK:

- DirectDraw—Provides efficient access to the video memory, resulting in smooth animation for game titles.
- Direct3D Immediate Mode—Provides high-performance rendering of 3D scenes, utilizing the latest in 3D accelerators.
- DirectSound—Provides audio playback and mixing, including 3D sound effects.
- DirectMusic—Provides interactive music capabilities, allowing for soundtracks that change with the game action.

1

- DirectInput—Allows input from keyboard, mouse, and game devices. Includes support for the latest force feedback devices.
- DirectPlay—Provides communications for multiplayer games over the Internet or local area network (LAN), or through a direct connection via modem or serial cable.

The DirectX Media SDK

The DirectX Media SDK provides multimedia extensions to supplement the foundation classes of the DirectX SDK, including:

- DirectX Transform—Transforms allow your application to create dynamic 2D and 3D graphics effects, such as alpha blending and surface distortions. The heart of the new Microsoft Chromeffects, DirectX Transform has numerous applications including Web content, entertainment software, and even creating filters for Adobe PhotoShop.
- DirectAnimation—DirectAnimation provides the means to embed DirectX applications into HTML pages, allowing for 3D presentation and gaming opportunities on the Web or intranet.
- DirectShow—DirectShow completes the package, adding video capabilities to DirectX. Features include streaming video playback for Internet-based video, as well as support for today's DVD players.
- Direct3D Retained Mode—Retained Mode provides an easier route to access 3D hardware by providing interfaces that handle creation and rendering of the scene.

Preparing to Use DirectX

The examples in this book were written for Microsoft Visual C++ 5.0 or above. Although it is recommended that you use Visual C++ to get the most from this book, it is possible to compile DirectX applications in other compilers and other languages.

Before you can start programming in DirectX, you will need to make modifications to your development environment. This will allow the compiler to properly locate and use the components of DirectX when building your application.

Three areas where you will need to configure your application to compile under DirectX are

- Setting your compiler to find the DirectX files. This will need to be done only once.
- Linking libraries into the application through the project settings. This will have to be applied to each application you build with DirectX.

• Including header files for the DirectX libraries. This will have to be done for each source code file that will access DirectX components.

Preparing the Compiler

To prepare Visual C++ for DirectX, you will need to set the directory paths for the Library and Include files that are provided with the SDK. First, bring up Visual Studio and open the Tools menu. Click on Options and select the Directories tab in the resulting dialog box, as shown in Figure 1.1.

FIGURE 1.1

Setting the path for SDK header files.

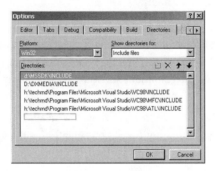

Through this dialog box, you can set what directories Visual C++ will search through when trying to find files specified in a project. The search directories are categorized into file types, which can be selected under the Show Directories For selection.

The first thing you will add is the Include files. Click the arrow below and to the right of Show Directories For, and a list will open, showing the file categories you can select. Click Include Files, and the existing directory list will appear.

To add the directories from the SDK, locate the directory under which you installed the DirectX SDK. A typical installation to drive C: will have a structure similar to this:

```
C:\
    C:\MSSDK
        C:\MSSDK\BIN
        C:\MSSDK\DOC
        C:\MSSDK\INCLUDE
        C:\MSSDK\LIB
        C:\MSSDK\SAMPLES
```

When you have made sure of the SDK location, double-click the first empty line in the directory list in Visual Studio and type the location of the Include directory under the SDK. For example, if DirectX was installed in C:\MSSDK\, as previously shown, you would enter C:\MSSDK\INCLUDE. You can also click the button to the right of the line marked ... to browse for the include directory.

When you have entered the Include directory, you will need to drag this directory to the top of the file list. This causes Visual Studio to look in this directory first, which is important because the existing Visual Studio directories will contain files for older versions of DirectX that ship with the compiler.

When you have finished adding the Include directory in the proper location, repeat this process for the Lib directory of the SDK, as shown in Figure 1.2. This folder must be listed under the Library Files category of the directory list.

FIGURE 1.2

Setting the path for SDK Library files.

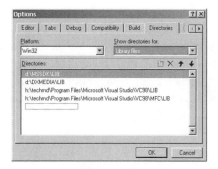

Including the SDK in Your Projects

Your compiler is now configured to use DirectX files. You will not need to repeat this process unless you re-install your compiler, move to another machine, or move the SDK directory.

Each project you write will have to be connected to libraries and header files in the DirectX SDK that provide the features of DirectX you want to use. These files are specific to each module of DirectX, and they will be covered in future chapters as you introduce them into your project.

A Brief Introduction to COM

Before you begin working with DirectX, you must first come to an understanding of the underlying technology that is used to interface with DirectX: the Component Object Model, or COM.

NEW TERM The *Component Object Model* is a widely supported specification for providing language-independent, reusable programming interfaces.

The COM definition provides for *interfaces* that are language independent, allowing COM-based libraries to be used in a variety of programming environments. COM objects are written to support an interface, and as such, are language independent. A COM object might be accessed using languages that do not recognize implementations by other languages, such as C accessing a C++ class. COM does this by providing an array of pointers to the methods the interface exports. This array borrows its name from the similar C++ implementation, and is known as the *vtable*.

One reason COM hides the implementation details behind an interface is because the objects become reusable and are easily versionable. If you write a DLL in C++, for example, the C++ proprietary *name-mangling algorithm* causes the DLL to be unusable to anyone but a client written with the same C++ compiler. Visual Basic users can't use it, nor can Java clients. Another sticky problem with plain DLLs is that versioning DLLs is problematic. If you, the developer, change and subsequently redeploy the DLL, you must be absolutely sure none of the DLL ordinals change. If they do, any client that statically links to your DLL will likely break (crash horribly). But interfaces never change—that is the definition of an interface. So clients of your COM object need not concern themselves about new and improved COM objects as long as the COM object supports the particular interface of interest.

New Term   All COM objects begin life with a universal interface, IUnknown. You'll learn more about IUnknown later in the chapter, but essentially IUnknown provides two important mechanisms—object *reference counting* and *interface determination*. The reference counting is important because the COM runtime will unload a COM object not currently being used (this conserves system resources). As you use the object, you increment a counter. As you finish with the object, you decrement the counter. When the counter reaches zero, COM will clean things up for you. Interface determination is important because COM objects that implement only IUnknown aren't very useful. However, IUnknown does enable you to ask the COM object if it supports a particular interface. If it does, the COM object will provide a pointer to that interface. If it doesn't, you'll receive a NULL pointer (and an error return code) instead. I'll now go into a bit more detail—this is important stuff!

Reusable Interfaces and Backward Compatibility

One of the peculiarities of the COM definition is that it does not allow for modification of existing interfaces. This means that when a new version of DirectX is released, the existing interfaces cannot be modified. Instead, new interfaces must be created to allow for additional functionality.

Although this leads to a proliferation of interfaces that provide the same functionality, it provides seamlessly for backward compatibility. For example, if you had written an

1

application that uses the basic IDirectDraw interface under DirectX 3, you can rest assured that if the DirectX developers did their work correctly, the same code will operate under DirectX 7.

The reason for this is that the `IDirectDraw` interface provided by DirectX 7 is the same as that provided under earlier revisions. To use the newer features provided by later versions, you must use newer interfaces, such as `IDirectDraw2` or `IDirectDraw7`.

This does not mean that you can disregard the earlier interfaces in new applications. When you initialize DirectDraw, for example, you will receive a pointer to the legacy `IDirectDraw` interface. This interface is then used to expose the newer interfaces that you might want to use, as will be seen in the following sections.

The `IUnknown` Base Class

All COM interfaces are based on the `IUnknown` interface. `IUnknown` acts much like an abstract base class in C++, providing a minimum set of functions that must be implemented and allowing for additional functions to be added by each interface.

Three functions are defined under the `IUnknown` definition:

Function	Description
QueryInterface	Used to attain pointers to interfaces that are derived through the current interface.
AddRef	Increments the reference count of the interface. See the upcoming section "Reference Counting in COM" for more information.
Release	Used to release an interface when it's no longer needed. Decrements the reference count and destroys the object if the reference count reaches zero.

Querying for Interfaces

DirectX provides functions that you will use to attain pointers to the most fundamental interfaces, such as `IDirectDraw`. Additional interfaces, including later iterations of an interface such as `IDirectDraw7`, can be attained by simply asking an existing interface for a pointer.

This is achieved using the `QueryInterface` method, which is defined under the base class `IUnknown`. To attain an interface pointer, a Globally Unique Identifier (GUID) for the desired interface is passed to `QueryInterface`.

NEW TERM   *A Globally Unique Identifier*, or GUID, is a unique value used to represent a
           COM interface. For example, if you wanted to attain a pointer to the
`IDirectDraw7` interface, having already attained a pointer to an `IDirectDraw` interface
stored in `lpDD`, you would call the `QueryInterface` function of the existing interface.
The function is passed the desired GUID and a pointer to be filled with a pointer to the
new interface, as shown in Listing 1.1.

LISTING 1.1   Querying for a New Interface

```
// query for IDirectDraw7 interface

LPDIRECTDRAW7 lpDD7;
HRESULT ddVal;

if (FAILED(ddVal=lpDD->QueryInterface(IID_IDirectDraw4,
                                      (void **) &lpDD7))) {
    // error retrieving interface, handle error code stored in ddVal
}
```

If successful, `QueryInterface` returns a value of `S_OK`. Otherwise, an interface-specific
error code will be returned. The `FAILED()` macro can be used to determine the success or
failure of any COM function. This macro, provided in Visual C++, returns `False` if the
return value is `S_OK` or `True` on an error.

Reference Counting in COM

Another interesting feature of COM is the capability for multiple elements of a program
to use an interface, without having to worry about the life and scope of the object. For
example, a worker thread might be passed a pointer to an existing interface and continue
to use it even after the main thread has released the object. In essence, this allows for
multiple owners of the same object.

This is achieved through a technique known as *reference counting*. When an interface is
initially created, it contains an internal count, called the reference counter, which is initialized to 1. This represents the number of pointers that reference the interface.

Each time a pointer to the object interface is provided through `QueryInterface()`, or
through a DirectX function that returns an interface pointer, the reference count is
increased by one. Each time the `Release()` function is called using a pointer to an interface, the reference count is reduced by one. The reference count is then tested, and if it
has reached 0, the object is destroyed.

The reference count can also be increased using the AddRef() function, defined in the IUnknown base class. This is useful if your program is going to maintain multiple copies of a pointer; for example, if a worker thread will maintain its own pointer to an interface.

> Be sure that every reference to an object has one (and only one) call to Release(), whether returned from a DirectX function, through QueryInterface(), or incremented by AddRef(). Experienced COM programmers typically set the pointer variable to NULL to preclude further use after the object is released.

Summary

In this hour, you got your first glimpse at DirectX. You took a look at the scope and capabilities of the DirectX SDK and the DirectX Media SDK. You learned how to set up the Microsoft Visual C++ compiler for use with the DirectX SDKs, as well as the basics of COM that will be required to access DirectX.

Q&A

Q How can DirectX enable me to develop software that will work properly with future hardware?

A When you work with DirectX, you never deal directly with the hardware devices. Instead, access to hardware is through a series of standardized software interfaces established in DirectX. Hardware vendors, in turn, develop drivers that allow DirectX to interface with their hardware and implement each of the interfaces required by DirectX. Although the actual hardware implementation might change, the software interface that the developer must use remains the same.

Q Will software written for the current version of DirectX need to be rewritten to work with future releases of DirectX?

A No. The underlying COM definition requires that future versions of DirectX must provide the same interfaces that are present now. In fact, for new functions to be added to DirectX, new interfaces must be provided. No changes can be made to the existing interfaces, guaranteeing that your software will be compatible with future revisions.

Workshop

The Workshop is designed to help you anticipate possible questions, review what you've learned, and begin thinking ahead to put your knowledge into practice. The answers to the quiz are in Appendix A, "Answers."

Quiz

1. What does the acronym COM stand for?
2. What macro can be used to test the result of `QueryInterface()`?
3. Which DirectX interface supports game controllers?
4. What is the base class from which all COM objects are constructed?

Exercises

There are no exercises for this hour.

PART II

Getting Started with DirectDraw

Hour

HOUR 2

Our First Step— DirectDraw in a Windows Application

In this hour, you will get your first taste of writing a DirectX program. But before you start coding, you will need to understand the structure behind DirectDraw.

In this hour, you will

- See how the video system works
- See the components of DirectDraw
- Learn the process of drawing on a surface
- Create your first DirectDraw application

Taking a Look at the Video System

When developing an application that uses the video screen, your task is essentially to control the flow of data between the CPU and the video adapter, which generates the image on the screen. Figure 2.1 shows the components involved in this process.

FIGURE 2.1

Components of the video system.

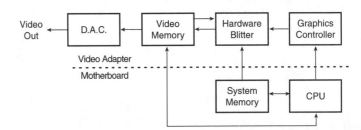

As you can see, two separate memory components exist in this model. The first, which is probably quite familiar to you, is the system memory. This is the memory that is linked to the CPU and used to store applications and data.

The second memory component is video memory. This is memory that resides on the display adapter and is used to store images for display. A region of this memory, known as the "frame buffer," contains the image that is currently being displayed.

The image you see onscreen is created by the DAC, or Digital to Analog Converter. This unit is responsible for converting the digital values stored in the frame buffer into a corresponding voltage, creating the analog signal that drives the monitor.

To get an image to the screen, an application's job is to transfer image data into the frame buffer, which will then be displayed on the monitor. Although this can be fairly straightforward, how the transfer is performed can greatly affect the performance of the product.

In particular, it is important to use the video hardware to its fullest extent. Although data can be transferred piece by piece by the CPU, many video adapters contain specialized hardware that can efficiently transfer blocks of data to the video memory, either from system memory or another location in video memory.

Fortunately, DirectDraw handles much of this issue for you, as you will see.

The Components of DirectDraw

DirectDraw is used for all access to the video screen. Whether you are using it directly for 2D graphics or are using one of the modules of Direct3D or DirectMedia, all access is actually achieved through DirectDraw. This being the case, it is important that you gain a good understanding of this interface from the start.

Five basic components, or interfaces, that make up DirectDraw are as follows:

- `IDirectDraw7` provides access to DirectDraw and allows creation of various other DirectDraw objects.

- `IDirectDrawClipper` maintains a list of clipping rectangles to control the display of DirectDraw applications that are constrained to a window.

- `IDirectDrawSurface7` objects represent a region of video or system memory into which an image can be drawn.

- `IDirectDrawPalette` objects are used to store an indexed array of colors and to establish the palette used for color translation when implementing 8-bit graphics modes.

- `IDirectDrawVideoPort` provides control of video adapters that have provisions for live video, such as TV tuner and video capture cards.

The `IDirectDraw7` Interface

All access to DirectDraw is achieved through the `IDirectDraw7` interface. Acquiring a pointer to this interface, then, is your first step in writing any DirectX Application that will use the video screen. Because your application does not initially have any interfaces from DirectX that you can query, you will use a helper function provided by the DirectDraw implementation:

The Syntax for `DirectDrawCreateEx`

```
HRESULT WINAPI DirectDrawCreateEx(
  GUID FAR *lpGUID,
  LPDIRECTDRAW7 FAR *lplpDD,
  REFIID iid,
  IUnknown FAR *pUnkOuter
);
```

The `DirectDrawCreateEx()` function is used to acquire a pointer to an `IDirectDraw7` interface. If this function is successful, `DD_OK` is returned.

Parameters:

lpGUID   Globally unique identifier (GUID) of a video display driver. Use NULL to indicate the default driver, or use one of the following values:

DDCREATE_EMULATIONONLY restricts the driver from using any hardware-accelerated features.

▼

DDCREATE_HARDWAREONLY restricts the driver from emu-
lating features that are not hardware accelerated.

lplpDD   Address of a variable that will receive a pointer to an
                                IDirectDraw7 interface.

iid   GUID specifying the type of interface to return. Must
                                be set to IID_IDIRECTDRAW7.

▲   pUnkOuter   Reserved for future use. Must be NULL.

When you have an interface to DirectDraw, you must establish in what role it will perform. For example, you might want to derive direct access to video in a windowed application, or you might want DirectDraw to take sole control of the video hardware,
allowing you to set the display resolutions as you want and use the entire screen surface.
To accomplish this, make a call to the SetCooperativeLevel() method, described in the
following.

The Syntax for IDirectDraw7::SetCooperativeLevel()

```
HRESULT SetCooperativeLevel(
  HWND hWnd,
  DWORD dwFlags
);
```

▼ **SYNTAX**

Sets the cooperative level for a DirectDraw object. Returns DD_OK if successful.

Parameters:

hWnd   Handle for the topmost window of the application.

dwFlags   Flags defining the cooperative level for DirectDraw.
                                Multiple flags might be bitwise ORed to define the
▲   cooperative level required.

A wide variety of behaviors can be defined through SetCooperativeLevel(). For your
purposes, you must be aware of a handful of them to get started:

DDSCL_NORMAL   The application will behave as a normal
                                         Windows application. Cannot be used
                                         with DDSCL_EXCLUSIVE or
                                         DDSCL_FULLSCREEN.

DDSCL_EXCLUSIVE   The application will have exclusive use
                                         of the video hardware. Must be used with
                                         DDSCL_FULLSCREEN.

DDSCL_FULLSCREEN	The application will use the full video screen rather than operate in a window. Must be used with DDSCL_EXCLUSIVE.
DDSCL_ALLOWREBOOT	Allows reboot using Ctrl+Alt+Delete to function while in full-screen mode. Without this flag, this key sequence is ignored.

DirectDraw Surfaces

NEW TERM To manipulate images in DirectDraw, you will create objects known as *surfaces*. A surface provides a rectangular region of memory that can be used for image storage. As you will see, DirectDraw surfaces can be used in a variety of forms, from bitmap storage to representation of the video screen.

The IDirectDrawSurface7 interface is used to define a surface. To create an IDirectDrawSurface7 interface, use the CreateSurface() method of the IDirectDraw7 interface.

The Syntax for IDirectDraw7::CreateSurface()

```
HRESULT CreateSurface(
  LPDDSURFACEDESC2 lpDDSurfaceDesc2,
  LPDIRECTDRAWSURFACE7 FAR *lplpDDSurface,
  IUnknown FAR *pUnkOuter
);
```

This function creates a DirectDraw surface. Returns DD_OK on success.

Parameters:

lpDDSurfaceDesc2	Pointer to a DDSURFACEDESC2 structure that contains a description of the surface to be created.
lplpDDSurface	Address of a variable that will receive a pointer to an IDirectDrawSurface7 interface.
pUnkOuter	Reserved for future use. Must be NULL.

> Be sure to clear all unused values in the DDSURFACEDESC2 structure and to initialize the dwSize member of this structure to sizeof(DDSURFACEDESC2). Failure to do so results in application errors and possible corruption of memory.

Surfaces in Differing Roles

DirectDraw surfaces appear in a great many roles. Ways in which surfaces will be used include the following:

- Offscreen surfaces are used to store images for later use.
- The primary surface represents the video frame buffer. Images written to this surface appear immediately on the screen.
- Back buffers are surfaces in video memory that can be exchanged with the primary surface. These surfaces are used to create an image that will not be displayed until complete, providing smoother animation.
- Z-buffers can be used in Direct3D to determine the visibility of objects.

Keeping Inside the Lines with the DirectDraw Clipper

When you create the primary surface in DirectDraw, you receive an interface that represents the entire screen surface, even if you only intend to draw to the area within your application window. To deal with this, DirectDraw provides the `IDirectDrawClipper` object. This object keeps track of the window location and size and tracks the overlap of other windows, allowing your application to be Windows friendly.

To use a clipper, you need do nothing more than create it from the `DirectDraw` object, provide a pointer to the topmost window of the application, and attach it to the primary surface. Its creation is performed with the `IDirectDraw7::CreateClipper()` function.

▼ SYNTAX

```
HRESULT CreateClipper(
  DWORD dwFlags,
  LPDIRECTDRAWCLIPPER FAR *lplpDDClipper,
  IUnknown FAR *pUnkOuter
);
```

This function returns `DD_OK` on success.

Parameters:

`dwFlags`	Currently unused. Must be set to 0.
`lplpDDClipper`	Address of a variable that will receive a pointer to an `IDirectDrawClipper` pointer.
`pUnkOuter`	Currently unused. Must be set to `NULL`.

The clipper must be created after you have set the cooperative level, but before creation of your primary surface. When the primary surface has been created, the clipper is attached using the `IDirectDrawSurface7::SetClipper()` function. This will be detailed later in the section "Creating the Primary Surface."

Drawing on a Surface

NEW TERM *Blitting* is the process of transferring blocks of image data from one surface to another. For example, to place an image on a surface, you must move the pixel data of the image into the surface's memory. Several ways to do this are as follows:

- By using the `Blt()` and `BltFast()` functions provided by `IDirectDrawSurface7`.
- By accessing the surface memory directly. This is achieved by calling the `IDirectDrawSurface7` function `Lock()`.
- A handle to a temporary drawing context can be acquired using the `IDirectDrawSurface7::GetDC()` function. This allows the use of standard GDI functions, such as those offered by the CDC class.

A Function to Load Bitmaps to a DirectDraw Surface

To illustrate a transfer to a DirectDraw surface, start off by creating a function that loads a bitmap from a file, creates a surface of matching size, and copies the bitmap to the surface.

To do this, you will use Graphics Device Interface (GDI), as described in the previous section. Note the following advantages and disadvantages to using GDI with DirectDraw:

Disadvantages:

- Poor performance in GDI compared to DirectDraw blits
- Locks the surface, preventing other processes from using the surface
- Sets a system flag known as Win16MuteX, which essentially stalls other threads, causing a loss of performance and possible deadlocks

Advantages:

- All the functionality of GDI available
- Automatic color format conversion
- Built-in functions for loading bitmaps

As you can see, GDI is not ideal when you need performance. Where it does come in quite handy is in the initial loading of bitmaps for later use. The availability of bitmap loading and color conversion saves you from having to re-invent the wheel. And, because image loading is normally performed at application startup or other controlled times, your overall performance will not be affected.

So, to begin with, you will define a function that accepts a pointer to a filename string and returns a pointer to a newly created surface on success, or returns NULL on failure.

Listing 2.1 shows the beginning of the function, with the loading of the bitmap using standard GDI functions. Note that this function assumes the existence of an `IDirectDraw7` pointer, stored in the global variable lpDD.

LISTING 2.1   Function Definition and Bitmap Loading Code

```
1: LPDIRECTDRAWSURFACE7 bitmap_surface(LPCTSTR file_name)
2: {
3:     HDC hdc;
4:     HBITMAP bit;
5:     LPDIRECTDRAWSURFACE7 surf;
6:     // load the interface bitmap
7:
8:     bit=(HBITMAP) LoadImage(NULL,file_name,IMAGE_BITMAP,0,0,
    ➥ LR_DEFAULTSIZE¦LR_LOADFROMFILE);
9:
10:    if (!bit)
11:
12:        // failed to load, return failure to caller
13:
14:        return NULL;
```

If the bitmap is created successfully, you will retrieve the dimensions of the bitmap and attempt to create a `IDirectDrawSurface7` of the same dimensions in system memory, as shown is Listing 2.2. Note that because you do not specify a pixel format, the pixel format of the primary surface will be used. GDI will automatically convert the pixel formats for you when transferring the image.

LISTING 2.2   Creating a Matching Surface

```
 1: // get bitmap dimensions
 2:
 3: BITMAP bitmap;
 4: GetObject( bit, sizeof(BITMAP), &bitmap );
 5: int surf_width = bitmap.bmWidth;
 6: int surf_height = bitmap.bmHeight;
 7:
 8: // create surface
 9:
10: HRESULT ddrval;
11: DDSURFACEDESC2 ddsd;
12: ZeroMemory(&ddsd,sizeof(ddsd));
13: ddsd.dwSize = sizeof(DDSURFACEDESC2);
14: ddsd.dwFlags = DDSD_CAPS ¦ DDSD_WIDTH ¦ DDSD_HEIGHT ;
15: ddsd.ddsCaps.dwCaps = DDSCAPS_OFFSCREENPLAIN¦DDSCAPS_SYSTEMMEMORY;
16: ddsd.dwWidth = surf_width;
17: ddsd.dwHeight = surf_height;
18:
19: // attempt to create surface
20:
21: ddrval=lpDD->CreateSurface(&ddsd,&surf,NULL);
```

Take a look at the surface creation. You define the parameters of the surface to be created within the DDSURFACEDESC2 that is passed to CreateSurface().

As mentioned before, start off by clearing the structure, effectively setting all member values to zero. Set the dwSize element to the required memory for the structure as required.

Now that the structure is ready to be used, set the dwFlags member, which defines which portions of the structure contain valid parameters that are to be applied to the surface. The following flags are set:

- DDSD_CAPS—The ddsCaps member contains valid parameters for the surface.
- DDSD_WIDTH—The dwWidth member contains the required width in pixels of the surface to be created.
- DDSD_HEIGHT—The dwHeight member contains the required height in pixels of the surface to be created.

Then set the members of dwCaps to specify that you want to create an offscreen surface in system memory.

When this is complete, check to see whether you have succeeded at creating the surface. If you have, you will attain a handle to a drawing context for the surface, as shown in Listing 2.3. On failure, the surface pointer is set to NULL, which will be returned to the caller to indicate the error.

LISTING 2.3   Checking Surface Creation and Getting a Surface DC

```
 1:  // created ok?
 2:
 3:  if (ddrval!=DD_OK) {
 4:
 5:      // no, release the bitmap and return failure to caller
 6:
 7:      DeleteObject(bit);
 8:      return NULL;
 9:
10: } else {
11:
12:      // yes, get a DC for the surface
13:
14:      surf->GetDC(&hdc);
```

At this point, you are ready to perform a standard GDI BitBlt function: to transfer the image between a temporary DC you have created for the loaded bitmap, and the off-screen surface you have created to store the image.

LISTING 2.4 Transferring Image Between Drawing Contexts

```
1: // generate a compatible DC
2:
3: HDC bit_dc=CreateCompatibleDC(hdc);
4:
5: // blit the interface to the surface
6:
7: SelectObject(bit_dc,bit);
8: BitBlt(hdc,0,0,surf_width,surf_height,bit_dc,0,0,SRCCOPY);
```

Finally, you are ready to clean up, releasing all the temporary objects that you used for this transaction. You deallocate the bitmap and the temporary context, and call IDirectDrawSurface7::ReleaseDC() to release the surface drawing context. Note that failure to release a surface drawing context will cause any further attempts to write to the surface to fail.

LISTING 2.5 Cleaning Up

```
 1:     // release the DCs
 2:
 3:     surf->ReleaseDC(hdc);
 4:     DeleteDC(bit_dc);
 5: }
 6:
 7: // clear bitmap
 8:
 9: DeleteObject(bit);
10:
11: // return pointer to caller
12:
13: return surf;
14: }
```

That completes the function. You will use this function in your first application to prepare for writing an image to the screen, using the Blt() functions in DirectDraw.

Your First DirectDraw Application

Before going through more technical details, we will get to the moment you've been preparing for—writing your first DirectX application. Your first venture will be to write a simple application that creates a window and blits a bitmap into the client rectangle of the window.

Setting Up the Project

To begin, bring up Visual C++ and select New from the File menu. Open the Projects tab, and select Win32 Application from the program options provided. Choose a location for the files, enter the name EXAMPLH2 for the filename, and click OK, as shown in Figure 2.2.

FIGURE 2.2

Creating the project.

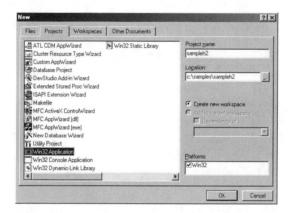

In the dialog that follows, select to create a Simple Win32 application, which you will use as the basic framework to create your program.

Before moving on to coding your application, you need to prepare the project to use DirectDraw by adding the library file DDRAW.LIB to the project settings for the linker. This library contains all the functions needed to use DirectDraw, and will be included. The library uses DirectDraw or a module that relies upon DirectDraw, such as Direct3D.

To use the library, open the Project menu and click the Settings option. In the Project Settings dialog that opens, click the Link tab to access the linker options, as shown in Figure 2.3.

FIGURE 2.3

Accessing the Project linker options.

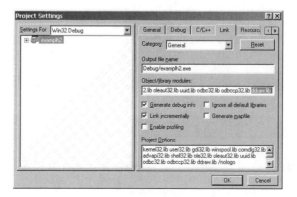

In the Settings For drop box, set All Configurations, which will allow you to insert the library in both the debug and release build settings at the same time. Next, select the Object/Library Modules field, and add DDRAW.LIB to the end of the list. Click OK to complete the setup.

> If you have not already done so, ensure that the paths to the library and header files of the SDK are set under Tools, Options, and that they are the first directories listed (see the section, "Preparing the Compiler," in Hour 1).

Creating a Windows Framework

At this point, you are ready to begin coding your application. Begin by setting up the necessary resource files, including required headers, and creating your window's framework, including the WinMain loop and message handler.

Your resource files will be very simple for this application. The only resource you will define is a File menu with a single entry for Exit. The program will load a default image on startup, so no other options are required.

Listings 2.6 and 2.7 show the required definitions in your RESOURCE.H and EXAMPLH2.RC.

LISTING 2.6   The EXAMPLH2.RC Resource File

```
1: #include "resource.h"
2:
3: IDR_MENU MENU DISCARDABLE
4: BEGIN
5:     POPUP "&File"
6:     BEGIN
7:         MENUITEM "E&xit",    IDM_EXIT
8:     END
9: END
```

LISTING 2.7   The RESOURCE.H Resource Header

```
1: #define IDR_MENU                    102
2: #define IDM_EXIT                    40001
```

For this application, you will need to start off with a set of includes, as shown in Listing 2.8. In addition to the standard headers you are accustomed to, two lines have been added that allow you to use DirectDraw.

LISTING 2.8   Required Header Definitions

```
1: #include "stdafx.h"
2: #include "resource.h"
3: #define INITGUID
4: #include <ddraw.h>
```

2

The definition of INITGUID prior to including DirectDraw provides you with access to the GUID library. The compiler needs access to interpret the GUIDs that are used to refer to the DirectX interfaces.

The second addition is the inclusion of the DDRAW.H file. This contains the function prototypes, class and structure definitions, and enumerations that are necessary to communicate with the DirectDraw library.

After you have included the header files, a number of global variables need to be defined for your application, as shown in Listing 2.9. These include the following:

- Interface pointers for your DirectDraw interface, clipper, and surfaces.
- The class name and window caption for your application window.
- A string pointer that will be used to pass error messages to your exit routine.
- String constants for the messages that might be returned by this application.

LISTING 2.9   Global Variable Definitions

```
 1: //------ Image Loading and Initialization Flags ------//
 2:
 3: BOOL bInit=FALSE;
 4:
 5: //------ Global Interface Pointers ------//
 6:
 7: LPDIRECTDRAW7          lpDD=NULL;          // DirectDraw object
 8: LPDIRECTDRAWSURFACE7   lpDDSPrimary=NULL;   // DirectDraw
    ➥primary surface
 9: LPDIRECTDRAWCLIPPER    lpClip=NULL;        // DirectDraw Clipper Object
10: LPDIRECTDRAWSURFACE7   lpBmp=NULL;         // Bitmap surface
11:
12: //------ Window Class Information ------//
13:
14: static char szClass[] = "XmplHr2Class";
15: static char szCaption[] = "Example - Hour 2";
16:
17: //------ Error Return String ------//
18:
19: const char *ErrStr=NULL;
20:
```

continues

LISTING 2.9   continued

```
21: //------ Error Messages ------//
22:
23: const char Err_Reg_Class[]         = "Error Registering Window Class";
24: const char Err_Create_Win[]        = "Error Creating Window";
25: const char Err_DirectDrawCreate[]   = "DirectDrawCreate FAILED";
26: const char Err_Query[]             = "QueryInterface FAILED";
27: const char Err_Coop[]              = "SetCooperativeLevel FAILED";
28: const char Err_CreateClip[]        = "CreateClip FAILED";
29: const char Err_CreateSurf[]        = "CreateSurface FAILED";
30: const char Err_LoadBMP[]           = "Error Loading Image";
```

Note that you have initialized all pointer values to NULL. This makes it easy to determine whether a pointer has been initialized, so you can prevent faults caused by invalid pointers.

Next you will create the WinMain function. Because the real functionality of this program will be driven by Windows events, the real functionality will be programmed in the message handler. This leaves you with a very simple WinMain function, shown in Listing 2.10.

LISTING 2.10   The WinMain Function

```
 1: int PASCAL WinMain(   HINSTANCE hInstance,
 2:               HINSTANCE hPrevInstance,
 3:             LPSTR lpCmdLine,
 4:             int nCmdShow)
 5: {
 6:     MSG msg;        // windows message structure
 7:
 8:     // initialize the application, exit on failure
 9:
10:     if (!Init(hInstance, nCmdShow)) {
11:         Cleanup();
12:         return FALSE;
13:     }
14:
15:     // handle the message loop till we exit
16:
17:     while (GetMessage(&msg, NULL, NULL, NULL)) {
18:         TranslateMessage(&msg);
19:         DispatchMessage(&msg);
20:     }
21:
22:     // exit returning final message
23:
24:     return (msg.wParam);
25: }
```

Initializing DirectDraw and Creating a Clipper

The Init function called in WinMain is a function you will write to handle all initialization, including creation of the application window, initialization of DirectDraw, and creation of a clipper and primary surface.

The first portion of your initialization code is familiar territory because you must start off by creating an application window and establishing its styles and resources. Listing 2.11 shows the beginning of the Init function.

LISTING 2.11   Creating the Application Window

```
 1: static BOOL Init(HINSTANCE hInstance, int nCmdShow)
 2: {
 3:     WNDCLASS            wc;
 4:     HRESULT             hRet;
 5:     DDSURFACEDESC2      ddsd;
 6:
 7:
 8:     // Set up and register window class
 9:
10:     wc.style = CS_HREDRAW | CS_VREDRAW;
11:     wc.lpfnWndProc = (WNDPROC) WindowProc;
12:     wc.cbClsExtra = 0;
13:     wc.cbWndExtra = sizeof(DWORD);
14:     wc.hInstance = hInstance;
15:     wc.hIcon = NULL;
16:     wc.hCursor = LoadCursor(NULL, IDC_ARROW);
17:     wc.hbrBackground = (HBRUSH) GetStockObject(BLACK_BRUSH);
18:     wc.lpszMenuName = MAKEINTRESOURCE(IDR_MENU);
19:     wc.lpszClassName = szClass;
20:     if (!RegisterClass(&wc)) {
21:     ErrStr=Err_Reg_Class;
22:         return FALSE;
23:     }
24:
25:     // Get dimensions of display
26:
27:     int ScreenWidth = GetSystemMetrics(SM_CXSCREEN);
28:     int ScreenHeight = GetSystemMetrics(SM_CYSCREEN);
29:
30:     // Create a window and display
31:     HWND hWnd;
32:
33:     hWnd = CreateWindow(szClass,                    // class
34:                     szCaption,                      // caption
35:                 WS_VISIBLE|WS_POPUP,        // style
36:                 0,                  // left
37:                 0,                  // top
```

continues

LISTING 2.11 continued

```
38:              ScreenWidth,          // width
39:              ScreenHeight,        // height
40:                   NULL,                // parent window
41:                   NULL,                // menu
42:                   hInstance,          // instance
43:                   NULL);           // parms
44:     if (!hWnd) {
45:     ErrStr=Err_Create_Win;
46:        return FALSE;
47:     }
48:     ShowWindow(hWnd, nCmdShow);
49:     UpdateWindow(hWnd);
```

After the window has been created, you are ready to get an interface for the `DirectDraw`
object. Shown in Listing 2.12, this portion of the initialization consists of three steps:

1. Call `DirectDrawCreateEx()` to get a pointer to the `IDirectDraw` interface.
2. Next, set the cooperative level for DirectDraw, which in the case of windowed
   applications is always `DDSCL_NORMAL`.
3. Finally, create the clipper and associate it with the application window.

LISTING 2.12 Initializing DirectDraw

```
 1: // Create the main DirectDraw object
 2:
 3:     hRet=DirectDrawCreateEx(NULL,(LPVOID*)&lpDD,IID_IDirectDraw7,NULL);
 4:     if (hRet != DD_OK) {
 5:         ErrStr=Err_DirectDrawCreate;
 6:      return FALSE;
 7:     }
 8:
 9:
10:     // Set our cooperative level
11:
12:     hRet = lpDD->SetCooperativeLevel(hWnd, DDSCL_NORMAL);
13:     if (hRet != DD_OK) {
14:         ErrStr=Err_Coop;
15:     return FALSE;
16:     }
17:
18:     // create the clipper
19:
20:     hRet=lpDD->CreateClipper(NULL,&lpClip,NULL);
21:     if (hRet != DD_OK) {
22:         ErrStr=Err_CreateClip;
23:     return FALSE;
24:     }
25:     lpClip->SetHWnd(0,hWnd);
```

Creating the Primary Surface

Before you can use the services of DirectDraw to write to the screen, you must first create a primary surface that will provide access to the screen. To accomplish this, you will create a surface description matching the surface you need to acquire and call `CreateSurface()`. This is illustrated in Listing 2.13.

> When working with DirectX interfaces, be careful to ensure that they are initialized correctly. Data structures should be cleared before initialization, and the `dwSize` member present in many of the DirectX structures must be properly set to the size of the structure. If this is not done, unpredictable results or outright failure will occur.

LISTING 2.13   Creating the Primary Surface and Attaching the Clipper

```
 1:    // Create the primary surface
 2:
 3:    ZeroMemory(&ddsd, sizeof(ddsd));
 4:    ddsd.dwSize = sizeof(ddsd);
 5:    ddsd.dwFlags = DDSD_CAPS;
 6:    ddsd.ddsCaps.dwCaps = DDSCAPS_PRIMARYSURFACE;
 7:    hRet = lpDD->CreateSurface(&ddsd, &lpDDSPrimary, NULL);
 8:    if (hRet != DD_OK) {
 9:        ErrStr=Err_CreateSurf;
10:    return FALSE;
11:    }
12:
13:    // Set the Clipper for the Primary Surface
14:
15:    lpDDSPrimary->SetClipper(lpClip);
16:
17:    // flag initialization as completed
18:
19:    bInit=TRUE;
```

The clipper created in Listing 2.12 has now been attached to the surface. This will test your transfers to the video screen to make sure they stay within bounds, clipping them if needed.

At this point, you are able to perform DirectDraw operations directly to the screen by using the primary surface. You have set the `bInit` flag to indicate this to your functions, so they can test for DirectDraw initialization before attempting to access it.

Loading the Image

However, you don't have anything to put on the screen yet. For this you will use the
bitmap surface() function I discussed earlier in this chapter. The code for this function
can be found starting in Listings 2.1 through 2.5.

When this is complete, you are ready to load the bitmap and create an offscreen surface
to store it in. This is illustrated in Listing 2.14, which completes your initialization code.

LISTING 2.14   Loading the Default Bitmap Image

```
 1:      // load the default bitmap
 2:
 3:      lpBmp=bitmap_surface("vista.bmp");
 4:
 5:      // display the image
 6:
 7:      DrawImage();
 8:
 9:      return TRUE;
10: }
```

Blitting an Image to the Screen

Now that you have loaded your image into memory, you can finally write it to the screen.
This is performed in the DrawImage routine that you first call in your initialization, and
which you will call in your message loop in response to refresh commands. The code for
your drawing routine is provided in Listing 2.15.

LISTING 2.15   The Draw Routine

```
 1: void DrawImage()
 2: {
 3:      // return if not ready to draw at this time
 4:
 5:      if (!lpBmp||!bInit)
 6:          return;
 7:
 8:      // draw the image full screen
 9:
10:      lpDDSPrimary->Blt(NULL,lpBmp,NULL,DDBLT_WAIT,NULL);
11: }
```

Note that it is possible this function could be called in response to a message before the
image is loaded, or before DirectDraw has been initialized. To safeguard against this, the
function first checks the bInit flag to ensure that DirectDraw has been loaded and veri-
fies that the pointer to the bitmap surface is valid. If not, the function returns to the caller
without attempting to blit to the screen.

Tying It All Together in the Message Loop

To provide control over program operation, you will override the default Windows procedure by creating a function named WindowProc(). This function will handle the following conditions:

- On receipt of a WM_COMMAND message, check to see whether the Exit option in the menu has been selected.

- In the result of a WM_PAINT message, used by Windows to notify applications that they must redraw. This message will be processed with a call to the DrawImage() function that you have created.

- When a WM_DESTROY message is posted to the application, the Cleanup() function will be called to allow release of DirectDraw surfaces and interface.

A copy of this function can be found in Listing 2.16.

LISTING 2.16   Window Message Handler

```
 1: LRESULT CALLBACK WindowProc(HWND hWnd, unsigned uMsg, WPARAM wParam,
    ➥ LPARAM lParam)
 2: {
 3:     switch (uMsg)
 4:     {
 5:         case WM_COMMAND:
 6:             switch (LOWORD(wParam))
 7:             {
 8:                 case IDM_EXIT:
 9:
10:                     DestroyWindow(hWnd);
11:                     break;
12:             }
13:             break;
14:
15:         case WM_PAINT:
16:             PAINTSTRUCT ps;
17:
18:             BeginPaint(hWnd, &ps);
19:             DrawImage();
20:             EndPaint(hWnd, &ps);
21:             break;
22:
23:         case WM_DESTROY:
24:             Cleanup();
25:             PostQuitMessage(0);
26:             break;
27:
28:         default:
```

continues

LISTING **2.16**   continued

```
29:             return DefWindowProc(hWnd, uMsg, wParam, lParam);
30:     }
31:     return 0L;
32: }
```

Deallocating the Interfaces

On exit, you must release the DirectX interfaces that you have created during execution
of the program. Two important things to remember when doing this are as follows:

- You must release the interfaces in the reverse order in which they were created.
  This ensures that you do not release an interface that is still in use by other interfaces which are still in existence.

- Attempting to release an interface that was never created will cause a program
  fault. To this end, you will create and use a macro called SafeRelease(), which
  checks the validity of an interface pointer before attempting to release it.

The Cleanup() function is shown in Listing 2.17.

LISTING **2.17**   Cleaning Up on Exit

```
1: //------ Cleanup Function to Release Objects ------//
2:
3: #define SafeRelease(x) if (x) { x->Release(); x=NULL; }
4:
5: void Cleanup(void)
6: {
7:     // release the interfaces
8:
9:     SafeRelease(lpBmp);
10:     SafeRelease(lpDDSPrimary);
11:     SafeRelease(lpClip);
12:     SafeRelease(lpDD);
13:     // display error if one thrown
14:
15:     if (ErrStr)
16:         MessageBox(NULL, ErrStr, szCaption, MB_OK);
17: }
```

 That completes the creation of your first DirectX program. When it has successfully
compiled, place the VISTA.BMP file from the CD-ROM that comes with this book in the
working directory and run the program. The output of this sample program is illustrated
in Figure 2.4.

FIGURE 2.4

Program output.

If you want, you might substitute a bitmap of your own and rename it VISTA.BMP. The image will automatically be scaled to fit into the application's full-screen window, and the colors remapped to match the current color depth.

Although support for stretching images is guaranteed, many display adapters do not support shrinking an image. Therefore, if you substitute the sample bitmap with one that is larger than the current display resolution, the image might not be properly displayed.

Summary

In this hour, you learned the basics of DirectDraw, including how to initialize DirectDraw, set up a clipper, and create DirectDraw surfaces. You also explored some of the functions necessary to allow use of bitmaps in a DirectX application, including loading bitmaps into an offscreen surface and blitting them to the screen.

Q&A

Q What advantages does DirectDraw offer over standard Windows GDI?

A The advantages of DirectDraw over GDI are twofold. First, it provides a more direct path to access the video hardware, which amounts to much greater performance. In addition to this, it provides a standard for accelerated hardware capabilities that allow the creation of high-speed special effects.

Q What kind of advanced hardware capabilities can I expect to use with DirectX?

A This will vary depending on the end user's system. With accelerated video hardware, you can perform special effects in DirectDraw such as blending images together or placing live video streams into your application. The really exciting advances will be found on the 3D side, where you will be able to generate effects such as shadows, smoke, flames, and explosions.

Workshop

The Workshop is designed to help you anticipate possible questions, review what you've learned, and begin thinking ahead to put your knowledge into practice. The answers to the quiz are in Appendix A, "Answers."

Quiz

1. Which window handle should be passed to a DirectDraw clipper object?

2. What type of DirectDraw surface is created to represent the screen surface?

3. What type of surface is used to store images for later use?

4. What is the definition of blitting?

Exercises

1. Add a Load command to the menu to provide interactive loading of images. Remember to check for and release existing image surfaces when loading a new image.

2. Modify the program to run in a resizable window. This will require reading the client rectangle coordinates and converting them to absolute screen coordinates because the primary surface represents the entire screen.

HOUR 3

Moving On—Grabbing Control of the System

When coding highly graphical applications, especially when those applications must be high-performance, you'll typically want to have as much control of the client system as possible. For example, perhaps you want to use the entire screen to render your scenes, or you want to make sure another application doesn't pop up and interfere with your rendering cycle. Of course, your artwork probably won't use the same color resolution as the client's current video setting. And wouldn't it be nice if there were an easy way to reduce or eliminate the screen flicker when animating your scene? All of these things are possible with DirectDraw, as you will see in this chapter.

In this hour, you will learn

- How to gain full-screen access to the video surface
- How to establish exclusive control of the screen, preventing other applications from appearing
- How to change the screen resolution and color depth
- How to use multiple-screen surfaces for flicker-free animation

Full-Screen Graphics

In the last hour, you learned how to use DirectDraw to access the video screen. However, you were still working under the Windows desktop, and if your goal is to develop entertainment software, this is not where you want to be.

Almost every entertainment title you find on the shelf today uses the full extent of the screen. This provides the best experience for the users because it immerses them into the game without the distraction of other windows on the screen. It also breaks out of the frame that normally surrounds a window.

Apart from the aesthetic issues, there are definite performance advantages to full-screen applications. They do not have to share the system with other applications, thus gaining more processing power for themselves. In addition, a program in Windows normally must deal with whatever resolution and color depth the user has chosen, which can result both in poor performance and degradation of graphics quality.

In DirectDraw we are able to break those shackles by taking control of the entire screen surface and setting the graphics resolution and color depth as we see fit. Most importantly, when our program is finished, the screen settings are reset to their original setting. This means that your programs will be user-friendly, instead of requiring the user to change his settings to accommodate the application.

Getting the System's Cooperation

The first step that you must take to create a full-screen application is to set the cooperative level, using the SetCooperativeLevel() function. If you want to review the use of this function, refer to "The IDirectDraw Interface" in Hour 2, "Our First Step— DirectDraw in a Windows Application."

There are two flags that you must use to set up for full screen: DDSCL_FULLSCREEN and DDSCL_EXCLUSIVE. To use multiple flags, you logically-OR the flags together:

```
lpDD->SetCooperativeLevel(hwnd, DDSCL_FULLSCREEN | DDSCL_EXCLUSIVE |
                          DDSCL_ALLOWREBOOT);
```

Ensure that the top-level window handle is passed to SetCooperativeLevel rather than to the handle of a child window. If this is not the case, messages will not properly be routed to your application.

Changing the Screen Resolution

When you have established this level of control, DirectDraw will allow you to set the screen resolution as you want. In the sample full-screen applications provided with this book, you will use 640×480 at a color depth of 16 bits, which provides you with 65,536 individual colors.

To set the resolution, call the `SetDisplayMode()` function of the `IDirectDraw7` interface. The syntax for the function is as follows.

SYNTAX ▼

The Syntax for `SetDisplayMode()`

```
HRESULT IDirectDraw7::SetDisplayMode(
    DWORD dwWidth,
    DWORD dwHeight,
    DWORD dwBPP,
    DWORD dwRefreshRate,
    DWORD dwFlags
);
```

The `SetDisplayMode()` function changes the current screen resolution and color depth. If this function is successful, `DD_OK` is returned.

Parameters:

dwWidth	Horizontal resolution.
dwHeight	Vertical resolution.
dwBPP	Color depth, in bits per pixel.
dwRefreshRate	Requested vertical refresh rate for the monitor. Specify 0 to use the default refresh rate.
dwFlags	Sets options for this function. At present, only `DDSDM_STANDARDVGAMODE` is provided, which causes VGA Mode 13 to be used if 320×240×8 is the requested resolution and color depth. Normally this value is set to 0.

▲

To set your screen mode to 640×480×16, perform the following call:

```
lpDD->SetDisplayMode(640,480,16,0,0);
```

The modes that can be set depend on the hardware capabilities and the video driver installed. I have elected to use 16-bit graphics at 640×480 because they provide a decent color depth, while at a resolution that can be supported by almost any DirectX-compatible video card, including older cards that have at least 2MB of video memory. To support cards with less memory, you can step the samples down to 8-bit color depth.

If you must determine what display modes are available at runtime, use the `EnumDisplayModes()` function of the `IDirectDraw7` interface. To learn more about enumerating display mode, see the documentation provided in the DirectX 7 documentation.

Page Flipping

As you might have previously experienced while programming Windows applications, creating an application that writes any significant amount of graphics to the screen can often cause the images to flicker as they are being drawn. This problem is known as "tearing" and is caused when your program redraws a portion of the screen that is currently being refreshed by the monitor.

To understand this, take a look at how the monitor places the image on the screen. Although the image appears continuous to our eyes, it is actually being repeatedly redrawn, usually at a rate of 60 times per second or more. This results in what is called "persistence of vision"—the illusion that an image is continuous, caused by the way our retinas react to very fast changes in light. If we could see what is really happening, the entire image is really nothing more than a moving dot!

NEW TERM   This dot is caused by a beam of electrons that is projected onto the phosphorus sputtered onto the back of the glass face of the monitor. The screen image is drawn starting in the upper-left corner, scanning each line from left to right. At the end of each line, drawing resumes at the start of the next scan line, as shown in Figure 3.1. After all the scan lines have been drawn, drawing again resumes in the upper-left corner so the image is redrawn. The rate at which this occurs is known as the *vertical refresh*.

FIGURE 3.1

The vertical refresh.

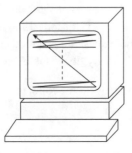

To prevent a diagonal line from appearing across the screen, however, the beam must be turned off while it traverses the screen. This period is known as the "vertical blanking interval," or VBI. During this period, you can get away with drawing to the screen, without the potential for tearing.

So, you just have to wait for the refresh, right? Well, it usually isn't quite that simple. The reason is that the blanking interval is very short compared to the amount of data that must be drawn to the screen each frame. Often it would be impossible to complete the task in time, and the refresh would catch you right in the middle of drawing on the screen.

The solution is to prepare your work ahead of time. Rather than drawing directly to the primary surface, as you did in the previous hour, you will create a second surface in video memory, a *back buffer*, which you can use to prepare your image while the previously drawn image is being displayed. When the blanking interval occurs, you can swap the two surfaces and have the next image on the screen long before the blanking interval is over (see Figure 3.2). This technique is known as *double buffering*.

FIGURE 3.2

Swapping buffers during the blanking interval.

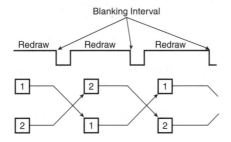

Creating the Flipping Chain

To use double buffering, you must create a second surface in video memory that is identical to the primary surface. There can be more than one back buffer, if needed—for example, two back buffers are sometimes used in a technique called, appropriately, triple buffering.

This collection of surfaces is collectively known as the *flipping chain*. To create the flipping chain, you must specify the number of buffers when you create your primary surface, as shown in Listing 3.1.

LISTING 3.1   Creating the Flipping Chain

```
1: // Create the primary surface with 1 back buffer
2:
3: DDSURFACEDESC2 ddsd;
4: DDSCAPS2 ddscaps;
5: ZeroMemory(&ddsd,sizeof(ddsd));
6: ddsd.dwSize = sizeof( ddsd );
7: ddsd.dwFlags = DDSD_CAPS ¦ DDSD_BACKBUFFERCOUNT;
```

continues

LISTING 3.1   continued

```
 8: ddsd.ddsCaps.dwCaps = DDSCAPS_PRIMARYSURFACE ¦
 9:                         DDSCAPS_FLIP ¦
10:                         DDSCAPS_COMPLEX;
11: ddsd.dwBackBufferCount = 1;
12: ddrval = lpDD->CreateSurface( &ddsd, &lpDDSPrimary, NULL );
```

As you can see in comparing this with the example from Hour 2, the following modifications were made to this code:

- We have added the DDSD_BACKBUFFERCOUNT flag to indicate to the CreateSurfaces() function that there is a valid back buffer count stored in ddsd.dwBackBufferCount.

- The dwBackBufferCount member of our surface description has been set to 1, to indicate that one back buffer should be created in addition to our primary surface.

- We have added DDSCAPS_FLIP and DDSCAPS_COMPLEX to the surface capabilities, indicating that the surface will be complex (consist of multiple surfaces), and that the surfaces can be exchanged, or "flipped."

The additional surfaces are created at the same time as your primary surface, but they are not returned by your call to CreateSurface(). They are instead created as "attached" surfaces. You can retrieve a pointer to the back buffer by using the GetAttachedSurface() command, as shown in Listing 3.2.

LISTING 3.2   Retrieving the Back Buffer

```
1: // Fetch back buffer interface
2:
3: ddscaps.dwCaps=DDSCAPS_BACKBUFFER;
4: ddrval=lpDDSPrimary->GetAttachedSurface(&ddscaps,&lpDDSBack);
5: if (ddrval!=DD_OK) {
6:     ErrStr=Err_CreateSurf;
7:     return FALSE;
8: }
```

Using Page Flipping

When you have created your surfaces, double buffering is easy to implement. The primary difference is that you blit to the back buffer rather than the primary surface. When a frame is completed, you use the Flip() function from the primary surface, as shown in the following:

```
lpDDSPrimary->Flip(NULL,DDFLIP_WAIT);
```

The Flip() command causes the primary surface to be exchanged with the back buffer. The flip might not occur immediately; instead, waiting for the next blanking interval before actually performing the exchange.

The syntax for Flip() is as follows.

The Syntax for Flip()

▼ SYNTAX

```
HRESULT IDirectDrawSurface7::Flip(
    LPDIRECTDRAWSURFACE7 lpDDSurfaceTargetOverride,
    DWORD dwFlags
);
```

The Flip() function causes DirectDraw to exchange surfaces, flipping the first back buffer to the screen and moving the screen surface to the end of the chain. If this function is successful, DD_OK is returned.

Parameters:

lpDDSurfaceTargetOverride	Surface to be exchanged with the primary surface. Normally this is set to NULL, which causes the function to set the first back buffer as the visible surface.
dwFlags	Flags that govern the behavior of this function. There are a variety of optional flags, which can be found in the SDK documentation. Normally, this is set to DDFLIP_WAIT, which causes the function to wait until the flip is properly set up if the hardware is waiting for another operation to complete.

▲

Slide Show—A Simple Surface-Flipping Application

To apply what you have learned, you will begin by creating a slide-show application. The program will allow the user to step through a series of screen shots from a 3D action game, using the arrow keys for navigation.

The images for this example can be found with the sample code for this hour on the CD-ROM. There are seven images, labeled SLIDE001.BMP through SLIDE007.BMP.

Setting Up the Application

To begin with, you will need to create a new Win32 project, just as you did in the section Setting Up the Project in Hour 2. Include the code from the `bitmap_surface()` function that you created in the last hour, as well as the error string assignments.

After the project is created, begin by loading the appropriate headers and establishing the global variables that are needed for this application (see Listing 3.3).

LISTING 3.3   Setting Up the Application

```
 1: /*------------------------------------------------------------*/
 2: // Sample Application
 3: //
 4: // Chapter 3
 5: //
 6: // Learn DirectX in 24 Hours
 7: // by Robert Dunlop
 8: //
 9: // Copyright (C) 1999
10: /*------------------------------------------------------------*/
11:
12: //------ Include Files ------//
13:
14: #include "stdafx.h"
15: #define INITGUID
16: #include <stdio.h>
17: #include <ddraw.h>
18: #include <mmsystem.h>
19:
20: //------ Window Class Information ------//
21:
22: static char szClass[] = "XmplHr3Class";
23: static char szCaption[] = "Example - Hour 3";
24:
25: //------ Global Interface Pointers ------//
26:
27: LPDIRECTDRAW7 lpDD=NULL;
28: LPDIRECTDRAWSURFACE7 lpDDSPrimary=NULL;
29: LPDIRECTDRAWSURFACE7 lpDDSBack=NULL;
30:
31: //------Define number of images and set up list of file names ------//
32:
33: #define IMAGE_COUNT              7
34:
35: char file_names[IMAGE_COUNT][256] = {  "slide001.bmp",
36:                                        "slide002.bmp",
37:                                        "slide003.bmp",
38:                                        "slide004.bmp",
39:                                        "slide005.bmp",
40:                                        "slide006.bmp",
```

```
41:                                    "slide007.bmp",
42: };
43:
44: //------ DirectDraw Surfaces for Image Storage ------//
45:
46: LPDIRECTDRAWSURFACE7 lpSlides[IMAGE_COUNT];
47:
48: //------ current image displayed------//
49:
50: int cur_image=0;
```

There are a few additions to the global code of this application, compared to the previous example. Here is an overview of the changes:

- A new surface pointer, lpDDSBack, is provided for the back buffer.
- The constant IMAGE_COUNT indicates the number of images in the slide sequence.
- The array file_names[] contains the names of the files to be loaded.
- lpSlides[] will contain an array of pointers to surfaces containing the slide images.
- The index of the currently displayed image is stored in cur_image.

Initializing the Application

Your initialization of the application window and the creation of a DirectDraw7 will remain the same as in the last hour. When that has been achieved, you are ready to switch to full-screen graphics, setting the cooperation level, and then the display mode as in Listing 3.4.

LISTING 3.4   Establishing Full-Screen Display

```
1: // Set our cooperative level
2:
3: ddrval = lpDD->SetCooperativeLevel( hWnd,
                                DDSCL_EXCLUSIVE | DDSCL_FULLSCREEN );
4: if (ddrval != DD_OK) {
5:      ErrStr=Err_Coop;
6:      return FALSE;
7: }
8:
9: // Set the display mode
10:
11: ddrval = lpDD->SetDisplayMode( 640, 480, 16, 0, 0);
12: if (ddrval !=DD_OK) {
13:      ErrStr=Err_DispMode;
14:      return FALSE;
15: }
```

Next, you will create your primary surface and back buffer (see Listing 3.5). This will form a flipping chain that you can use to preload the next slide onto the back buffer, avoiding any tearing that would otherwise occur.

LISTING 3.5   Creating the Flipping Chain

```
 1: // Create the primary surface with 1 back buffer
 2:
 3: DDSURFACEDESC2 ddsd;
 4: DDSCAPS2 ddscaps;
 5: ZeroMemory(&ddsd,sizeof(ddsd));
 6: ddsd.dwSize = sizeof( ddsd );
 7: ddsd.dwFlags = DDSD_CAPS | DDSD_BACKBUFFERCOUNT;
 8: ddsd.ddsCaps.dwCaps = DDSCAPS_PRIMARYSURFACE |
 9:                       DDSCAPS_FLIP |
10:                       DDSCAPS_COMPLEX;
11: ddsd.dwBackBufferCount = 1;
12: ddrval = lpDD->CreateSurface( &ddsd, &lpDDSPrimary, NULL );
13: if (ddrval!=DD_OK) {
14:     ErrStr=Err_CreateSurf;
15:     return FALSE;
16: }
17:
18: // Fetch back buffer interface
19:
20: ddscaps.dwCaps=DDSCAPS_BACKBUFFER;
21: ddrval=lpDDSPrimary->GetAttachedSurface(&ddscaps,&lpDDSBack);
22: if (ddrval!=DD_OK) {
23:     ErrStr=Err_CreateSurf;
24:     return FALSE;
25: }
```

Assuming that everything succeeded up to this point, you have only one item remaining: loading the slides. In Listing 3.6, note that we are only loading the first image. The reason for this is loading time—the files are 900KB each, and will take a significant amount of time to load.

LISTING 3.6   Retrieving the Back Buffer

```
 1:     // load the first image and display it
 2:
 3:     lpSlides[0]=bitmap_surface(file_names[0]);
 4:     if (!lpSlides[0])
 5:         return FALSE;
 6:     draw_slide();
 7:
 8:     // return success to caller
 9:
10:     return TRUE;
11: }
```

However, you only need to have the first image when you initially render the page. This allows you to get to the screen much faster.

When you have drawn your first image, you can load other images into memory, and most likely have them fully loaded before the user attempts to view the next slide. This provides the user with the illusion that all nine of the images have loaded in the time that it really took to load only the first image.

Cleaning Up

The cleanup function, Listing 3.7, will be almost identical to the previous example with the exception that you must release the slide images, which are stored in a different array than the previous sample used.

LISTING 3.7   Cleaning Up On Exit

```
 1: //------ Cleanup Function to Release Objects ------//
 2:
 3: #define SafeRelease(x) if (x) { x->Release(); x=NULL;}
 4:
 5: void Cleanup()
 6: {
 7:     // release loaded image surfaces
 8:
 9:     for (int i=0;i<IMAGE_COUNT;i++)
10:         SafeRelease(lpSlides[i]);
11:
12:     // release DirectDraw interfaces
13:
14:     SafeRelease(lpDDSPrimary);
15:     SafeRelease(lpDDSBack);
16:     SafeRelease(lpDD);
17:
18:     // display error if one thrown
19:
20:     if (ErrStr) {
21:         MessageBox(NULL, ErrStr, szCaption, MB_OK);
22:         ErrStr=NULL;
23:     }
24: }
```

Drawing a Slide

Now you are ready for the drawing of your slide. The function shown in Listing 3.8 will display the image referenced by the index stored in cur_image. The code implementation can be broken down into several operations:

- Ensure that the current slide image is loaded.
- Blit the current image to the back buffer.

- Get a device context and use it to place instructions on the back buffer.
- Call Flip() to exchange the primary surface with the back buffer.
- Load the next slide in the sequence if it is not already loaded.
- Load the previous slide in the sequence if it is not already loaded.

LISTING 3.8 Drawing the Current Image and Loading Adjacent Images

```
 1: //------ Function to Draw a Slide ------//
 2:
 3: void draw_slide()
 4: {
 5:     // make sure we have the current image, don't draw if we fail
 6:
 7:     if (!lpSlides[cur_image]) {
 8:         lpSlides[cur_image]=bitmap_surface(file_names[cur_image]);
 9:         if (!lpSlides[cur_image])
10:             return;
11:     }
12:
13:     // draw the object to the screen
14:
15:     lpDDSBack->BltFast(0,0,lpSlides[cur_image],NULL,DDBLTFAST_WAIT);
16:
17:     // draw instructions for slide show
18:
19:     HDC hdc;
20:     if (DD_OK==lpDDSBack->GetDC(&hdc)) {
21:         SetTextColor(hdc,0x00ff7f00);
22:         SetBkColor(hdc,0x000000);
23:         TextOut(hdc,20,400,"<- Previous Slide",16);
24:         TextOut(hdc,540,400,"Next Slide ->",13);
25:         SetTextColor(hdc,0x0000ffff);
26:         TextOut(hdc,235,440,"Press Arrow Keys to Change Slides",33);
27:         lpDDSBack->ReleaseDC(hdc);
28:     }
29:
30:     // flip to the primary surface
31:
32:     lpDDSPrimary->Flip(0,DDFLIP_WAIT);
33:
34:     // make sure we have the next and previous image
35:     // this insures that our next selection is quickly
36:     // available, while we only need to load one image
37:     // when the program starts.
38:
39:     int next_slide=(cur_image>=IMAGE_COUNT-1) ? 0 : cur_image+1;
40:     if (!lpSlides[next_slide])
```

```
41:          lpSlides[next_slide]=bitmap_surface(file_names[next_slide]);
42:
43:     int prev_slide=(cur_image<1) ? IMAGE_COUNT-1 : cur_image-1;
44:     if (!lpSlides[prev_slide])
45:          lpSlides[prev_slide]=bitmap_surface(file_names[prev_slide]);
46: }
```

Handling Slide Navigation

You can reuse the WinMain() function from Hour 2 to process your messages. To allow the user to navigate through the slide show, you will add processing of the WM_KEYDOWN message to your message handling in WindowProc().

When an arrow key is pressed, you increment or decrement the image number as requested, and ensure that the image index does not exceed the allowed values. If the index exceeds either end of the image list, it will be reset to the opposite end of the list. This causes the image list to wrap, allowing the user to continuously scroll through the list.

When the image number has been set, a call is made to the render_slide() that you just created, as seen in Listing 3.9.

LISTING 3.9 HandlingSlide Show Navigation

```
 1: //------ Windows Message Handler ------//
 2:
 3: LRESULT CALLBACK
 4: WindowProc(HWND hWnd, unsigned uMsg, WPARAM wParam, LPARAM lParam)
 5: {
 6:     switch (uMsg)
 7:     {
 8:
 9:         case WM_DESTROY:
10:             Cleanup();
11:             PostQuitMessage(0);
12:             break;
13:
14:         case WM_KEYDOWN:
15:             switch (wParam)
16:             {
17:                 case VK_LEFT:
18:
19:                     // Process the LEFT ARROW key.
20:
21:                     cur_image--;
```

continues

LISTING 3.9   continued

```
22:                          if (cur_image<0)
23:                              cur_image=IMAGE_COUNT-1;
24:                          draw_slide();
25:                          break;
26:
27:                      case VK_RIGHT:
28:
29:                          // Process the RIGHT ARROW key.
30:
31:                          cur_image++;
32:                          if (cur_image>IMAGE_COUNT-1)
33:                              cur_image=0;
34:                          draw_slide();
35:                          break;
36:
37:                      case VK_ESCAPE:
38:
39:                          // exit the program on escape
40:
41:                          DestroyWindow(hWnd);
42:                          break;
43:
44:                      // Process other non-character keystrokes.
45:
46:                      default:
47:                          break;
48:                  }
49:
50:          default:
51:              return DefWindowProc(hWnd, uMsg, wParam, lParam);
52:      }
53:      return 0L;
54: }
```

Sample Output

When the application is compiled, ensure that the bitmaps are in the working directory, and execute the application. You can use the right and left arrow keys to navigate through the slides. Pressing the Escape key or Alt+F4 will exit the application.

A sample image from the slide show is shown in Figure 3.3.

FIGURE 3.3
Sample of slide show display.

Summary

In this hour, you implemented your first full-screen DirectDraw application, taking full control of the video resources. Along the way, you have learned

* How to take full-screen control under DirectDraw
* The definition and purpose of double buffering
* How to create a flipping chain

Q&A

Q What kind of overhead does using page flipping add to your program? Doesn't it take a lot of time to transfer the entire screen image an extra time, after already having to construct the screen in the first place?

A No, there is actually little overhead at all because the image is not actually moved between the surfaces. Instead, there is a memory pointer on the video card that determines where the display memory starts. By simply setting this pointer to point to the back buffer, the next frame will be drawn from the new location without any need to move the image.

Q If I switch the surfaces in the flipping chain, and the primary surface gets shifted to the back, wouldn't I have to change which surface I write to each time?

A DirectDraw handles this for you, so you don't have to worry about keeping track of it. The surface pointers are actually pointers to a structure that points to the physical location of the surface. Internally, DirectDraw exchanges the pointers that your variables point to, so the primary surface pointer will always be the visible surface.

Workshop

The Workshop is designed to help you anticipate possible questions, review what you've learned, and begin thinking ahead to put your knowledge into practice. The answers to the quiz are in Appendix A, "Answers."

Quiz

1. What window handle must be used when setting the cooperative level?
2. What function can be used to determine the display modes available?
3. When using double buffering, which surface receives blits when you redraw the screen?
4. What is a complex surface?

Exercises

1. Modify the program to use triple buffering. To do this, simply set the back buffer count to 2 when creating the primary surface, and DirectDraw will do the rest.
2. Try using different standard resolutions, such as 800×600 or 1024×768. Note the difference in performance when working at higher resolutions.
3. With the application at the resolutions previously shown, insert your own images that match the new screen size. Note how much performance is gained by not having to stretch the images.

HOUR 4

Creating the Game Loop

In this hour, you will get your first look at the workings of an action game. You will create a sample application with a smooth scrolling background, which you will use as a framework to build upon in the next few hours.

In this hour, you will learn

- The mechanics of using a game loop to coordinate animation.
- How to implement a message loop that provides game-level performance while being friendly to other Windows applications.
- How to control motion of objects in a scrolling scene.
- How to clip images against the screen area.
- How to use timers to provide smooth motion at a predetermined rate.

Conceptual Overview of the Game Loop

At the heart of every good game is a small, efficient piece of code—as you will see, it is literally what makes it tick.

When creating a game, you create what is known as a *scene*—a collection of objects that make up the world of the game. This will often include a variety of different objects, including

- A background image that provides a place setting for the game.
- Static objects that are at fixed locations, such as buildings, trees, and other objects.
- Moving objects, including enemy characters and the players themselves.

To put all this in action, you must be able to handle the motion and interaction of the objects in the scene and display them in a realistic fashion.

NEW TERM A *scene* is a collection of objects that make up the world in which the player travels in a game.

Animation in a game occurs much like that in a cartoon flipbook—the scene is displayed repeatedly, each time moving the objects in small increments to provide the appearance of motion.

This is where the game loop comes in. The game loop begins after you have performed any initialization, and loops until the game is finished. During each pass through the loop, you calculate the new position for each object, deal with any action that occurs between objects, and display the scene in its new position. A flowchart of this is shown in Figure 4.1.

FIGURE 4.1

The structure of a typical game loop.

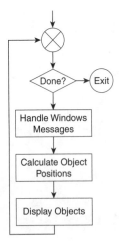

The game loop will take place within the `WinMain()` function and will be part of your Windows message loop. However, there are some distinct differences from a typical message loop, and there are some performance changes that you must make.

In some ways, this will depart from the normal recommendations for a Windows-based application. This is because the performance requirements for a game are much greater than a desktop-based application, and because of this, your program will demand as much of the processor's time slice as it can reasonably achieve.

This will change the way in which you handle messages, and it will also change the way in which you deal with performing program tasks in the game. In particular, you will be departing from the message-based structure of a Windows application, in which each task is prompted by a message sent to the application, and instead you will call routines directly from the message loop.

Writing a Better Message Loop

Probably the greatest difference between a desktop-based application and a game application is that the game doesn't sleep as much. This might seem like an odd analogy, but it is nonetheless an accurate one.

When writing the message loop, you typically use the GetMessage() command to receive the next message from the queue, as shown in Listing 4.1.

LISTING 4.1   A Typical Message Loop

```
1: MSG msg;
2: while GetMessage(&msg,NULL,NULL,NULL) {
3:     TranslateMessage(&msg);
4:     DispatchMessage(&msg);
5: }
```

The problem with this is in the definition of the GetMessage() command. The function checks for a message on the queue, and if one is found, it is returned—so far, so good. However, if there is no message in the queue, the idle loop is called, and then the application is suspended until there is a message available.

So, in essence, a Windows application spends most of its time suspended, coming to life only when an event prompts it into action.

For a game title, this will not do. The challenge of rewriting the entire screen many times a second, while dealing with sound, user input, and object motion, requires that you use every bit of processor time you can get your hands on.

To accomplish this, begin by replacing the GetMessage() command with PeekMessage(). It provides the same function as GetMessage(), but returns to the calling function even if no message is available. Listing 4.2 shows a revised message loop that uses this function. The new loop stays active even when there is not a message pending for the application to act upon.

LISTING 4.2   Revised Message Loop Using `PeekMessage()`

```
 1: BOOL notDone=TRUE;
 2: while (notDone) {
 3:
 4:     // is there a message to process?
 5:
 6:     if (PeekMessage( &msg, NULL, 0, 0, PM_REMOVE)) {
 7:
 8:         // yes, is it a quit message?
 9:
10:         if (msg.message==WM_QUIT)
11:             notDone=FALSE;
12:
13:         // dispatch the message
14:
15:         TranslateMessage(&msg);
16:         DispatchMessage(&msg);
17:
18:     } else {
19:
20:         // Handle game loop functions here
21:     }
22: }
```

There is one other major distinction in this loop: You are now calling your game functions from within the message loop rather than relying on the receipt of a timer message to activate them.

Achieving Smooth Playback

During each pass through the game loop, a new set of object positions is calculated and displayed. This set of positions, and the display that is rendered from it, is known as a frame.

NEW TERM   A *frame* is the image rendered from a scene at a specific point in time, based on the current location of the view and other objects within the scene.

To provide a smooth perception of motion, it is important that the time between the frames is even. To make sure that the time is even between frames, you will use a timer.

Using Timers in the Loop

In the last hour, you used a timer message, WM_TIMER, to notify you when you needed to display the next frame. Although this might work for a slide show, it does not provide sufficient performance for a game title. In addition to the normal overhead of message handling, WM_TIMER is considered to be of a lower priority than any other Windows message.

So, instead of relying on the timer message, you will need to read the time during each pass of the message loop and test to see whether it is time to render the next frame.

Selecting the Timer

When timing frame animations, it is important to use an accurate, high-resolution timer to set your tempo. The timeGetTime() function will provide an accuracy of 1 millisecond (1/1000ᵗʰ of a second, abbreviated "ms").

This function takes no parameters and returns a value of type DWORD containing the current system time. The starting point is arbitrary, so you cannot determine the time of day this way, but it will suit your needs—you can determine the elapsed time in milliseconds by subtracting a previously returned value.

Although this is sufficient for your needs, a higher resolution is preferred and will result in better performance and smoother playback. To achieve this, you can use the Performance Counter, a hardware timer that normally runs at 3.19MHz. This results in accuracy of better than one microsecond (1/1,000,000ᵗʰ of a second, abbreviated "us").

This timer is not available on all machines. It is supported on all current processors being produced, but some older processors did not support it. For this reason, it is necessary that you test for existence of the timer, and if it is unavailable, your program should fall back to using timeGetTime() instead.

Two functions are used to handle the performance counter. The first, QueryPerformanceFrequency(), is used to determine the frequency of the counter. This allows for support of hardware counters of any frequency, and using this function rather than assuming the frequency of this counter ensures that your program will be compatible with future hardware.

There is also a secondary purpose for this function—if the performance counter is not available, the function will fail. This allows you to test for the presence of the performance timer. The syntax for this function is shown in the following.

The Syntax for `QueryPerformanceFrequency()`

▼ SYNTAX

```
BOOL QueryPerformanceFrequency(
    LONGLONG *lpFrequency
);
```

The `QueryPerformanceFrequency()` function tests for the existence of a performance counter and determines the frequency if one exists. If successful, this function returns a non-zero value. If unable to locate a performance counter, this function will return zero.

Parameters:

`lpFrequency`	Pointer to a 64-bit integer that is to receive the frequency of the counter, measured in counts per second.

▲

The second function used with the performance counter is `QueryPerformanceCounter()`, which is used to read the current time count. Note that as with `timeGetTime()`, this function also returns a count that is based on an arbitrary starting time.

The Syntax for `QueryPerformanceCount()`

▼ SYNTAX

```
void QueryPerformanceCount(
    LONGLONG *lpCount
);
```

The `QueryPerformanceCount()` function reads the current value of the performance counter.

Parameters:

`lpCount`	Pointer to a 64-bit integer that is to receive the current count.

▲

By reading the frequency of the performance counter during initialization, you attain a value that can later be used to scale the counter value to a value in seconds.

To use `timeGetTime()` or the performance counter functions in an application, you will need to include mmsystem.h in your source code. Linking your application with the library winmm.lib is required as well.

Your First Piece of Animation: A Scrolling Background

Now that you have laid down the basis you need to create animation, you are ready to start out on your first animated scene. Your application will provide a scrolling background of a city, responding to keyboard input from the user.

The background that you use will be significantly wider than the screen surface. Images such as this can be difficult to store in memory because each bitmap must reside in a continuous block of memory. To deal with this, we have divided the image we will use in this exercise into *tiles*—smaller images that can be displayed side by side to form a larger, continuous image. In this case, the image is divided into three bitmaps, as illustrated in Figure 4.2.

FIGURE 4.2

Tiling images.

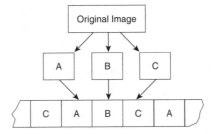

Note that in addition to dividing the images, the original image provided for this exercise also has matching ends so that when the scene loops, there is no visible seam.

Setting Up the Application

You are now ready to start the exercise. Start a new project for this exercise, and begin with the initialization code in Listing 4.3.

LISTING 4.3   Initial Setup of the Application

```
 1: //------ Include Files ------//
 2:
 3: #include "stdafx.h"
 4: #define INITGUID
 5: #include <stdio.h>
 6: #include <ddraw.h>
 7: #include <mmsystem.h>
 8:
 9: //------ Window Class Information ------//
10:
11: static char szClass[] = "XmplHr4Class";
12: static char szCaption[] = "Example - Hour 4";
```

This is the same as before, with one exception—we have added mmsystem.h to our includes to support the timing functions that we will need.

Next add the global variables and constant definitions, as shown in Listing 4.4.

LISTING 4.4   Globals and Constant Definitions

```
 1: //------ Define Position Limits ------//
 2:
 3: #define MIN_POS                 0.0
 4: #define MAX_POS                 50000.0
 5:
 6: //------ Global Interface Pointers ------//
 7:
 8: LPDIRECTDRAW7 lpDD=NULL;
 9: LPDIRECTDRAWSURFACE7 lpDDSPrimary=NULL;
10: LPDIRECTDRAWSURFACE7 lpDDSBack=NULL;
11:
12: //------ DirectDraw Surfaces for Object Storage ------//
13:
14: LPDIRECTDRAWSURFACE7 back_surf[3]={NULL,NULL,NULL};
15:
16: //------ Define Starting Position and Speed ------//
17:
18: double x_pos=25000.0;          // player position
19: double move_rate=0.0;          // player motion
```

The DirectDraw surfaces for the flipping chain, as well as the DirectDraw object itself, are just as they were in the previous hour. This time, however, we have added the following definitions:

- MIN_POS, MAX_POS—Defines the minimum and maximum position the player might scroll to.
- back_surf[3]—Array of surface pointers to contain the tiles of the background image.
- x_pos—Position of the player view, measured in pixels.
- move_rate—Rate of motion of the player view, measured in pixels per second.

This program will also use the error codes established in Hour 2, "Our First Step— DirectDraw in a Windows Application," (Listing 2.9), as well as the bitmap_surface() function (Listings 2.1 through 2.5) for loading bitmap files onto offscreen surfaces. Copy these functions from the previous examples and insert them into the new application.

Setting Up Initialization

The initialization of this application will proceed exactly as in the last hour, with the exception that you will load all three tile images before entering the message loop. At this point, copy the Init() function from Hour 3, "Moving On—Grabbing Control of the System," sample (Listings 3.4 and 3.5) into your new application.

To provide image loading, create a new function labeled load_images(), which will return True on success or False on failure. Replace the final return statement of the Init() function with the code shown in Listing 4.5 to call the function and test the results.

LISTING 4.5   Calling the Image Loading Function

```
 1:     // load the images and set up the layers
 2:
 3:     if (!load_images())
 4:
 5:         // return with error if failed
 6:
 7:         return FALSE;
 8:
 9:     // return success to caller
10:
11:     return TRUE;
12: }
```

Next, create the load_images() function, which will load the three image bitmaps into offscreen surfaces. The listing for this function is provided in Listing 4.6.

LISTING 4.6   The load_images() Function

```
 1: //------ Function to load object images and set up layers ------//
 2:
 3: BOOL load_images()
 4: {
 5:     // load the background images
 6:
 7:     back_surf[0]=bitmap_surface("city1.bmp");
 8:     if (!back_surf[0]) {
 9:         ErrStr=Err_LoadImage;
10:         return FALSE;
11:     }
12:     back_surf[1]=bitmap_surface("city2.bmp");
13:     if (!back_surf[1]) {
14:         ErrStr=Err_LoadImage;
15:         return FALSE;
16:     }
17:     back_surf[2]=bitmap_surface("city3.bmp");
18:     if (!back_surf[2]) {
19:         ErrStr=Err_LoadImage;
20:         return FALSE;
```

4

continues

LISTING 4.6   continued

```
21:     }
22:
23:     // return success to caller
24:
25:     return TRUE;
26: }
```

Controlling Motion Through Keyboard Input

To control the motion of our scrolling background, our program will accept keyboard input by providing a handler for the WM_KEYDOWN message. The windows message handler shown in Listing 4.7 will be used to handle the pressing of the right and left arrow to control motion, and will cause the program to exit if the Esc key is pressed.

LISTING 4.7   The Game Loop's Window Procedure with Keyboard Handling

```
 1: //------ Windows Message Handler ------//
 2:
 3: LRESULT CALLBACK
 4: WindowProc(HWND hWnd, unsigned uMsg, WPARAM wParam, LPARAM lParam)
 5: {
 6:     switch (uMsg)
 7:     {
 8:         case WM_KEYDOWN:
 9:             switch (wParam)
10:             {
11:                 case VK_LEFT:
12:
13:                     // Process the LEFT ARROW key.
14:
15:                     if (move_rate>-600.0)
16:                 move_rate-=120.0;
17:                     break;
18:
19:                 case VK_RIGHT:
20:
21:                     // Process the RIGHT ARROW key.
22:
23:                     if (move_rate<600.0)
24:                         move_rate+=120.0;
25:                     break;
26:
27:                 case VK_ESCAPE:
28:
29:                     // exit the program on escape
30:
```

```
31:                      DestroyWindow(hWnd);
32:                      break;
33:
34:                  // Process other non-character keystrokes.
35:
36:                  default:
37:                  break;
38:               }
39:
40:         case WM_DESTROY:
41:             Cleanup();
42:             PostQuitMessage(0);
43:             break;
44:
45:         default:
46:             return DefWindowProc(hWnd, uMsg, wParam, lParam);
47:      }
48:   return 0L;
49: }
```

Note that this routine increments the value of the move_rate variable each time the arrows
are pressed, increasing or decreasing the rate by 120 pixels per second. The velocity is
clipped to ensure that it does not exceed 600 pixels per second in either direction.

Cleanup on Exit

As before, you will implement a routine labeled Cleanup() that will be called on exit to
release the DirectDraw interfaces, including your three image surfaces. The revised function is shown in Listing 4.8.

LISTING 4.8   The Cleanup() Function

```
1: void Cleanup()
2: {
3:     // release loaded image surfaces
4:
5:     SafeRelease(back_surf[0]);
6:     SafeRelease(back_surf[1]);
7:     SafeRelease(back_surf[2]);
8:
9:     // release DirectDraw interfaces
10:
11:     SafeRelease(lpDDSPrimary);
12:     SafeRelease(lpDD);
13:
14:     // display error if one thrown
```

continues

LISTING 4.8   continued

```
15:
16:     if (ErrStr) {
17:         MessageBox(NULL, ErrStr, szCaption, MB_OK);
18:         ErrStr=NULL;
19:     }
20: }
```

Creating Your Game Loop

Now for the moment you've prepared for—writing the game loop that will put your animation into play. Begin by creating the WinMain() function (shown in Listing 4.9), initializing the window, and calling Init() to set up DirectDraw.

LISTING 4.9   The WinMain() Function

```
1: //------ Application Loop ------//
2:
3: int APIENTRY WinMain(HINSTANCE hInstance,
4:                       HINSTANCE hPrevInstance,
5:                       LPSTR     lpCmdLine,
6:                       int       nCmdShow)
7: {
8:     MSG msg;                  // message from queue
9:     LONGLONG cur_time;        // current time
10:     BOOL notDone=TRUE;        // flag for thread completion
11:     DWORD  time_count;     // milliseconds per frame
12:     LONGLONG perf_cnt;        // performance timer frequency
13:     BOOL perf_flag=FALSE;     // flag determining which timer to use
14:     LONGLONG next_time=0;     // time to render next frame
15:     LONGLONG last_time=0;      // time of previous frame
16:     double time_elapsed;      // time since previous frame
17:     double time_scale;         // scaling factor for time
18:
19:     // initialize the application, exit on failure
20:
21:     if (!Init(hInstance, nCmdShow)) {
22:       Cleanup();
23:         return FALSE;
24:     }
```

At this point, we have also defined several variables that we will be using in our timing
routines. These will become apparent as you use them.

Before you can begin the message loop, you must determine what timer is available and
set up timing parameters accordingly. The code for this is shown in Listing 4.10. This
code performs the following:

- Reads the frequency of the performance counter, if available, into `perf_cnt`.
- Sets `perf_flag` to `True` if the performance counter is available or `False` if it is not.
- Determines the number of ticks of the available timer that constitute 1/30th of a second, for a 30FPS frame rate.
- Calculates the scaling factor that must be multiplied by the timer count to convert them to seconds, and stores this value in `time_scale`.
- Saves the initial timer count in `last_time`, which will be used in each frame to determine the time the last frame was displayed.
- Sets the current time into the `next_time` variable, which will be set after each render to reflect the time the next frame should begin.

LISTING 4.10 Testing the Performance Counter

```
 1:     // is there a performance counter available?
 2:
 3:     if (QueryPerformanceFrequency((LARGE_INTEGER *) &perf_cnt)) {
 4:
 5:         // yes, set time_count and timer choice flag
 6:
 7:         perf_flag=TRUE;
 8:         time_count=perf_cnt/30;
 9:         QueryPerformanceCounter((LARGE_INTEGER *) &next_time);
10:         time_scale=1.0/perf_cnt;
11:
12:     } else {
13:
14:         // no performance counter, read in using timeGetTime
15:
16:         next_time=timeGetTime();
17:         time_scale=0.001;
18:         time_count=33;
19:     }
20:
21:     // save time of last frame
22:
23:     last_time=next_time;
```

With this accomplished, you are ready to enter your message loop (see Listing 4.11). As discussed in "Writing a Better Message Loop," earlier in this hour, we will use `PeekMessage()` to ensure that we retain control of the processor.

LISTING 4.11   The Message Loop

```
 1:     // run till completed
 2:
 3:     while (notDone) {
 4:
 5:         // is there a message to process?
 6:
 7:         if (PeekMessage( &msg, NULL, 0, 0, PM_REMOVE)) {
 8:
 9:             // yes, is it a quit message?
10:
11:             if (msg.message==WM_QUIT)
12:
13:                 notDone=FALSE;
14:
15:             // dispatch the message
16:
17:             TranslateMessage(&msg);
18:             DispatchMessage(&msg);
19:
20:         } else {
```

After you have received and dispatched messages, you are ready to check your timing for the frame.

When any available messages have been processed, you are ready to perform the timing for the loop. Your first step will be to read the appropriate timer function and compare it against next_time to determine whether it is time to render a new frame as seen in Listing 4.12.

LISTING 4.12   Checking the Frame Time

```
 1:         // use the appropriate method to get time
 2:         // and calculate elapsed time since last frame
 3:
 4:         if (perf_flag)
 5:             QueryPerformanceCounter((LARGE_INTEGER *) &cur_time);
 6:         else
 7:             cur_time=timeGetTime();
 8:
 9:         // is it time to render the frame?
10:
11:         if (cur_time>next_time) {
```

The initial value of next_time is set to the starting time, so the next time the counter is read, this test will pass. Each time you render a frame, increment this to reflect the period that should transpire before the next frame.

If this test should pass, it means that it is time to render the frame. In this case, you must calculate the time that has elapsed and move the background an appropriate distance. This is illustrated in Listing 4.13.

LISTING 4.13   Moving the Objects According to Elapsed Time

```
 1:                          // yes, calculate elapsed time
 2:
 3:                          time_elapsed=(cur_time-last_time)*time_scale;
 4:
 5:                          // save frame time
 6:
 7:                          last_time=cur_time;
 8:
 9:                          // move the screen position
10:
11:                          x_pos+=move_rate*time_elapsed;
12:                          if (x_pos<MIN_POS) {
13:                              x_pos=MIN_POS;
14:                              move_rate=0;
15:                          }
16:                          if (x_pos>MAX_POS) {
17:                              x_pos=MAX_POS;
18:                              move_rate=0;
19:                          }
20:
21:                          // render the frame
22:
23:                          render_frame();
24:
25:                          // set time for next frame
26:
27:                          next_time = cur_time + time_count;
28:                      }
29:                  }
30:          }
31:
32:      // exit returning final message
33:
34:      return (msg.wParam);
35: }
```

As you can see, the preceding code finishes off the message loop, after it places a call to render_frame() and calculates the time for the next frame.

Rendering a Scrolling Background

All that remains now is the rendering of the scene, which is encompassed in the render_frame() function that you will call from the message loop.

NEW TERM   The background in this image is *tiled*, meaning that images are displayed side by
             side to form a single, continuous image. Three background images, each 400
pixels wide, will form an apparent background of 1200 pixels.

The images are placed in order, side by side, with the first image starting at an x coordinate of 0, the next image starting at 400, and the final starting at 1200. In both directions,
the pattern will repeat so that you can scroll continuously in either direction.

You must address two issues to properly display this background. You must scroll the
images (move them side to side), and then you must determine what area of the images
are visible and "clip" them to the screen.

NEW TERM   *Clipping* is the process of removing the areas of an image that exceed the limits
             of the screen, prior to rendering it.

To do this, you do not actually change the image. Instead, you will adjust the coordinates
of the source and destination rectangle so that they only encompass those portions of the
image that are on the screen.

To achieve scrolling, offset the x position of the images by the value that you have calculated and stored in `tile_pos`. This will cause the images to move sideways in relation to
the screen, providing a perception that the viewer is moving side to side.

For example, Figure 4.3 illustrates the effect of setting x_pos to a value of –500.0. Each
of the images slides to the left, moving the first image off the screen and revealing part
of the third image in the process.

FIGURE 4.3

The effect of applying
an offset of –500 to the
scene.

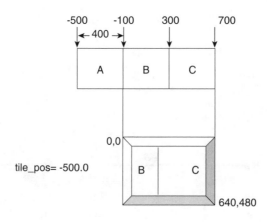

The code listing for render_frame(), which implements scrolling and clipping of the images as discussed, is shown in Listing 4.14.

LISTING 4.14   The render_frame() Function

```
 1: //------ Function to Draw a Frame ------//
 2:
 3: void render_frame()
 4: {
 5:     RECT rct;              // source rectangle of blit
 6:     long tile_pos;         // position of viewable tile
 7:
 8:     // loop through the tiles
 9:
10:     for (int i=0;i<3;i++) {
11:
12:         // calculate position of viewable tile
13:
14:         tile_pos=400*i+((long) (x_pos)/1200)*1200;
15:         if (tile_pos+1200<x_pos+640) tile_pos+=1200;
16:
17:         // is this object on the screen?
18:
19:         if (tile_pos+400>=x_pos) {
20:
21:             // yes, calculate the offset to the left edge of the
              ➥screen
22:
23:             int screen_x=tile_pos-x_pos;
24:
25:             // clip the object if necessary
26:
27:             rct.left=0;
28:             rct.top=0;
29:             rct.right=400;
30:             rct.bottom=480;
31:
32:             // test for clipping
33:
34:             if (screen_x<0) {
35:                 rct.left-=screen_x;
36:                 screen_x=0;
37:             } else if (screen_x+rct.right>640) {
38:                 rct.right=640-screen_x;
39:             }
40:
41:             // draw the object to the screen
42:
43:             lpDDSBack->BltFast(screen_x,0,back_surf[i],&rct,
```

continues

4

LISTING 4.14 continued

```
                    ➥DDBLTFAST_WAIT);
44:          }
45:      }
46:
47:      // flip to the primary surface
48:
49:      lpDDSPrimary->Flip(0,DDFLIP_WAIT);
50: }
```

That completes the creation of your first DirectX program. When it has successfully compiled, place the CITY1.BMP, CITY2.BMP, and CITY3.BMP files from the CD-ROM that comes with this book in the working directory and run the program. The output of this sample program is illustrated in Figure 4.4.

FIGURE 4.4

Program output.

Summary

In this hour, you have learned how to create the underlying structure of a high-performance entertainment title. This new knowledge includes

- Creating a high-performance game loop
- Synchronizing motion to time
- Clipping to the screen surface
- Utilizing high-performance timers

Q&A

Q **The sample program in this hour was set to run at 30FPS, which is equivalent to the refresh rate achieved on video. What are the practical limits for frame rates on today's computers, and how will this change in the future?**

A With the video accelerators that are widely available, frame rates of 60FPS or higher are readily achieved. In many cases, the video card is actually limited by the refresh rate of the monitor, even with some monitors now achieving refresh rates well over 100HZ.

Q **In the message loop that we created, the game only renders in the `else` statement, in the event that there are no messages. Why is this? Don't we want to render at the first available chance?**

A Although this does give some leverage over our execution to the messaging system, this is a necessary compromise. This prevents the queue from overflowing when the system is heavily loaded. Imagine, for example, that your rendering function caused messages to be sent to the queue. If the frame rate was not able to be sustained, the frame would render each pass through the loop. This would generate more messages each frame, even though only one message would be processed—leading to a growing queue of unprocessed messages.

Workshop

The Workshop is designed to help you anticipate possible questions, review what you've learned, and begin thinking ahead to put your knowledge into practice. The answers to the quiz are in Appendix A, "Answers."

Quiz

1. What is the standard frequency for the performance counter?
2. What is the resolution of the `timeGetTime()` function?
3. True or false: The Performance Counter is available on all systems.
4. True or false: The `WM_TIMER` message has a higher priority than other messages in the message queue.

Exercises

1. Put your own images into the engine, and adjust the scrolling routine to deal with different width images.
2. Try images that exceed the height of the screen. Add vertical scrolling and clipping to accommodate them.

Hour **5**

Make It Move— DirectDraw Animation Techniques

In this hour, you will study techniques that allow you to form complex animations using DirectDraw. This will include

- Blitting nonrectangular shapes using transparency
- Compositing objects together to form a scene
- Learning about Z-Ordering and parallax, and using them to create the perception of 3D in your application
- Adding an interface to your program with a nonrectangular viewport

Transparent Blits

In previous hours, you learned how to draw a rectangular portion of an image to the screen. However, often you will need to draw objects to the screen that are not rectangular. To create a scene, you must be able to composite objects of varying shapes to create a layered image.

NEW TERM The answer to this problem is one that you have probably seen on television every day—it is how a reporter appears in front of a weather map on the nightly news, and it is the same power that allowed Superman to fly. Both use a technique called *color keying*, which replaces any pixels of a specified color in one image with corresponding pixels from a second image.

In video and film, this is accomplished by recording the subject in front of a colored matte, usually using blue or green. When the image is processed, this color is replaced by pixels from a background image, as shown in Figure 5.1.

FIGURE 5.1

Color keying objects over a background.

Note that the subject image cannot contain the key color or these areas will not appear in the final image. For example, if a subject were to wear blue pants and the key color was blue, his legs would not be displayed.

In DirectDraw, the same method can be used to blit objects of any shape onto a DirectDraw surface. For example, if you wanted to draw a tree over a background previously blitted to the surface, you would create an image of the tree surrounded by a unique color filling unwanted portions of the rectangle.

The Two Flavors of Color Key

Two methods for color keying defined under DirectDraw are source color keying and destination color keying. The difference is in which surface is tested for the key color—the foreground (source) surface or the background (destination) surface:

- Source keying is the most commonly used. As in the video methods described previously, the portions of the image that are not a specified color will be drawn onto the target. The object appears to be in front of the image it is being drawn to. If this capability is not available in hardware, it will be emulated through DirectX's Hardware Emulation Layer (HEL).

- Destination keying replaces only those sections of the target surface that contain the key color. This technique is useful for filling masked areas in a background and gives the appearance that the drawn image is behind the existing background, being seen through gaps in the background where the color key was set. No emulation is available for destination color keying, so it must be available in hardware.

The majority of applications will use source color keys because they do not depend on the capability of the user's video adapter.

Choosing a Key Color

The first step in color keying is choosing a key color—this must be done before you can create the images that will be used in your application. Two major concerns exist when choosing a key color. They are as follows:

- The key color must be unique. That is, the color must not appear in any part of the image that you want to appear onscreen. Avoid colors that are close to object colors as well because reduction in color depth might cause these colors to be indistinguishable from the key color.
- Because the color format of the surface might differ from the original bitmap, you must be able to reliably determine what the color key will convert to in any pixel format you intend to use.

The first criteria depends on your material. The second one might not be as clear at first. Basically, three choices exist that you will find work well for key colors. They are as follows:

- Black—No matter what pixel format you convert it to, it will always be zero (0). However, black is common in images, and if you use this key, you must settle for levels of gray in your images rather than a true black.
- White is convenient, too, because you can determine the new value by turning all the bits in the given pixel format on. But once again, white is a common color, and features such as highlights will often reach pure white.
- The final option, which we will use in our examples, is to use a saturated primary color (red, green, or blue). *Saturated* means that the maximum value is set for the color and all other colors are absent. This is usually the most practical option because images rarely approach complete saturation of a primary color.

Converting the Key Color

In our color-keyed images, we will use saturated green—that is, an RGB value of (0,255,0). To set this as the key color, we must determine how this color will be represented in our current pixel format. Because we are using a 16-bit format for our screen, this is trickier than most. The reason is that when we set 16-bit color, we might have to deal with either of two color formats, as shown in Table 5.1.

5

TABLE 5.1   Common 16-Bit Pixel Formats

Color Element	15-Bit (5/5/5)	16-Bit (5/6/5)
Red	5-Bits	5-Bits
Green	5-Bits	6-Bits
Blue	5-Bits	5-Bits
Bitmask	XRRRRRGG GGGBBBBB	RRRRRGGG GGGBBBBB

To determine the final value of your key color, you must first find out what bits in the pixel correspond to green (your key color). To do this, you can use the GetPixelFormat() command to retrieve information on the color format of the primary surface, as shown in Listing 5.1.

LISTING 5.1   Determining the Pixel Format

```
1: DDPIXELFORMAT ddpf;
2: ddpf.dwSize=sizeof(ddpf);
3: lpDDSPrimary->GetPixelFormat(&ddpf);
```

This function provides format information, written to the DDPIXELFORMAT structure passed to it, for a variety of different surface types. This includes information for alternative surfaces such as video buffers and depth buffers, which are not of concern to you at this point. The following members are of interest in determining the pixel format:

dwRGBBitCount	The number of bits per pixel
dwRBitMask	The bitmask for red bits
dwGBitMask	The bitmask for green bits
dwBBitMask	The bitmask for blue bits
dwAlphaBitDepth	The bitmask for alpha bits

The bitmasks are 32-bit double words with the bits for the corresponding color set to true. To better understand color bitmasks, take a look at Figure 5.2 to see how the bitmasks assemble to form an RGB color value.

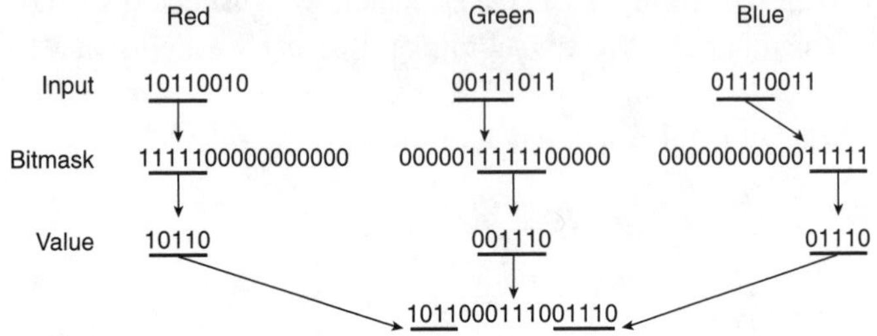

FIGURE 5.2

Conversion of color value to 16-bit (5/6/5) color.

With the bitmasks in hand, it is easy to convert any RGB value into the current pixel format. For example, to convert an RGB value that contains 25 percent red, 50 percent green, and 75 percent blue, multiply each bitmask by the desired percentage and then logically AND the result with the original bitmask. The calculation for this value is shown in Listing 5.2.

LISTING 5.2   Converting an RGB Color Value to the Current Pixel Format

```
1: Color = (((DWORD)(DwRBitMask * 0.25)) & DwRBitMask) +
2:          (((DWORD)(DwGBitMask * 0.50)) & DwGBitMask) +
3:          (((DWORD)(DwBBitMask * 0.75)) & DwBBitMask);
```

Because the bitmasks have all the bits for a specific color set, they represent the brightest value for that color. By multiplying each bitmap by a factor between 0.0 and 1.0, you can scale the brightness of each color over its entire range.

Going back to the desired key color of RGB (0,255,0), which would be expressed in this format as (0.0,1.0,0.0), it becomes apparent that the equation can be simplified. The unused colors, red and blue, have factors of zero and can thus be eliminated from the calculation. Green has a factor of 1.0, representing the full brightness of green, so you can simply use your bitmask for green without scaling it, as shown in Listing 5.3.

LISTING 5.3   Shortcut to Determining Key Color for RGB 0,255,0

```
1: // Determine proper key for pixel format
2:
3: DWORD KeyColor = ddpf.dwGBitMask;
```

5

Setting the Color Key in DirectDraw

▼ SYNTAX

The use of color keying is determined by the settings of the DirectDraw surfaces involved in the blit. To set the color key for an object's surface to a given key color, use the SetColorKey() function.

```
HRESULT SetColorKey(
  DWORD dwFlags,
  LPDDCOLORKEY lpDDColorKey
);
```

This function returns DD_OK on success.

Parameters:

▼ DwFlags provides information on the color key and might be one of the following values:

▼

DDCKEY_COLORSPACE	Indicates that a range of colors is requested.
DDCKEY_DESTBLT	Indicates that destination color keying will be used for blitting.
DDCKEY_DESTOVERLAY	Indicates that destination color keying will be used for overlays.
DDCKEY_SRCBLT	Indicates that source color keying will be used for blitting.
DDCKEY_SRCOVERLAY	Indicates that source color keying will be used for overlays.
lpDDColorKey	Pointer to a DDCOLORKEY structure containing the desired key color.

▲

The code shown in Listing 5.4 will set the color key for an object to the value previously stored in KeyColor.

LISTING 5.4   Setting the Color Key for a Surface

```
1:  // set color key
2:  DDCOLORKEY key;
3:  key.dwColorSpaceLowValue = KeyColor;
4:  key.dwColorSpaceHighValue = KeyColor;
5:  surface->SetColorKey(DDCKEY_SRCBLT, &key);
```

The first step you will perform is setting up a structure of type DDCOLORKEY, which provides a means for you to define a key color as a specific color or range of colors.

In our case we will be using a single key color, so set this color as both the upper and lower limit for the key color. We will stick with this in our examples because hardware support is required to perform color keys over a range of colors.

If you want to, and if the hardware supports it, you can specify a range of colors that will be interpreted as the key color. For example, using the method demonstrated earlier for converting to the current pixel format, you could define low and high values of (0.0,0.9,0.0) and (0.1,1.0,0.1) for your color key. This would interpret any pixel red and blue values from 0 percent–10 percent AND a green value between 90 percent and 100 percent as being set to the key color.

Such methods are often used when working with color keys in photographs or video, where you cannot rely on having the key color being read as a consistent pixel value.

Making It Look Like 3D

By now you should be quite comfortable working with x and y coordinates to represent locations on the screen. To represent a scene in 3D, we are missing something—depth.

In 3D graphics, points are represented using three coordinates—x, y, and z. x and y are similar to the familiar 2D coordinates: x represents the position to the right or left of the viewer, whereas y represents the location above or below the horizon.

The new value, z, is used to represent the depth of a coordinate—that is, the distance ahead or behind the viewer. Although we do not have a z coordinate in DirectDraw surfaces, you can simulate objects with different depths by simulating the visual cues that your mind uses to determine where an object lies in a scene.

Z-Ordering

Depth perception, or the ability to judge distance, is one function of the brain that we tend to take for granted—mostly because it is so automatic. In real life, we determine much of our information about depth, particularly for close objects, from the difference between the images perceived in our eyes. The closer an object is, the greater the difference there will be between what right and left eyes see. A quick illustration of this can be performed by holding your finger a couple of inches in front of your nose and alternately closing one eye and then the other. The finger will appear to shift from one side to the other. If you try this again with your finger at arm's length, the effect is not as great.

But there must be more than this at play because we can determine the depths of objects in 2D images such as photographs and video. So how does this happen, and what can we do to trick the brain into thinking our image is 3D?

One of the cues that we use is how images overlap in a scene. For example, consider Figure 5.3.

5

FIGURE 5.3

The effect of drawing order on perceived distance.

A Drawn First

B Drawn First

Each image contains two objects that are of identical size and shape. However, the perception of depth is quite different between them. In the image on the left, the circle obscures a portion of the square, and thus we assume the circle to be in front. In the image on the right, by contrast, the square obscures a portion of the circle—and thus we assume the square to be in front.

Looking back on our definition of source color keying, which is the method we will be using, you will see that images drawn to a surface appear to be located in front of previously drawn images. This feature allows us to generate an overlap in the order we chose, providing the viewer with an illusion of depth.

To use this, all you must do is control the order in which objects are drawn. This is accomplished by dividing the objects in your scene into layers. A *layer* is a group of objects that you want to appear to be at a certain distance from the viewer and do not overlap each other.

Creating a scene requires that you draw the objects in the proper order, known as the *Z-Order*. The objects in the back are drawn first, and then the next layer forward, and then finally the foreground.

Parallax—Depth Perception of Moving Objects

Being able to simulate overlap is just half of the picture, however. Other effects come into play over distance and become even more apparent when we put the scene in motion.

When we move, objects that are close to us appear to move in the opposite direction. This is a phenomenon known as *relative motion*. The objects aren't really moving, we are. But something interesting happens when we look at objects that are farther away—they do not seem to move as fast. Consider the scene in Figure 5.4, which illustrates the same scene viewed from different angles.

FIGURE 5.4

Parallax in action.

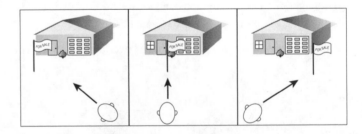

Note how the sign has moved much farther than the house in the background. This effect is known as *parallax* and is key to how we perceive depth in a moving scene.

To use this in your program, you will associate a floating-point value with each layer that you will multiply against the motion of the scene. Higher values will be used for those layers that are to appear closer to the user, causing them to move faster than those objects in the background.

Putting It All Together

At this point, you are ready to start making modifications to last hour's example. You will display the cityscape that you used in the last hour in a scrolling engine, but this time you will use multiple layers to provide a 3D effect.

There will be four separate layers, each of which you will tile as you did in the previous example. In addition to this, you will add a taxi cab that will move across the scene independent of your position.

To begin with, define a structure to contain information on each layer, and create an array to hold the definition of the four layers. The definition of the structure is shown in Listing 5.5.

LISTING 5.5   A Structure for Storing Layer Information

```
 1: // define number of layers
 2:
 3: #define     NUM_LAYERS        4
 4:
 5: // define structure for layers
 6:
 7: struct LAYER {
 8:      LPDIRECTDRAWSURFACE7      surf;
 9:      BOOL                     blit_flags;
10:      WORD                     start_x;
11:      WORD                     start_y;
12:      WORD                     interval;
13:      double                    parallax;
14:      WORD                     width;
15:      WORD                     height;
16: } layers[NUM_LAYERS];
```

The members of this structure contain the following information:

Variable Description

| surf | Contains a pointer to the surface containing the image for this layer. |
| blit_flags | Contains the flags to be used when calling BltFast(), including color key flags if required. |

continues

Variable	Description
start_x	Defines the location of the left-most occurrence of the image on this layer. Images will be repeated to the right of this point every *interval* pixels.
start_y	Defines the Y coordinate for all copies of this image.
interval	Defines the distance on the x-axis between copies of this image.
parallax	Defines the parallax factor for this layer. This is a multiplier applied to the scroll rate attained from the keyboard controls.
width	Defines the surface width of the source image.
height	Defines the surface height of the source image.

This array will be filled as you load the images at startup, and will then be used to sequence through the layers in the rendering loop.

Before loading the images, you will need to define global pointers to reference the DirectDraw surfaces in which you will store them. The global definitions for our surfaces is shown in Listing 5.6.

LISTING 5.6 Surfaces for Storing Layer Images

```
1: //------ DirectDraw Surfaces for Object Storage ------//
2:
3: LPDIRECTDRAWSURFACE7 int_surf=NULL;
4: LPDIRECTDRAWSURFACE7 back1_surf=NULL;
5: LPDIRECTDRAWSURFACE7 back2_surf=NULL;
6: LPDIRECTDRAWSURFACE7 ground_surf=NULL;
7: LPDIRECTDRAWSURFACE7 light_surf=NULL;
```

And, of course, you will need to release these surfaces when you are finished by adding the commands from Listing 5.7 to the Cleanup() function.

LISTING 5.7 Releasing the Image Surfaces

```
1: // release loaded image surfaces
2:
3: SafeRelease(back1_surf);
4: SafeRelease(back2_surf);
5: SafeRelease(int_surf);
6: SafeRelease(ground_surf);
7: SafeRelease(light_surf);
8: SafeRelease(taxi_surf);
```

Remember, you must always release surfaces before releasing interfaces on which they are dependent—so be sure to add these commands prior to the release of either the primary surface or the DirectDraw interface.

Loading the Layers

Now that you have allocated image storage and a means to store specifications for each layer, you are ready to load the images. Begin by creating a new version of the load_images() function of the existing example.

You will begin by loading a user interface. This image will be drawn over the final image, with a color keyed area that will act as a viewport through which the scene is seen. The loading of the interface is shown in Listing 5.8.

LISTING 5.8 Loading the User Interface

```
1: BOOL load_images()
2: {
3:     // load the interface image
4:
5:     int_surf = bitmap_surface("ntrface.bmp");
6:     if (!int_surf) {
7:         ErrStr=Err_LoadImage;
8:         return FALSE;
9:     }
```

Next, load your first background layer, which contains a cloud image for the sky, and set up a record for the rendering of this layer as shown in Listing 5.9.

LISTING 5.9 Loading the First Background Layer

```
1: // load the background image
2:
3: RECT rct;
```

5

continues

LISTING 5.9 continued

```
 4: back1_surf=bitmap_surface("back.bmp",&rct);
 5: if (!back1_surf) {
 6:     ErrStr=Err_LoadImage;
 7:     return FALSE;
 8: }
 9:
10: // set up layer record
11:
12: layers[0].surf=back1_surf;
13: layers[0].blit_flags=DDBLTFAST_WAIT;
14: layers[0].start_x=0;
15: layers[0].start_y=0;
16: layers[0].parallax=0.8;
17: layers[0].interval=layers[0].width=rct.right;
18: layers[0].height=rct.bottom;
```

Note that the parallax is set to 0.8—this layer will move slightly slower than the standard rate your keyboard routine determines.

Now you are ready to load your additional layers, for the various layers of the city. The code in Listing 5.10 provides for loading the additional layers, as well as loading the taxi sprite, which you will integrate into the scene.

LISTING 5.10 Loading the Layers

```
 1:     // load the cityscape layer
 2:
 3:     back2_surf=bitmap_surface("back2.bmp",&rct);
 4:     if (!back2_surf) {
 5:     ErrStr=Err_LoadImage;
 6:     return FALSE;
 7:     }
 8:
 9:     // set up layer record
10:
11:     layers[1].surf=back2_surf;
12:     layers[1].blit_flags=DDBLTFAST_WAIT|DDBLTFAST_SRCCOLORKEY;
13:     layers[1].start_x=0;
14:     layers[1].start_y=45;
15:     layers[1].parallax=1.4;
16:     layers[1].interval=layers[1].width=rct.right;
17:     layers[1].height=rct.bottom;
18:
19:     // load the light layer
20:
21:     light_surf=bitmap_surface("light.bmp",&rct);
22:     if (!light_surf) {
23:     ErrStr=Err_LoadImage;
```

```
24:     return FALSE;
25:     }
26:
27:     // set up layer record
28:
29:     layers[2].surf=light_surf;
30:     layers[2].blit_flags=DDBLTFAST_WAIT¦DDBLTFAST_SRCCOLORKEY;
31:     layers[2].start_x=0;
32:     layers[2].start_y=8;
33:     layers[2].parallax=1.8;
34:     layers[2].interval=600;
35:     layers[2].width=rct.right;
36:     layers[2].height=rct.bottom;
37:
38:     // load the ground layer
39:
40:     ground_surf=bitmap_surface("ground.bmp",&rct);
41:     if (!ground_surf) {
42:     ErrStr=Err_LoadImage;
43:     return FALSE;
44:
45:
46:     // set up layer record
47:
48:     layers[3].surf=ground_surf;
49:     layers[3].blit_flags=DDBLTFAST_WAIT;
50:     layers[3].start_x=0;
51:     layers[3].start_y=106;
52:     layers[3].parallax=2.4;
53:     layers[3].interval=layers[3].width=rct.right;
54:     layers[3].height=rct.bottom;
55:
56:     // load the sprite for the taxi
57:
58:     taxi_surf=bitmap_surface("taxi.bmp",&rct);
59:     if (!taxi_surf) {
60:     ErrStr=Err_LoadImage;
61:     return FALSE;
62:     }
63:
64:     // save taxi dimensions
65:
66:     taxi_width=rct.right;
67:     taxi_height=rct.bottom;
```

5

For these three layers, you have set successively higher parallax values, so they will move faster and provide the appearance that each is closer to you than the previous layers.

You have also added an extra flag to your blit_flags field, which will be passed to the BltFast() function when you draw the layers. This will cause DirectDraw to use the color key you specified to perform source color keying. Note that the first layer does not have a color key flag because it has nothing under it. The last layer also has no color key because it is rectangular and will have no color keyed areas.

Speaking of color keys, you have not set one yet. Now that you have loaded all your images, you will start off by finding the proper color for saturated green, which is the key used in the sample images. The code for this is shown in Listing 5.11.

LISTING 5.11   Determining Color Key for Current Pixel Format

```
1:      // get the pixel format
2:
3:      DDPIXELFORMAT ddpf;
4:      ddpf.dwSize=sizeof(ddpf);
5:      lpDDSPrimary->GetPixelFormat(&ddpf);
6:
7:      // Determine proper key for pixel format
8:
9:      KeyColor = ddpf.dwGBitMask;
```

With this value in hand, create a DDCOLORKEY structure and use it to set the color key for the interface and the foreground objects, using the SetColorKey() function. The code is shown in Listing 5.12.

LISTING 5.12   Setting the Color Key

```
1: // set color keys
2:
3: DDCOLORKEY key;
4: key.dwColorSpaceLowValue = KeyColor;
5: key.dwColorSpaceHighValue = KeyColor;
6: int_surf->SetColorKey(DDCKEY_SRCBLT, &key);
7: back2_surf->SetColorKey(DDCKEY_SRCBLT, &key);
8: light_surf->SetColorKey(DDCKEY_SRCBLT, &key);
9: taxi_surf->SetColorKey(DDCKEY_SRCBLT, &key);
```

That concludes the setup of surfaces for the layers of your scene. Now the only thing remaining is to rewrite the existing render_frame() function to draw the layers in the proper order. Start off by looping through the layers, as shown in Listing 5.13.

LISTING 5.13   Beginning of the Frame Rendering Function

```
1: void render_frame()
2: {
3:    RECT rct;
4:
```

```
5:    // loop through the layers
6:
7:    for (int i=0; i<NUM_LAYERS; i++) {
```

Now for the 3D magic! The keyboard routine keeps track of your scrolling position in x_pos; however, the position of each layer is determined by the parallax factor for the layer.

To determine the position for a layer, simply take your normal scrolling position and multiply it by the parallax for the layer (see Listing 5.14).

LISTING 5.14   Calculating Parallax Based Position for a Layer

```
1: // calculate parallax position of layer
2:
3: int screen_pos = x_pos*layers[i].parallax;
```

Next, determine the position of the first instance of the object in the layer and loop through the copies until you have found all the ones that are in the viewing area (see Listing 5.15).

LISTING 5.15   Finding Objects That Are Onscreen

```
1: // set position of first object
2: int obj_pos=layers[i].start_x;
3: // loop until off right side of screen
4: while (obj_pos<screen_pos+640) {
5:     // is this object on the screen?
6:     if (obj_pos+layers[i].width>=screen_pos) {
```

For each object on the screen, Listing 5.16 will calculate its screen position and clip the object to the screen if necessary, as you learned in Hour 4, "Creating the Game Loop."

LISTING 5.16   Clipping to the Screen Rectangle

```
1: // yes, calculate the offset to the left edge of the screen
2:
3: int screen_x=obj_pos-screen_pos;
4:
5: // clip the object if necessary
6:
7: rct.left=0;
8:  rct.top=0;
```

continues

5

LISTING 5.16 continued

```
 9:  rct.right=layers[i].width;
10:  rct.bottom=layers[i].height;
11:  if (screen_x<0) {
12:      rct.left-=screen_x;
13:      screen_x=0;
14:  } else if (screen_x+rct.right>640) {
15:      rct.right=640-screen_x;
16:  }
```

Finally, you are ready to render the object to the screen. You will use the `blit_flags` member of the layer record to set the flags for `BltFast()`, setting the flag for color keying on those layers that need it (see Listing 5.17).

LISTING 5.17 Blitting to the Screen

```
 1:              // draw the object to the screen
 2:
 3:              lpDDSBack -> BltFast( screen_x,layers[i].start_y,
                 ➥layers[i].surf,
 4:          &rct,layers[i].blit_flags);
 5:          }
 6:
 7:      // increment to next object position
 8:
 9:          obj_pos+=layers[i].interval;
10:      }
11:  }
```

After you have drawn all the layers, you are ready to handle your taxi sprite. We have saved it for last because it is the closest object in the scene. The taxi will travel from right to left across the scene and loop back around to the right of the scene when it goes off the edge of the scene. Listing 5.18 shows you how to do this.

LISTING 5.18 Moving and Displaying the Taxi Sprite

```
 1:      // calculate screen position for taxi parallax
 2:
 3:      screen_pos=x_pos*3.0;
 4:
 5:      // is the taxi on the screen?
 6:
 7:      if (taxi_pos+taxi_width > screen_pos&&taxi_pos<screen_pos+640) {
 8:
```

```
 9:            // yes, calculate the offset to the left edge of the screen
10:
11:            int screen_x=taxi_pos-screen_pos;
12:
13:            // clip the object if necessary
14:
15:            rct.left=0;
16:            rct.top=0;
17:            rct.right=taxi_width;
18:            rct.bottom=taxi_height;
19:            if (screen_x<0) {
20:                rct.left-=screen_x;
21:                screen_x=0;
22:            } else if (screen_x+rct.right>640) {
23:                rct.right=640-screen_x;
24:            }
25:
26:            // draw the object to the screen
27:
28:            lpDDSBack->BltFast(screen_x,220,taxi_surf,&rct,
                    ➥DDBLTFAST_WAIT¦DDBLTFAST_SRCCOLORKEY);
29:    }
30:
```

Now you are ready to apply the interface, blitting with a source color key so that the drawn scene shows through. Finally, flip the back buffer to the front, showing the completed image. The code shown in Listing 5.19 provides the finishing touches on this exercise.

LISTING 5.19   Displaying the Interface

```
 1:    // blit the interface to the back buffer with color key
 2:
 3:    rct.left=0;
 4:    rct.top=0;
 5:    rct.right=640;
 6:    rct.bottom=480;
 7:    lpDDSBack -> BltFast (0,0,int_surf,&rct,DDBLTFAST_WAIT
 8:            ¦DDBLTFAST_SRCCOLORKEY);
 9:    // flip to the primary surface
10:
11:    lpDDSPrimary->Flip(0,DDFLIP_WAIT);
12: }
```

That completes the rendering of your scene. This technique, known in the gaming engine as *side scrolling*, provides a good illusion of 3D without the cost of creating a 3D world and rendering engine. A sample of the final scene is shown in Figure 5.5.

FIGURE 5.5

The composition of the final scene.

Summary

In this hour, you learned what color keys are and how to use them, including choosing a key color, converting that key, and setting the color key in DirectDraw. You also learned about depth in 3D by using Z-Order and how to load different layers in a parallax environment.

Q&A

Q What are the practical limitations of color keyed scenes, such as the one demonstrated in this hour? How complex can they be?

A If such scenes are properly optimized, they can easily reach seven or eight layers in depth. The biggest loss of performance is from what is known as *overdraw*. Overdraw is a measurement of how many times a given pixel is drawn in a single frame. In commercial games, regions of overlapping objects are often determined before rendering, and background objects that are obscured are not drawn.

Q With the increasing popularity of 3D games, is there still a market for 2D games based on this kind of technology?

A Yes, there will still be for some time. Although this style of game will require an increased quality in both media and game play to compete, they are far less demanding in their system requirements and thus reach a broader market.

Workshop

The Workshop is designed to help you anticipate possible questions, review what you've learned, and begin thinking ahead to put your knowledge into practice. The answers to the quiz are in Appendix A, "Answers."

Quiz

1. What are the two most common 16-bit pixel formats?

    a. 5,5,5 5,5,6

    b. 6,5,6 5,6,5

    c. 5,6,5 5,5,5

2. What are the two types of color keying?

3. Which function is used to set the color of a surface in DirectDraw?

4. Using Z-Ordering, the first image drawn is

    a. in the foreground

    b. in the background

5. True or false: During cleanup you should release DirectDraw surfaces before releasing DirectDraw object interfaces.

Exercises

1. Change the values for each parallax layer by increasing or decreasing its value. See how it affects the effect of 3D.

2. Add an additional layer or two and adjust the parallax speeds according to their depth.

5

PART III

Adding Music and Sound

Hour

HOUR 6

DirectSound—Adding Ambience and Sound Effects to Your Game

DirectSound is the audio portion of DirectX that supports high-performance audio mixing and playback. Using DirectSound, you can create games with very rich sound effects that help add excitement and realism. The main benefit to using DirectSound is the ability to get close to the sound hardware. More specifically, DirectSound automatically uses hardware acceleration if it detects that the sound hardware supports it.

This hour introduces you to DirectSound and lays the groundwork for using DirectSound to play sound effects in games. You will learn about the architecture of DirectSound along with some specifics regarding how certain DirectSound objects are used.

In this hour, you will learn

- The benefits of using DirectSound
- The main objects used in DirectSound

- The relationship between primary and secondary sound buffers
- How to alter the volume, panning, and frequency of a sound buffer
- The difference between static and streaming sound buffers

DirectSound Basics

DirectSound is the sound component of DirectX, and it provides support for efficient wave mixing, direct access to sound hardware, and the capability of utilizing 3D audio. You can think of DirectSound as an audio buffer manager. The primary design goal behind DirectSound is to provide an efficient, device-independent interface to sound hardware that can use hardware acceleration. DirectSound pulls off this feat by providing default software functionality that is superceded by hardware functionality if the hardware is available. This open-ended design allows DirectSound to take advantage of new audio features as sound hardware evolves.

DirectSound accesses the sound hardware through the DirectSound HAL (Hardware Abstraction Layer). The HAL is a layer of software implemented by the DirectSound device driver that provides a uniform interface to the sound hardware. The HAL is implemented as an extension to the standard audio device driver. This means that a DirectSound driver is really just a Windows device driver with HAL extensions.

Don't let all this HAL talk get you to thinking that you need to understand how to program low-level device drivers to use DirectSound. DirectSound's driver model is actually very similar to the DirectDraw driver model. And similar to DirectDraw, it isn't imperative that you understand the inner workings of a device driver to develop DirectX applications.

The DirectSound HAL provides the following functionality:

- It describes the capabilities of the sound hardware
- It acquires and releases control of the sound hardware
- It performs an operation when the sound hardware is available
- It fails an operation when the sound hardware is unavailable

Although it's important to have a general understanding of how DirectSound communicates with the sound hardware, it's much more important to understand exactly what DirectSound can do for you at the application level. The next few sections uncover some of the main benefits of using DirectSound.

Low-Latency Audio Mixing

NEW TERM   The most important feature of DirectSound is low-latency audio mixing. *Latency* is the delay between when a sound is played programmatically and when the user actually hears it. Low-latency means that this delay is very small, which is a good thing. Ideally, the latency would be so small that the user doesn't notice any delay. DirectSound is supposed to have no more than a 20 millisecond latency, which is practically instantaneous, at least in terms of human perception.

Low-latency mixing is extremely important to games and other high-performance multimedia applications because you will often want to play a sound in conjunction with a graphical animation of some sort. Suppose, for example, that you're developing a game and you want to play an explosion sound to go along with an animated explosion visual effect. You don't want the boom to come a half second after the smoke clears; you want it to come right as the explosion animation starts. DirectSound offers suitable performance to alleviate this type of problem.

DirectSound isn't perfect when it comes to low-latency mixing, however. If the user doesn't have a suitable DirectSound driver, DirectSound has to rely on HAL emulation, which results in a higher latency. This means that if the user doesn't have a DirectSound driver, there will more than likely be noticeable latency delays. Fortunately, most Windows 98 sound card drivers support DirectSound, so this is rarely an issue.

Hardware Acceleration

Another major feature of DirectSound is its capability of taking advantage of hardware acceleration. DirectSound is designed to carry out all of its functionality in software, but it always attempts to use hardware acceleration whenever possible. This means that the actual mixing of sound buffers takes place in hardware sound buffer memory, as opposed to being handled in software. Because hardware is inherently faster than software, any functions that can be performed in hardware improve performance.

The really nice thing about DirectSound's hardware acceleration feature is that it is completely automatic. You don't have to write any special code to detect hardware and enable hardware acceleration; DirectSound takes on all the responsibility of querying the hardware and using hardware acceleration if it is available. Just in case you don't see the significance of this, let me assure you that this is a huge benefit for developers. By simply developing your application to use DirectSound, you can boast that it fully supports hardware acceleration.

6

3D Audio

When I first heard people talking about 3D audio a few years back, I thought that it was just a gimmick. How could you possibly give the effect of 3D audio with a couple of speakers? Well, the idea behind 3D audio doesn't have as much to do with the speakers as it does with the context of a game or multimedia application. 3D audio has to do with assigning a spatial position to a piece of audio so that its playback attributes (volume, panning, frequency, and so on) can be altered accordingly. Typically this involves altering these attributes based on the position of the audio with respect to a player's character in a game. If an explosion occurs to your right, the sound should primarily come from the right speaker.

DirectSound 3D adds a spatial dimension to audio by taking into account the subtleties of human audio perception. The most obvious spatial audio cue is volume, which varies based on how close a sound is to the listener. Another more subtle cue is the slightly muffled effect a sound has when heard from behind. DirectSound 3D takes these cues into account to make the user of an application or game feel as if sounds are coming from different locations.

DirectSound and Windows Waves

DirectSound supports all the standard Windows wave formats. Not only does it support using all the formats, but it also enables you to mix waves in any of the formats, handling appropriate conversions automatically. Even so, it is smarter and more efficient to try and keep all your waves in the same format so that DirectSound has to do as little conversion as possible. DirectSound supports all combinations of the following wave formats:

- 8- or 16-bit sample data width
- 11kHz, 22kHz, or 44kHz sample rate
- mono or stereo

Inside DirectSound

Now that you have an idea as to the benefits of using DirectSound, take a look inside DirectSound to see how it is structured. DirectSound is implemented as a set of COM objects for representing both physical sound devices and sound data buffers. You might not ever need all the objects, but it still helps to know what they are. Following are the DirectSound objects involved in the playback of audio:

- `DirectSound`—represents a physical hardware sound device
- `DirectSoundBuffer`—represents a stream of audio data

- DirectSound3DBuffer—represents a stream of audio data positioned in 3D space
- DirectSound3Dlistener—represents an audio listener positioned in 3D space
- DirectSoundNotify—provides a mechanism for notifying an application of DirectSound events

To keep things relatively simple, I'm going to stick with 2D audio in this lesson and show how to mix 2D audio clips using DirectSound. To play 2D audio, you really only need to use the DirectSound and DirectSoundBuffer objects. So, I will focus on these two objects and you will learn more about their role in DirectSound.

The DirectSound Object

The DirectSound object is a software representation of a physical audio hardware device (a sound card). Because most computers have only one sound card, you will typically be using only one DirectSound object. This means that multiple applications that use DirectSound will have to share the DirectSound object because they all use the same physical audio hardware. Fortunately, DirectSound automatically tracks the input focus of each application and produces sound only for the application with input focus. In other words, you don't have to worry about sharing the DirectSound object.

You create a DirectSound object by calling the global DirectSoundCreate() function, which returns a pointer to an IDirectSound interface:

```
HRESULT WINAPI DirectSoundCreate(LPGUID lpGuid, LPDIRECTSOUND * ppDS,
➥LPUNKNOWN  pUnkOuter);
```

The first parameter to DirectSoundCreate(), lpGUID, is a global identifier for the audio device that the DirectSound object represents. This identifier can be determined from calling DirectSoundEnumerate(), or it can be set to NULL. In the latter case, DirectSound uses the default Windows sound device. The second parameter, ppDS, is a pointer to a DirectSound object pointer. This parameter is set to the DirectSound object pointer after successful creation, and it serves as the basis for performing future DirectSound operations. The final parameter to DirectSoundCreate() is pUnkOuter, which might be used to support aggregation in a future release of DirectSound, but for now must be set to NULL. If the DirectSound object is successfully created, DirectSoundCreate() will return DS_OK.

I mentioned that you could call the DirectSoundEnumerate() function to determine an audio device identifier. Following is the prototype for this function:

```
HRESULT WINAPI DirectSoundEnumerate(LPDSENUMCALLBACK lpDSEnumCallback,
➥LPVOID lpContext);
```

You must use DirectSoundEnumerate() only if you're concerned that multiple audio devices might be available. DirectSoundEnumerate() will return a list of these devices,

6

from which you can choose one. You provide DirectSoundEnumerate() with a callback function in the first parameter, which is called by DirectSound and provided with information about each available sound device. You can also provide additional information of your own to the callback function by using the second parameter to DirectSoundEnumerate(). Because the default sound device is suitable in most cases, I won't spend any more time on the DirectSoundEnumerate() function. Just understand that if you want to support a system with eleven sound cards, you certainly have the flexibility to do so!

After successfully creating a DirectSound object, you're ready to get to work manipulating it. DirectSound objects are manipulated through the IDirectSound COM interface. The IDirectSound interface methods are used to get and set DirectSound object attributes, as well as to create DirectSoundBuffer objects. Following are the methods defined in the IDirectSound interface, some of which you will use in the next lesson when you add DirectSound support to an application:

- Initialize()
- SetCooperativeLevel()
- CreateSoundBuffer()
- DuplicateSoundBuffer()
- GetCaps()
- Compact()
- GetSpeakerConfig()
- SetSpeakerConfig()
- AddRef()
- QueryInterface()
- Release()

Creating a Sound Buffer

The CreateSoundBuffer() method is used to create sound buffers, which are actually DirectSoundBuffer objects. Following is the prototype for this function:

```
HRESULT CreateSoundBuffer(LPCDSBUFFERDESC lpcDSBufferDesc,
    LPLPDIRECTSOUNDBUFFER lplpDirectSoundBuffer, IUnknown FAR * pUnkOuter);
```

You will typically use the CreateSoundBuffer() method to create secondary sound buffers to represent different sounds in a game. The first parameter, lpcDSBufferDesc, is a pointer to a DSBUFFERDESC structure. This structure contains a description of the sound buffer to be created, including the size of the buffer, among other things:

```
typedef struct {
    DWORD          dwSize;
    DWORD          dwFlags;
    DWORD          dwBufferBytes;
    DWORD          dwReserved;
    LPWAVEFORMATEX lpwfxFormat;
} DSBUFFERDESC, *LPDSBUFFERDESC;
typedef const DSBUFFERDESC *LPCDSBUFFERDESC;
```

You will learn how to create and fill-in the details of a DSBUFFERDESC structure in the next hour. Getting back to the CreateSoundBuffer() method, the second parameter, lplpDirectSoundBuffer, points to a location to store a pointer to the newly created DirectSoundBuffer object. This is the pointer you will use to manipulate the sound buffer. The last parameter to CreateSoundBuffer(), pUnkOuter, might be used to support aggregation in a future release of DirectSound, but for now must be set to NULL.

Getting Device Capabilities

Sometimes it is useful to query the sound hardware for its device capabilities to see what you have to work with. The GetCaps() method performs this task:

```
HRESULT GetCaps(LPDSCAPS lpDSCaps);
```

The only parameter to GetCaps() is a pointer to a structure that is filled in with details regarding the sound hardware. The DSCAPS structure contains a wide variety of fields with detailed device information about the sound hardware. You should refer to the DirectSound documentation for more information about the specifics of this structure.

Releasing DirectSound

When you're finished using a DirectSound object, you must make sure to free it, so it releases the sound hardware and any other resources that it has tied up. You do this by calling the Release() method, which takes no parameters:

```
ULONG Release();
```

A call to Release() actually results in the reference count of the DirectSound object being adjusted. Not surprisingly, the reference count on a COM object keeps up with how many times the object is being referenced. When the reference count reaches 0, the DirectSound object is automatically freed. When a DirectSound object is finally freed, all the DirectSoundBuffer objects created for it are released as well. In other words, releasing a DirectSound object results in all associated DirectSoundBuffer objects being released too.

Setting the Cooperative Level

The last method of interest in the IDirectSound interface is SetCooperativeLevel(), which must be called on a DirectSound object before any sound buffers can be played.

6

SetCooperativeLevel() establishes the cooperative (priority) level for the sound device represented by the DirectSound object. There are four priority levels, listed in order of increasing priority:

- Normal
- Priority
- Exclusive
- Write-primary

The normal priority level has the lowest priority, whereas write-primary has the highest priority. You must use the write-primary priority level to write directly to the primary sound buffer; this is something that you will rarely need to do.

The SetCooperativeLevel() method is defined as follows:

```
HRESULT SetCooperativeLevel(HWND hwnd, DWORD dwLevel);
```

The first parameter, hwnd, is the handle of the application's main window. The second parameter, dwLevel, is a flag that indicates the desired priority level. The DSSCL_NORMAL flag represents the normal priority level and is recommended in most situations. Because the DSSCL_NORMAL flag specifies the lowest priority level, it provides the safest sharing of sound resources with other applications. You should use DSSCL_NORMAL unless you have a compelling reason for using a higher priority level.

The DirectSoundBuffer Object

The DirectSoundBuffer object represents a stream of wave audio, and comes in two forms: the primary sound buffer and secondary sound buffers. The primary sound buffer represents the audio buffer being played on the physical audio device. Secondary sound buffers represent individual audio streams that are mixed into the primary buffer for output. Figure 6.1 shows the relationship between the primary and secondary buffers.

FIGURE 6.1

The relationship between the primary and secondary sound buffers.

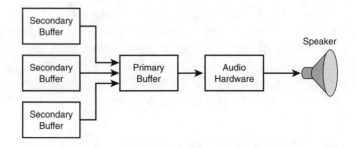

Figure 6.1 shows how the primary sound buffer represents the output of the `DirectSound` object and effectively serves as the result of mixing secondary buffers together. Secondary sound buffers are equivalent to the inputs on an audio mixer, except that in DirectSound there are no limits to the number of secondary sound buffers. Each secondary sound buffer is capable of being mixed with any other secondary buffer, with the resulting sound residing in the primary buffer for output.

Practically speaking, secondary sound buffers are used to represent each discrete sound in a game or multimedia application. You can create and mix as many secondary buffers as you need within a given application.

`DirectSoundBuffer` objects are manipulated through the `IDirectSoundBuffer` COM interface. You create `DirectSoundBuffer` objects by calling the `CreateSoundBuffer()` method on the `DirectSound` object, which returns a pointer to an `IDirectSoundBuffer` interface. The `IDirectSoundBuffer` interface methods are used to get and set `DirectSoundBuffer` object attributes, as well as to write audio data and play the sound buffers. Following are the methods defined in the `IDirectSoundBuffer` interface:

- `GetCaps()`
- `GetFormat()`
- `SetFormat()`
- `GetStatus()`
- `Initialize()`
- `Restore()`
- `GetCurrentPosition()`
- `SetCurrentPosition()`
- `Lock()`
- `Unlock()`
- `Play()`
- `Stop()`
- `GetFrequency()`
- `SetFrequency()`
- `GetPan()`
- `SetPan()`
- `GetVolume()`
- `SetVolume()`

6

- AddRef()
- QueryInterface()
- Release()

You'll be using several of these methods in the next hour to add DirectSound functionality to an existing application. The next few sections highlight these functions and how they work.

Locking and Unlocking a Sound Buffer

A sound buffer is really just a chunk of memory containing sound data. Before you can play a sound buffer, you must first write sound data to it. You do so by locking the buffer and obtaining a pointer to the buffer memory. The Lock() method is used to lock a sound buffer:

```
HRESULT Lock(DWORD dwWriteCursor, DWORD dwWriteBytes, LPVOID lplpvAudioPtr1,
➡LPDWORD lpdwAudioBytes1, LPVOID lplpvAudioPtr2, LPDWORD lpdwAudioBytes2,
➡DWORD dwFlags);
```

The first parameter, dwWritePosition, specifies a position, relative to the start of the buffer, where the buffer is to be locked. The second parameter, dwWriteBytes, specifies how many bytes are to be locked for writing, starting at dwWritePosition. The third parameter, lplpvAudioPtr1, points to a value that will contain a pointer to the first block of writable audio data. The lpdwAudioBytes1 parameter points to a DWORD that will be filled with the number of bytes that can actually be written. If lpdwAudioBytes1 is equal to dwWriteBytes, then lpdwAudioBytes1 points to the entire requested block of data. If not, then the fifth parameter, lplpvAudioPtr2, points to a second block of audio data. The lpdwAudioBytes2 parameter points to a DWORD, which will be filled with the number of bytes that can actually be written to the second block. The last parameter to Lock(), dwFlags, specifies the buffer lock flags, which can be either DSBLOCK_FROMWRITECURSOR or DSBLOCK_ENTIREBUFFER. The former flag locks the buffer from the current position at which it is safe to write new data (the write cursor)—usually about ten milliseconds ahead of the play cursor. You can use the latter flag if you want to write to the entire buffer.

NEW TERM   *play cursor:* the position in a sound buffer at which the data is being played.

NEW TERM   *write cursor:* the position in a sound buffer at which it is safe to write new data; usually about ten milliseconds ahead of the play cursor.

You're probably thinking that the Lock() function is unnecessarily confusing—I know I did when I first worked with DirectSound. The big question is why do you need two memory blocks? This is necessary because sound buffers are circular, which means that if you read or write past the end of a buffer, you will wrap around and continue from the beginning. Figures 6.2 and 6.3 reveal the circular nature of sound buffers by visually showing two approaches to a 2KB lock within a 3KB buffer.

FIGURE **6.2**

A 2KB lock performed from the beginning of a 3KB sound buffer.

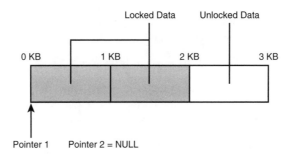

FIGURE **6.3**

A 2KB lock performed at 2KB into a 3KB sound buffer, resulting in a circular wraparound.

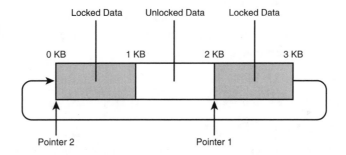

In Figure 6.3, the buffer data is circular because there isn't room to write 2KB of data when there is only 1KB left until the end of the buffer. So, the remaining 1KB is wrapped around to the beginning of the buffer. Two data pointers are necessary to account for the wraparound. Although this is a nice feature, in most cases you will lock the entire buffer, which means that you'll only use the first data pointer passed to the Lock() method.

It's very important not to leave buffers locked for long periods of time. This is because of the fact that you might be playing a buffer as you are writing to it, and keeping the buffer locked for too long might result in the play cursor catching up with the locked data. This can result in random noise, which is a bad thing. You call the Unlock() method to unlock a sound buffer:

```
HRESULT Unlock(LPVOID lpvAudioPtr1, DWORD dwAudioBytes1, LPVOID lpvAudioPtr2,
➡DWORD dwAudioBytes2);
```

As you can see, the Unlock() function takes four of the same parameters that you passed into Lock(). This allows it to properly free the memory that was locked down.

6

Playing and Stopping a Sound Buffer

The `Play()` method is used to play sound buffers. Playing a buffer actually means that the buffer is mixed into the primary buffer, which is then output to the sound device. If `Play()` is called on a buffer that is already playing, the call succeeds without interrupting play. Following is the prototype for the `Play()` function:

```
HRESULT Play(DWORD dwReserved1, DWORD dwReserved2, DWORD dwFlags);
```

The first two parameters to `Play()` are reserved and must be passed as 0. The last parameter is a flag that specifies how the buffer is to be played. The only flag defined in DirectSound is `DSBPLAY_LOOPING`, which indicates that the buffer is to continue playing over and over until it is explicitly stopped. You pass 0 to indicate that the buffer is to only be played once.

To stop playing a sound buffer, you call the `Stop()` method. `Stop()` is most commonly used to stop the play of looping sound buffers, which don't stop playing on their own. Following is the prototype for the `Stop()` function:

```
HRESULT Stop();
```

There isn't too much more to say about `Stop()`; just call it on a buffer to stop it.

Getting Sound Buffer Status

You can obtain information about the status of a sound buffer by calling the `GetStatus()` method:

```
HRESULT GetStatus(LPDWORD lpdwStatus);
```

The only parameter to `GetStatus()` is a pointer to a `DWORD`, `lpdwStatus`, which is where the resulting buffer status is stored. The status of the buffer consists of whether the buffer is currently playing, whether it is looping, and whether the buffer has been lost. Of course, a buffer must be playing for it to be looping. The three corresponding status flags are `DSBSTATUS_PLAYING`, `DSBSTATUS_LOOPING`, and `DSBSTATUS_BUFFERLOST`.

In the event of a buffer being lost, as indicated by the `DSBSTATUS_BUFFERLOST` flag, you must call the `Restore()` method and then reinitialize the sound buffer data. You learn how to do this in the next hour when you put DirectSound to work.

Setting Sound Buffer Volume

You get and set the volume of a `DirectSoundBuffer` object by calling the `GetVolume()` and `SetVolume()` methods:

```
HRESULT GetVolume(LPLONG lplVolume);
HRESULT SetVolume(LONG lVolume);
```

Volume is measured in hundredths of decibels (dB), which results in possible values ranging from –10,000 to 10,000. Negative volumes attenuate a sound whereas positive volumes amplify a sound; a volume of zero results in a sound being played at its recorded level.

Controlling Sound Buffer Panning

To get and set the panning of a `DirectSoundBuffer` object, you must call the `GetPan()` and `SetPan()` methods:

```
HRESULT GetPan(LPLONG lplPan);
HRESULT SetPan(LONG lPan);
```

The panning of a sound buffer determines how the sound is played with respect to the left and right speakers. Panning is expressed in hundredths of decibels (dB), which determines how much a channel is attenuated. Panning values range from –10,000 to 10,000, with negative values attenuating the right channel and positive values attenuating the left channel; a panning value of zero results in both channels at full volume. It's important to note that panning is applied in addition to volume settings.

Altering Sound Buffer Frequency

You get and set the frequency of a `DirectSoundBuffer` object by calling the `GetFrequency()` and `SetFrequency()` methods:

```
HRESULT GetFrequency(LPDWORD lpdwFrequency);
HRESULT SetFrequency(DWORD dwFrequency);
```

Frequency is measured in Hertz (Hz), with possible values ranging from 100 to 100,000. Keep in mind that sounds are typically recorded at 11,250Hz (11kHz), 22,500Hz (22kHz), or 44,100Hz (44kHz). So, you can effectively slow down a 22kHz sound by setting its frequency to 15,000Hz, for example.

Static and Streaming Sound Buffers

NEW TERM   It's worth pointing out that the `DirectSoundBuffer` object supports both static and streaming sound buffers. A *static* sound buffer is a buffer that contains an entire sound in memory, whereas a *streaming* sound buffer usually contains only part of a sound and requires the application to write new data to the sound buffer as the buffer is being played. Static buffers are more efficient because DirectSound will store them directly in the memory of a hardware audio device if possible. If a static buffer can be stored in the hardware audio device's memory, the sound hardware takes on the task of mixing the audio, which is much faster than leaving it up to the system CPU. It is also possible to use hardware mixing with streaming sound buffers providing that the system data bus is fast enough to transfer the stream of data to the audio hardware as it is delivered.

6

Unless you are building an application that pulls audio from the Internet, you will more than likely want to use static sound buffers because they are more efficient. It is important to point out that audio hardware memory is limited, which means that there might not be enough room for it to hold all the static sound buffers you are using. Therefore, you should prioritize sound buffers so that the most commonly played buffers have the best chance of being stored directly in audio hardware memory. You do this by simply creating and initializing the most commonly played sound buffers first.

Summary

In this hour, you became acquainted with DirectSound, the high-performance audio portion of DirectX. You began the lesson by learning some basics about DirectSound, including the major benefits it offers. You then took a look inside the DirectSound API, exploring the DirectSound architecture and learning some details about DirectSound COM objects along the way. You focused on the DirectSound and DirectSoundBuffer objects, which are the most commonly used objects for playing 2D sound.

The next hour shows you how to apply what you learned today. More specifically, you use the DirectSound and DirectSoundBuffer objects to add some interesting sound effects to the cityscape application from the previous hour.

Q&A

Q I understand that a 44kHz sampling rate results in a better quality sound than 22kHz and that 16-bit audio is better quality than 8-bit. Why is this so?

A Because the sampling rate determines how many discrete samples are taken per second, a higher sampling rate results in more samples being taken. This in turn results in higher sampled sound quality because you're obtaining more information about the physical sound. The same applies to the data width of the sample, which can be 8- or 16-bit. 16 bits provide more discrete amplitude levels than 8 bits, and ultimately make the sampled sound more closely match the physical sound.

Q If a DirectSound object can be shared among multiple applications, how does it know when to produce sound for a given application?

A The DirectSound object automatically tracks the input focus, which is always set to the currently active window. The DirectSound object only produces sound for the application with the input focus. So, when an application loses the input focus, all audio being played through DirectSound is muted. This helps to ensure that two applications can't play sounds on top of each other.

Workshop

The Workshop is designed to help you anticipate possible questions, review what you've learned, and begin thinking ahead to put your knowledge into practice. The answers to the quiz are in Appendix A, "Answers."

Quiz

1. What is the purpose of the DirectSound HAL?
2. How is the DirectSound HAL implemented?
3. What is the most important feature of DirectSound?
4. To what does the term *latency* refer?
5. What happens if the user doesn't have a DirectSound driver?
6. What DirectSound COM object represents a physical hardware sound device?
7. How do you initially create a `DirectSound` object?
8. What priority level provides the safest sharing of sound resources with other applications?
9. What happens to any associated `DirectSoundBuffer` objects when a `DirectSound` object is released?
10. What happens to the playback of a sound if you set the panning value to 10,000?

Exercises

1. Take some time to get acquainted with the DirectSound documentation, which ships with DirectX. You'll find a handy DirectSound API reference, along with additional information about the architecture and usefulness of DirectSound.
2. Try your hand at recording some sound effects of your own using sound editing software. You can either use the Sound Recorder application that ships with Windows, or try a third-party sound editing application. Most third-party applications provide lots of extra features for manipulating sounds. Be sure to take note of the format in which you store the sounds.

6

Hour 7

Applying DirectSound

You learned in the previous hour that DirectSound provides support for playing mixed audio with very low latency. This hour continues with the examination of DirectSound by showing you how to use DirectSound in the context of a real application. More specifically, you build upon the cityscape application from Hour 5, "Make It Move—DirectDraw Animation Techniques," and add some interesting sound effects.

In addition to learning the practical ins and outs of playing sounds using DirectSound, this hour also shows you how to control the properties of sounds. You learn how to control the volume and frequency of individual sounds, as well as the panning between left and right speakers.

In this hour, you will learn

- How waves fit into the DirectSound equation
- How to load and extract information from waves
- How to initialize and play mixed audio using DirectSound
- How to alter the volume, frequency, and panning of DirectSound buffers

DirectSound and Games

It helps to understand how sounds are used in games and multimedia applications before jumping into the details of a real DirectSound application. Wave sounds are typically used in games to represent sound effects and speech. These sounds are usually played in response to some event in the game, such as a bomb exploding or a character talking. Generally speaking, you don't need to concern yourself with whether you are playing multiple sounds at once. DirectSound automatically handles the mixing of sounds even though you play them independently of each other programmatically.

A `DirectSoundBuffer` object represents each sound in a game. You create each of these sound objects after creating the main `DirectSound` object. Keep in mind that this doesn't include interactive music, which is handled completely differently in DirectX. You will learn how to use DirectMusic to generate interactive music in the next two hours.

It's handy to place a group of sounds in an array of `DirectSoundBuffer` objects that is initialized at the start of the game by locking, writing sound data, and then unlocking the sounds. You will likely have the sounds stored as waves; in which case, you need to extract the raw sound data from wave files stored on disk or wave resources stored in the executable application or a DLL. When the sound buffers are initialized, you are free to play any of the sounds at any time.

It is important to structure your sounds so that they are either static or streaming, based upon their size and usage. Static buffers should be used for frequently played sounds (preferably short) that you want mixed in hardware. The order in which you create sounds affects their accessibility to hardware mixing. The first sounds that you create have a better chance of being mixed in hardware because a limited amount of memory is available on sound devices. For this reason, you should prioritize your sounds so that short, frequently used sounds are created and initialized first. Streaming buffers are less efficient and are often used to store partial sounds.

Some games have lots of levels with sounds that vary from level to level. Because you don't want to have too many sounds loaded at once, it makes sense to have an array of sounds and rewrite the buffer data at each level change. In this scenario, you would have all your sounds divided among different levels, and then load a sound into a buffer only if the player is on the level where the sound is used. You would initialize the sound array at the start of each new level. You could then have a separate sound buffer array that holds common sounds across all levels, such as sounds for footsteps, gunfire, and explosions.

This brief description of a DirectSound usage scenario should be a good start for you to develop a sound model for your own games. Later in the hour, you put these ideas to the test by adding sound support to the cityscape application from Hour 5.

Working with Waves

Waves serve as the basis for sounds that are played using DirectSound. The most popular digital sound format used in Windows is the wave format, which is denoted by the .wav file extension. Windows .wav files are actually RIFF files, which stands for Resource Interchange File Format. The RIFF format serves as the basis for many of the Windows media file formats.

From the perspective of a multimedia application, waves are just another type of resource, like bitmaps and icons. This means that you can include waves as resources in the resource script for an application.

 You can create your own waves using the Sound Recorder application that ships with Windows. Although Sound Recorder is primitive compared to commercial wave editors, it gets the job done. If you have a microphone connected to your sound card, you can record just about anything you want. You can also record audio directly from an audio CD in your CD-ROM drive.

A High-Level Use for Waves

Before getting into the details of how waves are used with DirectSound, it's worth pointing out that the Win32 API includes a function that can be called to play waves: PlaySound(). Following is the prototype for the PlaySound() function:

```
BOOL PlaySound(LPCSTR pszSound, HMODULE hmod, DWORD fdwSound);
```

The first parameter to the PlaySound() function, pszSound, is the name of the wave audio clip, which can be the name of a wave file, the name of a wave resource, or a pointer to a wave image in memory. In the case of playing a wave resource, the second parameter, hmod, is the module instance handle where the resource is located. Otherwise, you can pass NULL as this parameter. The last parameter, fdwSound, specifies flags that determine how the sound is played. Table 7.1 lists the flags supported by the PlaySound() function, along with their usage.

TABLE 7.1   Flags Supported by the PlaySound() Win32 API Function

Flag	Description
SND_FILENAME	Specifies that the pszSound parameter is a wave filename
SND_RESOURCE	Specifies that the pszSound parameter is a wave resource identifier
SND_MEMORY	Specifies that the pszSound parameter points to a wave image in memory

continues

7

TABLE 7.1 continued

SND_ASYNC	Plays the sound asynchronously, which means that the function returns immediately after starting the playing of the sound
SND_SYNC	Plays the sound synchronously, which means that the function doesn't return until the sound finishes playing
SND_LOOP	Plays the sound repeatedly until it is explicitly stopped; looped sounds must be asynchronous, which means that you must use the SND_ASYNC flag with SND_LOOP
SND_NOSTOP	Specifies that the sound won't interrupt any other sound that is already playing; the sound won't be played if another sound is being played
SND_NODEFAULT	Specifies that the default system sound won't be played if the wave sound isn't located

This table alludes to a few interesting points regarding the PlaySound() function. First, the PlaySound() function can only be used to play one sound at a time. This gives you an idea why DirectSound is necessary for multimedia applications that require the mixing of multiple sounds, such as most games. Second, the PlaySound() function will play the default system event sound if the specified wave sound cannot be located. The SND_NODEFAULT flag can be used to circumvent this default behavior.

The PlaySound() function is part of the original Windows multimedia support and isn't technically part of DirectX. However, it is useful in situations where you don't need the extensive audio capabilities of DirectSound. I wanted to let you know about it just so you understand the full range of audio support in Windows.

Following is an example of playing a looped wave file asynchronously using the PlaySound() function:

```
PlaySound("Siren.wav", NULL, SND_NODEFAULT | SND_ASYNC | SND_LOOP);
```

Although the PlaySound() function is useful in some situations, it can't compare to the rich audio features offered by DirectSound. The good news is that you still use waves when working with DirectSound. However, it is necessary to extract the wave data from a wave in order to play the wave using DirectSound. This involves digging into a wave and navigating through it to extract wave data.

Creating the CWave Class

To make using waves easier in C++, it is helpful to create a class, CWave, which encapsulates the functionality of a wave. This class could actually serve two purposes:

1. Provide a high-level means of playing wave audio via the PlaySound() Win32 API function

2. Provide a low-level means of mixing wave audio with advanced playback capabilities via DirectSound

Not surprisingly, supporting the PlaySound() Win32 API function in the CWave class is very straightforward. Supporting DirectSound, however, is not so easy. Listing 7.1 contains the declaration of the CWave class, which gives you an idea about the methods that you can use to work with waves.

LISTING 7.1   The Wave.h Header File for the CWave Class

```
 1: #ifndef __WAVE_H__
 2: #define __WAVE_H__
 3:
 4: //--------------------------------------------------------------
 5: // Inclusions
 6: //--------------------------------------------------------------
 7: #include <MMSystem.h>
 8:
 9: //--------------------------------------------------------------
10: // CWave Class - Wave Object
11: //--------------------------------------------------------------
12: class CWave {
13:     // Public Constructor(s)/Destructor
14: public:
15:             CWave();
16:             CWave(const char* pszFileName);
17:             CWave(UINT uiResID, HMODULE hmod);
18:     virtual ~CWave();
19:
20:     // Public Methods
21: public:
22:     BOOL    Create(const char* pszFileName);
23:     BOOL    Create(UINT uiResID, HMODULE hmod);
24:     BOOL    IsValid() const { return (m_pImageData ? TRUE :
25:             FALSE); };
26:     BOOL    Play(BOOL bAsync = TRUE, BOOL bLooped = FALSE) const;
27:     BOOL    GetFormat(WAVEFORMATEX& wfFormat) const;
28:     DWORD   GetDataLen() const;
29:     DWORD   GetData(BYTE*& pWaveData, DWORD dwMaxToCopy) const;
30:
```

continues

7

LISTING 7.1   continued

```
31:     // Protected Methods
32: protected:
33:     BOOL    Free();
34:
35:     // Private Data
36: private:
37:     BYTE* m_pImageData;
38:     DWORD m_dwImageLen;
39:     BOOL  m_bResource;
40: };
41:
42: #endif
```

As you can see, the CWave class supports three different constructors: a default constructor, a file constructor, and a resource constructor. The default constructor simply creates an empty CWave object with no actual wave data. The file constructor takes a wave file name as the only parameter and constructs a CWave object from the wave file. Finally, the resource constructor takes a module instance handle and a resource identifier as parameters and creates a CWave object from the resource image of the wave. The destructor for the CWave class is responsible for freeing the image data associated with the wave. This will make more sense in a moment.

The Create() methods take on the task of reading a wave from a file or resource. Both Create() methods call the Free() method to free any previous wave data before loading a new wave. The IsValid() method checks to see if the object contains valid wave data.

The Play() method is used to play a wave using the Win32 PlaySound() function. However, it doesn't enter the picture when using the CWave object with DirectSound. For that, you must use the GetFormat(), GetDataLen(), and GetData() methods. These methods allow you to retrieve information about the format of the wave, the length of the raw wave data, and the raw wave data itself.

The definition of the CWave class is where you learn how these methods are implemented. Listing 7.2 contains the code for the three constructors and the single destructor for CWave.

LISTING 7.2   The Constructors for the CWave Class

```
 1: CWave::CWave() : m_dwImageLen(0), m_bResource(FALSE),
 2:     m_pImageData(NULL)
 3: {
 4: }
 5:
 6: CWave::CWave(const char* pszFileName) : m_dwImageLen(0),
 7:     m_bResource(FALSE), m_pImageData(NULL)
 8: {
 9:     Create(pszFileName);
10: }
```

```
11:
12: CWave::CWave(UINT uiResID, HMODULE hmod) : m_dwImageLen(0),
13:     m_bResource(TRUE), m_pImageData(NULL)
14: {
15:     Create(uiResID, hmod);
16: }
17:
18: CWave::~CWave() {
19:     // Free the wave image data
20:     Free();
21: }
```

Notice in the code listing that the file- and resource-based constructors call the `Create()` method to initialize the object. If you use the default constructor to create a `CWave` object, you must call `Create()` yourself in order to properly initialize the object. This is a common object initialization approach in MFC and is referred to as two-phase construction. The code for these `Create()` methods is shown in Listing 7.3.

LISTING 7.3   The `Create()` Methods for the `CWave` Class

```
 1: BOOL CWave::Create(const char* pszFileName)
 2: {
 3:     // Free any previous wave image data
 4:     Free();
 5:
 6:     // Flag as regular memory
 7:     m_bResource = FALSE;
 8:
 9:     // Open the wave file
10:     ifstream fileWave(pszFileName);
11:
12:     // Get the file length
13:     fileWave.seekg(0, ios::end);
14:     m_dwImageLen = (DWORD)fileWave.tellg();
15:
16:     // Allocate and lock memory for the image data
17:     m_pImageData = (BYTE*)GlobalLock(GlobalAlloc(GMEM_MOVEABLE |
18:         GMEM_SHARE, m_dwImageLen));
19:     if (!m_pImageData)
20:         return FALSE;
21:
22:     // Read the image data from the file
23:     fileWave.seekg(0, ios::beg);
24:     fileWave.read(m_pImageData, m_dwImageLen);
25:
26:     return TRUE;
27: }
28:
```

7

continues

LISTING 7.3   continued

```
29: BOOL CWave::Create(UINT uiResID, HMODULE hmod)
30: {
31:     // Free any previous wave image data
32:     Free();
33:
34:     // Flag as resource memory
35:     m_bResource = TRUE;
36:
37:     // Find the wave resource
38:     HRSRC hresInfo;
39:     hresInfo = FindResource(hmod, MAKEINTRESOURCE(uiResID),
40:         "WAVE");
41:     if (!hresInfo)
42:         return FALSE;
43:
44:     // Load the wave resource
45:     HGLOBAL hgmemWave = LoadResource(hmod, hresInfo);
46:
47:     if (hgmemWave)
48:     {
49:         // Get pointer to and length of the wave image data
50:         m_pImageData= (BYTE*)LockResource(hgmemWave);
51:         m_dwImageLen = SizeofResource(hmod, hresInfo);
52:     }
53:
54:     return (m_pImageData ? TRUE : FALSE);
55: }
```

You might notice that both of the Create() methods call the Free() method to free any old wave data before creating a new wave. Listing 7.4 contains the code for the Free() method.

LISTING 7.4   The GetData() Method for the CWave Class

```
1: BOOL CWave::Free()
2: {
3:     // Free any previous wave data
4:     if (m_pImageData) {
5:         HGLOBAL  hgmemWave = GlobalHandle(m_pImageData);
6:
7:         if (hgmemWave) {
8:             if (m_bResource)
9:                 // Free resource
10:                FreeResource(hgmemWave);
11:            else {
12:                // Unlock and free memory
13:                GlobalUnlock(hgmemWave);
14:                GlobalFree(hgmemWave);
15:            }
16:
```

```
17:                    m_pImageData = NULL;
18:                    m_dwImageLen = 0;
19:                    return TRUE;
20:            }
21:        }
22:        return FALSE;
23: }
```

The implementation of the Play() method shows how the PlaySound() Win32 API function is used to provide a high-level means of playing waves using the CWave class (Listing 7.5) .

LISTING 7.5 The Play() Method for the CWave Class

```
1: BOOL CWave::Play(BOOL bAsync, BOOL bLooped) const
2: {
3:     // Check validity
4:     if (!IsValid())
5:         return FALSE;
6:
7:     // Play the wave
8:     return PlaySound((LPCSTR)m_pImageData, NULL, SND_MEMORY ¦
9:         SND_NODEFAULT ¦ (bAsync ? SND_ASYNC : SND_SYNC) ¦
10:        (bLooped ? (SND_LOOP ¦ SND_ASYNC) : 0));
11: }
```

Although the Play() method has its place in making CWave a well-rounded class, this book is about DirectX, which means that you're interested in using the CWave class to play waves using DirectSound. More important to DirectSound are the GetFormat(), GetDataLen(), and GetData() methods (Listings 7.6–7.8) .

LISTING 7.6 The GetFormat() Method for the CWave Class

```
1: BOOL CWave::GetFormat(WAVEFORMATEX& wfFormat) const
2: {
3:     // Check validity
4:     if (!IsValid())
5:         return FALSE;
6:
7:     // Setup and open the MMINFO structure
8:     CMMMemoryIOInfo mmioInfo((HPSTR)m_pImageData, m_dwImageLen);
9:     CMMIO          mmio(mmioInfo);
10:
11:     // Find the WAVE chunk
12:     CMMTypeChunk mmckParent('W','A','V','E');
13:     mmio.Descend(mmckParent, MMIO_FINDRIFF);
14:
15:     // Find and read the format subchunk
```

7

continues

LISTING 7.6   continued

```
16:     CMMIdChunk mmckSubchunk('f','m','t',' ');
17:     mmio.Descend(mmckSubchunk, mmckParent, MMIO_FINDCHUNK);
18:     mmio.Read((HPSTR)&wfFormat, sizeof(WAVEFORMATEX));
19:     mmio.Ascend(mmckSubchunk);
20:
21:     return TRUE;
22: }
```

LISTING 7.7   The GetDataLen() Method for the CWave Class

```
1: DWORD CWave::GetDataLen() const
2: {
3:     // Check validity
4:     if (!IsValid())
5:         return (DWORD)0;
6:
7:     // Setup and open the MMINFO structure
8:     CMMMemoryIOInfo mmioInfo((HPSTR)m_pImageData, m_dwImageLen);
9:     CMMIO           mmio(mmioInfo);
10:
11:     // Find the WAVE chunk
12:     CMMTypeChunk mmckParent('W','A','V','E');
13:     mmio.Descend(mmckParent, MMIO_FINDRIFF);
14:
15:     // Find and get the size of the data subchunk
16:     CMMIdChunk mmckSubchunk('d','a','t','a');
17:     mmio.Descend(mmckSubchunk, mmckParent, MMIO_FINDCHUNK);
18:     return mmckSubchunk.cksize;
19: }
```

LISTING 7.8   The GetData() Method for the CWave Class

```
1: DWORD CWave::GetData(BYTE*& pWaveData, DWORD dwMaxLen) const
2: {
3:     // Check validity
4:     if (!IsValid())
5:         return (DWORD)0;
6:
7:     // Setup and open the MMINFO structure
8:     CMMMemoryIOInfo mmioInfo((HPSTR)m_pImageData, m_dwImageLen);
9:     CMMIO           mmio(mmioInfo);
10:
11:     // Find the WAVE chunk
12:     CMMTypeChunk mmckParent('W','A','V','E');
13:     mmio.Descend(mmckParent, MMIO_FINDRIFF);
14:
15:     // Find and get the size of the data subchunk
16:     CMMIdChunk mmckSubchunk('d','a','t','a');
```

```
17:        mmio.Descend(mmckSubchunk, mmckParent, MMIO_FINDCHUNK);
18:        DWORD dwLenToCopy = mmckSubchunk.cksize;
19:
20:        // Allocate memory if the passed in pWaveData was NULL
21:        if (pWaveData == NULL)
22:            pWaveData = (BYTE*)GlobalLock(GlobalAlloc(GMEM_MOVEABLE,
23:                dwLenToCopy));
24:        else
25:            // If we didn't allocate our own memory, honor dwMaxLen
26:            if (dwMaxLen < dwLenToCopy)
27:                dwLenToCopy = dwMaxLen;
28:        if (pWaveData)
29:            // Read waveform data into the buffer
30:            mmio.Read((HPSTR)pWaveData, dwLenToCopy);
31:
32:        return dwLenToCopy;
33: }
```

These three methods use a couple of multimedia support classes, CMMMemoryIOInfo and
CMMIO, to retrieve information about the format of a wave and the raw data associated
with a wave. This is necessary because DirectSound utilizes waves at a low-level and
must have access to raw wave data.

> The code for the CMMMemoryIOInfo and CMMIO multimedia support
> classes can be found on the accompanying CD-ROM. This code doesn't
> have much to do directly with DirectSound, so it's not terribly important to
> delve into the details of it here.

You might notice that the GetFormat(), GetDataLen(), and GetData() methods operate
on chunks of data. Chunks form the basis of RIFF files, which represent the format wave
files are stored in. It isn't critical that you understand the structure of RIFF files, but I
thought it was worth mentioning to help make the CWave code a little clearer. For more
information on RIFF files and how to navigate through them, refer to the multimedia I/O
data structures and functions in the Win32 API. On the other hand, you could just use the
CWave class and not worry about the hassles of navigating RIFF files.

Using the CWave Class

Now that you've seen how the CWave class is implemented, you're probably curious to
see how it works. Following is an example of playing a wave using the high-level Play()
method in the CWave class:

```
CWave wavExplode("Explode.wav");
wavExplode.Play();
```

7

Although the high-level approach to playing waves is certainly simple and effective, it doesn't offer the power and flexibility of DirectSound. The remainder of the hour focuses on how to use the CWave class with DirectSound.

Playing Sound Effects with DirectSound

To get a feel for using DirectSound, you're going to add sound effects to the cityscape example application from Hour 5. The remainder of the hour focuses on the coding required to pull this off. In the process, you'll learn how to mix sound effects such as footsteps, thunder, and sirens at random intervals, and with random volume, and varying panning and frequency values. By altering the volume, panning, and frequency of sounds, you can add significantly to the mood and effect of the cityscape.

> Because the cityscape application you develop in this hour simulates sounds occurring at different spatial locations, it might make sense to use DirectSound's 3D audio features. However, I wanted to keep things relatively simple. Even so, you might be surprised at how effective it is to vary the volume, panning, and frequency of sound effects to give an application a realistic feel.

The cityscape application uses a total of nine sound effects, which are stored in the lpDSBSounds array. Following are the different sound effects used in the application, which help to add realism and ambience:

- Siren
- Car skid
- Car horn
- Clock
- Dog bark
- Lightning
- Thunder
- Gunshot
- Footstep

Following are the declarations for the sound-related variables used in the application:

```
LPDIRECTSOUND        lpDS;
LPDIRECTSOUNDBUFFER  lpDSBSounds[NUMSOUNDS];
LONG                 lSirenPan;
LONG                 lSirenPanInc;
```

The lpDS variable stores a pointer to the DirectSound object. The lpDSBSounds array stores an array of pointers to the DirectSound buffers for each sound effect. The lSirenPan and lSirenPanInc variables are used to control the panning of the siren sound effect, which is moved from right to left or left to right between channels (speakers) when played.

In addition to these new variables, some new error messages are required to notify the user of any problems encountered while using DirectSound:

```
const char Err_DirectSoundCreate[]  = "DirectSoundCreate FAILED";
const char Err_CreateBuff[]         = "CreateBuffer FAILED";
const char Err_LoadWAV[]            = "Error Loading Sound";
```

The DirectSound object itself is created and initialized in the Init() function. The new code added to this function is shown in Listing 7.9.

LISTING 7.9   DirectSound Initialization Code that Is Added to the Init() Function

```
 1: // Create the DS object
 2: if (DirectSoundCreate(NULL, &lpDS, NULL) != DS_OK)
 3: {
 4:     ErrStr = Err_DirectSoundCreate;
 5:     return FALSE;
 6: }
 7:
 8: // Set the cooperation level for the DS object
 9: if (lpDS->SetCooperativeLevel(hWnd, DSSCL_NORMAL) != DS_OK)
10: {
11:     ErrStr = Err_Coop;
12:     return FALSE;
13: }
14:
15: // Initialize the DS buffers
16: if (!load_sounds())
17: {
18:     return FALSE;
19: }
```

The Init() function first calls the DirectSoundCreate() function to create a DirectSound object. The cooperative level of the DirectSound object is then set with a call to SetCooperativeLevel(). Setting the cooperative level is a strict requirement before using a DirectSound object. In this case, the cooperative level is set to DSSCL_NORMAL, which provides the smoothest multitasking and resource-sharing behavior for the DirectSound object. The last step in the Init() function is to load and initialize the sounds with a call to load_sounds(), which you learn about in a moment.

7

A single line of code is all that is required to cleanup the remnants of DirectSound. The following line of code, which is added to the `Cleanup()` function, accomplishes this task:

```
SafeRelease(lpDS);
```

`SafeRelease()` is actually a macro that calls the `Release()` method and then sets the object pointer to `NULL`:

```
#define SafeRelease(x) if (x) { x->Release(); x=NULL;}
```

It's important to note that releasing the `DirectSound` object also releases the DirectSound buffers associated with the object.

Listing 7.10 contains the code for the `load_sounds()` function, which loads and initializes the sounds for the application. Keep in mind that all the sounds are actually stored in `DirectSoundBuffer` objects.

LISTING 7.10   The `load_sounds()` Function that Is Used to Initialize the Waves and DirectSound Buffers

```
 1: BOOL load_sounds()
 2: {
 3:      // Initialize waves
 4:      CWave waves[NUMSOUNDS];
 5:      waves[0].Create("Siren.wav");
 6:      waves[1].Create("CarSkid.wav");
 7:      waves[2].Create("Clock.wav");
 8:      waves[3].Create("Dog.wav");
 9:      waves[4].Create("Lightning.wav");
10:      waves[5].Create("Thunder.wav");
11:      waves[6].Create("GunShot.wav");
12:      waves[7].Create("CarHorn.wav");
13:      waves[8].Create("Footstep.wav");
14:
15:      // Initialize secondary DS buffers
16:      for (int i = 0; i < NUMSOUNDS; i++) {
17:          // Get the wave information
18:          DWORD         dwDataLen = waves[i].GetDataLen();
19:          WAVEFORMATEX  wfFormat;
20:          waves[i].GetFormat(wfFormat);
21:
22:          // Setup the DS buffer description
23:          DSBUFFERDESC dsbdDesc;
24:          ZeroMemory(&dsbdDesc, sizeof(DSBUFFERDESC));
25:          dsbdDesc.dwSize = sizeof(DSBUFFERDESC);
26:          dsbdDesc.dwFlags = DSBCAPS_CTRLFREQUENCY | DSBCAPS_CTRLPAN |
                        ➥DSBCAPS_CTRLVOLUME | DSBCAPS_STATIC;
27:          dsbdDesc.dwBufferBytes = dwDataLen;
28:          dsbdDesc.lpwfxFormat = &wfFormat;
29:
```

```
30:          // Create the DS buffer
31:          if (lpDS->CreateSoundBuffer(&dsbdDesc,
32:              &lpDSBSounds[i], NULL) != DS_OK)
33:          {
34:              ErrStr = Err_CreateBuff;
35:              return FALSE;
36:          }
37:
38:          // Lock the DS buffer
39:          BYTE* pDSBuffData;
40:          if (lpDSBSounds[i]->Lock(0, dwDataLen, (void**)&pDSBuffData,
41:              &dwDataLen, NULL, 0, 0) != DS_OK)
42:          {
43:              ErrStr = Err_LoadWAV;
44:              return FALSE;
45:          }
46:
47:          // Write wave data to the DS buffer
48:          dwDataLen = waves[i].GetData(pDSBuffData, dwDataLen);
49:
50:          // Unlock the DS buffer
51:          if (lpDSBSounds[i]->Unlock(pDSBuffData, dwDataLen, NULL, 0) !=
52:              DS_OK)
53:          {
54:              ErrStr = Err_LoadWAV;
55:              return FALSE;
56:          }
57:      }
58:
59:      return TRUE;
60: }
```

The load_sounds() method is called by Init() to create and initialize a sound buffer
for each sound effect wave. This is where the CWave class enters the picture with
DirectSound. The CWave class includes support methods necessary to handle creating a
sound buffer of the correct size and with the correct wave format, along with copying the
wave data into the buffer. load_sounds() creates an array of CWave objects as a means of
initializing DirectSound buffers. The CWave objects are created directly from wave files
stored on disk. The static DirectSound buffers are then created based on each of the
CWave objects.

Before you learn how to play sounds using DirectSound, it's important to understand that
the memory associated with a DirectSound buffer can potentially be freed. This can pose
a big problem because it isn't possible to play a sound that is no longer in memory. The
solution is to restore the buffer before attempting to play it. The RestoreDSBuffers()
method (Listing 7.11) restores the memory for the sound effect buffers and reinitializes
them with wave data. RestoreDSBuffers() simply calls the Restore() method on each
buffer and then reinitializes them with a call to load_sounds().

7

LISTING 7.11 The `RestoreDSBuffers()` Function that Is Used to Restore DirectSound Buffers

```
 1: BOOL RestoreDSBuffers()
 2: {
 3:     // Restore the buffers
 4:     for (int i = 0; i < NUMSOUNDS; i++)
 5:         if (lpDSBSounds[i]->Restore() != DS_OK)
 6:             return FALSE;
 7:
 8:     // Re-initialize the buffers
 9:     return load_sounds();
10: }
```

Most of the sound effects in the cityscape application are played in the main timing loop of the `WinMain()` function. This loop was established in previous lessons to establish a frame rate for the DirectDraw animation. You're now going to use it as a basis for generating random sound effects. Listing 7.12 contains the code added to the timing loop of the `WinMain()` function.

LISTING 7.12 Code Added to the `WinMain()` Function that Randomly Plays Sound Effects

```
 1: DWORD dwStatus;
 2: lpDSBSounds[8]->GetStatus(&dwStatus);
 3: if (move_rate != 0) {
 4:     // Check to make sure the buffer hasn't been lost
 5:     if (dwStatus & DSBSTATUS_BUFFERLOST)
 6:         RestoreDSBuffers();
 7:
 8:     lpDSBSounds[8]->SetFrequency(16000 + abs(move_rate) * 40);
 9:     if (!(dwStatus & DSBSTATUS_LOOPING))
10:         lpDSBSounds[8]->Play(0, 0, DSBPLAY_LOOPING);
11: }
12: else
13:     if (dwStatus & DSBSTATUS_LOOPING)
14:         lpDSBSounds[8]->Stop();
15:
16:
17: // play a random sound (1 in 50 chance per frame)
18:
19: if (rand() % 50 == 0)
20: {
21:     // Determine which sound to play
22:     int nIndex = rand() % (NUMSOUNDS - 2);
23:     if (lpDSBSounds[nIndex] != NULL)
24:     {
25:         DWORD dwStatus;
26:         lpDSBSounds[nIndex]->GetStatus(&dwStatus);
27:
```

```
28:            // Check to make sure the buffer hasn't been lost
29:            if (dwStatus & DSBSTATUS_BUFFERLOST)
30:                RestoreDSBuffers();
31:
32:            // Check to make sure the sound isn't already playing
33:            if (!(dwStatus & DSBSTATUS_PLAYING))
34:            {
35:                if (nIndex > 0)
36:                {
37:                    // Set the panning of the sound
38:                    lpDSBSounds[nIndex]->SetPan((rand() % 2000) - 1000);
39:
40:                    // Set the volume of the sound
41:                    lpDSBSounds[nIndex]->SetVolume((rand() % 3) * -250);
42:
43:                    // Play the sound
44:                    lpDSBSounds[nIndex]->Play(0, 0, 0);
45:                }
46:                else
47:                {
48:                    // Set the panning of the siren
49:                    LONG lStart = (rand() % 2) ? -1 : 1;
50:                    lSirenPan = lStart * 8000;
51:                    lSirenPanInc = -(lStart * 25);
52:                    lpDSBSounds[nIndex]->SetPan(lSirenPan);
53:
54:                    // Play the siren sound
55:                    lpDSBSounds[nIndex]->Play(0, 0, DSBPLAY_LOOPING);
56:                }
57:            }
58:        }
59: }
60:
61: // If siren sound is playing, see if we should stop it
62: lpDSBSounds[0]->GetStatus(&dwStatus);
63: if (dwStatus & DSBSTATUS_LOOPING)
64: {
65:     if ((lSirenPan < -8000) || (lSirenPan > 8000))
66:         lpDSBSounds[0]->Stop();
67:     else
68:     {
69:         lSirenPan += lSirenPanInc;
70:         lpDSBSounds[0]->SetPan(lSirenPan);
71:         lpDSBSounds[0]->SetVolume(-(abs(lSirenPan) / 5));
72:     }
73: }
```

7

The timing loop in the WinMain() function is entered every 16 milliseconds by default, as determined by code inherited from Hour 5. The timing loop first checks to see if a sound effect should be played, which is given a 1 in 50 likelihood of happening. This results in a sound effect being played an average of every 0.8 seconds (50×0.016).

This might sound like a short span between sound effects, but it actually works pretty well with the types of sounds used in this example. You can always tweak this number to get a different result.

The first sound effect code plays the footstep sound effect in response to the user moving. In other words, the move_rate variable is checked to see if the footstep sound effect needs to be played. If so, the sound effect is looped with its frequency based on the value of move_rate. This yields an audible effect of the user walking faster or slower based on the rate at which she is scrolling.

Most of the other sound effects in the application are simply played at random by selecting one from the array of DirectSound buffers. The GetStatus() method is then called on the selected sound buffer to make sure that the buffer hasn't been lost. If it has been lost, the RestoreDSBuffers() method is called to restore all the sound buffers. WinMain() also checks to make sure that the selected sound buffer isn't already playing. If the sound buffer isn't the siren sound effect, a random panning and volume is set and the sound buffer starts playing.

If the buffer is the siren sound effect, the panning and volume are specially set so that the siren sounds like it is flying by. This also requires WinMain() to update the settings of the siren sound effect buffer periodically, which is reflected by the last block of code in the timing loop. The siren sound effect is played looped, which means that it is played repeatedly until it cycles from one speaker to the other and fades out. This logic is entirely controlled by the code in the timing loop.

Along with the sound effects played in the WinMain() timing loop, the cityscape application also plays a sound in the render_frame() function. This might seem like a strange place to play sounds, but it happens to work out because it is the best place to ascertain the location of the taxi. This is useful because the car horn sound is only played when the taxi is visible on the screen. Furthermore, the car horn sound is panned based on the location of the taxi on the screen. Following is the code added to the render_frame() function to accomplish this task:

```
DWORD dwStatus;
lpDSBSounds[7]->GetStatus(&dwStatus);
if (!(dwStatus & DSBSTATUS_PLAYING) && (rand() % 25 == 0)) {
    lpDSBSounds[7]->SetPan((taxi_pos + (taxi_width / 2) -
        screen_pos - 320) * 20);
    lpDSBSounds[7]->Play(0, 0, 0);
}
```

That wraps up the DirectSound enhancements to the cityscape application. Feel free to play around with the code and add sound effects of your own to further spice up the application.

Summary

This hour tackled the practical side of DirectSound by showing you how to use DirectSound to add sound effects to an existing application. You began the hour by taking a step back and laying some ground rules regarding how DirectSound is used in the context of game development. You then moved on to exploring waves and how they are loaded and manipulated. This was necessary because DirectSound buffers are initialized using raw wave data.

With a handy class for manipulating waves in hand, you finally moved on to the important stuff: putting DirectSound to use. You learned how to create and use DirectSound buffers that store sound effects. You also found out how to play, loop, and stop these sound buffers. You even learned how to alter the properties of sound buffers, including volume, panning, and frequency.

Q&A

Q How does DirectSound establish the format of the primary sound buffer?

A By default, the primary sound buffer is set to 8-bit 22 kHz mono regardless of the format of the secondary sound buffers. You should explicitly set the format of the primary sound buffer to match the secondary buffers if you plan on using a higher quality sound format. However, this requires you to use a higher priority level flag for the DirectSound object: DSSCL_PROIRITY.

Q How do I use waves as resources?

A You can store waves as resources by including them in an application's resource file and giving them the resource type WAVE. This will result in the waves being included in the application's executable file; you can also compile wave resources into a DLL. To load a wave resource, you simply use the CWave constructor that is designed to load waves from resources.

Workshop

The Workshop is designed to help you anticipate possible questions, review what you've learned, and get you thinking about how to put your knowledge into practice. The answers to the quiz are in Appendix A, "Answers."

Quiz

1. What do you do to give a sound buffer a better chance of being mixed in hardware?
2. What Win32 API structure do you use to contain format information about a wave?
3. What method in the CWave class is used to obtain raw wave data?

4. What file format serves as the basis for Windows waves?

5. What is the purpose of the lSirenPan variable in the cityscape application?

6. What value do you pass to the SetVolume() method to completely silence a sound?

7. Why do you not need to call the Release() method on DirectSound buffers?

8. What should you do if the memory associated with a sound buffer is freed?

9. How does the move_rate variable impact the footstep sound in the cityscape application?

10. What method do you call on a sound buffer to see if the buffer memory has been lost?

Exercises

1. Experiment with changing the values of the sounds in the cityscape application. More specifically, try adjusting the panning of the siren sound to make it move faster from speaker to speaker. Also, try adjusting the frequency of the footstep sound so that the footsteps speed up and slow down more dramatically.

2. Come up with some sound effects of your own and integrate them into the cityscape application. Make sure to save the sound effects as 22 kHz, 8-bit, mono sounds so that they match the other sounds in the application. Also, keep in mind that you'll have to create and initialize new DirectSoundBuffer objects in the application to accommodate these sounds.

PART IV
Welcome to 3D

Hour

HOUR 8

DirectMusic—Interactive Music

In the previous hour, you learned how to create sounds by using DirectSound. In this hour, we will discuss another component of the DirectX SDK that deals with sound called DirectMusic. DirectMusic is a relatively new component of DirectX. With the release of DirectX 7.0, DirectMusic joins DirectSound in enriching a player's environment with sound and music.

DirectMusic gives a programmer the capability of creating musical scores to enrich a player's experience. Music can involve the player more deeply in a game. It can push him along, or perhaps give him a sense of trepidation about a particular area of the game. By using the features of DirectMusic, you can create a musical score that adapts itself based on the player's actions. It can seem to react to the current state of the game. As the player begins the game or enters a particular area, the music moves slowly. Then, as the player gets into a tough area of the game, the music speeds up and seems to match the intensity of the moment. You can accomplish these things and more using DirectMusic.

The lesson in this hour begins by introducing you to the `IDirectMusicPerformance` interface, which we will eventually use to add music to our game. We will begin with a discussion of Microsoft's Software Synthesizer and how using interactive music can enhance any game. We then follow with a few details on the interface, a primer on music, and finally the concept of interactive music.

In this hour, you learn

- The Microsoft Synthesizer and its features
- The concepts of interactive music
- About the `IDirectMusicPerformance` interface
- The concepts of digital music
- The concepts of creating dynamic music

The Features of DirectMusic

The mood and atmosphere of today's games owe a lot to music. When driving our cars, most people listen to some kind of music on the radio. The music can calm us or get us excited and can make the trip a little more enjoyable. Like driving in a real car, a racing game seems more enjoyable when it has a range of music available for the player to listen to. This music helps involve the player in what is happening in the game. Virtually any game can use music to enhance the user experience.

Creating this enjoyable music requires the use of some type of audio hardware. This hardware is usually a general audio card of some type. The audio cards produced today are capable of much higher fidelity sound than what was available only a few years ago. These cards can play more sounds at one time and can play those sounds more richly. Using the features of DirectMusic will allow you to play many instruments at one time, as though a full orchestra were playing from the computer. This is often referred to as polyphony.

NEW TERM   *Polyphony* refers to the nature of music having more than one voice. It derives from the Latin words *poly*, meaning many and *phonic*, meaning sound.

The large number of voices of these cards gives us the ability to make our music sound richer with more instruments playing at the same time. With this capability, of course, comes an increase in complexity. Thanks to DirectMusic, though, a lot of the complexities of playing music through an audio card can be greatly reduced. In fact, within the next two hours, you will see just how easy using DirectMusic to add music to that next big project of yours really is.

DirectMusic, like many of the other components of the DirectX SDK, also adjusts to the capabilities of the hardware platform it is running on. DirectMusic does not support a HAL, like the DirectSound interface does, but it supports a similar concept using software synthesizers. For people who have older audio cards, DirectMusic can use the standard, built-in Microsoft Synthesizer, to create a rich, uniform sound that the cards might not be capable of producing through hardware.

DirectMusic also throws a few twists on being just a general song player. Many games available today have music that seems stagnant, and the music does not seem interactive at all. The capabilities of DirectMusic will allow you to go beyond playing just songs, changing your music in reaction to the player's actions. You can add this capability to your own games by adding interactive music to your other list of features. Imagine the tempo of the music increasing as the player nears a tough point in the game, and the tempo slowing back down as the situation becomes easier. By adjusting at runtime the music that you created during development, you can create music that seems to follow the player and becomes a reactive element of your game.

Perhaps the most useful feature that DirectMusic provides is the abstraction from having to deal with actual sound production via wave data. With DirectSound, you have to be concerned with streams of sound data and managing the buffers containing that data. With DirectMusic, you can describe your music in terms of a composer: with tempo changes, notes, keys, and so on. This general way to describe music data is called MIDI, which stands for Musical Instrument Digital Interface.

MIDI, as a standard, began its history as a hardware standard to describe essentially the same things that DirectMusic describes: notes in a song. It is important to realize the two different ways to describe sound using DirectX: DirectSound uses waveform data to describe sounds, and DirectMusic uses MIDI to describe notes.

The Microsoft Synthesizer

The major component of DirectMusic's actual music production is the synthesizer. It is the synthesizer's responsibility to turn the music data provided by the IDirectMusicPerformance into the actual waveform data that will be played by the audio hardware. The synthesizer operation can be handled by the hardware directly, or it can be handled through software. DirectMusic even has interfaces to allow third parties to develop their own custom software synthesizers.

For DirectMusic to allow music played on virtually any piece of audio hardware to sound the same on any other hardware, Microsoft includes a standard software synthesizer with DirectMusic. This synthesizer is called, amazingly enough, the Microsoft Software Synthesizer. Its job is to take the general music data that is created during playback of music by IDirectMusicPerformance and translate it into the actual waveform data that will be played by the audio hardware. This data is then fed into the audio card for actual waveform playback.

> Coincidentally, the actual audio playback is handled through a connection to DirectSound. As you learned earlier, DirectSound is capable of playing sounds incredibly fast and without bogging down the CPU. This helps DirectMusic achieve some of its speed.

The Microsoft Synthesizer supports the downloadable sounds (DLS) standard. DLS allows waveform samples to be loaded into memory and assigned to any specified bank or instrument location. Because these samples are typically wave files, anything that can be stored in a wave file can be played as an instrument. The Microsoft Synthesizer also comes with its own DLS instrument file. This file contains a set of General MIDI instruments that are licensed from Roland.

> A MIDI instrument refers to a standard sound that represents a particular musical instrument. The first instrument of the General MIDI set represents a piano. 128 standard instruments exist within the standard General MIDI set. The General MIDI set licensed from Roland contains these 128 instruments and an additional 126 instruments that are unique to the Roland instrument set.

With the large number of sound cards available today, it is difficult to get consistent sounding music from any two sound cards. The reason for this is because of the fact that each audio card vendor uses a different wave table for internal MIDI synthesis. This is not to say that any particular audio card is more or less adequate than any other; it just means that the way your music sounds on any one machine will depend greatly on the particular audio card playing your music. In the past, you were lucky if every player was using the same audio hardware as you. Now by using DirectMusic and the Microsoft Synthesizer, you won't have to worry what audio card the player has.

NEW TERM *Wave-table* refers to a collection of waveform samples, usually stored in memory on a sound card. This is very similar, in fact, to DLS, except a proprietary interface is often used to load and manage the wave table on a particular card.

DLS architecture and the use of Roland's General MIDI instruments gives the Microsoft Synthesizer the capability to play the same piece of music on two totally different sound cards and still have the music sound exactly the same. This ensures that the way your music sounds when you play it on your development machine will be the way that any user playing your music will hear it. This power extends to any waveforms you create yourself. Simply ensure that you include any DLS file you used as instruments while creating your music. It is because of the inclusion of the Roland instruments with DirectMusic, as a standard installation item, that you should consider using these instruments where possible.

The Age of Interactive Music

Today's gamers are becoming more and more demanding of game developers to "push the envelope." And although the graphical components of these games seems to move forward with leaps and bounds, music still seems to be lacking. Sure, some games come with audio tracks on the CD that you can play in the background. Other games have background music in the game, but unfortunately I usually find myself turning it off because of its repetitiveness.

What if you could create many blocks of reusable musical patterns and set parameters about how to use them in sequence? You could then rearrange blocks of these patterns in a different order to create a new musical score without having to create any additional music. Or better yet, let DirectMusic do the arranging for you! You can then simply change some of the parameters of the music, depending on player actions. The music would seem to react to the player. By adding this interactive power to your games, you should be able to bring the mood and aura of your games to a new level. DirectMusic makes creating interactive music simple and easy, as we will see in the next hour.

Dynamic Creation of Music

By applying the power of DirectMusic, you can create music in your game that is actually dynamic. This can be accomplished several different ways. You could use some of the capabilities of the DirectMusic Producer to create your music. During creation, you assign properties to the musical patterns that will allow the `IDirectMusicPerformance` object to randomize your musical piece during playback. You could also use another piece of music editing software to create linear MIDI pieces of music. Then during playback, simply change the properties of the music using `IDirectMusicPerformance`.

NEW TERM   A *pattern* is a series of musical notes usually comprising only a measure or two. These notes describe the actual note pitch that is played, at what volume the note is played, and for how long. Patterns are normally used to create dynamic compositions, either within the editor or during runtime.

DirectMusic has the capability to make changes to the music you create. During playback, DirectMusic can change the currently played notes to other notes or to other octaves. DirectMusic can also rearrange the patterns into different sequences. Depending on the exact arrangement chosen during playback, your music will actually seem to be created on-the-fly. This of course depends greatly on the way the music was composed. DirectMusic can't create music algorithmically, or on its own. A human composer still needs to create the components of the music. DirectMusic simply knows of ways to rearrange music you have composed to create a unique piece every time your music is played.

By using the DirectMusic Producer application, discussed in more detail in the next hour, you can create patterns of music that will be played back randomly. You can create different bands that can be loaded to play the same patterns with different instruments. Motifs can be created to add flare to the pattern combinations, adding breaks and fills, interesting intros, and endings. To play a certain set of patterns, you can create segments that allow you to have greater control over how your patterns are played back.

NEW TERM   A *motif* is a specialized pattern of music that is generally very short. Motifs are played over other patterns to indicate solo pieces that do not interrupt the current musical score.

NEW TERM   A *segment* is the actual arrangement of music. It represents all the musical data, usually made up of other patterns arranged in a particular order.

For greater randomness, you can apply templates, which allow you to further randomize your music using chordmaps. During playback, `IDirectMusicPerformance` will randomly select certain chords from the chord maps you created and transpose the next section of music to the selected chord. Because the chord selection is a random process, your music will sound different every time it is played.

NEW TERM   A *chord* is several musical notes that are played at the same time to provide a harmonic component to the melody. Chords are typically made up of three or four notes.

NEW TERM   A *chordmap* is a listing of chords created by a human composer that DirectMusic will use to determine the next available chord during dynamic music creation.

If you would rather just create your MIDI songs using another music editing package, during playback you can still change some of the parameters by which your music will be played. For example, you could set the tempo very low at the beginning of a level. Then as the player got closer to the main boss at the end of the level, you increase the tempo. If the player turns back and goes the other way, you could decrease the tempo. Although this method does not provide the flexibility offered by DirectMusic Producer, it still allows you to change some of the dynamics of your music and helps make it seem a little more interactive.

Another option you might consider is to create your musical patterns in whatever musical editing software you prefer and output the patterns as a MIDI file. You can then import the MIDI files as patterns into DirectMusic Producer. When imported, you can use the Producer to add different bands or create different styles with the patterns you have imported. This will allow you to add more flexibility to your MIDI music, while still allowing you to use the composing environment you might already be using.

Composition of Music in the Digital Realm

Music creation used to involve a lot of time in experimenting with the music on a keyboard or other instrument, and then composing the music on paper. With the number of music editing packages on the market today, it is easy for the do-it-yourself person to find a decent musical editing package for as little as a hundred dollars or so.

Many of the music editing packages that are available produce standard MIDI files. The whole process of music creation can be made simpler by using a MIDI keyboard. Most audio cards today, in addition to outputting waveform data, usually have the capability of connecting to MIDI devices. This is usually accomplished through a cable attached to the joystick port on the audio card. What this allows you, as keyboardist, to do is capture the notes from your keyboard. But suppose that you don't have a MIDI keyboard to record your music with. That's oaky because most software packages today allow you to create your musical score visually on the screen using either a musical staff or virtual keyboard.

After recording your performances using a keyboard or by using the virtual keyboard, you can make any adjustments necessary to your musical score. Using any one of the music editing software packages, you can adjust the duration of notes, the actual pitch the note is played at, add other notes, and even copy entire measures to other parts of the musical score. The creation of music on the computer allows greater control over the time it takes to create music. More time can be spent fine-tuning your music rather than inputting it in the first place.

A Quick Primer on Musical Structure

Before delving into the details of DirectMusic, we should probably start with a quick primer on musical structure. I won't try to bore you with a lot of fundamental details, but having an understanding of some of the basics of music will help during the next hour where we use DirectMusic Producer. We will be using the Producer application to create some elementary music, and having at least a cursory understanding of music principle should help with your DirectMusic endeavors. If you are relatively new to music, this hour should help explain some of the components of musical structure. For the rest of you, consider this a refresher course on music.

So what is music? Music, in its simplest form, is comprised of sounds that are played over a period of time. A more technical description would be several musical notes or rhythmic beats that follow a particular rhythm. The period of time is known as the *score*. Musical instruments create the sounds; although, as you already know, you can actually use any kind of sound you want. A trumpet, a drum, a flute, a bird chirp, and a doorbell are all examples of an instrument.

Each musical score has a certain measure of time. This is known as the *tempo* of the score. The tempo is the number of beats that occur within a minute. During the score, it is possible that the tempo might change, and it might change at different rates. When the tempo increases, the music is played faster; when the tempo decreases, the music is played slower. There can also be distinct points within the score that the tempo will change.

Given a particular tempo, there occurs a certain number of beats within a controlled period of time. The controlled period of time is called a *measure*. The most common length for a measure is four beats, also known as 4/4 time. The two fours are actually found on top of each other when seen on a sheet of music. The number on the top, or left, gives the number of beats contained within a measure. The number on the bottom, or right, gives the note length that is given each beat. I will explain this in a little more detail in a moment.

NEW TERM   A *measure* is a certain number of beats that occur within a specified period, usually four beats. Measures are used to break up a musical score into smaller pieces, consisting of a small number of actual notes.

A musical note is the smallest part of a musical score and represents a sound played at a particular pitch for a particular duration. The *pitch* of a note determines the actual sound that you hear, and the *duration* is how long the sound is played. The pitches of a note are actually written on sheet music using the letters from A to G. Each of these notes can be played at a particular octave, which is the same note played at a higher pitch. If you look

8

at Figure 8.1, you can see a set of standard piano keys. The white key on the far left is the C key. This is also the lowest octave on the piano, or low C. The next keys in series are shown, but notice that the thirteenth key to the right of low C is another C. This key plays a pitch that is the same note as low C, just at a different octave.

FIGURE 8.1
Piano keys.

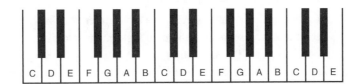

NEW TERM An *octave* is a particular range of normally eight pitches (12 distinct pitches when counting the black keys on a keyboard). The difference between one of the pitches in an octave and the same pitch one octave higher is that the pitch is exactly twice the frequency of the pitch below it. There exists a large number of octaves, although most musical instruments typically have a range of only three to five.

Notes also have a particular duration. This duration is measured in some fraction of a measure. A whole note is a note that is played over the entire measure. A half note is half as long as a whole note, or a note played during half of a measure. A quarter note is half as long as a half note and so on, down to a thirty-second note. These notes are played for the duration specified by their length. In a 4/4 measure, a quarter note is one beat in duration. Because a half note is twice as long as a quarter note, it is played twice as long, or for two beats.

Storing Compositions with the MIDI Format

Most of the musical editing software packages available today allows saving the musical scores you create as a MIDI file. This file format contains all the necessary MIDI data to be sent through the MIDI out port on your audio card, or through a software synthesizer, like the Microsoft Synthesizer.

The MIDI format consists of a few basic messages. One of them deals with instrument selections, which are accomplished through bank and instrument selection commands. There are also pan messages that refer to which channel a note is played through (right versus left) and volume messages that change the overall volume of a note.

With the number of MIDI music applications available, it is easy to create and save MIDI files, which end with the extension .MID. They are also quite handy because the Windows Media Player has the capability of playing them. Most audio cards also come with some piece of software that allows them to load and play MIDI files. The DirectMusic Producer application that comes with the DirectX 7.0 SDK also allows

importing MIDI files. This allows you to create MIDI music using another editing
package and to import the entire MIDI song into Producer for easier musical editing
capability.

Multitrack Music Synthesis

Within a given section of a musical score are different tracks that make up the score
itself. Each track represents an individual instrument's notes for the score. This allows
the composer to create the music that will be played by each instrument in its own track.
Can you imagine what it would be like trying to create a score with 10 instruments without seeing each instrument in its own track?

Using MIDI creation software, such as DirectMusic Producer, you can create music that
consists of many hundreds of tracks. Each track is assigned to a particular channel. To
each channel, you assign an instrument. The tracks consist of the actual note information
that will be played by the attached instruments. Each note has a particular pitch, duration, and volume. By playing back all the tracks at the same time, the entire musical
piece can be heard. Think of it like a symphony orchestra. Each group of instruments
represents a different track. If you play all the tracks at the same time, the entire orchestra plays.

Ideally, you should at least create a rhythm track that uses either the General MIDI drum
kit or a percussion instrument. To this, you should add your melody track or tracks,
depending on the number of instruments you are using for the melody. Then add some
background accompaniment, perhaps using two or three tracks. How many tracks you
actually use in your musical pieces will obviously differ depending on the exact music
you are trying to create.

DirectMusic Architecture

DirectMusic includes several components that allow in-depth control over its features.
For the purposes of this hour, we are going to discuss `IDirectMusicPerformance`, as
well as some of its companion interfaces. It is through these interface music, when a particular music segment is played, and when different patterns should be played. We will
be using the companion interfaces in-depth later in the next hour. We will also briefly
discuss a few of them here.

The `IDirectMusicPerformance` Interface

The `IDirectMusicPerformance` interface is, like the rest of DirectX, based on COM. It
has the following list of methods:

8

- AddNotificationType()
- AddPort()
- AdjustTime()
- AllocPMsg()
- AssignPChannel()
- AssignPChannelBlock()
- CloseDown()
- DownloadInstrument()
- FreePMsg()
- GetBumperLength()
- GetGlobalParam()
- GetGraph()
- GetLatencyTime()
- GetNotificationPMsg()
- GetParam()
- GetPrepareTime()
- GetQueueTime()
- GetResolvedTime()
- GetSegmentState()
- GetTime()
- Init()
- Invalidate()
- IsPlaying()
- MIDIToMusic()
- MusicToMIDI()
- MusicToReferenceTime()
- PChannelInfo()
- PlaySegment()
- ReferenceToMusicTime()
- RemoveNotificationType()
- RemovePort()
- RhythmToTime()

- SendPMsg()
- SetBumperLength()
- SetGlobalParam()
- SetGraph()
- SetNotificationHandle()
- SetParam()
- Stop()
- TimeToRhythm()
- AddRef()
- QueryInterface()
- Release()

Like all DirectX interfaces, the last three functions: AddRef(), QueryInterface(), and Release() are inherited from the IUknown interface.

We will be getting into the nitty-gritty of actually using the IDirectMusicPerformance object in the next hour. The rest of this hour we will cover a lot of the concepts you will need to know in order to create music in any of your work. Much of what you will need to know to use DirectMusic lies in understanding some of the principles behind DirectMusic and what its capabilities are. These will help during the next hour where we actually apply what we are covering in this hour.

Interfaces Used with the Performance Object

For the IDirectMusicPerformance object to actually play the musical score, it relies on several different DirectMusic interfaces for actually defining the various components of the music. It might be helpful to think of these interfaces as different views of a musical score.

The IDirectMusicSegment object represents the actual musical data that can be played using the IDirectMusicPerformance object. The IDirectMusicSegment object has methods that control the looping of the musical data, the timing of playback, event notification, and contains some number of IDirectMusicTrack objects. This object, and its collection of IDirectMusicTrack objects, contains all the data that will be used to play the actual music. Also, because IDirectMusicSegment objects are what IDirectMusicPerformance plays, implementing dynamic music involves creating segments at runtime.

The `IDirectMusicTrack` object is used to contain most of the actual data that makes up `IDirectMusicSegment` objects. Each track object can contain different types of timed data. This timed data might include tempo changes, band changes, other timed events, and even note data. For example, one track object might contain a band selection message, whereas another contains tempo change messages. The `IDirectMusicTrack` objects usually contain most of the data contained within an `IDirectMusicSegment` object.

Putting Together the Band

To make our music, we must first determine who is going to play in our band. We might decide that for a racing game, we want a lot of metal sounding instruments, lots of percussion, and a racing electric guitar. If creating a fantasy role-playing game, perhaps a harpsichord and a classic guitar should make up the band. For any music we want to create, we must first decide which instruments we want to include in the musical score.

DirectMusic allows us to actually create different bands for use within the same musical piece. Each band can consist of completely unique instruments or the same instruments, and instruments from different MIDI instrument sets can all be used within the same band. For example, you can use instruments from the General MIDI set and others from Roland's MIDI set, all within the same band.

Because of the capabilities of DLS, we can also create instruments out of virtually any wave file we choose. For example, we could record a bird chirping as a wave file. Then using the Wave Editor from within DirectMusic Producer, you can create a DLS instrument from it. Try and be creative in your choices for instruments. Or, if you prefer, you can stick to just the basic MIDI instruments included with DirectMusic.

DirectMusic can be configured to handle all the loading of the instruments for you. This can be accomplished by configuring the `IDirectMusicPerformance` object to automatically load necessary instruments. For those who want to have greater control of which band instruments are loaded and when they are loaded, you can also load instruments manually. DirectMusic gives you as little or as much control as you need.

Musical Templates

In a previous section, we discussed how `IDirectMusicSegment` objects are what the `IDirectMusicPerfomance` object actually plays. But the segments we discussed then represented human composed pieces of music. Earlier, we also discussed using blocks or patterns of music that could be rearranged into new pieces of music. This concept is called dynamic music. We now turn our attention to how DirectMusic actually allows you to implement this concept.

We begin with the template object. This object is really just a special kind of segment object. The template object, however, is not like a normal segment object. We will not use it directly to play music. Instead, we will use an interface called IDirectMusicComposer to create an actual IDirectMusicSegment object from the template object. It is this new segment object that will actually be played back by the performance object. These new segments are derived from authored components, but are not actually authored themselves.

During runtime, you can compose music by simply using the IDirectMusicComposer interface itself. This is accomplished by loading music composition files and calling a method of the IDirectMusicComposer object to create a new segment. For most purposes, this will provide the most basic level of randomness to your music. Of course, the actual amount of randomness is determined by the complexity of the initial composition files you create.

For those individuals wanting more control over the actual musical segment being created, you can change some of the parameters of the IDirectMusicSegment object created by the composer object yourself. Because the composer object relies on two interfaces for music composition, controlling them allows even greater control over the actual new music segments that will be generated. The other two interfaces are IDirectMusicChordMaps and IDirectMusicStyle.

The IDirectMusicStyle interface deals with the actual note patterns themselves. It can be comprised of several different note patterns. IDirectMusicStyle can also have several different bands that are associated, and by calling its different methods, these different bands can be selected. Certain patterns of notes can also be ordered for playback at a specific time, adding a little more control to the randomness of the entire template object.

The IDirectMusicChordMaps interface contains a list of available chords to be selected by the template object. Depending on the overall feel of the musical piece, there might be a large number of chords available for selection, or only one or two. The number of available chords depends on how sophisticated you want to make your music.

To create the actual random music, IDirectMusicComposer relies on the original composer to create the elements that will be put together to create the dynamic music. During the course of playing the new segment, certain markers, called *signposts*, will tell DirectMusic that another chord can be selected from a chordmap object. DirectMusic might then select a new chord from the list of chords in the chordmap and transpose all the following notes to the new chord. The transposed music will then play until another marker is reached. DirectMusic will then randomly select another chord and transpose again.

8

NEW TERM
A *signpost* is a point within a style that indicates to DirectMusic that another chord can be selected from the chord map.

NEW TERM
Transposing changes the actual pitch value of a note or notes, usually because of a specific chord chosen. By transposing music, the actual notes are changed to new values. Because selecting a chord that does not coincide with the notes being played would not sound appropriate, the notes are changed to values that do coincide with the new chord.

The power of musical templates lies with the fact that because each chord is chosen at random, the same pattern of music could sound completely different from performance to performance without the composer making any changes to the actual score. The selection of chords and the transpositions of notes occur within DirectMusic and require no programming on your part. This does, however, require some amount of setup by the composer in the first place. A chord map must be created that gives DirectMusic the chords to transpose the music by. Signposts must also be added to the patterns you create to mark where a new chord might be chosen.

For really creative individuals, you can take advantage of the `IDirectMusicComposer` interface described earlier to create dynamic music that includes a certain amount of interactivity. You could take advantage of all the components, creating your own `IDirectMusicStyle` and `IDirectMusicChordMap` interfaces, and create special short segments that are to be played in response to user events. You could then play these segments at the appropriate place in your game, even as another template is playing. This is the power of musical templates and demonstrates creating dynamic and interactive music that your players will love.

Summary

In this hour, you learned about the Microsoft Synthesizer and how it can provide consistency to the music your game plays. By applying the concept of making interactive music, you should have a greater understanding of how DirectMusic goes beyond being just another song player. Adding the concept of dynamic music to your next game should help make your music seem alive and spontaneous.

By covering some of the concepts of musical structure and music creation, you should have some of the general knowledge required to create music of your own. This knowledge will be invaluable when attempting to create your music for that next big game. In addition to these concepts, we also discussed the concepts of creating multiple tracks of music and incorporating MIDI files into our scores.

And of course, we also dug a little into the actual interfaces of DirectMusic. Looking at the `IDirectMusicPerformance` interface and the interfaces used in musical composition paves the way for actually implementing DirectMusic in your own projects. These concepts should give you the foundation necessary to discuss the application of DirectMusic in the next hour.

Q&A

Q Where does the `IDirectMusicPerformance` object come into play?

A The `IDirectMusicPerformance` object is the master controller of the musical score. Think of it as the orchestra conductor. Although it doesn't directly make the actual sounds you hear as the music plays, it directs everything and makes sure that everything plays on queue. We will cover how to apply the `IDirectMusicPerformance` interface and the other interfaces required for making music in more detail in the next hour.

Q Can I use DirectMusic to just play standard MIDI files, or do I have to create my music using the DirectMusic Producer application mentioned earlier?

A The answer to this question is easy: Yes you can just play standard MIDI files. One of the nice features of DirectMusic is that you could just create linear music scores and simply use the `IDirectMusicPerformance` object as a MIDI player. This shields you from having to stream the wave data directly to the audio card using DirectSound yourself. For those who want to implement some of the more powerful capabilities of DirectMusic, you should use the DirectMusic Producer to create patterns of music, which in turn allows you to create dynamic music. You might also want to use another music editing package and just use Producer to bring all the components together. We will cover using DirectMusic Producer in the next hour.

Workshop

The Workshop is designed to help you anticipate possible questions, review what you've learned, and get you thinking about how to put your knowledge into practice. The answers to the quiz are in Appendix A, "Answers."

Quiz

1. What is the purpose of a synthesizer?

2. What are two of the primary features of the Microsoft Synthesizer?

3. How does DLS architecture allow the Microsoft Synthesizer to produce exact music sounds on different audio cards?

4. What is meant by the phrase interactive music?

5. What is the purpose of the IDirectMusicPerformance object?

6. What kind of instruments can DirectMusic use?

7. What is the difference between a segment object and a template object?

8. What is an advantage of multi-track music synthesis?

9. What is the difference between interactive music and dynamic music?

Exercises

1. Be sure to check out the DirectMusic samples in the DirectX SDK. Most of the samples are games that actually use a lot of other DirectX features, but now incorporate DirectMusic. There is also the DirectMusic Shell application. This application actually demonstrates some of the amazing interactive capabilities of DirectMusic. After loading, it will begin playing music and will place a small DirectX icon in your system tray. Click on the DirectX system tray icon and select one of the other types of music. You will notice that it reacts to any activities you perform, such as opening windows or typing into any window. You will be hearing interactive music that is being created dynamically!

2. Try your hand at some music composition. You can use any of the music editing software packages on the market today. Most of them should be able to output standard MIDI files. You could also install the DirectMusic Producer application from the DirectX 7.0 SDK. Using the Producer application might seem a little complex at first, but if you find yourself a little lost, don't worry. We will discuss how to create music using DirectMusic Producer in the next hour.

HOUR 9

Applying DirectMusic

In the previous hour, we covered a lot of concepts about DirectMusic and what it can offer you in terms of adding music to your games. In this hour, we will discuss DirectMusic in much more detail, including actually implementing the different interfaces of DirectMusic. We will also discuss using the DirectMusic Producer application that comes with the DirectX 7 SDK to create music.

The lesson in this hour begins with a quick tutorial of the DirectMusic Producer application. This application allows you to compose music using a number of different tools, and you will learn how to create compositions using these editing tools. We then follow with the details of how to implement DirectMusic and its different interfaces to play music in your games. We will also cover adding the music we will create during this hour to our game.

In this hour, you will learn

- How to use the DirectMusic Producer application to create music
- How to implement the different interfaces of DirectMusic
- How to change music in response to game events
- How to add DirectMusic to our game

Using the DirectMusic Producer to Create a Simple Score

To create the music you use in your games, you can use any kind of musical editing package. For the purposes of the first part of this hour, we will be discussing how to use the DirectMusic Producer application that comes with DirectX 7. This application typically installs into your Program Files directory, although you can change the installation directory during the installation process.

The Producer application will allow us to create all the elements needed to create music for our games. We will create most of these elements using one or more of the editors or designers within Producer. Each editor has a specific purpose, but they are well integrated, so you might not notice that you are using individual editors. It is not important to remember the individual editor or designer names, only how to launch each of the editors to perform whatever editing is necessary. This will become clearer after using the Producer application for a while.

We will begin by opening the DirectMusic Producer application. Selecting the Producer application from Programs from the Start menu will launch the application. When the application is running, it should have a window with a lot of toolbars, and the lower portion of the display should be empty. We will first create our project. Select the New button from the toolbar. The window that appears should look like Figure 9.1. Select Project from the list. After clicking OK, the New Project window appears. Enter a name for the project like Chapter 9 as shown in Figure 9.2. We now have an open project that will wind up containing all the elements for the music we are going to play.

FIGURE 9.1

Getting started with DirectMusic Producer.

FIGURE 9.2

Name the new project.

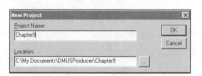

Selecting the Instruments

Now that we have created a new project, it is time to start putting together the elements of our music. For any piece of music to be heard, we must choose the instruments that will play the music. When selecting our instruments, we can actually create more than one band of instruments. This allows us to create two different bands with slightly different sounding instruments. Then during playback, we can play the segment with the first band, and then play the segment again with the second band.

To select our instruments we first create a new band object. This can be accomplished by selecting the New button from the Producer toolbar. This will add a new category to the Producer's project tree called Band.bnp and will add an initial band object called Band1. The first level in the hierarchy is important because it indicates the file in which this band, and subsequent band objects added to this file, will be located. The second level in the hierarchy is the name of our band. You can rename the band to anything you like, and you can change the name of the band file as well.

Now we must actually assign some instruments to the band object. We do this within the Band Editor. To bring up the Band Editor, simply double-click on the Band1 object we just created. You should now see the Band Editor window. Within the editor window is a list of PChannels on the left. Double-click on the first PChannel in the list and the PChannel Properties window will appear.

NEW TERM   *PChannel* is an acronym for Performance Channel. A Performance Channel contains all the information for a particular instrument. This includes MIDI instrument selections, volume, pan, octave, and transposition values.

> By looking at Figure 9.3, you can see that our band has 16 instruments. Remember from the discussion in the last hour that we could have virtually an unlimited number of instruments. So why are only 16 listed here? Because we can add additional instruments to this band if needed; in fact, as many as 999 of them. For our purposes, however, 16 will be more than enough.

FIGURE 9.3

Selecting instruments.

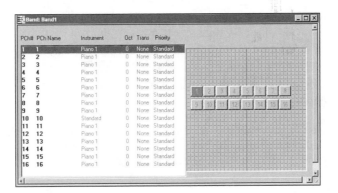

To actually select a specific instrument for a given PChannel, we must check off the Instrument check box. We can then select an instrument by pressing on the button just to the right of the check box. For the first instrument in our band, we will select the first piano, Piano 1, from the list of piano instruments. For the second instrument, let's pick Steel Guitar from the list of guitar instruments.

We will also need some instruments for creating a rhythm track. Fortunately for us, a PChannel has been set aside for us to use as a rhythm track. If you look at Figure 9.3, you can see that PChannel ten already has Standard as an instrument. This is because of the fact that, by default, MIDI uses channel ten for a drum kit. To take advantage of this, turn on the instrument for PChannel ten. Open PChannel ten, and check off the Instrument check box. You can also select one of the other seven drum kits if you want by clicking on the button marked Standard.

Now that we have selected our instruments, a few more things must be touched on. Until now we only discussed the left side of the Band Editor. If you look at the right side, you will notice a grid with some numbers in it. This grid actually has more than just a pretty aesthetic purpose. The position of the numbers on the grid indicates some of the properties of the instruments. The left and right halves of the grid represent the pan of the instrument. If the number is positioned on the left side of the grid, the instrument will be played more from the left speaker than from the right. The further left the number, the more the left speaker plays than the right. The reverse is also true as you move the number right. The top and bottom halves of the grid represent the volume of the instrument. Moving an instrument to the top half raises the volume of that instrument. The further up the number, the louder the instrument will be played. You can also adjust the volume and pan properties from the PChannel Properties window where you selected the instruments initially.

Creating a Rhythm

Now that we have determined which instruments we are going to use, it is time to start creating the actual music we are going to be playing. The most basic element of any piece of music is usually rhythm. Most people think of rhythm as being created by a drum or other percussion instrument. However, other instruments can set the rhythm of the music such a bass guitar or other instrument playing regularly timed notes. Regardless of the actual instrument or instruments creating the rhythm, it usually sets the overall beat of the music.

To begin entering in music, we will need a track to enter in the note data. As we covered in the last hour, a segment object is comprised of one or more tracks of timed data. So start by creating a new segment object. Select the New button from the toolbar and select

Segment from the list. This will create a new segment file and a single segment object. Now we will need to open the segment object to enter our rhythm notes. By double-clicking on the segment object, you can open the segment editor, which is shown in Figure 9.4. This editor allows modifying the parameters about the segment itself as well as adding in tracks of musical data. We will only need twelve measures for our small composition, so we will need to change the segment to be only twelve measures, or bars long. Right-click on the segment object itself and select Properties. When the Segment Properties window appears, change the length to twelve measures, or bars.

9

FIGURE 9.4

Creating a segment.

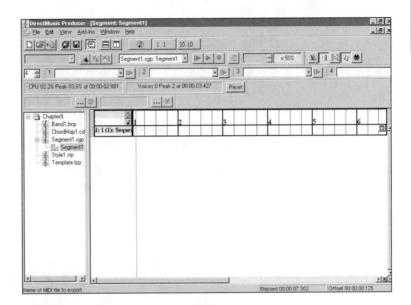

To enter our rhythm track, we will need a note track. To create a note track, right-click on the editor window and select Add Track to open the Add New Tracks window. From this window, select Sequence Track and then click the OK button. A sequence track is created that contains a part for the first instrument. Along the top, a series of numbers are spaced apart evenly. These numbers represent the measures for the sequence track, which can be seen in Figure 9.4.

Now that we have a sequence track, we must actually add a sequence for the PChannel we are using for our rhythm. We assigned the standard drum kit to the number ten PChannel earlier, so right-click on the sequence track area and select Add New Part. When the Add New Part window appears, change the PChannel box to ten and click the Create New Part button. This should add a sequence for the number ten PChannel.

On the far right side of the sequence area is a button that minimizes and maximizes the sequence window (see Figure 9.5). Click this button to display the sequence in its maximized state. On the left side of the window are what appear to be the keys of a piano, only the keys are flipped on their sides and some words are written all over them. The words are actually the different components of the drum kit. Scroll up or down the list of instruments using the scrollbar to the right of the piano keys until you locate the instrument Snare Drum 1. Right-click on the sequence area to the right, select Snap To from the drop-down list and then select Beat. This will align any notes that we add to a single beat of the measure.

FIGURE 9.5

Putting melody in the segment.

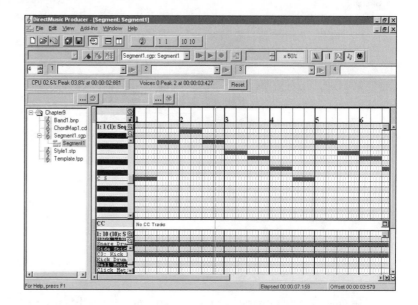

We are now ready to add the actual musical notes. Start by placing your cursor in the first column just to the right of the Snare Drum 1 piano key. Either press the insert key on the keyboard, or right-click and select Insert Note. You might find it easier to use the keyboard's arrow keys to move around the measures, and through the instruments or notes. After you have entered the first note, repeat the process for each beat for the next twelve measures. This creates a one beat note for each beat in the entire segment. You could also repeat the same note creation step for the Kick Drum 1. Now that you have actually created some kind of music, let's listen to it! From the Transport Controls toolbar, select the green Play From Start button to play the segment.

Making a Simple Melody

Now that we have some music to play, we must add some kind of melody to it. For expedience, we are going to create a simple melody for "Twinkle, Twinkle, Little Star." This process is very similar to creating the rhythm track, except that we are using a regular instrument, rather than a drum kit. Normally we would have to create a sequence for the instrument, but because the sequence for PChannel number one was created by default, we only need to maximize sequence one's window. You should also change the Snap To for the sequence to Beat like you did before.

Notice that the piano keys on the left side only have markers for the different octaves of C. This will be your guide for which note you are actually creating. We must now create the actual notes so that the entire song is comprised of quarter notes and half notes. The half notes are positioned at the last half of every second measure. The note progression for the song is C, G, A, G, F, E, D, C, G, F, E, D, G, F, E, D, C, G, A, G, F, E, D, C. When creating the half notes, you can change the length of any note, by left-clicking on the right edge of the note and dragging it left until it takes up two whole beats. Look at Figure 9.5 to get an idea of what the sequences should look like at this point. After you have entered all the notes, try playing your new segment again. It should sound like "Twinkle Twinkle Little Star." You now have a completed piece of music that we could load into DirectMusic and play through a performance object.

Creating Musical Templates

Now we actually have a piece of music that we can play. The segment object contains note data for the three instruments, one being the standard drum kit, and we have a band file that specifies the information for each of those instruments. In the previous hour, we discussed using template objects to create music that would be created dynamically at runtime. We will now create a simple musical template to show what is possible using Producer. Because a lot of capabilities of template objects exist and only those who have a strong music composition background will be able to use them all, we will only be brushing the surface of what is possible through template objects.

First, create a new template object. We will also need to create a style object as well as a chordmap object. The template object uses the note patterns and band objects that are contained within the style object to actually create the music. Notice that the style object has a number of children objects, namely band, motif, and pattern objects. We will only concern ourselves with the pattern objects, although you should experiment with creating multiple band objects and perhaps creating motifs on your own.

To provide some musical notes to be played by the template, we will import one of the MIDI files from those that come with Windows. Right-click on the patterns object and select Import MIDI File as Pattern. From the window that appears, change to the media directory under your Windows directory. Select any of the MIDI files there, such as the Bach's Brandenburg Concerto No. 3. When you have selected the MIDI file, Producer will import the music as a pattern, and will in most cases create a band file as well. The band file represents the instruments that were selected in the original MIDI file. You can then delete the default Band1 and Pattern1 objects that were created when you created the style initially.

Now we must create a couple of chords for the template object to use for transpositions of the MIDI pattern we just created. Open the chordmap object by double-clicking on the Chordmap1 object. We will use the area on the right to create our chords. First, under the SP column, left-click on the word New. This will open the Signpost Chord Scale/Inversion Properties window. This window might seem a little confusing at first, but it can be relatively simple to create a different chord. The first box you see is the base note of the chord; we can change our chord by simply raising or lowering this base note. For our first chord, we will leave it at 2C, so simply close the window. There should now be a line under the column headers, with 2 C M under the SP column. Now we will need to indicate at what signpost markers this chord could be selected. The signpost markers will be created from within the template object, but we must indicate here which chords are usable at a given signpost. Ideally, you will want a number of chords available at each signpost because that allows for greater randomness. So let's set at which signposts the 2CM chord can be used. Left-click in the boxes to the right of the chord, marked with the numbers one through five. Then select the word New under the SP column again. This time change the chord's base note from 2C to 2E and close the window. As with the 2CM chord, check off the one through 5 boxes to the left of the 2EM chord. Finally, create one more chord as 2A and check off the same five boxes once more. Your chordmap should look like Figure 9.6.

There are a lot of little elements to consider when creating a musical template, and unfortunately there are too many to cover here. You should try experimenting on your own because changing just a single chord at a signpost can have a significant impact on the way your music sounds. This represents a good demonstration of the power of designing music with the Producer application. Create once and use many times is the general philosophy here.

FIGURE 9.6

Editing the chordmap.

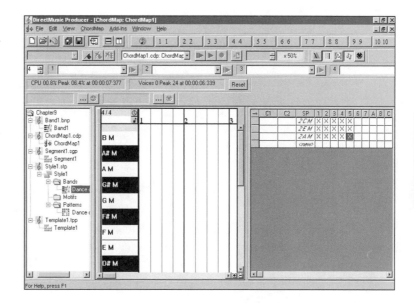

The chords have been created, but we have one final step to actually hear music that is dynamic. We must create the signposts within the template object that indicate where a new chord can be selected. Open the template object by double-clicking on it. There should be a single track called a Signpost Track. Because we attached our chords to five signposts, we will assign five signposts to our template. In the signpost track, right-click in the first measure and select Insert. The Signpost Group Properties window will appear. The combo box should already be set to one, so simply close the window to create the signpost. Now we will want to create another signpost and give it the group number one, so right-click in the fifth measure of the signpost track. Select the number two from the combo box and close the window. Now create three more signposts for groups three, four and five, at measures nine, thirteen, and seventeen. You can also reuse a particular signpost group again, so create another signpost at measure nineteen and set it to group three.

Now to create a random set of chords, select the little musical note button next to the track's title. A new Chord Track should be created, and chords should now be listed in the track. Try playing the template. Notice how the music changes when it gets to a new chord. This is not magic. Some musical pieces change chords during their play. In fact, you could add a chord track to your own segment object and accomplish what we just set up with one exception: by clicking on the little musical note button again, the chords in the chord track change. This process will be performed automatically when creating a segment from a template object at runtime. We've covered a lot so far, but now we have a regular segment we could use and a template object, which we will use later to create a new segment for our game during runtime.

It is possible to add a signpost track to a regular segment object. Doing so changes the segment to a template object, but will not change its name. This will mean that you will have to use the `IDirectMusicComposer` interface to create a new segment from this segment at runtime. This can be handy when you have a particularly long segment, or perhaps one that was imported from a MIDI file, and you want to add a little bit of dynamics to the segment. It will still require a chordmap and a style object just like a regular template object.

Saving the Performance

When you are satisfied with your music, you can simply select the Save All button on the toolbar, and all your music compositions will be saved. You can also save at any time during creation, and you might want to consider doing just that, for safety's sake. This saving process saves your compositions into the directory that you specified when we created the project in the beginning.

There is also a detail about saving the performance that you should consider. For each of the composition files, there are design and runtime file locations. These are used to separate the design-time files and runtime files, respectively. When you are finished with your compositions, you will want to create a runtime version of your files for inclusion in your game. The reason is elements exist within the initial files that are used by the Producer application. By saving your compositions as runtime files, you can reduce the overall size and create the files that DirectMusic will use to play your music. Saving the runtime versions is as simple as selecting either Runtime Save As or Runtime Save All from the File Menu. You can then include the saved files with your application.

Setting Up DirectMusic

Now that we have some musical material created, it is time to begin digging into the innards of DirectMusic. In the last hour you learned about some of the interfaces of DirectMusic. The main interface we are going to use is `IDirectMusicPerformance`. This interface is the object that is going to play our music for us. We will also cover how to use other interfaces, such as those used to load and create music during runtime.

Initializing the Performance Interface

To begin our journey into the nitty-gritty of DirectMusic, we must first obtain a pointer to an `IDirectMusicPerformance` interface. You can accomplish this with a call to the COM function `CoCreateInstance`. An example of doing this follows:

```
HRESULT hresult;
LPDIRECTMUSICPERFORMANCE lpDirectMusicPerformance;

hresult = CoCreateInstance( CLSID_DirectMusicPerformance,
        NULL, CLSCTX_INPROC_SERVER,
        IID_IDirectMusicPerformance, (LPVOID*)&lpDirectMusicPerformance);
if ( FAILED(hresult) )
        HandleFailure();
```

After creating a reference and obtaining an interface, we are ready to begin setting up our IDirectMusicPerformance COM object. Before we begin using our new performance object, we will need to initialize it. This must be performed before any other method is called. Initialization can be accomplished through a call to the Init() method.

```
HRESULT Init(IDirectMusic** ppDirectMusic,
             LPDIRECTSOUND pDirectSound, HWND hWnd);
```

Notice that the first parameter passed to the Init method is the address of a reference to an IDirectMusic interface. For most purposes, you can simply leave this parameter as NULL. The IDirectMusicPerformance object will then create its own internal IDirectMusic interface object. The IDirectMusicPerformance object uses the IDirectMusic object to create and manage ports and buffers and to manage the master clock.

If you want, you can retrieve a reference to the IDirectMusic interface by passing in the address of a pointer to an IDirectMusic object. IDirectMusicPerformance will then populate your pointer with a reference to the IDirectMusic object it created. This can be accomplished by the following:

```
IDirectMusic *pDirectMusic;
HRESULT Init(IDirectMusic** &pDirectMusic,
 LPDIRECTSOUND pDirectSound, HWND hWnd);
```

You can also initialize your own IDirectMusic object before calling Init, and simply pass the address of the pointer to that object to the Init method. To obtain a reference to an IDirectMusic interface, simply call the CoCreateInstance function.

```
HRESULT hresult;
LPDIRECTMUSIC lpDirectMusic;

hresult = CoCreateInstance( CLSID_DirectMusic, NULL, CLSCTX_INPROC_SERVER,
        IID_IDirectMusic, (LPVOID*)&lpDirectMusic);
if ( FAILED(hresult) )
        HandleFailure();
```

If you intend to use a synthesizer different than the default one, you will need to either create your own `IDirectMusic` object or retrieve a reference to the one created by `IDirectMusicPerformance`. Using the reference to the `IDirectMusic` object enables you to make changes to the default synthesizer, as well as make changes to the master clock. Because the default synthesizer is the synthesizer we want—that is, the Microsoft Synthesizer—we will not be using the `IDirectMusic` interface directly.

The second parameter passed to the `Init` method shown previously is a pointer to a DirectSound object. Like the `IDirectMusic` object, you could pass in an existing reference to a DirectSound object. For most purposes, we will have no need to pass in a DirectSound object, so simply pass in the value of `NULL`. If you have already initialized a DirectSound object to play sounds for the existing window, you can pass in the reference to that object to the `Init` method.

The third parameter is a handle to the window with which the DirectSound object will be associated. If you are passing your own pointer to a DirectSound object to the `Init` method, you should pass in the value of `NULL`. Otherwise, pass in the handle to the window associated with the DirectSound object. If you are going to let the `IDirectMusicPerformance` object obtain its own DirectSound object and want to use the current window, simply pass in a value of `NULL`.

Loading Composition Files

After `Init` has been called, the `IDirectMusicPerformance` object is ready to be used. To play any music at all, however, we must load some music data so that the `IDirectMusicPerformance` object has something to play. Thankfully for us, DirectMusic uses a simple method for loading composition files, and this method is very similar for all the different composition files being loaded. Loading is provided by an interface that we haven't discussed yet called the `IDirectMusicLoader`.

Some of the composition files we will be loading contain references to other composition files. When we created our style object using the Producer application earlier, we created a band object and a pattern object. These objects were saved in the file with the style object. Fortunately for us, the `IDirectMusicLoader` interface will handle the creation of the band and pattern objects for us transparently. We only need to load the style object itself, and when the references to the band and pattern objects occurs, the `IDirectMusicLoader` interface creates them as well. This transparent loading holds true for any objects referenced by either segment or template objects.

To load a file, we must first obtain a reference to an `IDirectMusicLoader` interface. The `IDirectMusicLoader` object will handle the actual loading of the data for you. The `IDirectMusicLoader` object can also cache the loaded objects, so additional load calls will only retrieve the already loaded object and not cause unnecessary loading. For this reason, you should consider creating a global `IDirectMusicLoader` object that you use to load all your files, and then free the reference when all loading is complete. A reference to an `IDirectMusicLoader` interface can be obtained by the following code:

```
IDirectMusicLoader* m_pLoader;
HRESULT hr = CoCreateInstance(CLSID_DirectMusicLoader, NULL, CLSCTX_INPROC,
        IID_IDirectMusicLoader, (void**)&m_pLoader);
```

For most of the operations with the DirectX SDK, structures are used to set some of the operating parameters of the methods that are called. The `IDirectMusicLoader` interface uses one of these structures, called `DMUS_OBJECTDESC`, to indicate what type of file should be loaded and how it should be loaded. This structure allows setting things like the name of the composition file to load, the path that the file should be loaded from, and the type of file being loaded. We will be using the `IDirectMusicLoader` interface to load the segment, template, chordmap and style objects we created earlier with the Producer application.

We can load the segment object we created earlier using the `IDirectMusicLoader` interface. We simply populate the `DMUS_OBJECTDESC` structure and then call the `GetObject` method. This can be accomplished by a wrapper function like this:

```
void myLoadSegment(IDirectMusicSegment **ppIDMSegment)
{
        IDirectMusicLoader *pIDMLoader;     // Loader interface.
        // You could alternatively use a glogal loader object
        CoCreateInstance(CLSID_DirectMusicLoader,NULL, CLSCTX_INPROC,
        IID_IDirectMusicLoader, (void **) &pIDMLoader);
        if (pIDMLoader)
        {
                DMUS_OBJECTDESC Desc;

                // Start by initializing Desc with the file name and
                // class GUID for the band object.

                wcscpy(Desc.wszFileName, L"C:\\MyMusic\\Work\\Segment1.sgp");
                Desc.guidClass = CLSID_DirectMusicSegment;
                Desc.dwSize = sizeof (DMUS_OBJECTDESC);

                // Since we are including the Class ID and the file name
                // and full path to the file, we need to inform the Loader object

                Desc.dwValidData = DMUS_OBJ_CLASS |
                        DMUS_OBJ_FILENAME | DMUS_OBJ_FULLPATH;

                pIDMLoader->GetObject(&Desc, IID_IDirectMusicSegment,
```

```
                (void **) ppIDMSegment);
        pIDMLoader->Release();
    }
}
```

We now have a reference to the loaded segment object. We will use this reference later to play the actual segment. By changing the Class ID to that of whatever object you want to load and providing the address of a pointer to the same object, you can load any of the files that are created by the Producer application.

Establishing the Instruments

When creating your compositions using the Producer application, you set up the instruments that you will use to play your music in band objects. Whenever you load a segment or style file, a default band object is created for it. This band file will represent the first band file that existed in the project when you created it.

The band objects we will be using can be loaded in a number of different ways. Let's look at loading them from a separate file first because this process is very similar to loading other objects and will provide a reference when loading other objects.

```
void myLoadBand(IDirectMusicBand **ppIDMBand)
{
        IDirectMusicLoader *pIDMLoader;     // Loader interface.
        // You could alternatively use a glogal loader object
        CoCreateInstance(CLSID_DirectMusicLoader,NULL, CLSCTX_INPROC,
        IID_IDirectMusicLoader, (void **) &pIDMLoader);
        if (pIDMLoader)
        {
                DMUS_OBJECTDESC Desc;

                // Start by initializing Desc with the file name and
                // class GUID for the band object.

                wcscpy(Desc.wszFileName, L"C:\\MyMusic\\Work\\Band1.bnp");
                Desc.guidClass = CLSID_DirectMusicBand;
                Desc.dwSize = sizeof (DMUS_OBJECTDESC);

                // Since we are including the Class ID and the file name
                // and full path to the file, we need to inform the Loader object

                Desc.dwValidData = DMUS_OBJ_CLASS |
                        DMUS_OBJ_FILENAME | DMUS_OBJ_FULLPATH;

                pIDMLoader->GetObject(&Desc, IID_IDirectMusicBand,
                        (void **) ppIDMBand);
                pIDMLoader->Release();
        }
}
```

If you look at the preceding `GetObject` call, you will see that we pass in the address of a reference to the band object as a parameter. This method looks similar to the method used to load the segment in the previous section. When the function returns, the band object reference should contain a valid band object. We will use this object to create and play a new segment.

```
/* Automatic downloading should be turned on,
   and a reference to the loaded band object retrieved. */

HRESULT myPlayBand(IDirectMusicBand *pIDMBand,      // Pointer to band object
            IDirectMusicPerformance *pIDMPerf,      // Performance to use band
            REFERENCE_TIME rfTime,                  // Time to play the band at
            DWORD dwFlags)                          // Performance flags
{
      IDirectMusicSegment *pIDMSegment;             // Used to cue the band change
      HRESULT hResult = pIDMBand->CreateSegment(&pIDMSegment);
      if (SUCCEEDED(hResult))
      {
            hResult = pIDMPerf->PlaySegment(pIDMSegment,
                              dwFlags | DMUS_SEGF_SECONDARY,
                              rfTime, NULL);
            pIDMSegment->Release();
      }
      return hResult;
}
```

 If automatic downloading isn't enabled, it will be necessary to download the instrument's wave data to the `IDirectMusic` port. This can be accomplished with a call to the `Download` method of the `IDirectMusicBand` object. If automatic downloading isn't enabled and the data isn't downloaded, you will not hear any notes played by that band.

The preceding code creates what is called a secondary segment object. Secondary segment objects are segment objects that perform operations just like a primary segment, except that they usually have a smaller purpose. For example, a secondary segment can be used to cue messages such as band changes, tempo changes, instrument solos, and small specific note pieces called motifs. Although only a single primary segment can be playing at once, many secondary segments can be played at any time, and are typically used to enhance or change the music playing from the primary segment.

NEW TERM A *motif* is a short pattern of music that is usually played over a primary segment.

As you look at the preceding code, notice that the `CreateSegment` method of the band object is called. The newly created segment is then played by the performance using the `PlaySegment` method of the performance object. Because the segment is cued immediately, it is no longer needed and can be released. This methodology is used to cue a number of different changes to the music, and we will discuss it a little further in a few moments.

When we saved the performance earlier, the band object was saved as well, and it is located in a separate file. As mentioned earlier, when loading a segment or style that contains references to bands or other objects, those objects are in turn loaded with the segment or style automatically. It might be necessary in some cases to obtain references to those band objects to alter properties about them. This can be accomplished by retrieving a reference to the band object directly.

The `IDirectMusicLoader` interface uses caching by default, so a direct loading of the band object isn't necessary because a reference to the already loaded band object can be returned. You could either load the band object directly, which results in an immediate return of the reference to the already cached object, or if the band is part of a style object, simply retrieve the band object from the style object that contains it. This is accomplished through a call to the `GetBand` method of the `IDirectMusicStyle` interface.

```
hr = pStyle->GetBand(bstrBandName, &pIDMBand);
```

This will retrieve the band from the style so that you could use the band object elsewhere. You could, for example, create a segment from the band object and play the new segment to change the band that is being used by the currently playing segment. You might also need the band object reference to download the instrument data to the port using the `Download` method of the `IDirectMusicBand` object.

DirectMusic Playback

Until now, we have managed to create a musical composition and have loaded the related composition files into memory. Now we must play the music to hear it. Depending on the complexity of the music you want to create, you will need to determine when will be the appropriate time within your game's loading routines to load the music. You could, for example, create your DirectMusic objects very early and use them to play an opening segment as you load the opening components of your game. Then, you could play another segment while the user navigates any game menus. When game play has begun, you could play yet another segment, or perhaps a template.

Playing Segments

We now arrive at probably the most important step in this lesson, and one I am sure you have been looking forward to. We now actually play the music we have created and loaded previously. As we discussed in the last hour, the IDirectMusicPerformance object is responsible for playing our musical pieces. We will start with how to a play a segment object.

```
DMUS_OBJECTDESC Desc;
HRESULT hr;
IDirectMusicSegment* pIDMSegment;

Desc.dwSize = sizeof(DMUS_OBJECTDESC);
Desc.guidClass = CLSID_DirectMusicSegment;
wcscpy(Desc.wszFileName, L"Segment1.sgt");
Desc.dwValidData = DMUS_OBJ_CLASS | DMUS_OBJ_FILENAME | DMUS_OBJ_FULLPATH;
lpIDMLoader->GetObject(&Desc, IID_IDirectMusicSegment2, (void**) pIDMSegment);

hr = pIDMPerf->PlaySegment(pIDMSegment, 0, 0, NULL);
```

The preceding code loads a primary segment, and then plays the segment through the performance object. The first parameter takes a pointer to the segment object to be played, the second parameter contains any flags associated with the segment, the third indicates when to play the segment, and the fourth parameter takes the address of a pointer to a IDirectMusicSegmentState object. We pass in the segment we loaded, and set the flag parameter to zero to indicate that it should play as a primary segment. For the time parameter, we enter zero to indicate that it should occur whenever the next available start time would be. If another primary segment is still playing, it will stop and this segment will begin playing. The last parameter is the address to a reference of an IDirectMusicSegmentState object. This object can be used to retrieve some parameters about the currently playing music. For our purposes, we do not need the reference, so we simply pass in NULL.

Real-Time Changes to Tempo and Structure

We have the ability to make a number of different changes to the overall structure of our music as it is playing. We will start with a very simple change that you will probably use often. We will adjust the overall tempo of the playing segment. When we created the segment initially using the Producer application, we created a tempo track that set the initial tempo to 120 beats per minute. Let's start by adjusting the tempo of the currently playing segment to 140 beats per minute.

To make changes to the currently playing music, we will need to feed different messages into the performance object. When received by the performance object, the messages will

be either processed immediately, or cued for the time you specify. The following shows
how to create one of these messages, a tempo message, and how to send it to a performance object.

```
// We will need to disable the tempo track in the segment
// that is playing, so that it doesn't reset the tempo on us

// Disable tempo track in segment so that it does not reset tempo
lpIDMSegment->SetParam( GUID_DisableTempo, 0xFFFF,0,0, NULL );

DMUS_TEMPO_PMSG* pTempo;
if( SUCCEEDED(lpIDMPerformance->AllocPMsg(sizeof(DMUS_TEMPO_PMSG),
            (DMUS_PMSG**)&pTempo)))
{
        // Queue tempo event
        ZeroMemory(pTempo, sizeof(DMUS_TEMPO_PMSG));
        pTempo->dwSize = sizeof(DMUS_TEMPO_PMSG);
        pTempo->dblTempo = DEFAULT_TEMPO;
        pTempo->dwFlags = DMUS_PMSGF_REFTIME;
        pTempo->dwType = DMUS_PMSGT_TEMPO;
        lpIDMPerformance->SendPMsg((DMUS_PMSG*)pTempo);
}
```

We can also change our music using a template object. During runtime, we can create a
new segment from the template object, additionally selecting the associated style and
chordmap objects we want to use. We created one style and one chordmap object earlier
and we will use those here. We are, however, going to need a reference to an
IDirectMusicComposer interface. As you might recall from our discussion last hour, the
composer object is used to create the actual segment we will play. You can create a reference to the IDirectMusicComposer object the same way you create an
IDirectMusicPerformance object.

```
IDirectMusicComposer* m_pIDMComposer;
HRESULT hr = CoCreateInstance(CLSID_DirectMusicComposer, NULL, CLSCTX_INPROC,
        IID_IDirectMusicComposer, (void**)&m_pIDMComposer);
```

When we have this reference, we can use the ComposeSegmentFromTemplate method to
create a new segment object based on the template. The following code demonstrates
creating the new segment.

```
// The style, chordmap and template objects are assumed to have been
// loaded previous using a loader object.
IDirectMusicSegment **ppIDMSegment;

HRESULT ComposeSegmentFromTemplate(pIDMStyle, pIDMTempSeg, w_Activity,
            pIDMChordMap, ppIDMSegment);
```

The preceding `ComposeSegmentFromTemplate` method takes in a style, chordmap, template object, and an activity value and populates the reference to the segment object. Because we included a reference to the style and chordmap objects when we created our template earlier, we can simply pass nulls in for those values. The activity parameter represents the amount of harmonic activity that DirectMusic should apply to the specified template. The valid range is between zero and three. The lower the number, the more the chords will fluctuate, the higher the number, the less they will fluctuate. The segment reference we passed in is now a new copy of our template that has been created and can now be played through the performance object.

Adding DirectMusic to Our Game

Now we must apply what we have covered here to the game that we have been developing. There are a number of additional objects that we will need, so we begin by adding references to all the objects as seen in Listing 9.1.

LISTING 9.1 The Variable Declarations, Defines, and Other Values

```
1: #include <dmusici.h>
2: //------ DirectMusic Objects ------//
3: IDirectMusicPerformance        *lpIDMPerformance;
4: IDirectMusicLoader             *lpIDMLoader;
5: IDirectMusicComposer          *lpIDMComposer;
6: IDirectMusicSegment            *lpIDMSegment;
7: IDirectMusicSegment            *lpIDMTemplate;
8: IDirectMusicStyle             *lpIDMStyle;
9: IDirectMusicChordMap          *lpIDMChordMap;
10:
11: //------ Define Stand-Still Tempo ------//
12: #define DEFAULT_TEMPO    60
13:
14: //------ Used to watch speed for tempo changes to music --------//
15: BOOL fMoveChange=TRUE;         // Used to determine if tempo change needed.
16:
17: //------ Error Messages ------//
18: const char Err_DMPerfCreate[] =
    ➥"Error creating DirectMusicPerformance object";
19: const char Err_DMLoadCreate[] =
    ➥"Error creating DirectMusicLoader object";
20: const char Err_DMCompCreate[] =
    ➥"Error creating DirectMusicComposer object";
21: const char Err_DMLoadMusic[]        = "Error loading music";
```

Creating the Interfaces

In Listing 9.2, the code creates the IDirectMusicPerformance, IDirectMusicLoader, and IDirectMusicComposer objects. From the references that were created, we can begin initializing the DirectMusic objects we will need. We begin by calling the Init method of the performance object and then after turning on the automatic downloading of instrument data, we ensure that a default port is created. We then call the routine to load the composition files, and begin playing the music. When the music is playing, we immediately adjust the tempo of the music to the default tempo, which is set for sixty beats a minute.

LISTING 9.2   The Changes to the Init() Function That Create the Necessary DirectMusic Components and Start the Music Playing

```
 1: // Create the DM objects
 2: CoInitialize(NULL);
 3:
 4: dmrval = CoCreateInstance(CLSID_DirectMusicPerformance,
                  NULL, CLSCTX_INPROC_SERVER,
 5:               IID_IDirectMusicPerformance, (LPVOID*)&lpIDMPerformance);
 6: if (FAILED(dmrval))
 7: {
 8:         ErrStr = Err_DMPerfCreate;
 9:         return FALSE;
10: }
11:
12: dmrval = CoCreateInstance(CLSID_DirectMusicLoader, NULL, CLSCTX_INPROC,
13:                    IID_IDirectMusicLoader, (LPVOID*)&lpIDMLoader);
14: if (FAILED(dmrval))
15: {
16:         ErrStr = Err_DMLoadCreate;
17:         return FALSE;
18: }
19:
20: dmrval = CoCreateInstance(CLSID_DirectMusicComposer, NULL, CLSCTX_INPROC,
21:                    IID_IDirectMusicComposer, (LPVOID*)&lpIDMComposer);
22: if (FAILED(dmrval))
23: {
24:         ErrStr = Err_DMCompCreate;
25:         return FALSE;
26: }
27:
28: // Initialize the Performance object
29: dmrval = lpIDMPerformance->Init(NULL, NULL, NULL);
30:
31: // Turn on automatic downloading of instruments
32: BOOL fAutoDownload = TRUE;
33: lpIDMPerformance->SetGlobalParam(GUID_PerfAutoDownload, &fAutoDownload,
    ➥sizeof(BOOL));
```

```
34:
35: // Tell the Performance to create the default port
36: lpIDMPerformance->AddPort(NULL);
37:
38: // Load the DM musical data
39: if (!load_music())
40: {
41:         ErrStr = Err_DMLoadMusic;
42:         return FALSE;
43: }
44:
45: // Since we want the music in the background, start playing the music
46: lpIDMPerformance->PlaySegment(lpIDMSegment, 0, 0, NULL);
47:
48:
49: // Disable tempo track in segment so that it does not reset tempo
50: lpIDMSegment->SetParam( GUID_DisableTempo, 0xFFFF,0,0, NULL );
51:
52: DMUS_TEMPO_PMSG* pTempo;
53: if( SUCCEEDED(lpIDMPerformance->AllocPMsg(sizeof(DMUS_TEMPO_PMSG),
    ➡(DMUS_PMSG**)&pTempo)))
54: {
55:         // Queue tempo event
56:         ZeroMemory(pTempo, sizeof(DMUS_TEMPO_PMSG));
57:         pTempo->dwSize = sizeof(DMUS_TEMPO_PMSG);
58:         pTempo->dblTempo = DEFAULT_TEMPO;
59:         pTempo->dwFlags = DMUS_PMSGF_REFTIME;
60:         pTempo->dwType = DMUS_PMSGT_TEMPO;
61:         lpIDMPerformance->SendPMsg((DMUS_PMSG*)pTempo);
62: }
```

Loading the Performance Components

Now that we have created our interfaces, we must load the composition files we created
with DirectMusic Producer. We will use the IDirectMusicLoader reference to load the
template object and the associated style and chordmap objects (see Listing 9.3).

LISTING 9.3   The load_music() Function That Loads in the Template, Style, and
Chordmap Objects and Creates a New Segment

```
1: BOOL load_music()
2: {
3:     DMUS_OBJECTDESC    Desc;
4:     HRESULT            dmrval;
5:
6:     // Enable object caching for the Loader object
7:     lpIDMLoader->EnableCache(GUID_DirectMusicAllTypes, TRUE);
```

continues

LISTING 9.3   continued

```
 8:
 9:     // Start by initializing Desc with the file name and
10:     // class GUID for the band object.
11:     ZeroMemory(&Desc, sizeof(Desc));
12:     wcscpy(Desc.wszFileName, L"Template.tpl");
13:     Desc.guidClass = CLSID_DirectMusicSegment;
14:     Desc.dwSize = sizeof (DMUS_OBJECTDESC);
15:
16:     // Since we are including the Class ID and the name,
17:     //   we need to inform the Loader object
18:     Desc.dwValidData = DMUS_OBJ_CLASS|DMUS_OBJ_FILENAME|DMUS_OBJ_FULLPATH;
19:     dmrval = lpIDMLoader->GetObject(&Desc,
        ➥IID_IDirectMusicSegment, (void**) &lpIDMTemplate);
20:
21:     if (!(lpIDMTemplate))
22:     {
23:         return FALSE;
24:     }
25:
26:     // Load the style associated with the template
27:     Desc.guidClass = CLSID_DirectMusicStyle;
28:     wcscpy(Desc.wszFileName, L"Style1.sty");
29:     dmrval = lpIDMLoader->GetObject(&Desc,
        ➥IID_IDirectMusicStyle, (void**)&lpIDMStyle);
30:     if (!(lpIDMStyle))
31:     {
32:         return FALSE;
33:     }
34:
35:     // Load the chordmap associated with the template
36:     Desc.guidClass = CLSID_DirectMusicChordMap;
37:     wcscpy(Desc.wszFileName, L"Chordmap1.cdm");
38:     dmrval = lpIDMLoader->GetObject(&Desc, IID_IDirectMusicChordMap,
        ➥(void**)&lpIDMChordMap);
39:
40:     if (!(lpIDMChordMap))
41:     {
42:         return FALSE;
43:     }
44:
45:     // Now that we have the template loaded, we need to create an actual
46:     // segment that we can play
47:     dmrval = lpIDMComposer->ComposeSegmentFromTemplate(lpIDMStyle,
        ➥lpIDMTemplate, 1, lpIDMChordMap, &lpIDMSegment);
48:
49:     if (dmrval != S_OK)
50:     {
51:         return FALSE;
52:     }
```

```
53:
54:      // Set the music to loop infinitely
55:      lpIDMSegment->SetRepeats(999);
56:
57:      return TRUE;
58: }
```

The routine loads the template, style, and chordmap objects. When they are all loaded, they are used by the `ComposeSegmentFromTemplate` method of the composer object to create a new segment. We set the repeat value for the segment to 999 so that it loops almost indefinitely. Upon returning, the segment is played by the performance object in the `Init()` function as shown in Listing 9.2.

Changing the Music to Reflect the Scene

Now the game has music, but we want to make the music a little interactive. Wouldn't it be marvelous if we could speed up the music as the player starts walking in either direction, and slows back down as the player stops walking? Listing 9.4 shows how to change the music based on the user movement, and Listing 9.5 shows how to pick up the changes in the Windows message handler.

LISTING 9.4 The Addition to the `WinMain()` Function to Change the Tempo of the Music as the Player Starts Moving

```
 1: // We need to check whether or not we should change the tempo of the music
 2: // We will key the tempo of the music to the speed the player is walking.
 3: // Since the move rate varies from -300 to +300 ticks, we will change the
 4: // tempo 10 beats a minute for every 60 ticks away from zero.  Starting at
 5: // 60 beats per minute this will equate to a tempo range of 60 to 110.
 6:
 7: // We first check the flag value to see if the player moved.
 8: // This prevents sending unnecessary tempo changes.
 9: if (fMoveChange)
10:     {
11: // Take the move_rate and determine the exact tempo change
12: double lNewTempo;
13:
14:     if (move_rate == 0)
15:     lNewTempo = DEFAULT_TEMPO;
16:     lNewTempo = (abs(move_rate) / 60)  * 10 + DEFAULT_TEMPO;
17:
18:     // Send a tempo message to the performance object with the new tempo
19:     DMUS_TEMPO_PMSG* pTempo;
20:     if( SUCCEEDED(lpIDMPerformance->AllocPMsg(sizeof(DMUS_TEMPO_PMSG),
      ➥(DMUS_PMSG**)&pTempo)))
```

continues

LISTING 9.4 continued

```
21:     {
22:         // Queue tempo event
23:         ZeroMemory(pTempo, sizeof(DMUS_TEMPO_PMSG));
24:         pTempo->dwSize = sizeof(DMUS_TEMPO_PMSG);
25:       pTempo->dblTempo = lNewTempo;
26:         pTempo->dwFlags = DMUS_PMSGF_REFTIME;
27:         pTempo->dwType = DMUS_PMSGT_TEMPO;
28:         lpIDMPerformance->SendPMsg((DMUS_PMSG*)pTempo);
29:     }
30:     fMoveChange = FALSE;
31: }
```

LISTING 9.5 The Addition to the `WindowProc()` Function to Change the Movement Flag when the Player Moves

```
1: case WM_KEYDOWN:
2:     switch (wParam)
3:     {
4:         case VK_LEFT:
5:         // Process the LEFT ARROW key.
6:         if (move_rate>-300.0)
7:         {
8:         fMoveChange = TRUE;
9:         move_rate-=60.0;
10:         }
11:         break;
12:         case VK_RIGHT:
13:     // Process the RIGHT ARROW key.
14:     if (move_rate<300.0)
15:     {
16:         fMoveChange = TRUE;
17:         move_rate+=60.0;
18:     }
19: break;
20: case VK_ESCAPE:
21:         // exit the program on escape
22:         DestroyWindow(hWnd);
23:         break;
24:     default:
25:     // Process other non-character keystrokes.
26:     break;
27: }
28: break;
```

As the player walks in either direction, the tempo change flag gets set. Then, during the normal looping process, the flag is checked. If the flag is checked, a new tempo is calculated from the current player speed. After this new tempo is calculated, a tempo message is sent to the performance object and the tempo changes. Because the piece of music that is playing is based on a template, the music will seem to change even when the player is standing still. Obviously, if many small patterns had been used instead of the imported MIDI file, the music would seem even more dynamic. Now we have added interactive, dynamic music to our game!

9

Summary

In this hour, you learned how to create music using the DirectMusic Producer application. We covered how to create a band object and add in instruments. You learned how to put together a rhythm and melody track as well as how to create template objects to dynamically create music at runtime. Using what you have learned about the DirectMusic Producer application, you should be able to create musical compositions of your own to use in your own games.

Also in this hour, we covered a lot of the nitty-gritty of the DirectMusic interface. We discussed how to load instruments and the other compositional files we created using the Producer application. We also covered how to load and play these compositions through the IDirectMusicPerformance interface. By adjusting some of the parameters of playback, you learned how you can make modifications to your musical pieces while they play. Finally, we incorporated what has been covered in this and the previous hour to add the musical score we created to our game.

Q&A

Q **The DirectX Help files mention downloadable sounds (DLS). What are these, and will I want to use them?**

A Downloadable Sounds are essentially Windows .wav files that you import into DirectMusic Producer and use as instruments. There is a process to this, which we didn't cover in this chapter because our sample projects used General MIDI sounds rather than DLS. The primary advantages of DLS are consistency and flexibility. Because the instrument sound is carried along with the project when using DLS, as opposed to being hard-wired into a wavetable on the sound card, they will always sound the same when playing the music on different machines. Also, DLS obviously lets us use a wider palette of sounds than General MIDI. For example, with a simple .wav file of a dog barking, we could easily play one of our segments with the sound rather than, say, General MIDI Piano. The primary disadvantage of DLS is overhead; DLS files take much more time to download to a port than a simple General MIDI patch selection, and the CPU also must do some work at runtime to transform the .wav file to all the various notes being played in the piece.

Q Do I want to use automatic downloading of instruments, or is it preferable to manually download them?

A Automatic downloading is turned off by default. However, in all the sample code here, we have it turned on. You might want this turned off so you don't have to load all the instruments at the same time. If you decide to use the DLS format for your instruments, they will usually be the largest single chunks of data you work with in DirectMusic. Therefore, there will be significant hard drive work going on during their loading; for most real-time applications (such as most games) it is undesirable to load very large chunks of data because it will hang up the system during the load. Note that if you choose to use manual downloading to get around this, you must do a little extra work. I will summarize it here, although there are concrete examples in the DirectMusic help files.

You must obtain a DirectMusicCollection object (which can be obtained with the Loader) and `Enumerate` and `Get` the instruments off the Collection object. Then call the `DownloadInstrument()` function on your `Port` object to download the instruments one by one. Note that you must retain the `IDirectMusicDownloadedInstrument` interfaces that this function passes back to pass to `UnloadInstrument()` on the `Port` object when you are finished playing.

Q There are so many interfaces in DirectMusic, do I need to learn more about all of them?

A The interfaces covered in this chapter provide most of the functionality you would need for an application that plays songs such as a game. There are so many interfaces because DirectMusic is intended for use in all musical applications; for example, someone writing a sequencer with the SDK would probably use more of the interfaces. Some of the interfaces do rather novel and unique things, such as the concept of a DirectMusic "tool." We will not go into detail here on what all these interesting extras can accomplish because that could turn this chapter into a book in itself, but you should know that you can get away with the interfaces discussed in this chapter for most playing type activity, and the others are the "bells and whistles."

Q Do I need to know about music to code for DirectMusic? And do I need to know about programming to compose for DirectMusic?

A In short, not really. Programmers can get away without knowing what is going on musically, as long as they understand all the necessary elements required for a complete DirectMusic song. This could vary, depending on the level of interactivity desired. For example, very few interfaces are needed to simply play a linear MIDI file, but if you want to get interactive, you must begin introducing more interfaces (styles, templates, and so on). Likewise, the musician doesn't really need to know how the programmers will be accomplishing their work with code, but the musician must understand the amount of resources required for the programmers to write their code.

All this is not to say that the two jobs have little communication between them; it is important to collaborate on a suitable format for the music in the project. For example, the music might just be MIDI files, or it might be elaborate interactive music consisting of styles, chordmaps, templates, DLS collections, and so on. It is a good idea to work these things out before composing or coding because both sides will surely undergo major changes if you decide to change the format of the music after starting.

Workshop

The Workshop is designed to help you anticipate possible questions, review what you've learned, and get you thinking about how to put your knowledge into practice. The answers to the quiz are in Appendix A, "Answers."

Quiz

1. How can I change the instruments that are playing the current segment to a different set of instruments?

2. What are the differences between pan and volume, and where can these values be changed within the Producer application?

3. What different methods can I use to change my music as it is playing?

Exercises

1. Some capabilities can be achieved by controlling the objects that the
   `IDirectMusicPerformance` object creates during initialization. For example, you
   could create your own DirectSound reference and pass it into the `Init` method. You
   could then apply some of the capabilities of DirectSound such as using 3D sound
   buffers. It would be possible to create a 3D sound buffer and change the locations
   of the instruments in 3D space. Try applying what was covered about DirectSound
   earlier to change the parameters of the actual sound data that DirectMusic produces. After covering 3D sound buffers in a later hour, try experimenting with
   applying the techniques discussed there to create 3D music.

2. Be sure and read the help files that come with the DirectMusic Producer application. The help files are quite extensive, and although they seem to be written for
   people with a musical background, they should be helpful to anyone. Also be sure
   to check out the code samples that come with DirectMusic. The different samples
   cover a range of concepts from loading a simple segment, to creating many different segments from template objects. The code samples can be a great reference and
   can even serve as a starting point for code for your own game.

3. Try to create different template objects. Because templates have such a dynamic
   flow, it might be difficult for most of us to really produce professional quality
   music without using templates. It is entirely possible, however, for even the novice
   to create a truly interesting piece of dynamic music. I often find that experimentation is the key. Try starting with around ten or so small patterns that are only a couple of measures long. Then create a few different band objects with only slight
   changes in them, such as pan or volume changes, or entire instrument changes.
   Add more chords to the associated chordmap object, and add more signposts to the
   template. The more material you add to the template, the more random
   DirectMusic will be able to make it.

HOUR 10

Introduction to 3D Concepts

It is now time for you to get your feet wet in the basic concepts of 3D. You will move into Direct3D over the next few hours, but first you must understand some basic concepts that we will use to describe a 3D world and the interaction of objects in a scene.

In this hour, you will learn what it takes to create objects and scenes in 3D, including

- The basic components of the 3D pipeline
- Describing locations with 3D coordinates
- How polygons are used to create solid 3D objects
- What matrixes are, and how they can be used to manipulate 3D space
- How to use matrices to move objects and establish the user's point of view

An Overview of the 3D Process

Before we delve into the specifics of the 3D engine, let's explore the overall process that allows a 3D scene to appear on our screen by looking at how 3D models are defined and ultimately rendered by the computer's video hardware.

Object Definitions

Just as creating artwork is a first step in developing a two-dimensional game title, in 3D the task begins with the creation of 3D artwork. Unlike the flat images you are accustomed to, however, you must now create objects that describe the actual shape and contours that define them.

These object definitions, which are composed of groups of interconnected points, are known as 3D *models*. By connecting the dots, the computer can generate a representation of the object from any angle. A model in this format is commonly called a *wireframe* model (or *mesh*) because of its appearance when rendered in this state. Wireframes are interesting, but what you're really after is a realistic 3D model. For that, you must go one step further.

NEW TERM   After the shape has been defined, colors and lighting effects might be added, and a 2D image can be stretched over the surface of the wireframe model to form a skin that provides a realistic appearance. This process is known as *Texture Mapping*. Essentially, you take a 3D wireframe model and "shrink-wrap" a bitmapped image to the model.

The 3D Pipeline

After you have defined the models that will populate your world, quite a few steps still must be completed before the models hit the screen. The software and hardware that processes 3D models and translates them to the screen is known as the 3D pipeline. The pipeline gets its name from the sequential nature of these processes; in essence forming a conduit that all models must flow through on their way to the screen.

NEW TERM   The *3D pipeline* is a series of processes that must be executed on a collection of models to generate a 2D representation of the scene.

This section provides an overview of the 3D pipeline, so you will be able to put the upcoming details into perspective. Note that you will often hear individual portions of the process described as pipelines, such as the "transformation pipeline," referring to the processing of models through a specific task in the 3D engine.

To begin, 3D image manipulation and graphics rendering requires a tremendous amount of mathematical calculation to take place to properly visualize a given scene. In a larger sense, this is what the 3D pipeline's role involves—lightning-fast calculations and quick data manipulation. For example, the 3D models must all be moved into their respective 3D positions, which is known as transformation. Some models might be translated to the edge of the viewable scene such that parts of them must be snipped off, a process known as clipping. If the scene has light sources defined, to increase the realism of the scene, the lighting pipeline manages the myriad of calculations required to place the light sources and accurately simulate the reflected light from each 3D model.

Of course, you begin with 3D wireframes, so the textures must be applied to each to improve each model's appearance. Clearly, some models will be located in front of others, so the portions of models set farther back in the scene that are hidden from view because of closer models must not be rendered, a process known as hidden surface removal. And, of course, the final scene must be rendered to the screen, something known as rasterization. Let's look at each of these pipelines in more detail.

Transformation

The first step along the way is to manipulate the models into their proper place in relation to each other. This process in known as "transformation."

NEW TERM *Transformation* is the process of manipulating the coordinates in a model, to determine the location and orientation.

Each object is subjected to a series of transforms, which is a mathematical means to translate coordinates from one position and orientation to another.

The first such transform, called the "World Transform," is used to position the object in 3D space. Each object will typically be subjected to a different transform, identifying its place in the scene.

After objects have been translated into the scene, the next step in the transformation pipeline is determining their position relative to the viewer. This is known as the "View Transform."

Finally, the objects are submitted to a third transform, the "Perspective Transform." This transform is responsible for shaping the scene into the perspective you desire, and basically has the same function as the lens of a camera. By selecting different perspective transformations, you can greatly change the user's field of view and perception of depth.

10

Clipping

After the objects in the scene have been shifted to reflect the viewer's perspective, the next step is to determine what is within the viewing area of the screen. Each object is tested to determine whether it is on or off the screen. Objects that are partially within the viewing area are trimmed to the edges of the screen; a process known as *clipping*.

Lighting

To provide a higher level of realism, the objects can be subjected to light sources within the 3D world. The amount of light is calculated for each area, and highlights are calculated to provide an illusion of reflective shine on objects that require it.

Texturing

After lighting has been applied, a texture map might be stretched over objects to apply additional realism. These textures are combined with the lighting values previously calculated in the lighting pipeline to provide shading of the object surface.

Hidden Surface Removal

Just as you experienced in Hour 5, "Make It Move—DirectDraw Animation Techniques," with the creation of a parallax engine, objects in a 3D scene will often overlap as well. To allow for this, the rendering engine must determine which objects are obscured, and prevent their display. This process is known as hidden surface removal.

NEW TERM   *Hidden surface removal* is the process of removing those parts of a 3D scene that should not be visible to the viewer.

Rasterization

Rasterization is the final step of the rendering pipeline. This is the process of converting 3D surfaces—after they have been transformed, clipped, lit, and textured—into pixels on the screen. In most video cards available on the market today, this process is provided by accelerated hardware on the video adapter.

Now that you've seen some of the tools the 3D graphics system provides, it's time to take a closer look at what your responsibilities involve when modeling a 3D scene. A good place to start is to understand how to define where your 3D models should be located when viewed from a 3D perspective.

Defining Locations in 3D Space

When working with 2D images, you specify a location by providing the distance from the upper-left corner of the screen, expressed as x, y (see Figure 10.1).

FIGURE **10.1**

2D versus 3D coordinates.

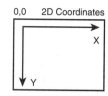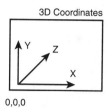

When working with 3D coordinates, you add a third axis to the coordinate, known as z. You might recognize this from Hour 5, where you used Z-Ordering to provide an appearance of 3D to what was actually a series of flat images.

Notice that the y-axis points up, rather than down as in 2D. Also note that the z-axis points away from us, into the screen.

The New Origami—Building Objects in 3D

One of the greatest challenges in creating a 3D world is to represent the objects we encounter in a realistic manner, while keeping the detail to a level that is practical for real-time rendering.

When you create 3D objects for DirectX, you represent them as a series of interconnected triangles. For example, if you wanted to represent a cube as a 3D model, you could do so by dividing each face into two triangles, as shown in Figure 10.2.

FIGURE **10.2**

A cube defined as a 3D mesh.

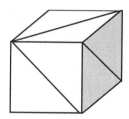

When you look at objects in the real world, you see them as being composed of continuously varying surfaces. Most naturally occurring objects, as well as many of those that are man-made, consist of curving or organic surfaces. Because of the angular nature of polygon-based models, 3D models only provide an approximation of organic shapes, as seen in Figure 10.3.

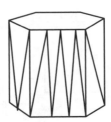

FIGURE 10.3
Approximating curves in 3D objects.

Relative Coordinates—Origins and Vectors

To define a 3D coordinate in Direct3D, the following D3DVECTOR structure is used.

The Syntax for a D3DVECTOR Structure

SYNTAX

```
typedef struct _D3DVECTOR {
    union {
        D3DVALUE x;
        D3DVALUE dvX;
    };
    union {
        D3DVALUE y;
        D3DVALUE dvY;
    };
    union {
        D3DVALUE z;
        D3DVALUE dvZ;
    };
} D3DVECTOR, *LPD3DVECTOR;
```
▲

NEW TERM However, this definition is a bit tricky. A *vector* is actually defined as a line of a fixed direction and a fixed length. They can be used for a variety of purposes, including as a measure of location, orientation, distance, and speed of travel within 3D space.

So why do you use vectors to represent points in space? The answer might seem a bit vague at first: in 3D, all things are relative.

When defining a point in space, its location is defined relative to an arbitrary point in space, known as the *origin*. In dealing with 2D screen space, you reference points relative to the upper-left corner of the screen. This is our origin in 2D space; the point at which all axis have a value of zero.

The same is true in 3D coordinates, although the point in space we use does not have to be relative to a specific screen coordinate.

In some ways, this is similar to our experience in DirectDraw with sprites. When working in 2D, each of the images that you add to the scene have a starting point of 0,0.

However, when you blit them onto the screen, you select their position relative to the origin of the video surface.

When working with 3D models, there is another level of complexity to deal with. Not only are you able to move along three axis rather than two, but you also have the flexibility to move objects freely through space, including rotation and scaling as well (see Figure 10.4).

FIGURE 10.4

An object with separate origin relative to scene.

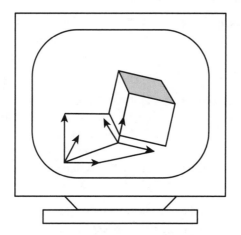

Matrixes—Making the World Go Round

You place the objects in a 3D scene through a series of transforms, as you previously looked at in the review of the 3D pipeline. These transformations are accomplished mathematically, by using an object known as a matrix.

NEW TERM A *matrix* is a two dimensional array of values, which together are used to express a transformation, forming new coordinates that are based on a different origin and orientation than the original. In this case, you will be using a 4×4 matrix; that is, an array that is four columns wide and four rows high. The values are stored in a D3DMATRIX structure, as shown in the following.

The Syntax for a D3DMATRIX Structure

```
typedef struct _D3DMATRIX {
    D3DVALUE _11, _12, _13, _14;
    D3DVALUE _21, _22, _23, _24;
    D3DVALUE _31, _32, _33, _34;
    D3DVALUE _41, _42, _43, _44;
} D3DMATRIX, *LPD3DMATRIX;
```

To transform a vector, its coordinates are multiplied against the values of the matrix, in the following manner:

```
New_X = _11*x + _21*y + 31*z + _41
New_Y = _12*x + _22*y + 32*z + _42
New_Z = _13*x + _23*y + 33*z + _43
```

This might seem a bit confusing at first, but if you take a little time to follow the equation through its steps, you will see a pattern emerging.

Each column represents the values necessary to calculate the result for an axis. Reading from left to right, the first columns provide the formulas for the x-, y-, and z-axis, respectively. The fourth column is basically a placeholder because some matrix math functions require that the matrix be square.

Just as the columns serve as our output, the rows of the matrix serve as our inputs. You will see, for example, that elements _11, _12, and _13 are all factors that are multiplied by the original x value of the coordinate. As before, the first three rows from the top down correspond to x, y, and z. In this case, however, the fourth row has a purpose—it determines what offset will be applied on each axis, independent of the original value of the vector.

The math involved in matrix creation can get a bit complicated. Fortunately, you will not need to understand the inner workings of matrixes because a variety of helper functions are included with Direct3D to assist in matrix and vector calculations.

For example, the preceding operation can be performed using the D3DMath_VectorMatrixMultiply function, as shown in the following.

The Syntax for D3DMath_VectorMatrixMultiply

```
HRESULT D3DMath_VectorMatrixMultiply (
    D3DVECTOR &vDest,
    D3DVECTOR &vSrc,
    D3DMATRIX &mat
);
```

The D3DMath_VectorMatrixMultiply() function multiplies a vector by a transformation matrix and stores the result in a second vector structure. On success, this function returns S_OK or will return E_INVALIDARG if the matrix supplied is invalid.

Parameters:

vDest	Vector that will receive results of the transformation
vSrc	Vector containing coordinates to be transformed
mat	Matrix containing the desired transformation

▲

This and other such helper functions, which are provided in the D3DFRAME directory of the SDK Direct3D Immediate Mode Samples, are provided as a ready means to implement common functions. These are not an integral part of the Immediate Mode API, so you are free to use these functions or create your own as you see fit.

Now that you have a basic understanding of the purpose of matrices, take a look at the transforms that form the transformation pipeline in Direct3D. Along the way, you will see how matrices are created and learn a bit more about the capabilities they provide.

The World Transform

In a typical 3D scene, several models must be placed within the scene, each with their own independent location. Within each model, the coordinates given are relative to an origin that is specific to the 3D model. These coordinates are said to be in "model space."

To define your scene, you will need to transform these coordinates so that they represent locations relative to a new origin, which will represent their position within the world you are creating. The results of this transformation are thus said to be in "world space."

All the models in the scene will be transformed to their desired location in world space so that the coordinates now share a common origin (see Figure 10.5). You might even include multiple instances of the same model, by providing a separate transform for each copy of the model.

FIGURE 10.5

Transforming objects into the world view.

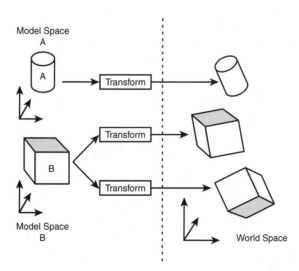

The world matrix will often be the transformation that you apply the most because each object that moves within the scene will have its own world matrix which must be updated every frame to reflect the object's motion. This is in contrast to the view matrix, which must be set once per frame for the entire scene, or the projection matrix, which you'll commonly set once and leave alone from that point on.

Three Types of Transforms

The transformations that are required for object control fall into three categories: translation, scaling, and rotation.

NEW TERM   *Translation* is an operation that moves an object in a linear fashion, without rotating the object or affecting its size. The object can be translated in any of the three directions, X, Y, and Z.

NEW TERM   *Scaling* an object changes the object's size. The object can be scaled to be larger or smaller than the original model.

NEW TERM   *Rotation* spins the object in 3D space. Objects can be rotated about any of the three coordinate axes, X, Y, and Z.

These three operations can be combined to describe any position, orientation, and size that an object might occupy. Each operation requires its own matrix to describe the transformation. Each coordinate of the 3D model will be run through the transformation matrix to calculate a final coordinate, which is ultimately where the object will be rendered when rasterized. Tables 10.1 through 10.5 provide a summary of how the matrices are set up for each of these three operations along with their respective DirectX 3D utility functions used to initialize the matrix for each case. You'll find the functions in the D3Dutil.cpp file, which ships with the DirectX SDK.

Translation moves the 3D object along the vector (a,b,c), shown in Table 10.1. Scaling resizes the object according to scaling factors, one for each coordinate direction. The X value is adjusted by a, Y by b, and Z by c, as you see in Table 10.2. Rotation is the most complicated—you can rotate about any of the coordinate axes, as delineated in Tables 10.3 through 10.5. In these cases, R is the rotation angle (in radians) about a given axis.

In each case, note the three coordinates are involved (X, Y, and Z) as well as a new term, *H*. H is generally considered a convenience term to make the mathematics somewhat simpler, and though it does have theoretical significance, for this purpose you can ignore it. Simply carry it along with your calculations. For example, translation by a vector (a,b,c) becomesthe vector (a,b,c,1) when multiplied through the translation matrix. The resulting H value can generally be thrown away, at least when dealing with transformations.

TABLE 10.1   3D Translation Matrix (`D3DUtil_SetTranslateMatrix()`)

X	Y	Z	H
1	0	0	0
0	1	0	0
0	0	1	0
a	b	c	1

TABLE 10.2   3D Scaling Matrix (`D3DUtil_SetScaleMatrix()`)

X	Y	Z	H
a	0	0	0
0	b	0	0
0	0	c	0
0	0	0	1

10

TABLE 10.3   3D X-Axis Rotation Matrix (`D3Dutil_SetRotateXMatrix()`)

X	Y	Z	H
1	0	0	0
0	cos(R)	sin(R)	0
0	−sin(R)	cos(R)	0
0	0	0	1

TABLE 10.4   3D Y-Axis Rotation Matrix (`D3Dutil_SetRotateYMatrix()`)

X	Y	Z	H
cos(R)	0	−sin(R)	0
0	1	0	0
sin(R)	0	cos(R)	0
0	0	0	1

TABLE 10.5   3D Z-Axis Rotation Matrix (D3Dutil_SetRotateZMatrix())

X	Y	Z	H
cos(R)	sin(R)	0	0
–sin(R)	cos(R)	0	0
0	0	1	0
0	0	0	1

Combining Several Transforms into One

When multiple transformations are performed on a coordinate, taking the output from each matrix and using it as the input for the next, the effects of the matrix transformations are cumulative. Therefore, you can string together several matrices that will form a motion that, for example, will both translate the object and cause it to rotate around its y-axis.

However, having to perform a long series of transformations on each vertex in the scene would be very expensive in terms of CPU power. Fortunately, there is a way around this.

When two matrixes are multiplied together, through a process known as matrix concatenation, the result is a new matrix that performs the functions of both of the original matrices. Any number of matrix transforms can be combined in this manner. A helper function is available in the SDK called D3DMath_MatrixMultiply(), as shown in the following.

The Syntax for D3DMath_MatrixMultiply()

```
VOID D3DMath_MatrixMultiply (
    D3DMATRIX &q,
    D3DMATRIX &a,
    D3DMATRIX &b
);
```

The D3DMath_MatrixMultiply() function multiplies two matrices together, returning a concatenated matrix representing both of the input matrices.

Parameters:

q	Matrix that will receive results of the matrix multiplication
a	Matrix containing first transformation
b	Matrix containing second transformation

Note that the order in which matrices are multiplied determines the order in which the transformations will be evaluated. This must be taken into consideration if you expect to get the desired result from your transform. The reason for this is that matrix multiplication is not commutative. This means the resulting matrix derived by multiplying Matrix A by Matrix B is not the same as the resulting matrix when Matrix B is multiplied by Matrix A. They don't mean the same thing, and this directly results in an improper, or at least unexpected, visual effect.

Take Figure 10.6, for example. If you wanted to place an object at (0,10,0) with a rotation of 45 degrees around the y-axis, you first turn the object 45 degrees, then move the object upward 10 units from the origin.

FIGURE 10.6

Effects of rotation then translation.

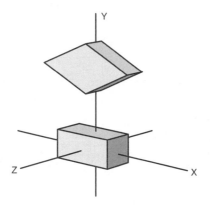

10

If, however, you were to translate the object first, the situation portrayed in Figure 10.7 would occur. After you translated the object, your attempt to rotate the object would not twist it on its axis. Instead, it would move in an arc around (0,0,0), causing it to move away from the desired (0,10,0) position.

FIGURE 10.7

Effects of translation then rotation.

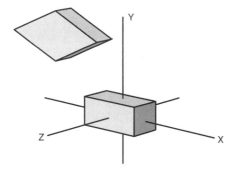

Now that you know how to locate objects in 3D space, it's time to see how they are presented to a viewer. The nice aspect about the 3D graphics calculations you've been using so far is the location of the objects is independent from the viewing aspect of the user.

That allows you to place the user's viewpoint anywhere within your 3D world without having to relocate the objects. To do this you use the view transform.

The View Transform

The real appeal of a 3D game is that it not only allows for control of object motion within the world, but also allows for the user to move through the world as well. In this way, you can immerse the user into the 3D world you have created, allowing them the illusion of traveling through your scene.

Just as you had to locate the models in world space, you must also place the viewer within the scene. However, because you cannot physically move the viewer, you must move the world to provide the proper view for the location and orientation you want to portray.

The effect of this is that the values you apply have their sign reversed to perform the proper transformation. For example, if you wanted to position the viewer at a location 10 units forward from the world origin on the z-axis (0,0,10), you would actually move the world 10 units back, ending up with a view from (0,0,–10).

Once again, helper functions are provided to assist in creating the view matrix. Several ways to construct the view matrix exist, but to start out we will be using the D3DUtil_SetViewMatrix() function. This function takes vectors corresponding to the viewer's location, a point that is directly in front of them, and a vector pointing upward from the user's point of view.

This function is a useful starting point, though it might be a bit cumbersome later when you are looking for more control of the view. But for now it basically lets you tell Direct3D that "I am standing here, looking over there." The syntax for this function is as follows.

The Syntax for D3DUtil_SetViewMatrix

▲ SYNTAX

▼

```
HRESULT D3DUtil_SetViewMatrix( D3DMATRIX& mat,
                               D3DVECTOR& vFrom,
                               D3DVECTOR& vAt,
                               D3DVECTOR& vWorldUp )
```

The D3DUtil_SetViewMatrix() function constructs a view matrix from vectors for the view location, up direction, and forward (look at) direction.

Parameters:

mat	D3DMATRIX that will receive the resulting matrix
vFrom	D3DVECTOR containing the location from which the scene is being viewed

▼ | vAt | D3DVECTOR containing a point that is in front of the user, to which the view origin will be translated

▲ | vWorldUp | A vector pointing upward from the user's perspective, with a length of 1.0

The Projection Matrix

With the view matrix constructed, only one transform is left before your object can hit the screen. But before you can understand the projection transform, you must take a closer look at how you perceive the world before you.

After being processed through the view matrix, the objects have been oriented to our view—but if you were to view the scene at this point, you would find that it lacks a feeling of perspective.

That is where the projection matrix comes in, providing a way to define your visual perception of the scene. However, a few more things must be considered before jumping in. Take time to review this hour and ensure that you have grasped the concept of transformations and vectors. In the next hour, we will dive into the remaining processes required to render the scene to the screen.

Summary

In this hour, you learned the essentials of defining a world in 3D. You have attained a basic understanding of how objects are created as 3D models, and learned how they are placed into a viewable 3D scene. You'll use the techniques you've seen here over and over again to move objects in your 3D world around, shift the viewpoint of the viewer, and make basic 3D models appear realistic. If some of this seemed complicated, that's because it is. However, you have DirectX on your side, and DirectX handles the majority of the gritty details for you. To your users, it looks like magic, which is the best effect of all.

Q&A

Q You said that the helper functions provided with the SDK are provided for convenience, and I can replace them with my own functions if I want. What are the advantages in doing so?

A The helper functions are generic functions, which are made to support most situations. As such they are easily integrated into your application, and they provide a decent level of performance. However, as generic routines, they might provide more than you need, and that can eat up performance. Each case is unique, but at some point—when you are confident of the rest of your application—it pays off to sit down and evaluate each aspect of your program.

Q   You said that you usually rotate and then translate when concatenating matrices, but I found examples in earlier versions of DirectX that do it in the opposite order. Why is that?

A   The `D3Dmath_MatrixMultiply()` helper function in earlier versions of DirectX had an error in that it actually multiplied matrices B×A rather than A×B. If you look at the implementation of the function in DirectX 7, you'll notice a comment indicating that the error was corrected for this version. This makes the examples look like they are translating then rotating.

Workshop

The Workshop is designed to help you anticipate possible questions, review what you've learned, and begin thinking ahead to put your knowledge into practice. The answers to the quiz are in Appendix A, "Answers."

Quiz

1. The world transform converts coordinates

   a. From view coordinates to world coordinates

   b. From model coordinates to world coordinates

   c. From world coordinate to screen coordinates

   d. From model coordinates to view coordinates

2. Name the three transformation matrixes that are used in the transformation pipeline.

3. Name the three kinds of matrix transformation.

4. What type of transform is used to move an object in a straight line?

5. True or false: Multiplication of matrices is commutative, meaning that it is the same in either order.

Exercises

No Exercises

HOUR 11

Rendering the 3D Scene

Now that you have had a look into the creation and organization of a 3D world, you will delve deeper into the 3D rendering process. Your studies in this hour will include the following:

- Learning the inner workings of the viewing frustum, which is the cross-section of space that is visible from a given perspective.
- Learning how to set up the viewing frustum by establishing a projection matrix and setting viewport parameters.
- Learning how to set up the rendering viewport.
- Looking at how back-face culling and z-buffering are used to provide hidden surface removal in Direct3D.

Hierarchy of Direct3D Immediate Mode

Before you continue exploring the theory behind 3D rendering, you need to look at the interfaces you will be using to implement Direct3D applications. This will allow you to better understand how these methods are applied.

Direct3D sits atop DirectDraw, using the methods established in DirectDraw to access the video hardware, and renders a 3D scene onto a DirectDraw surface. As with DirectDraw, it also supports interfaces for HAL, the Hardware Abstraction Layer, and HEL, the Hardware Emulation Layer. This ensures that you can use accelerated functions in 3D accelerators, while still providing compatibility for systems that do not support such features in hardware.

The `IDirect3D7` Interface

The backbone of Direct3D consists of two interfaces. The `IDirect3D7` interface is the base interface that associates Direct3D with an existing DirectDraw interface. To create an `IDirect3D7` interface, query the DirectDraw interface using `QueryInterface()`:

```
hResult = lpDD->QueryInterface (IID_IDirect3D7, (void **)&lpD3D);
```

This interface will be used to create the remainder of the Direct3D interfaces.

The `IDirect3DDevice7` Interface

Although the `IDirect3D7` interface initializes Direct3D and associates it with DirectDraw, it does not provide any connection to video hardware.

Connecting to the hardware is the job of our second interface: `IDirect3DDevice7`. This is created by using the `CreateDevice()` member of the `IDirect3D7` interface you have created. The syntax for this function is shown in the following.

The Syntax for `IDirect3D7::CreateDevice`

```
HRESULT CreateDevice(
REFCLSID rclsid,
LPDIRECTDRAWSURFACE7 lpDDS,
LPDIRECT3DDEVICE7 *lplpD3DDevice,
LPUNKNOWN pUnkOuter
);
```

▼ SYNTAX

`CreateDevice()` creates an `IDirect3DDevice7` that is bound to the video hardware represented by the provided surface. The function returns `D3D_OK` on success.

Parameters:

`rclsid`	Class ID representing the hardware support required
`lpDDS`	Surface to which the device will write
`lplp3DDevice`	Pointer that will receive a pointer to the newly created device
`pUnkOuter`	Reserved for future use, must be set to `NULL`

▲

As you will learn in the upcoming sections, the Direct3D device interface that is created is the window to the Direct3D graphics engine. This is where the 3D pipeline, which you learned about in the last hour, dwells. You will use this device to define your viewing parameters, define how the scene is lit, and create and render your 3D objects.

Now you will resume your studies of 3D rendering and learn how the pieces fall into place.

The Viewing Frustum

In the last hour, you learned of the transformations that take place to locate objects in their proper places in relation to the viewer. When this is complete, you must determine what objects are within the viewing area, and where they will appear on the screen.

As we observed in our study of parallax (Hour 5, "Make It Move—DirectDraw Animation Techniques"), objects appear to grow larger as they get closer, taking up a greater portion of our view. This is because our view of the world, though it might not appear so, is actually a cone. As illustrated in Figure 11.1, our view covers a larger area as distance increases.

FIGURE 11.1
The viewing frustum.

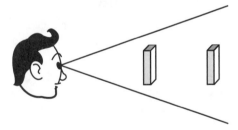

This cone, known as the *viewing frustum*, is defined by the limits of our peripheral vision. In Direct3D, you will determine how the frustum is shaped, and thus how you perceive distance, by providing a field of view. This value is defined by the angle formed by either side of the frustum.

Our field of view is roughly circular. However, when viewing a scene on the screen, our view of the world is rectangular. To compensate for this, the frustum that Direct3D creates is a four-sided pyramid.

Clipping the Frustum to the Field of View

The first step in generating the viewing frustum is to provide an angle for the field of view, which defines how wide the viewing frustum is. Anything outside this angle will be clipped and not be visible to the user.

The effect of the field of view parameter is analogous to using a zoom lens on a camera. The smaller the field of view, the greater the zoom. This has two effects, which can be seen in Figure 11.2. As the zoom increases, objects become larger and appear to be closer. However, at the same time, the area we are able to see grows smaller, and the perception of depth decreases as well.

FIGURE 11.2
The effect of field of view on perspective of depth.

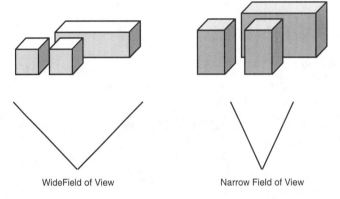

WideField of View   Narrow Field of View

Front and Rear Clipping Planes

In addition to defining the width of the viewing frustum, you must also define what the limits of the frustum are, in terms of distance away from the viewer along the z-axis.

Two limits that you must specify along the z-axis are as follows:

- The far clipping plane, which determines how far into the distance you can see.
- The near clipping plane, which determines how close an object can be before it is considered to be behind you.

The far clipping plane is fairly straightforward. Any objects that extend beyond this distance will not be displayed, so you must consider how far away an object might be in your scene and still be visible.

The near clipping plane is a little more difficult to grasp at first. It is, however, necessary that you limit how closely you can look at an object, both for reasons of performance and because the realism of a 3D scene breaks down at close distances.

The Projection Matrix, Revisited

From the last hour, recall that the third matrix in the transformation pipeline was responsible for giving a perception of depth to the scene. This is where the shape of the frustum is defined.

To define the projection matrix, we will use a helper function, `D3DUtil_SetProjectionMatrix()`. This function is defined as follows.

The Syntax for `D3DUtil_SetProjectionMatrix`

▶ SYNTAX

```
HRESULT D3DUtil_SetProjectionMatrix (
D3DMATRIX& mat,
FLOAT fFOV,
FLOAT fAspect,
FLOAT fNearPlane,
Float fFarPlane
);
```

The `D3DUtil_SetProjectsionMatrix` function creates a projection matrix from the provided parameters. It returns `S_OK` on success, or `E_INVALIDARG` if there is an invalid argument.

Parameters:

mat	Reference to an existing matrix that is to receive the projection matrix
fFOV	Field of view, in radians
fAspect	Aspect ratio of the viewport
fNearPlane	Distance of near clipping plane from the viewer
fFarPlane	Distance of far clipping plane from the viewer

The field of view parameter, `fFOV`, determines how wide or narrow the viewing frustumwill be (see Figure 11.2). Note that the angle is provided in radians, not degrees. In case you are not familiar with this unit of measure, we will take a moment to define our angular measurements.

When expressing angles in layman's terms, we usually express angles in degrees. A degree, expressed using the symbol ° is a unit of measure that is equal to 1/360th of a revolution, as illustrated in Figure 11.3.

By contrast, radians are measured in terms of pi (π), which is equal to approximately 3.14159. A value of π radians is equal to 180°. Thus, 2π radians represents a complete circle.

The next parameter, `fAspect`, provides the aspect ratio of the viewing area. This is calculated by dividing the height of the viewport, in pixels, by the width, in pixels.

Finally, you provide the distance to the near and far clipping planes. As mentioned previously, units in Direct3D are arbitrary. A distance of one (1.0) might represent an inch, a foot, or a meter—it is up to you to determine.

FIGURE **11.3**
Measuring angles in degrees and radians.

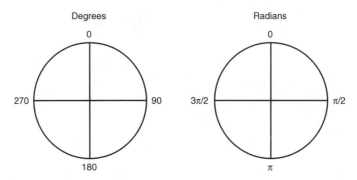

How you define the clipping planes will put the unit of measure into perspective. For example, if you were measuring in feet, you might set the front and rear clipping planes at 10 and 500, respectively. However, if your unit of measure were inches, values of 120 and 6000 would be more appropriate.

Defining the Viewport

After you have defined the shape of the frustum, you must define how it is mapped onto the screen. To accomplish this, you must define a viewport.

A viewport describes the area of the screen to which the frustum will be mapped, and also provides the minimum and maximum values for each axis that will fit within the viewport. The viewport is defined using a D3DVIEWPORT7 structure, described in the following.

The Syntax for **D3DVIEWPORT7**

```
typedef struct _D3DVIEWPORT7 {
    DWORD       dwX;
    DWORD       dwY;
    DWORD       dwWidth;
    DWORD       dwHeight;
    D3DVALUE    dvMinZ;
    D3DVALUE    dvMaxZ;
} D3DVIEWPORT7, *LPD3DVIEWPORT7;
```

▼ SYNTAX

Members:

dwX	Pixel coordinate of the left side of the viewport.
dwY	Pixel coordinate of the top of the viewport.
dwWidth	Width of the viewport, in pixels.
dwHeight	Height of the viewport, in pixels.

▼

▼ dvMinZ	Minimum transformed Z value for near clipping plane, usually set to 0.0.
dvMaxZ ▲	Maximum transformed Z value for far clipping plane, usually set to 1.0.

After you have filled a structure with the desired parameters, set the device to that viewport structure. If you wanted to set a viewport for a full-screen 640×480 application using the entire screen, Listing 11.1 would apply.

LISTING 11.1   Setting a 640×480 Viewport

```
 1: // set up the viewport info
 2: D3DVIEWPORT7 view;
 3: view.dwX=0;
 4: view.dwY=0;
 5: view.dwWidth=640;
 6: view.dwHeight=480;
 7: view.dvMinZ=0.0f;
 8: view.dvMaxZ=1.0f;
 9:
10: // set the device to the viewport
11: lpD3DDevice7->SetViewport(&viewport);
```

11

Hidden Surface Removal

When rendering a complex scene, it is important that you deal not only with displaying the objects within your view, but also that you hide those that are not. This process is known as hidden surface removal, and it is achieved through several mechanisms discussed here.

Several types of hidden surfaces that will have to be dealt with are as follows:

- Surfaces that are on the back side of an object that is in your view.
- Objects, or portions of objects, that are obscured by other items in the scene.
- Objects that are not within your field of view because they are too far away or in a different direction from that you are facing.

Techniques for hidden surface removal are quite involved. Fortunately, DirectX provides built-in support for these issues, and you will not have to deal with them directly.

However, that does not mean you don't need to understand them—as you will see, it is important to understand the methods that DirectX uses, so that you can work with it rather than against it.

Back-Face Culling

Looking back at the geometric models in Figures 10.2 and 10.3, you will notice that many of the triangles that make up the surface are not visible from the angle you are viewing them. No matter what angle you see them from, portions will always be hidden.

Although this might be obvious, however, it is not so apparent to a computer. When we look at an object, we are able to instantly identify that the object takes up a volume of space, and recognize that one side of this volume is facing us.

The computer, on the other hand, has no way of seeing the finished image or recognizing it in this manner. All that it has to work with is a list of coordinates that form a series of triangles, so we must rely upon computational means to determine visibility.

Before you look at the method Direct3D uses to provide back-face culling, you need to take a closer look at how you construct triangles and connect them together in a model.

When defining a triangle within 3D space, you provide coordinates for three points. The area defined has two sides, or faces. One of these faces, the front face, is usually on the outside of the object. By definition, Direct3D assumes the front face of a triangle to be the face where the points are defined in clockwise order. The other face (counter-clockwise definition) is known as the back face. It is triangles whose back face is visible to the viewer you must detect and remove.

In creating a polygon, you also implicitly supply an order. Although changing the order of the vertexes used to define a triangle does not affect its shape, it does affect what is known as the winding order of the triangle.

The winding order represents a direction of travel around the triangle, either clockwise or counterclockwise (see Figure 11.4). One more feature of winding order is quite useful. When a triangle is rotated 180°, its winding order reverses—this means that the winding order of the front face and back face will always be opposites.

This is how DirectX determines whether our view of a polygon is facing the front or back face of a triangle. It is assumed that all clockwise triangles are visible and that counterclockwise triangles are not.

Although it provides a computationally inexpensive means of determining orientation, it is also a potential pitfall. This is because it depends on you, as the developer, to always provide triangles with a clockwise winding order. This is a common mistake, and one to keep in mind if you find that your 3D code is missing polygons or simply failing to display a model.

FIGURE 11.4
Winding order versus
orientation.

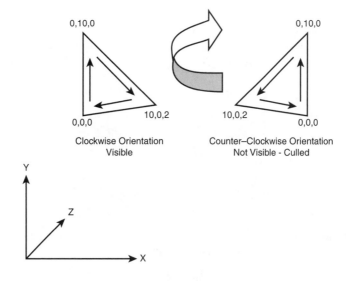

Clockwise Orientation
Visible

Counter–Clockwise Orientation
Not Visible - Culled

Z-Buffering

As you learned in Hour 5, you can depict overlapping objects by drawing them in the proper order. Whichever object is rendered last will appear to be closest to the viewer because it hides any other objects that were previously rendered. This method is often known as the Painter's Algorithm because it relies upon painting over parts of the scene that are no longer relevant.

This method can be used in 3D rendering as well, but it has a couple of downfalls. First, all polygons must be sorted from back to front and rendered in order. Whenever objects move, the list must be re-sorted.

Besides the additional processing required to use this method, it is unable to properly render in certain situations. Consider Figure 11.5.

FIGURE 11.5
Intersecting surfaces in
a 3D scene.

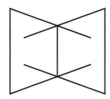 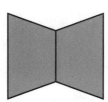

In this scene, two surfaces intersect to form a corner. Portions of both polygons are obscured by the other—so which one do you render first?

Using the painter's algorithm, there is no acceptable order to render these polygons. Figure 11.6 demonstrates the results of rendering the scene in left to right and right to left. You can see that in each case, a portion of one of the polygons that should be obscured is rendered on top of the other polygon, completely spoiling the 3D effect.

FIGURE 11.6

Failure of the Painter's Algorithm with overlapping objects.

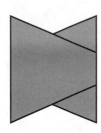 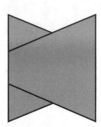

The answer to this dilemma is that you must deal with surface visibility on a pixel-by-pixel basis, rather than judging the whole polygon as visible or obscured.

NEW TERM In DirectX, this is accomplished using a *z-buffer*. The z-buffer is a special type of DirectDraw surface that is used to store depth of field information while rendering the scene.

As each object is rendered, each pixel is checked against the z-buffer to see if an object that is closer to the user has already been displayed at that pixel. If so, that portion of the object is obscured, and the pixel is not written. If the value in the z-buffer is farther away or has not been written to previously, the pixel is written to the screen. The distance from the viewer of the object being rendered is then written to the corresponding pixel. An illustration of this is provided in Figure 11.7.

FIGURE 11.7

Using a z-buffer to properly render a scene.

Screen   Z Buffer

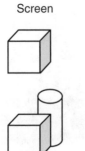 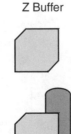

Summary

In review of this hour, you have learned the following:

- You studied the physics behind your perception of depth and how it works to create your field of view.
- You have learned how to set up the projection matrix and viewport to define the viewing frustum.
- You took a look at two hidden surface removal techniques that are used in Direct3D.

Now that you have taken a look at the processes that are responsible for rendering your 3D scene, you are ready to move on to writing your first Direct3D application.

Q&A

Q If I want to provide multiple views at the same time, how can this be done? Is it possible to have multiple viewports?

A Yes, you can use multiple viewports during the render cycle. When it comes time to render, you change the viewport on the device and render the geometry you want visible in that viewport.

Q You stated that normally the projection matrix is set only once, when I set up my 3D device. Is it possible, with multiple viewports, to use a different projection matrix for each viewport?

A Yes it is. However, the projection matrix is associated with the device, not the viewport. Because of this, it will be necessary to reset the projection matrix before rendering to each viewport.

Workshop

The Workshop is designed to help you anticipate possible questions, review what you've learned, and begin thinking ahead to put your knowledge into practice. The answers to the quiz are in Appendix A, "Answers."

Quiz

1. Back-face culling in Direct3D by default removes which faces?
2. A viewport is set on which interface?
3. How many radians represent a complete revolution?
4. An angle of 45 degrees is equal to what angle in radians?
5. What value determines how far the viewer can see?

Exercises

1. If culling a triangle is faster than rendering it, it follows that not having to cull it in the first place would be faster yet. Go to the DirectX documentation and examine the description of `IDirect3DDevice7::ComputeSphereVisibility`. Consider ways you can use sphere visibility to avoid sending objects to the device and improve your application's performance.

2. Z-buffers are useful in most rendering situations but are not always a perfect solution. Sketch some display you might present as a function of your DirectX application. Assume you don't want to blit, but just render everything in 3D. What do you think would be the optimal render order, and can you identify things you might want to render with the z-buffer turned off?

PART V

Input Devices

Hour

Hour **12**

Creating Our First Direct3D Application

Now your studies of 3D concepts will finally pay off—you are ready to start your first 3D application!

In this hour, you will

- Learn the different types of vertices that can be defined under Direct3D.
- Learn how to set up a collection of vertices that will define a 3D object.
- Learn the various forms in which 3D mesh data can be stored.
- Look at the various rendering methods that are used to determine the appearance and quality of 3D images.
- Create your first Direct3D application.

Creating Objects in Direct3D

In the last couple of hours, you have learned much about how a 3D scene is rendered. However, before you can render a scene, you will need to populate it with 3D models.

As you learned previously, objects in 3D are stored in meshes, which are composed of a series of triangles that form the surface of the object. We will now take a detailed look at how they are constructed and stored in Direct3D.

Vertices—A Thousand Points of Light

Just as we are composed of a massive collection of atoms that are interconnected to form the whole, 3D models are also composed of fundamental, interconnected building blocks.

We know that meshes are made of triangles, but we can break a triangle down farther—each triangle consists of three sides. These are in turn defined by the three points that define the corners of the triangle. Each point is a *vertex*, a point where two or more lines converge.

NEW TERM   To define a mesh, I begin by defining a list of the vertices (plural of vertex) that will be used to create the polygons of the mesh. *Vertices* contain the location in 3D space, as well as other information regarding the point that will be used to apply color, lighting, and textures to the polygons that are constructed from them.

Direct3D provides methods for us to create our own "flexible vertex format," defining exactly what parameters we want to include with each vertex. Most of the time, however, you will not need to define a custom format. Three standard formats are provided with Direct3D that will suit your needs for most situations:

- D3DVERTEX—This vertex structure is used when lighting and transformation are to be performed by DirectX. It includes the model space coordinates of the vertex and the information needed for Direct3D to light the vertex.

- D3DLVERTEX—This is known as a *pre-lit* vertex. Using this structure specifies that, while DirectX is to perform transformation, the application has already applied lighting and added the light values to the vertex.

- D3DTLVERTEX—This structure provides a pre-lit and pre-transformed vertex. This structure is often used when you want to specify a screen location directly to Direct3D.

These preset vertex types each have their advantages, depending on the application to which they are put. In the next few hours, you will get a chance to see how all three of these structures fit into place. But first, let's take a look at how we string the vertices together into a mesh.

The Three Mesh Formats

When we have decided where the vertices in our mesh will be, the next consideration is how they are interconnected into polygons. To accommodate the many forms a mesh might take, there are three basic methods for defining a mesh: triangle lists, triangle strips, and triangle fans. These forms are known as *primitives* and are the building blocks that we use to form complex objects.

Triangle Lists

The simplest and most versatile form of a mesh is the triangle list. The vertices of the list are provided in an array, and each consecutive group of three vertices are assumed to form a triangle (see Figure 12.1). Thus, in an array of nine vertices, the first three vertices (0,1,2) would form a triangle, as would the next three vertices (3,4,5), and the last three vertices (6,7,8). Note that a triangle list must always contain a multiple of three vertices, or attempts to render it will fail.

FIGURE 12.1

The construction of a triangle list.

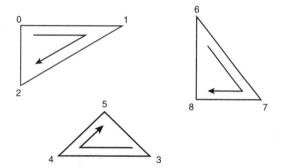

Although this might be the simplest and most flexible means of defining a mesh, it is also the least efficient. In most cases, a mesh will share many of its vertices between two or more polygons. In a triangle list, these vertices must nonetheless be created individually for each polygon.

There are sometimes advantages to this, however. Even though vertices are shared, they might have different characteristics aside from their common location, and thus a triangle list will be merited.

Note that the preceding triangles all contain a clockwise winding order. Be sure to maintain the proper winding order when defining a mesh, or back-face culling will cause the polygons not to be displayed except when they are facing away from the viewer.

Triangle Strips

Triangle strips are used to define a series of polygons, in cases in which each polygon shares a side with the previous polygon. This provides us a significant savings in the number of polygons that must be included in the mesh.

The first three points in a triangle strip define the first triangle and must be provided in a clockwise winding order. Each additional point is then combined with the previous two points to form an additional triangle, as shown in Figure 12.2. Note that the winding order is reversed internally for every other triangle so that back face culling will work properly.

FIGURE 12.2

The construction of a triangle strip.

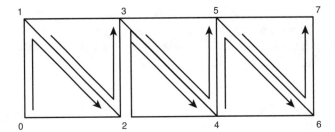

Triangle Fans

The third form that meshes can take is that of a *triangle fan*. A *fan* is a series of triangles that share 2 points with each of their neighbors, one of which is common to all the triangles. This forms a series of connected triangles that fan out from a central point, as shown in Figure 12.3.

FIGURE 12.3

The construction of a triangle fan.

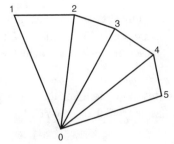

Drawing a Mesh

After you have constructed a mesh as an array of vertices in one of the preceding forms, you can render it to the screen by using the DrawPrimitive() function. The syntax of the DrawPrimitive() function is as follows.

The Syntax for IDirect3Ddevice7::DrawPrimitive()

```
HRESULT DrawPrimitive(
    D3DPRIMITIVETYPE dptPrimitiveType,
    DWORD dwVertexTypeDesc,
    LPVOID lpvVertices,
    DWORD dwVertexCount,
    DWORD dwFlags
);
```

The DrawPrimitive() function renders a primitive, applying transformation and lighting if required. On success, this function returns DD_OK.

Parameters:

dptPrimitiveType	A value defining the type of primitive to render. Valid values include D3DPT_TRI-ANGLELIST, D3DPT_TRIANGLESTRIP, and D3DPT_TRIANGLEFAN. Additional values are available for lists of lines or points. See the DirectX SDK documentation for further details.
dwVertexTypeDesc	A combination of vertex format flags that specify the type of vertex structure being passed to this function.
lpvVertices	Pointer to an array of vertices containing the primitive.
dwVertexCount	Number of vertices in the array.
dwFlags	Optional flag to wait for completion of function before return. This flag is rarely used, and should normally be set to zero.

12

▲

The DrawPrimitive function might only be used within the confines of a 3D scene. See "Rendering the Scene," later in this hour for more details.

Indexing a Mesh

To provide better flexibility and efficiency, Direct3D provides one more option that you can use with any of the preceding forms: indexing.

As you will begin to see when you attempt to apply the primitive forms to real world shapes, objects often do not fall into a fixed mold.

Consider, for example, a simple cube. Four of its surfaces can easily be made into a strip, but you would then have to make separate strips for either end. This would require storing 16 vertices, even though there are only 8 unique points that define the cube. Switching to a triangle list would allow you to draw the cube as a single primitive, but would require 36 vertices instead!

When rendering an indexed primitive, you provide an array of vertices, as before. You also pass a list of WORDs, which represent the order the vertices are to be used to construct a primitive. The advantage of this is that you can re-use the points in the array, and they only need to be transformed and lit once for the entire primitive.

An example of this is shown in Figure 12.4, illustrating how an index would be created to construct the cube we discussed as a triangle list, using only 8 vertices.

FIGURE **12.4**

Constructing a cube using an indexed triangle list.

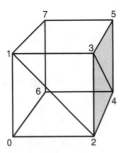

Index Values

```
0 1 2      6 7 0
2 1 3      0 7 1

2 3 4      1 7 3
4 3 5      3 7 5

4 5 6      0 2 6
6 5 7      2 4 6
```

Drawing an Indexed Primitive

Drawingan indexed primitive is very similar to drawing a normal primitive. The DrawIndexedPrimitive() function uses the same parameters as the DrawPrimitive() function, except for the addition of a pointer and length of an array of indices.

The Syntax for `IDirect3Ddevice7::DrawIndexedPrimitive()`

```
HRESULT DrawPrimitive(
    D3DPRIMITIVETYPE dptPrimitiveType,
    DWORD dwVertexTypeDesc,
    LPVOID lpvVertices,
    DWORD dwVertexCount,
```

▼
```
    LPWORD lpwIndices,
    DWORD dwIndexCount,
    DWORD dwFlags
);
```

The `DrawPrimitive()` function renders a primitive, applying transformation and lighting if required. On success, this function returns `DD_OK`.

Parameters:

dptPrimitiveType	A value defining the type of primitive to render. Valid values include `D3DPT_TRIANGLELIST`, `D3DPT_TRIANGLESTRIP`, and `D3DPT_TRIANGLEFAN`. Additional values are available for lists of lines or points. See the DirectX SDK documentation for further details.
dwVertexTypeDesc	A combination of vertex format flags that specify the type of vertex structure being passed to this function.
lpvVertices	Pointer to an array of vertices containing the primitive.
dwVertexCount	Number of vertices in the array.
lpwIndices	Pointer to an array of type `WORD` that contains indices into the vertex list.
dwIndexCount	Number of indices in the index array.
dwFlags	Optional flag to wait for completion of function before return. This flag is rarely used, and should normally be set to zero.

▲

12

Setting Out on Your First Direct3D Adventure

By now, I imagine you are itching to start putting some of this knowledge to use. Well, now is the time—you are ready to code your first application in Direct3D.

The sample application you will create in this hour will create a series of rectangular blocks aligned to a grid, and will allow you to view them from any angle using keyboard controls. Over the hours to come, you will evolve this application into a virtual city.

Creating a Simple 3D Object

You will begin this project by defining a simple 3D object, using what you have learned about vertices and the various types of primitives available.

To implement the rectangular blocks in your soon to be constructed city, you will create a class of type CCube. The class will construct an array of indexed vertices, and provide a function to draw the object using a Direct3DDevice7 object.

Begin by creating a new Win32 project, as you have done in previous hours. If you are using Visual C++, create a generic class from the class view window, and title it as CCube. The files CUBE.CPP and CUBE.H will be created. For other compilers, create these files and add them to the project in the appropriate manner for your compiler.

First, you will create a class definition, which will be contained in the CUBE.H file. The definition is shown in Listing 12.1.

LISTING 12.1   Class Definition for CCube

```
1: class CCube
2: {
3:     public:
4:         CCube(D3DVECTOR origin,D3DVECTOR size,float R,float G,float B);
5:         virtual ~CCube();
6:         void draw(LPDIRECT3DDEVICE7 device);
7:         D3DLVERTEX *verts;
8: };
```

As you can see, this class has three functions and only one data member. The following list is a brief overview of what these pieces do.

- CCube() is the constructor and is responsible for allocating the vertices and calculating their positions. The parameters include a starting location with the minimum X,Y, and Z values, a vector specifying the size of the object along each axis, and the RGB values that determine the color of the block.
- ~CCube() is the destructor, and is responsible for releasing the memory that was allocated for storage of the object's vertices.
- The draw() function draws the block to a 3D device.
- The *verts* member is a pointer that will be used to point to an array of pre-lit vertices that will be used to define the object.

Next you will create the class member functions in the CUBE.CPP file. To begin with, you will include the header files for Direct3D, as well as the header for the class definition of CCube, as shown in Listing 12.2.

LISTING 12.2   Header Files Included in CUBE.CPP

```
1: #include "stdafx.h"
2: #define D3D_OVERLOADS
3: #include "d3d.h"
4: #include "Cube.h"
```

The D3D.H file provides basic access to Direct3D. The addition of the D3D_OVERLOADS prior to loading the header causes the Direct3D header to make certain overloaded operators and constructors available. I will introduce some of these helpful tools along the way, and you can find additional information through the SDK documentation in the Direct3D Immediate Mode Reference.

Our next step will be to define the index that will be used to create the triangles that constitute the block, from the eight points that define its corners. For an illustration of how the vertices and indices of the block will be mapped, see Figure 12.4. The definition of the index array is shown in Listing 12.3.

LISTING 12.3   Defining the Index Values for a Block

```
 1: WORD cube_index[36]={0,1,2,
 2:                 2,1,3,
 3:                 2,3,4,
 4:                 4,3,5,
 5:                 4,5,6,
 6:                 6,5,7,
 7:                 6,7,0,
 8:                 0,7,1,
 9:                 1,7,3,
10:                 3,7,5,
11:                 0,2,6,
12:                 2,4,6
13: };
```

12

Note that this is a global array, which will be shared by all CCube instances. Because the order of construction is the same for all blocks, this only needs to be defined once. The location, shape, and size of the blocks will be determined by the values that are set in the vertices and are independent of the index.

At this point, you are ready to set up the constructor for the CCube class. The function will be passed a starting coordinate, corresponding to the minimum value on each axis, as well as a vector containing the dimensions of the block and color values.

A couple of things should be noted about this class. The first is that the blocks can only be oriented along the X, Y, and Z axis because you do not have a definition of an angle to offset the block. This can be achieved at render time, by modifying the world matrix.

The other item of note is that you are using *pre-lit* vertices to define the cube. What this means is that you provide the final color for each vertex within the vertex structure. This would not be the case if we were using Direct3D to provide lighting of the object.

Because I have not yet covered this issue, we will use pre-lit vertices and create some generalized lighting values to provide an appearance of lighting on the object. This method also has the advantage of higher performance because it does not require lighting to be calculated for each frame. This is often a means for fast rendering of objects, such as buildings viewed in sunlight, that are subject to static lighting conditions.

Pre-lit vertices are defined using the D3DLVERTEX structure, which is defined as follows.

The Syntax for a D3DLVERTEX Structure

▼ SYNTAX

```
typedef struct _D3DLVERTEX {
    union {
        D3DVALUE x;
        D3DVALUE dvX;
    };
    union {
        D3DVALUE y;
        D3DVALUE dvY;
    };
    union {
        D3DVALUE z;
        D3DVALUE dvZ;
    };
    DWORD       dwReserved;
    union {
        D3DCOLOR color;
        D3DCOLOR dcColor;
    };
    union {
        D3DCOLOR specular;
        D3DCOLOR dcSpecular;
    };
    union {
        D3DVALUE tu;
        D3DVALUE dvTU;
    };
    union {
        D3DVALUE tv;
        D3DVALUE dvTV;
    };
} D3DLVERTEX, *LPD3DLVERTEX;
```

As with the D3DVECTOR structure that I introduced in Hour 10, "Importing 3D Objects and Animations into the Scene," the first three members of the structure provide a 3D
▼ coordinate for the vertex.

▼ The `color` and `specular` elements determine the color of the object. The `color` variable
▲ sets what is known as the *diffuse* color, which is the overall color that will be applied for
that region of any polygons that incorporate the vertex. The *specular* component is used
to apply a glossy shine to polygons.

You will learn more about how these are applied in the next couple of hours, as you learn
more about how the lighting pipeline of Direct3D is used to light a scene. We will also
explore the *tu* and *tv* variables in the next hour, when I cover the application of textures
to a surface. These values are used to determine how a texture lines up with the vertices
of an object, and correspond to a relative location along the X and Y axis of the two-
dimensional textures. These values range from 0.0 to 1.0.

So let's start building our constructor. As shown in Listing 12.4, we begin by allocating
an array for the eight(8) vertices that will store the corners of the block. We then calculate the maximum values for X, Y, and Z by adding the *size* vector passed to the function
to the *origin* vector.

LISTING 12.4   Allocating Vertices and Calculating Extents

```
1: CCube::CCube(D3DVECTOR origin,D3DVECTOR size,float R,float G,float B)
2: {
3:     // allocate the vertex array
4:
5:     verts=new D3DLVERTEX[8];
6:
7:     // calculate far corner of the cube
8:
9:     D3DVECTOR extent=origin+size;
```

Note that we are able to calculate the extents by adding the two vectors, even though
they are complex structures. This is because of our definition of the constant `D3D_`
`OVERLOADS` that I discussed earlier. It includes simple mathematical operations on various
structures defined in Direct3D, saving us from handling each member variable individually.

In Listing 12.5, we calculate lighting values for the vertices. The lighting will be created
from a precalculated table that will determine the light intensity for each point. This esti-
mation of lighting values, though a bit rough, will provide a reasonably realistic set of
highlights and shadows that Direct3D will stretch evenly across the surfaces when they
are rendered.

12

LISTING 12.5 Precalculating Lighting Values for the Vertices

```
 1:     // calculate highlight, midtone, and shadow colors
 2:
 3:     D3DCOLOR clr[8];
 4:     float luma[8]={0.7f,1.0f,0.5f,0.8f,0.15f,0.45f,0.35f,0.65f};
 5:     for (int i=0;i<8;i++)
 6:         clr[i]=D3DRGB(R*luma[i],G*luma[i],B*luma[i]);
```

Finally, we will define the location and light color for each vertex, as shown in Listing 12.6. Note the construction of D3DVECTOR and D3DLVERTEX structures using a single statement. This is yet another benefit of the D3D_OVERLOADS definition.

LISTING 12.6 Defining the Vertices

```
 1:     // set up the 8 corners of the cube
 2:
 3:     verts[0]=D3DLVERTEX(D3DVECTOR(origin.x,origin.y,origin.z),
                          clr[0],0,0.0f,0.0f);
 4:     verts[1]=D3DLVERTEX(D3DVECTOR(origin.x,extent.y,origin.z),
                          clr[1],0,0.0f,0.0f);
 5:     verts[2]=D3DLVERTEX(D3DVECTOR(extent.x,origin.y,origin.z),
                          clr[2],0,0.0f,0.0f);
 6:     verts[3]=D3DLVERTEX(D3DVECTOR(extent.x,extent.y,origin.z),
                          clr[3],0,0.0f,0.0f);
 7:     verts[4]=D3DLVERTEX(D3DVECTOR(extent.x,origin.y,extent.z),
                          clr[4],0,0.0f,0.0f);
 8:     verts[5]=D3DLVERTEX(D3DVECTOR(extent.x,extent.y,extent.z),
                          clr[5],0,0.0f,0.0f);
 9:     verts[6]=D3DLVERTEX(D3DVECTOR(origin.x,origin.y,extent.z),
                          clr[6],0,0.0f,0.0f);
10:     verts[7]=D3DLVERTEX(D3DVECTOR(origin.x,extent.y,extent.z),
                          clr[7],0,0.0f,0.0f);
11: }
```

To complement the constructor, we must also create a destructor that will release the memory we have allocated for the vertices, as shown in Listing 12.7.

LISTING 12.7 Destructor for CCube Class

```
1: #define SafeDelete(x) if (x) {delete x;x=NULL;}
2:
3: CCube::~CCube()
4: {
5:     // de-allocate the vertex array
6:
7:     SafeDelete(verts);
8: }
```

Rendering the Object

To round up the class, we have one final function to complete. The `draw()` function requires only a single line of code to render the object, as shown in Listing 12.8.

LISTING 12.8   Function to Draw the `CCube` Object

```
1: void CCube::draw(LPDIRECT3DDEVICE7 device)
2: {
3:     device->DrawIndexedPrimitive(D3DPT_TRIANGLELIST,D3DFVF_LVERTEX,
4:                                  verts,8,
5:                           cube_index,36,
6:                           0);
7: }
```

Of course, although it might only require a single line, the parameter list is a bit intensive. Take a moment to review the definition of the `DrawIndexedPrimitive()` function, which I defined earlier in this hour in "Drawing an Indexed Primitive," and then let's take a look at how we have used this function.

To facilitate the reading of this statement, the preceding function call is broken into multiple lines, each of which contains one or more related parameters. The first pair of parameters tells Direct3D how the data that you are passing is formatted. `D3DPT_TRIANGLELIST` specifies that the primitive will be defined as a series of individual triangles. Each set of three (3) consecutive indices will constitute a triangle. The second parameter defines what format of vertex is being passed to the function. In this case, the `D3DVFVF_LVERTEX` flag indicates that an array of `D3DLVERTEX` structures will be provided.

> Remember that a triangle list must always consist of a multiple of three points. In the case of an indexed primitive, this means that the index count must be a multiple of three. The vertex count does not share this requirement, but must contain enough vertices to accommodate the highest value in the index array.

The second group contains a pointer to an array of vertices of the specified type, and a number specifying the number of vertices in the array.

Next, an array of indexes is provided, along with a count of the number of indexes present in the array. These indexes will correspond to the elements in the vertex array, with an index of 0 corresponding to the first vertex in the array.

The final parameter is used to determine the behavior of the `DrawIndexedPrimitive()` function. In this case, you use the `D3DDP_DONOTLIGHT` to notify Direct3D that you have already lit the vertices, so that it can skip the lighting pipeline for this primitive.

12

Getting Down to Business

Now that we have established a class-based object that you can use to define a 3D cube, it is time to start structuring your application.

You will begin, as with any project, by listing the required header inclusions and definitions, including the class name and caption for your application. Listing 12.9 exhibits the includes for the sample application.

LISTING **12.9**   Includes and Definitions for a 3D Application

```
 1: //------ Include Files ------//
 2:
 3: #include "stdafx.h"
 4: #define D3D_OVERLOADS
 5: #define INITGUID
 6: #include "windef.h"
 7: #include <mmsystem.h>
 8: #include <ddraw.h>
 9: #include <d3d.h>
10: #include <d3dtypes.h>
11: #include "d3dutil.h"
12: #include "d3dmath.h"
13: #include "cube.h"
14:
15: #define SafeRelease(x) if (x) { x->Release(); x=NULL;}
16: #define SafeDelete(x) if (x) {delete x;x=NULL;}
17:
18: //------ Window Class Information ------//
19:
20: static char szClass[] = "XmplHr12Class";
21: static char szCaption[] = "Example - Hour 12";
```

Note that I have added several header files that were not in previous applications. They are as follows:

- D3D.H provides definitions of the interfaces in Direct3D.

- D3DTYPES provides definitions of data structures used by Direct3D.

- D3DUTIL.H and D3DMATH.H are both found in the SDK sample directory for D3DIM, under the D3DFRAME directory. They provide helper functions that can be used for a variety of math and utility functions.

- CUBE.H, which we have previously created to contain the class definition for our CCube object.

Note that in addition to including the proper header files, you will need to add the D3DIM.LIB library file to the link list in the project settings. For more information on how these settings are accessed, refer to "Setting Up the Project" in Hour 2.

Global Interface Pointers

As in previous examples, I will establish global pointers to contain the DirectX interfaces that we create. In addition to the DirectDraw object and the surfaces of the flipping chain, two additional objects will be created for a Direct3D application. They are as follows:

1. A Direct3D7 object, which will provide access to the Direct3D API.

2. A Direct3DDevice7 interface, which will be used to access the rendering capabilities of the video adapter through Direct3D.

The global definitions for these interface pointers are illustrated in Listing 12.10.

LISTING 12.10   Global Interface Definitions

```
1: //------ Global Interface Pointers ------//
2:
3: LPDIRECTDRAW7 lpDD=NULL;
4: LPDIRECTDRAWSURFACE7 lpDDSPrimary=NULL;
5: LPDIRECTDRAWSURFACE7 lpDDSBack=NULL;
6: LPDIRECT3D7 lpD3D=NULL;
7: LPDIRECT3DDEVICE7 lpDevice=NULL;
```

To provide persistent storage of the viewing parameters, we will create global variables to store information on the viewer's current position and their rate of motion.

In this example, the view will orbit around the set of objects, always facing the center of the group. In addition, the user will be able to move the camera location up and down, while maintaining the same viewing target. This will allow the objects to be viewed from any angle.

As you will soon explore, you can use the location and viewing angle to calculate a vector that represents the direction the viewer is facing. By defining the location, and a point the user is looking at, you can then create an appropriate viewing matrix. This information will be contained in the variables defined in Listing 12.11.

LISTING 12.11   Storage of Viewer Location and Direction

```
1: //----- Rotation position and speed -----//
2:
3: float rotAngle=g_PI;              // current angle
4: float rotVel=0.0f;            // current velocity of spin
5:
6: //----- Elevation of viewer and vertical speed -----//
7:
8: float elevation=350.0f;            // current elevation
9: float liftVel=0.0f;           // rate of rise / decent
```

continues

12

LISTING **12.11**   continued

```
10:
11: //----- Define distance of viewer orbit from target ------//
12:
13: #define ORBIT            800.0f
```

Next, you will create an array of pointers that will reference a set of CCube objects that you will create. The blocks will be spaced along a two dimensional grid, four blocks wide and four blocks deep. The size specification and array declaration shown in Listing 12.12 will contain these objects.

LISTING **12.12**   Object Storage for an Array of Cubes

```
1: //------ Storage for Cube Objects -----//
2:
3: #define NUM_ROWS          4
4: #define NUM_COLUMNS       4
5:
6: CCube *cubes[NUM_ROWS][NUM_COLUMNS];
```

Finally, you will define a list of error strings to describe possible failure modes, as you have performed in your previous applications and shown in Listing 12.13. You will also create a list of function prototypes so that you do not have to depend on a specific order of function definition within the source code.

LISTING **12.13**   Error Strings and Function Prototypes

```
 1: //------ Error Return String ------//
 2:
 3: const char *ErrStr=NULL;
 4:
 5: //------ Error Messages ------//
 6:
 7: const char Err_Reg_Class[]        = "Error Registering Window Class";
 8: const char Err_Create_Win[]       = "Error Creating Window";
 9: const char Err_DirectDrawCreate[]   = "DirectDrawCreate FAILED";
10: const char Err_Query[]            = "QueryInterface FAILED";
11: const char Err_Coop[]             = "SetCooperativeLevel FAILED";
12: const char Err_CreateSurf[]       = "CreateSurface FAILED";
13: const char Err_DispMode[]         = "Error Setting Display Mode";
14: const char Err_Device[]           = "Device Creation Failed";
15: const char Err_SetView[]          = "Viewport settings failed";
16:
17: //------ Function Prototypes -----//
18:
19: void Cleanup();
```

```
20: void create_objects();
21: static BOOL Init(HINSTANCE hInstance, int nCmdShow);
22: BOOL init_d3d();
23: BOOL init_ddraw(HWND hWnd);
24: void render_frame(float elapsed);
```

Initializing the Application

The first function we will write is our program initialization. We will begin as we have in past applications by generating a window and initializing DirectDraw. Because our initialization function is growing, we will split the DirectDraw initialization into a separate function, init_ddraw(). This portion of the Init() function is shown in Listing 12.14.

LISTING 12.14   The Initialization of the Application Window and DirectDraw

```
 1: //------ Function to Initialize DirectDraw and the Application ------//
 2:
 3: static BOOL Init(HINSTANCE hInstance, int nCmdShow)
 4: {
 5:     WNDCLASS                    wc;
 6:
 7:     // Set up and register window class
 8:
 9:     wc.style = CS_HREDRAW | CS_VREDRAW;
10:     wc.lpfnWndProc = (WNDPROC) WindowProc;
11:     wc.cbClsExtra = 0;
12:     wc.cbWndExtra = sizeof(DWORD);
13:     wc.hInstance = hInstance;
14:     wc.hIcon = NULL;
15:     wc.hCursor = LoadCursor(NULL, IDC_ARROW);
16:     wc.hbrBackground = (HBRUSH) GetStockObject(BLACK_BRUSH);
17:     wc.lpszMenuName = NULL;
18:     wc.lpszClassName = szClass;
19:     if (!RegisterClass(&wc)) {
20:         ErrStr=Err_Reg_Class;
21:         return FALSE;
22:     }
23:
24:     // Get dimensions of display
25:
26:     int ScreenWidth = GetSystemMetrics(SM_CXSCREEN);
27:     int ScreenHeight = GetSystemMetrics(SM_CYSCREEN);
28:
29:     // Create a window and display
30:
31:     HWND hWnd;
32:
```

12

continues

LISTING 12.14   continued

```
33:     hWnd = CreateWindow(szClass,              // class
34:                         szCaption,            // caption
35:                   WS_VISIBLE|WS_POPUP,    // style
36:                   0,              // left
37:                   0,              // top
38:                   ScreenWidth,        // width
39:                   ScreenHeight,       // height
40:                         NULL,             // parent window
41:                         NULL,             // menu
42:                         hInstance,        // instance
43:                         NULL);            // parms
44:     if (!hWnd) {
45:         ErrStr=Err_Create_Win;
46:         return FALSE;
47:     }
48:     ShowWindow(hWnd, nCmdShow);
49:     UpdateWindow(hWnd);
50:
51:     // initialize DirectDraw
52:
53:     if (!init_ddraw(hWnd)) return FALSE;
```

To complete the initialization, we must initialize Direct3D and create the objects that will exist in our scene. These tasks will be performed in separate functions, which will be called from the Init() functions as shown in Listing 12.15.

LISTING 12.15   Initialization of Direct3D and the 3D Scene

```
 1:     // initialize Direct3D
 2:
 3:     if (!init_d3d()) return FALSE;
 4:
 5:     // create 3D objects
 6:
 7:     create_objects();
 8:
 9:     // return success to caller
10:
11:     return TRUE;
12: }
```

Initializing DirectDraw for Use with Direct3D

To use DirectDraw with Direct3D, one simple consideration must be made. For the DirectDraw surfaces to be compatible with the 3D device, the primary surface must be created with the DDSCAPS_3DDEVICE flag.

The `init_ddraw()` function that we call from `Init()` is listed in Listing 12.16. With the exception of being moved to a separate function, the only modification is the addition of the proper flag to inform DirectDraw that it will be used by Direct3D.

Listing 12.16   Initializing DirectDraw to be Compatible with Direct3D

```
 1: BOOL init_ddraw(HWND hWnd)
 2: {
 3:     // Create the main DirectDraw object
 4:
 5:     HRESULT ddrval = DirectDrawCreateEx(NULL, (void**)&lpDD,
                                        IID_IDirectDraw7, NULL);
 6:     if (ddrval != DD_OK) {
 7:         ErrStr=Err_DirectDrawCreate;
 8:         return FALSE;
 9:     }
10:
11:     // Set our cooperative level
12:
13:     ddrval = lpDD->SetCooperativeLevel(hWnd,
                    DDSCL_EXCLUSIVE | DDSCL_FULLSCREEN );
14:     if (ddrval != DD_OK) {
15:         ErrStr=Err_Coop;
16:         return FALSE;
17:     }
18:
19:     // Set the display mode
20:
21:     ddrval = lpDD->SetDisplayMode( 640, 480, 16, 0, 0);
22:     if (ddrval !=DD_OK) {
23:         ErrStr=Err_DispMode;
24:         return FALSE;
25:     }
26:
27:     // Create the primary surface with 1 back buffer
28:
29:     DDSURFACEDESC2 ddsd;
30:     ZeroMemory(&ddsd,sizeof(ddsd));
31:     ddsd.dwSize = sizeof( ddsd );
32:     ddsd.dwFlags = DDSD_CAPS | DDSD_BACKBUFFERCOUNT;
33:     ddsd.ddsCaps.dwCaps = DDSCAPS_PRIMARYSURFACE |
34:                           DDSCAPS_FLIP | DDSCAPS_3DDEVICE |
35:                           DDSCAPS_COMPLEX;
36:     ddsd.dwBackBufferCount = 1;
37:     ddrval = lpDD->CreateSurface( &ddsd, &lpDDSPrimary, NULL );
38:     if (ddrval!=DD_OK) {
39:         ErrStr=Err_CreateSurf;
40:         return FALSE;
41:     }
```

continues

Listing 12.16 continued

```
42:
43:     // Fetch back buffer interface
44:
45:     DDSCAPS2 ddscaps;
46:     ZeroMemory(&ddscaps,sizeof(ddscaps));
47:     ddscaps.dwCaps=DDSCAPS_BACKBUFFER;
48:     ddrval=lpDDSPrimary->GetAttachedSurface(&ddscaps,&lpDDSBack);
49:     if (ddrval!=DD_OK) {
50:         ErrStr=Err_CreateSurf;
51:         return FALSE;
52:     }
53:
54:     // return success to caller
55:
56:     return TRUE;
57: }
```

Initializing Direct3D

Now that you have initialized DirectDraw properly for use with Direct3D, you must
establish interfaces to allow you to render using Direct3D. As you saw in the last hour,
under "Hierarchy of Direct3D Immediate Mode," two interfaces must be created:
IDirect3D7 and IDirect3Ddevice7.

First, you will query your IDirectDraw7 interface for a pointer to an IDirect3D7 interface, which will be used for access to Direct3D. After this is complete, you will create a
3D device, which will handle rendering to the screen surface.

There will usually be several possible 3D devices to choose from, depending on what
hardware is available on the system. Ideally, you would ask the IDirect3D7 interface to
provide you with a list of these devices and select the optimum device for your application. However, for the purpose of your first application, you are going to take a bit of a
shortcut.

When you call CreateDevice(), you pass a GUID as the first parameter. This identifier
specifies which device you want to use to render 3D graphics. Rather than searching the
system, however, Direct3D provides a shortcut in the form of four pre-defined constants:

- IID_IDirect3DHALDevice—Requests that hardware acceleration be used, rendering 3D through the Hardware Abstraction Layer (HAL). Calling CreateDevice()
  with this identifier will fail if there is no 3D accelerator available on the system.

- IID_IDirect3DTnLHalDevice—Same as previous, but provides transformation and
  lighting acceleration in hardware.

- IID_IDirect3DRGBDevice—Specifies that software emulation (HEL) is to be used
  for 3D rendering. Although this does not take advantage of 3D hardware and offers

slow performance, it will always be available on any Direct3D compatible system. This provides a fallback solution for systems without 3D support in hardware.

• IID_IDirect3DMMXDevice—Requests that a special version of software emulation be used, optimized for processors that support the MMX instruction set. Calling CreateDevice() with this identifier will fail if MMX is not supported on the system.

With these identifiers in hand, you will use a trial and error approach to creating a device. That is, you will first attempt to create a HAL device because this will provide you with far greater performance than software emulation.

If this fails, you will not exit the program with an error. Instead, you will then attempt to create an MMX device. If this too fails, you will attempt to create a standard HEL device—the Hardware Emulation Layer provides a final safety net, allowing you to render on devices without hardware acceleration.

If all four attempts should fail, you will then exit the program with an error. The code for our 3D interface creation is shown in Listing 12.17.

LISTING 12.17   Creating the Direct3D Object and Device Interfaces

```
 1: BOOL init_d3d()
 2: {
 3:     // get master 3D interface
 4:
 5:     if (FAILED(lpDD->QueryInterface(IID_IDirect3D7, (LPVOID *)&lpD3D))) {
 6:         ErrStr=Err_Query;
 7:         return FALSE;
 8:     }
 9:
10:     // set up the best device interface
11:
12:     if (lpD3D->CreateDevice(IID_IDirect3DTnLHalDevice,
                               lpDDSBack,&lpDevice)!=D3D_OK)
13:         if (lpD3D->CreateDevice(IID_IDirect3DHALDevice,
                                   lpDDSBack,&lpDevice)!=D3D_OK)
14:             if (lpD3D->CreateDevice(IID_IDirect3DMMXDevice,
                                       lpDDSBack,&lpDevice)!=D3D_OK)
15:                 if (lpD3D->CreateDevice(IID_IDirect3DRGBDevice,
                                           lpDDSBack,&lpDevice)!=D3D_OK)
16:                     return FALSE;
```

12

Setting Up a Viewport

When you have successfully attained a 3D device, you next must set up a viewport to define the region of the screen that the scene will be rendered to. For this example, I will use the full 640×480 screen surface. The code for setting up the viewport is shown in Listing 12.18.

LISTING 12.18   Setting Up the 3D Viewport

```
 1:     // set up the viewport
 2:
 3:     D3DVIEWPORT7 view;
 4:     view.dwX=0;
 5:     view.dwY=0;
 6:     view.dwWidth=640;
 7:     view.dwHeight=480;
 8:     view.dvMinZ=0.0f;
 9:     view.dvMaxZ=1.0f;
10:     if (lpDevice->SetViewport(&view)!=D3D_OK) {
11:         ErrStr=Err_SetView;
12:         return FALSE;
13:     }
```

Next, we will create the projection matrix, which will determine our field of view and perception of depth. For this application, we will use a 45 degree field of view. We will set our near clipping plane to 10 and f to 2000 units.

Because angles are always expressed in radians, we will have to convert this angle by dividing by 2 pi. This results in an angle of 0.785 radians, as seen in Listing 12.19.

LISTING 12.19   Setting Up the Projection Matrix

```
 1:     // set the projection transform
 2:
 3:     D3DMATRIX proj_m;
 4:     D3DUtil_SetProjectionMatrix(proj_m, 0.785f, 1.333f, 10.0f, 2000.0f );
 5:     lpDevice->SetTransform(D3DTRANSFORMSTATE_PROJECTION,&proj_m);
 6:
 7:     // return success to caller
 8:
 9:     return TRUE;
10: }
```

Object Creation

The stage has now been set—the 3D engine is ready to go. As your final act of creation, all that is needed is to create 3D objects to populate the scene. For this application, create a two-dimensional array of CCubes, as shown in Listing 12.20.

LISTING 12.20   Creating the 3D Objects

```
void create_objects()
{
    // create cubes on a grid

    for (int i=0;i<NUM_ROWS;i++)
```

```
    for (int j=0;j<NUM_COLUMNS;j++)
        cubes[i][j]=new CCube(
                    D3DVECTOR(125.0f-100.0f*j, 0.0f, 125.0f-100.0f*i),
                    D3DVECTOR(50.0f,150.0f,50.0f),
                    0.95f,1.0f,0.8f);
}
```

Putting It in Motion

The render_frame() function will handle the 3D display generation, including calculating the movement of the viewing position and creating the view matrix.

The application will allow the user to fly around the set of blocks that you have constructed. By using the arrow keys, they will be able to circle around the periphery of the structures while the camera always tracks to the center of the scene (see Figure 12.5).

Figure 12.5

An orbital tour of the 3D city.

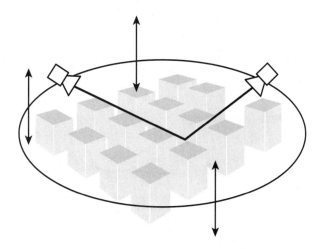

The rendering process will start by checking for lost surfaces and restoring them, and adjusting the elevation and rotation angle according to the velocity values that you will establish from keyboard input. The updated position will include the viewer's angle in relation to the circle, as well as their elevation off the ground. The code for this is shown in Listing 12.21.

LISTING 12.21   Getting Ready to Render

```
1: void render_frame(float elapsed)
2: {
3:     // recover any lost surfaces
```

continues

12

Listing 12.21   continued

```
 4:
 5:     if (lpDDSPrimary->IsLost()==DDERR_SURFACELOST)
 6:         lpDDSPrimary->Restore();
 7:     if (lpDDSBack->IsLost()==DDERR_SURFACELOST)
 8:         lpDDSBack->Restore();
 9:
10:     // increment viewer position
11:
12:     elevation+=liftVel*elapsed;
13:     rotAngle+=rotVel*elapsed;
```

After you have updated the position, you have all the information needed to determine their location on the circle. This is achieved through the use of the sin() and cos() functions. Because this might not be part of your normal routine, I will take a minute to review how this works—this is one of several math concepts you will have to work with quite a bit in the hours ahead.

Figure 12.6 illustrates graphs of both functions. A couple of interesting things can be noted about these functions, particularly in considering how they could be used to create a circle:

- It is cyclic, and will repeat indefinitely.
- It cycles back to the start every 2 pi.
- The two functions are identical, but out of sync.

FIGURE 12.6

Characteristics of the sin() *and* cos() *functions.*

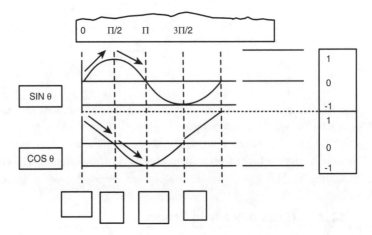

The first two characteristics are obvious similarities to the nature of a circle. The third similarity is a little harder to put your finger on. Take a look at Figure 12.7, which illustrates a circle mapped on the X, Z plane.

FIGURE **12.7**
Characteristics of a circle.

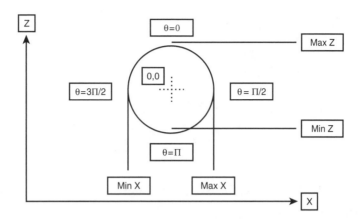

If you trace around the circle and observe the changes in the X and Z values, you will find that they exactly correlate to the sin() and cos() functions. During a complete cycle around the circle, both the X and the Z values cycle through a maximum and minimum value and return to the starting point at 2pi radians. The difference between X and Z, however, is that they are out of sync from each other by a quarter of a revolution.

Thus, sin() and cos() will be used to determine the x and z coordinate values of the circle. The y coordinate will be a set height, which can be modified by user input.

The output from sin() and cos() ranges from -1.0 to 1.0. To calculate a point of a circle of a given size, pass the angle from the center to that point in the sin() and cos() functions and multiply the results by the circle's radius. Listing 12.22 shows how this is implemented in the sample application.

LISTING 12.22 Calculating Viewer Location

```
1:      // calculate current viewer position
2:
3:      D3DVECTOR view_loc;
4:      view_loc.y=elevation;          // set elevation
5:      view_loc.x=sinf(rotAngle)*ORBIT;   // calculate position on x,z plane
6:      view_loc.z=cosf(rotAngle)*ORBIT;
```

When you have determined your location in 3D space, you can then create and set the view matrix using the helper function provided in the D3DUtil libraries. You will create a view pointing from the viewers location to the center of the 3D scene, as shown in Listing 12.23.

LISTING **12.23**   Setting the View Transform

```
1:      // create and set the view matrix
2:
3:      D3DMATRIX view_matrix;
4:      D3DUtil_SetViewMatrix(view_matrix,
5:                          view_loc,
6:                          D3DVECTOR(0.0f,0.0f,0.0f),
7:                          D3DVECTOR(0.0f,1.0f,0.0f));
8:      lpDevice->SetTransform(D3DTRANSFORMSTATE_VIEW,&view_matrix);
```

Rendering the Scene

The view has now been properly set so that the 3D scene can be rendered. This will be accomplished using the DrawPrimitive methods, but before rendering you must make preparations for the viewport to be rendered.

Before rendering each frame, it will be necessary to clear the surface of any previous images. This is accomplished using the IDirect3DDevice7::Clear() command, as shown in the following.

The Syntax for **IDirect3Ddevice7::Clear()**

▼ SYNTAX

```
HRESULT Clear(
    DWORD dwCount,
    LPD3DRECT lpRects,
    DWORD dwFlags,
    DWORD dwColor,
    D3DVALUE dvZ,
    DWORD dwStencil
);
```

The Clear() function is used to clear the rendering target, and can also clear associated z-buffers and stencil buffers. On success, this function returns D3D_OK.

Parameters:

dwCount	Number of rectangles defined by lpRects parameter. Must be set to 0 if lpRects is NULL.
lpRects	Pointer to a D3DRECTS structure that defines one or more rectangular regions to be cleared. Set to NULL to clear the entire surface.
flags	Flags defining the target of the clear operation:
	D3DCLEAR_TARGET Clear the rendering target to the color in dwColor.

▼

▼

	D3DCLEAR_ZBUFFER	Clear the depth buffer to the value in dvZ.
	D3DCLEAR_STENCIL	Clear the stencil buffer to the value in dwStencil.
dwColor, dvZ, dwStencil		Values to be written to rendering target, according to value of dwFlags as defined previously.

▲

Because you are not using depth buffering, your only concern is clearing the target surface, as shown in Listing 12.24.

LISTING 12.24   Clearing the Viewport

```
1:    // clear the viewport
2:
3:    lpDevice->Clear(0,NULL,D3DCLEAR_TARGET,0,1.0f,0);
```

Rendering a frame in a 3D engine is similar to the sequence used in your previous applications: clear the surface, render the scene, and flip the back buffer to the screen. However, it is necessary to notify Direct3D before rendering primitives to the pipeline, and to let it know when rendering is complete. This is accomplished with the IDirect3DDevice7::BeginScene() and IDirect3DDevice7::EndScene() functions, as shown in Listing 12.25.

LISTING 12.25   Scene Rendering

```
1:    // start the scene render
2:
3:     if( SUCCEEDED( lpDevice->BeginScene() ) ) {
4:
5:        // loop through the cubes and draw
6:
7:        for (int i=0;i<NUM_ROWS;i++)
8:            for (int j=0;j<NUM_COLUMNS;j++)
9:                if (cubes[i][j])
10:                    cubes[i][j]->draw(lpDevice);
11:
12:                // end the scene
13:
14:                lpDevice->EndScene();
15:    }
16:
17:    // flip to the primary surface
18:
19:    lpDDSPrimary->Flip(0,DDFLIP_WAIT);
20: }
```

12

The BeginScene() and EndScene() functions must always enclose any DrawPrimitive calls; otherwise, they will fail to render.

> Within the scope of the BeginScene() and EndScene() functions, avoid calling 2D functions such as Blt(). Doing so can cause poor performance, as well as causing the render to fail on some devices.

Handling User Input

To put the scene in motion, the program needs to be able to respond to user input. As noted in "Putting It in Motion," keyboard input will be used to set velocity controls for elevation and rotation around the scene.

Listing 12.26 shows the necessary code to implement the message handler for this application, which will set velocity according to input on the cursor keys.

LISTING 12.26   Windows Message Handler

```
 1: LRESULT CALLBACK
 2: WindowProc(HWND hWnd, unsigned uMsg, WPARAM wParam, LPARAM lParam)
 3: {
 4:     switch (uMsg)
 5:     {
 6:         case WM_DESTROY:
 7:
 8:             Cleanup();
 9:             PostQuitMessage(0);
10:             break;
11:
12:         case WM_KEYDOWN:
13:
14:             switch (wParam) {
15:
16:             case VK_UP:
17:
18:                 // move up
19:
20:                 liftVel=200.0f;
21:                 break;
22:
23:             case VK_DOWN:
24:
25:                 // move down
26:
27:                 liftVel=-200.0f;
```

```
28:                    break;
29:
30:                case VK_RIGHT:
31:
32:                    // rotate to the right
33:
34:                    rotVel=0.5f;
35:                    break;
36:
37:                case VK_LEFT:
38:
39:                    // rotate to the left
40:
41:                    rotVel=-0.5f;
42:                    break;
43:            }
44:            break;
45:
46:        case WM_KEYUP:
47:
48:            switch (wParam) {
49:
50:            case VK_UP:
51:
52:                // move up
53:
54:                liftVel=0.0f;
55:                break;
56:
57:            case VK_DOWN:
58:
59:                // move down
60:
61:                liftVel=0.0f;
62:                break;
63:
64:            case VK_RIGHT:
65:
66:                // rotate to the right
67:
68:                rotVel=0.0f;
69:                break;
70:
71:            case VK_LEFT:
72:
73:                // rotate to the left
74:
75:                rotVel=0.0f;
76:                break;
77:
78:            case VK_ESCAPE:
```

12

continues

LISTING **12.26**   continued

```
79:
80:                    // exit the program on escape
81:
82:                    DestroyWindow(hWnd);
83:                    break;
84:
85:                }
86:                break;
87:
88:          default:
89:              return DefWindowProc(hWnd, uMsg, wParam, lParam);
90:        }
91:
92:      return 0L;
93: }
```

The Finishing Touches

All that remains are the finishing touches: adding a game loop and a cleanup routine. The game loop resides in the WinMain() function and is unchanged from the routines we developed in previous 2D applications. The code for WinMain() is shown in Listing 12.27.

LISTING **12.27**   The WinMain Function

```
 1: //------ Application Loop ------//
 2:
 3: int APIENTRY WinMain(HINSTANCE hInstance,
 4:                      HINSTANCE hPrevInstance,
 5:                      LPSTR     lpCmdLine,
 6:                      int       nCmdShow)
 7: {
 8:     LONGLONG cur_time;        // current time
 9:     LONGLONG perf_cnt;        // performance timer frequency
10:     BOOL perf_flag=FALSE;     // flag determining which timer to use
11:     LONGLONG last_time=0;     // time of previous frame
12:     float time_elapsed;       // time since previous frame
13:     float time_scale;         // scaling factor for time
14:
15:     // initialize the application, exit on failure
16:
17:     if (!Init(hInstance, nCmdShow)) {
18:         Cleanup();
19:         return FALSE;
20:     }
```

```
21:
22:     // is there a performance counter available?
23:
24:     if (QueryPerformanceFrequency((LARGE_INTEGER *) &perf_cnt)) {
25:
26:         // yes, set timer info and get starting time
27:
28:         perf_flag=TRUE;
29:         QueryPerformanceCounter((LARGE_INTEGER *) &last_time);
30:         time_scale=1.0f/perf_cnt;
31:
32:     } else {
33:
34:         // no performance counter, read in using timeGetTime
35:
36:         last_time=timeGetTime();
37:         time_scale=0.001f;
38:     }
39:
40:     // Now we're ready to receive and process Windows messages.
41:
42:     BOOL bGotMsg;
43:     MSG  msg;
44:     PeekMessage( &msg, NULL, 0U, 0U, PM_NOREMOVE );
45:
46:     while( WM_QUIT != msg.message   )
47:     {
48:         bGotMsg = PeekMessage( &msg, NULL, 0U, 0U, PM_REMOVE );
49:         if( bGotMsg )
50:         {
51:             TranslateMessage( &msg );
52:             DispatchMessage( &msg );
53:         } else {
54:
55:             // use the appropriate method to get time
56:             // and calculate elapsed time since last frame
57:
58:             if (perf_flag)
59:                 QueryPerformanceCounter((LARGE_INTEGER *) &cur_time);
60:             else
61:                 cur_time=timeGetTime();
62:
63:             // calculate elapsed time
64:
65:             time_elapsed=(cur_time-last_time)*time_scale;
66:
67:             // save frame time
68:
```

continues

LISTING 12.27   continued

```
69:             last_time=cur_time;
70:
71:             // render the frame
72:
73:             render_frame(time_elapsed);
74:         }
75:     }
76:
77:     // return final message
78:
79:     return msg.wParam;
80: }
```

The Cleanup() routine, shown in Listing 12.28, handles de-allocation of interfaces and object storage. In addition to the DirectDraw interfaces, it also handles deletion of our mesh objects, as well as releasing the Direct3D object and device interfaces.

LISTING 12.28   Cleaning Up

```
 1: void Cleanup()
 2: {
 3:     // de-allocate block objects
 4:
 5:     for (int i=0;i<NUM_ROWS;i++)
 6:         for (int j=0;j<NUM_ROWS;j++)
 7:             SafeDelete(cubes[i][j]);
 8:
 9:     // release 3D interfaces
10:
11:     SafeRelease(lpDevice);
12:     SafeRelease(lpD3D);
13:
14:     // release DirectDraw interfaces
15:
16:     SafeRelease(lpDDSBack);
17:     SafeRelease(lpDDSPrimary);
18:     SafeRelease(lpDD);
19:
20:     // display error if one thrown
21:
22:     if (ErrStr) {
23:         MessageBox(NULL, ErrStr, szCaption, MB_OK);
24:         ErrStr=NULL;
25:     }
26:
27: }
```

Note that the `Cleanup()` routine releases the 3D interfaces prior to the DirectDraw interfaces. This is very important because the 3D objects are dependant on DirectDraw; and after DirectDraw has been released, the 3D interfaces will be invalid. Also note that the device interface must be deleted before the Direct3D interface.

Running the Application

The application is now ready for testing. Compile the application and use the arrow keys to navigate around the scene. The initial view of the scene is shown in Figure 12.8.

FIGURE 12.8
The initial view of the scene.

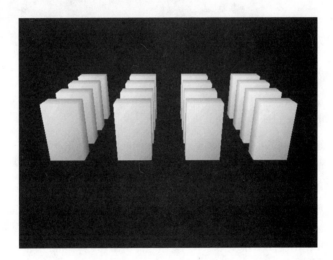

As you rotate the scene, you will notice a flaw in the drawing of the blocks, causing them to overlap as shown in Figure 12.9.

This is because the distance of the objects from your view changes as the scenes rotate, causing the z-order of them to change. In the next hour, you will learn how to use z-buffers to prevent overdraw.

12

FIGURE 12.9
*Object overlap
because of overdraw.*

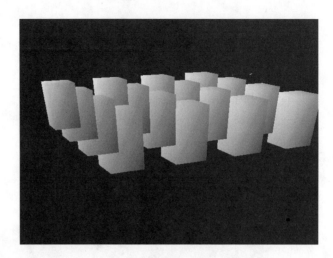

Summary

In this hour, you have created your first 3D application, which creates a simple 3D scene and allows the user to navigate around it.

In addition to building on the 3D concepts that you have studied in previous hours, several new concepts were learned and applied:

- Some of the various forms in which 3D meshes might be stored.
- How to use indexed storage to minimize the number of vertices required by a mesh.
- How to render objects with the `DrawPrimitive()` and `DrawIndexedPrimitive()` functions.
- How to clear the viewport.
- How to set up a scene rendering routine.

Q&A

Q What are the limitations of Direct3D? How many vertices are practical in a scene while still maintaining a smooth frame rate?

A Much depends on the hardware available, and how well the application has been optimized. In my experience, you can achieve an acceptable frame rate with hardware acceleration while displaying between 2000 and 4000 polygons per frame, depending on the rendering options used. This does not mean that a scene must be limited to this size, though. The scene can be much larger, in some cases over a hundred thousand vertices, if we take the time to filter the rendering task down to the objects that need to be displayed.

Q How large can a primitive be?

A In theory, a primitive can contain up to 65,536 vertices. However, for performance reasons, large primitives should always be broken into smaller groups of vertices and rendered in groups of 25-40 vertices at a time. This allows the CPU and the video adapter to be used to their fullest advantage because the video adapter can process vertices while the CPU prepares the next batch.

Workshop

The Workshop is designed to help you anticipate possible questions, review what you've learned, and begin thinking ahead to put your knowledge into practice. The answers to the quiz are in Appendix A, "Answers."

Quiz

1. Which mesh type is based on a central vertex to which all other vertices connect?
2. In which vertex format does the coordinates match the pixel coordinates of the screen?
3. Which mesh type requires the most vertices to create?
4. What is the advantage of indexing a primitive?
5. What is the purpose of applying a specular color to a vertex?

Exercises

1. Increase the number of objects in the scene and see how performance is affected.
2. Create new object classes using the CCube object as a template. Experiment with simple shapes such as pyramids and cones; then try to create more complex forms.

12

HOUR 13

Adding Textures and Z-Buffers to the Scene

In the previous hour you learned how to set up Direct3D and render a simple 3D scene. But did you notice one thing when turning the viewpoint in the previous hour's sample project? The polygons appear to be sorted the wrong way. In this hour you'll learn how to fix that problem using a z-buffer and add detail by texture mapping your rendered objects.

You already heard about the z-buffer and how it sorts polygons on a per pixel basis. Well, now is the time to implement the z-buffer so your polygons will be sorted correctly.

You could use other means of sorting. At my daytime job I work with Playstation programming. It doesn't have a z-Buffer, so we have to sort polygons on a triangle basis.

The results can be good but require the artists to make sure that their triangles don't overlap or lie too close to each other or sorting errors will occur.

Fortunately, the PC programmer doesn't have this problem. Almost every card that boasts 3D in its description has at least a hardware z-buffer, and you can be assured new and future hardware will include z-buffer functionality.

The z-buffer is a valuable tool but also has its limitations. If you are rendering an otherwise unsorted scene, the z-buffer will do a pretty good job of properly obscuring distant objects with nearer objects. When using DirectX immediate mode, there is no implicit scene management, and you must decide when things are rendered. I've found that sorting objects by distance, then rendering them from far to near gives the best results. You might think in that case you wouldn't really need the z-buffer, but it is still valuable because it assures proper overdraw not only object-to-object, but for polygons within an object. For example, if you render an airplane and the polygons for the wing hidden by the fuselage render after the fuselage, without the z-buffer the wing would overdraw, or cut into, the fuselage.

There are also times when you would want to disable the z-buffer before rendering. The best example is when rendering something that you want partially transparent; this is referred to as alpha blending, where alpha designates the level of opacity. A common pratice is to render, for example, a glowing projectile as a bitmap on a rectangular face turned toward the camera, which is known as a billboard. DirectX enables you to render it so that light areas of the map are more opaque and dark areas more transparent. In the extreme case, a black pixel is completely transparent. If you render that billboard with the z-buffer on, and then render something behind it, the z-buffer considers the black pixel closer and disallows rendering the pixel behind it—ugh! Obviously, you must render in the proper order, z-buffer or not, but I have found that rendering things that include transparency is usually done with the z-buffer off.

The other issue we will be covering in this hour is texture mapping.

NEW TERM *Texture mapping* is the process of associating a bitmap with the surface of your geometry. It enables you to add detail while keeping your geometry simple. This brings realism to your scene without sacrificing performance.

In this hour you will learn to

- Set up and use the z-buffer
- Load and set up textures
- Display textures on triangles
- Add this knowledge to our sample application

Preparing a Z-Buffered Device

If you decide to use a z-buffer in your application, the hard part is setting it up. After you have selected a z-buffer format, created the z-buffer, and attached it to the back buffer, you can pretty much forget about it. If you need to enable and disable it for situations like those mentioned earlier, you can do this with device states; in other words you don't detach and reattach it, you simply turn it on and off.

Preparing a z-buffered device is essentially the same as discussed in Hour 12, "Creating Our First Direct3D Application," except you must select, create, and attach the z-buffer. For completeness, we'll also examine how to enable and disable the z-buffer after it is attached.

Selecting a Z-Buffer

When you create a z-buffer, you must ask Direct3D for the desired z-buffer mode. Depending on hardware support and your specific needs, you can create specialized z-buffers known as stencil buffers or w-buffers, but most applications use simple z-buffer depth sorting functionality, which is what we'll cover here and use in our sample application.

Also dependent on the particular hardware, you can select different z-buffer bit depths. The larger the bit depth of the z-buffer, the greater the sorting precision. Later, when we set the near and far clipping planes, we will discuss how the depth of the viewport also affects the precision of the z-buffer.

> The far and near clipping planes simply remove (clip) polygons that get too far away or too close to the player, thus optimizing 3D performance.

To find the best z-buffer for your application, ask Direct3D to enumerate the available z-buffer formats. This is similar to other device enumerations and selections you've encountered in DirectX. In this case, you must create the IDirect3D7 interface, and then ask it to enumerate z-buffer formats as shown in Listing 13.1.

13

LISTING 13.1 Enumerating Z-Buffer Formats

```
1: BOOL init_d3d()
2:     {
3:     // Get Direct3D interface
4:     if (FAILED(lpDD->QueryInterface(IID_IDirect3D7,(LPVOID*)&lpD3D))) {
```

continues

LISTING 13.1 continued

```
 5:          // Set error string.
 6:          ErrStr=Err_Query;
 7:          // Return false
 8:          return FALSE;
 9:          }
10:     // First try hardware with accelerated transform and lighting.
11:     DDPIXELFORMAT m_ddpfZBuffer;
12:     ZeroMemory(&m_ddpfZBuffer,sizeof(m_ddpfZBuffer));
13:     m_ddpfZBuffer.dwSize=sizeof(m_ddpfZBuffer);
14:     m_ddpfZBuffer.dwFlags = DDPF_ZBUFFER;
15:     lpD3D->EnumZBufferFormats(IID_IDirect3DTnLHalDevice,
        ➥EnumZBufferFormatsCallback,(VOID*)&m_ddpfZBuffer);
16:     if (zbuf_flag) {
17:         zbuf_format=1;
18:         }
19:     else {
20:         lpD3D->EnumZBufferFormats(IID_IDirect3DHALDevice,
            ➥EnumZBufferFormatsCallback,(VOID*)&m_ddpfZBuffer);
21:         if (zbuf_flag) {
22:             zbuf_format=2;
23:             }
24:         else {
25:             lpD3D->EnumZBufferFormats(IID_IDirect3DMMXDevice,
                ➥EnumZBufferFormatsCallback,(VOID*)&m_ddpfZBuffer);
26:             if (zbuf_flag) {
27:                 zbuf_format=3;
28:                 }
29:             else {
30:                 lpD3D->EnumZBufferFormats(IID_IDirect3DRGBDevice,
                    ➥EnumZBufferFormatsCallback,(VOID*)&m_ddpfZBuffer);
31:                 if (zbuf_flag) zbuf_format=4;
32:                 }
33:             }
34:         }
```

Note that you must specify which device you want formats for in the call to Direct3D. This example checks each device type in order of preference, and quits searching when an acceptable z-buffer format is found and retained. For our example, we'll accept the first format that comes along, as shown in Listing 13.2.

LISTING 13.2 Handling Z-Buffer Format Callback

```
1:     // Variables used when looking for z-buffer
2:     BOOL zbuf_flag=FALSE;
3:     // Used to keep track of which z-buffer device we got.
```

```
 4:    char zbuf_format=0;
 5:
 6:    // Z-Buffer callback function
 7:    static HRESULT WINAPI EnumZBufferFormatsCallback(DDPIXELFORMAT* pddpf,
       ➥VOID* pddpfDesired)
 8:      {
 9:      // If parameters == NULL, don't enumerate more
10:      if (NULL==pddpf || NULL==pddpfDesired)
11:          return D3DENUMRET_CANCEL;
12:
13:      // If the current pixel format's match the desired ones (DDPF_ZBUFFER
14:      // possibly DDPF_STENCILBUFFER), lets copy it and return. This
15:      // function is not choosy...it accepts the first valid format that
16:      // comes along.
17:      if (pddpf->dwFlags==((DDPIXELFORMAT*)pddpfDesired)->dwFlags) {
18:          memcpy(pddpfDesired,pddpf,sizeof(DDPIXELFORMAT));
19:          // Set flag to TRUE, since we got a valid z-buffer format.
20:          zbuf_flag=TRUE;
21:          return D3DENUMRET_CANCEL;
22:          }
23:      return D3DENUMRET_OK;
24:      }
```

As you can see, we accept the first format that matches and pass it back by copying it into the callback's context parameter, which we associated with the local pixel format object when we started the enumeration. After we've captured the valid format, we tell Direct3D to cancel the enumeration.

Creating and Attaching the Z-Buffer

DirectX implements z-buffers as DirectDraw surfaces. As such, you create the z-buffer using functions you should already be familiar with, except you must set the proper flags and include the pixel format selected by the enumeration. Because the z-buffer resolves depth after all transforms are complete—that is, at the back buffer—it must also be the same size as the back buffer so there is a z-buffer pixel, or location, for each back buffer pixel. Listing 13.3 picks up where Listing 13.1 left off by using the selected z-buffer pixel format to create the z-buffer surface.

13

LISTING 13.3   Create and Attach Z-Buffer

```
1: // Create the zbuffer
2: DDSURFACEDESC2 ddsd;
3: HRESULT ddrval;
4: ZeroMemory(&ddsd,sizeof(ddsd));
5: ddsd.dwSize = sizeof( ddsd );
```

continues

LISTING 13.3 continued

```
 6: ddsd.dwFlags = DDSD_CAPS¦DDSD_WIDTH¦DDSD_HEIGHT¦DDSD_PIXELFORMAT;
 7:
 8: // Use counter to check if we should create z-buffer in [sr]
    ➥video or system memory
 9: // Note flag that specifies that this is a z-buffer surface.
10: if (zbuf_format<3)
11:     ddsd.ddsCaps.dwCaps = DDSCAPS_ZBUFFER¦DDSCAPS_VIDEOMEMORY;
12: else
13:     ddsd.ddsCaps.dwCaps = DDSCAPS_ZBUFFER¦DDSCAPS_SYSTEMMEMORY;
14:
15: // Set this to size of screen
16: ddsd.dwWidth=640;
17: ddsd.dwHeight=480;
18: ddsd.ddpfPixelFormat.dwSize=sizeof(DDPIXELFORMAT);
19: ddsd.ddpfPixelFormat.dwFlags=DDPF_ZBUFFER;
20: memcpy(&ddsd.ddpfPixelFormat,&m_ddpfZBuffer,sizeof(DDPIXELFORMAT));
21: ddrval = lpDD->CreateSurface( &ddsd, &lpDDSZBuf, NULL );
22: if (ddrval!=DD_OK)
23: {
24:     return FALSE; // Could not get z-buffer. Return false
25: } else {
26:
27:     // Attach z-buffer to surface
28:     lpDDSBack->AddAttachedSurface(lpDDSZBuf);
29: }
```

As you can see, you attach the z-buffer surface to the back buffer and it's ready to use. Device creation and setting up the viewport are the same as before, so I won't repeat that part here. However, you should consider the depth of the viewport and its affect on the z-buffer.

The viewport's depth is actually set by the projection matrix and is equal to the difference between the far clipping plane and the near clipping plane, as covered in Hour 11, "Rendering the 3D Scene." The z value will always fall between 0 and 1, where a z of 0 is at the near clipping plane and 1 is at the far clipping plane. Distances from the camera in world space do not transform to z-values in a linear fashion; if you want a linear transform, you'll want to investigate using a w-buffer (refer to DirectX documentation for more on w-buffers). However, it should be fairly obvious that a 24-bit z-buffer will have a finer granularity than a 16-bit z-buffer. What that means is if you use a shallow z-buffer and a deep viewport, the z-buffer will have trouble resolving between two objects that are close together. This can be a real problem in, for example, a space game, where you are simulating vast distances, so you'll want to carefully think out your scale factors and look for other tricks to avoid making your z-buffer too coarse-grained.

Enabling and Disabling the Z-Buffer

When you attach a z-buffer to the device, Direct3D enables the z-buffer by default. So, if you plan to always have it enabled, you must take no further action. However, if the people giving you requirements are even remotely like mine, you will quickly find that leaving this wonderful gadget enabled often produces not so wonderful results. The examples mentioned above barely scratch the surface.

The Direct3D device enables you to control the z-buffer by changing a device render state. There are quite a few types of render state that you can change on the device. The ones you'll likely use the most are lighting, alpha blending, alpha testing, and z-buffering. This snippet shows how to change the z-buffer's enable state:

```
// Enable z-buffering.
lpDevice->SetRenderState(D3DRENDERSTATE_ZENABLE,D3DZB_TRUE);
```

```
// Disable z-buffering.
lpDevice->SetRenderState(D3DRENDERSTATE_ZENABLE,D3DZB_FALSE);
```

You might want to review the DirectX help documentation of `SetRenderState()` because you assert so much control over how your rendered objects will appear with this function.

Adding Textures

Texture mapping is a fairly simple concept but can be quite involved if you use it for advanced effects. In the simple case, as demonstrated with our sample application, texture maps add detail to the surfaces of objects in your scene. DirectX enables you to associate up to eight textures to the device at one time and mix, blend, or combine them in a myriad of ways. Let's consider the basics first, and then touch on a couple examples of how textures can do more than just add details.

You need at least three things to render a texture mapped object in Direct3D.

- First, you must load the texture into a DirectDraw surface.
- Second, the vertices of the object must include data values, known as uv coordinates, that define how the bitmap is to be associated, or mapped, to the polygons—hence texture mapping.
- Third, the device must have the proper render, texture, and texture stage states set. When these things are set, you can render the geometry using the appropriate rendering function.

Before delving into our example of basic texture mapping, let's consider some of the other things you can do with textures. The Direct3D device enables you to layer textures

13

in stages. A common example is called an illumination map; in this case, you attach a map to stage 0 that expresses diffuse details and a map to stage 1 that is mostly black but has colored areas that you want visible whether the object is lit or not. You can use an add function when you render so the parts of the stage 1 map that are black (color value of 0) have no effect, but areas with color content are added into the diffuse color when rendered, which simulates localized illumination.

Bump mapping, which gives the impression of dimensionality to mapped details, is done much the same way. You can also use map combinations and modulate (rather than add) to designate areas of transparency, or emboss one image with another. This is a vast subject well beyond the scope of this book, but you'll probably want to look into this more as a means to create advanced effects. Beware, however, that although Direct3D supports up to eight texture stages, most current hardware can handle only two stages at once, so you'll probably want to limit your ambitions, at least for now.

Let's get back to basics: load a texture, prepare geometry, set up the device, and render!

Load a Texture

The texture itself is simply a DirectDraw surface, so loading it is not much different from loading bitmaps for 2D blitting. However, texture dimensions must always be a power of 2 to work properly, and you must flag the surface as a texture when it is created.

Textures can be stored as a file or as a resource within your project. You'll almost certainly want to store bitmaps as resources for any release product, but for simple efforts, you may leave them unpackaged. For now, we'll use a CreateTexture function that takes a Direct3D device and a string as parameters. The string is the name of the bitmap; the function shown in Listing 13.4 tries to load it from a resource and, if that fails, tries to load it from a file.

LISTING 13.4   Getting the Texture's Bitmap

```
 1: LPDIRECTDRAWSURFACE7 CreateTexture( LPDIRECT3DDEVICE7 pd3dDevice,
 2:                                     CHAR* strName )
 3: {
 4:     // Create a bitmap and load the texture file into it. Check the
 5:     // executable's resource first.
 6:     HBITMAP hbm = (HBITMAP)LoadImage( GetModuleHandle(NULL), strName,
 7:                          IMAGE_BITMAP, 0, 0, LR_CREATEDIBSECTION );
 8:     if( NULL == hbm )
 9:     {
10:         // If not in the resource, try to load the bitmap as a file.
11:         //   Real code would try to find the bitmap among many file paths.
12:         hbm = (HBITMAP)LoadImage( NULL, strName, IMAGE_BITMAP, 0, 0,
```

```
13:                                LR_LOADFROMFILE¦LR_CREATEDIBSECTION );
14:        if( NULL == hbm )
15:            return NULL;
16:    }
17:
18:    // The actual work of creating the texture is done
    ➥in this next function.
19:    return CreateTextureFromBitmap( pd3dDevice, hbm );
20: }
```

As you probably noticed, `CreateTexture` calls a function called
`CreateTextureFromBitmap`. This function, shown in Listing 13.5, creates a texture the
same way you would create a normal DirectDraw surface, except it takes into consideration texture size limitations and texture-specific flags.

LISTING 13.5 Loading the Bitmap Into the Texture Surface

```
 1: static LPDIRECTDRAWSURFACE7 CreateTextureFromBitmap(LPDIRECT3DDEVICE7
    ➥pd3dDevice,
    ➥HBITMAP hbm )
 2: {
 3:     LPDIRECTDRAWSURFACE7 pddsTexture;
 4:     HRESULT hr;
 5:
 6:     // Get the device caps so we can check if the device has any
 7:     // constraints when using textures (Voodoo cards for example,
    ➥have a limit of 256x256 texture size)
 8:     D3DDEVICEDESC7 ddDesc;
 9:     if( FAILED( pd3dDevice->GetCaps( &ddDesc ) ) )
10:         return NULL;
11:
12:     // Get the bitmap structure (to extract width, height, and bpp)
13:     BITMAP bm;
14:     GetObject( hbm, sizeof(BITMAP), &bm );
15:     DWORD dwWidth  = (DWORD)bm.bmWidth;
16:     DWORD dwHeight = (DWORD)bm.bmHeight;
17:
18:     // Setup the new surface desc for the texture.
    ➥Note how we are using the texture manage
19:     // attribute so Direct3D does alot of dirty work for us
20:     DDSURFACEDESC2 ddsd;
21:     ZeroMemory( &ddsd, sizeof(DDSURFACEDESC2) );
22:     ddsd.dwSize        = sizeof(DDSURFACEDESC2);
23:     ddsd.dwFlags       = DDSD_CAPS¦DDSD_HEIGHT¦DDSD_WIDTH¦
24:                          DDSD_PIXELFORMAT¦DDSD_TEXTURESTAGE;
25:     ddsd.ddsCaps.dwCaps = DDSCAPS_TEXTURE;
26:     ddsd.dwWidth       = dwWidth;
```

13

continues

LISTING 13.5 continued

```
27:     ddsd.dwHeight        = dwHeight;
28:
29:     // Turn on texture management for hardware devices
30:     if( ddDesc.deviceGUID == IID_IDirect3DHALDevice )
31:         ddsd.ddsCaps.dwCaps2 = DDSCAPS2_TEXTUREMANAGE;
32:     else if( ddDesc.deviceGUID == IID_IDirect3DTnLHalDevice )
33:         ddsd.ddsCaps.dwCaps2 = DDSCAPS2_TEXTUREMANAGE;
34:     else
35:         ddsd.ddsCaps.dwCaps |= DDSCAPS_SYSTEMMEMORY;
36:
37:     // Adjust width and height, if the driver requires it
38:     if( ddDesc.dpcTriCaps.dwTextureCaps & D3DPTEXTURECAPS_POW2 )
39:     {
40:         for( ddsd.dwWidth=1;  dwWidth>ddsd.dwWidth;   ddsd.dwWidth<<=1 );
41:         for( ddsd.dwHeight=1; dwHeight>ddsd.dwHeight; ddsd.dwHeight<<=1 );
42:     }
43:     if( ddDesc.dpcTriCaps.dwTextureCaps & D3DPTEXTURECAPS_SQUAREONLY )
44:     {
45:         if( ddsd.dwWidth > ddsd.dwHeight ) ddsd.dwHeight = ddsd.dwWidth;
46:         else                               ddsd.dwWidth  = ddsd.dwHeight;
47:     }
48:
49:     // Enumerate the texture formats and find the closest device-supported
50:     // texture pixel format. The TextureSearchCallback function for this
51:     // tutorial is simply looking for a 16-bit texture. Real apps may be
52:     // interested in other formats, for alpha textures, bumpmaps, etc..
53:     pd3dDevice->EnumTextureFormats(TextureSearchCallback,
          ➥&ddsd.ddpfPixelFormat );
54:     if( 0L == ddsd.ddpfPixelFormat.dwRGBBitCount )
55:         return NULL;
56:
57:     // Get the device's render target, so we can then use the render
58:     // target to get a ptr to a DDraw object. We need the DirectDraw
59:     // interface for creating surfaces.
60:     LPDIRECTDRAWSURFACE7 pddsRender;
61:     LPDIRECTDRAW7        pDD;
62:     pd3dDevice->GetRenderTarget( &pddsRender );
63:     pddsRender->GetDDInterface( (VOID**)&pDD );
64:     pddsRender->Release();
65:
66:     // Create a new surface for the texture
67:     if( FAILED( hr = pDD->CreateSurface( &ddsd, &pddsTexture, NULL ) ) )
68:     {
69:         pDD->Release();
70:         return NULL;
71:     }
72:
73:     // Done with DDraw
```

```
 74:        pDD->Release();
 75:
 76:        // Now, copy the bitmap to the texture surface. To do this, we are
 77:        //creating a DC for the bitmap and a DC for the surface, so we can
 78:        // use the BitBlt() call to copy the actual bits.
 79:
 80:        // Get a DC for the bitmap
 81:        HDC hdcBitmap = CreateCompatibleDC( NULL );
 82:        if( NULL == hdcBitmap )
 83:        {
 84:            pddsTexture->Release();
 85:            return NULL;
 86:        }
 87:        SelectObject( hdcBitmap, hbm );
 88:
 89:        // Get a DC for the surface
 90:        HDC hdcTexture;
 91:        if( SUCCEEDED( pddsTexture->GetDC( &hdcTexture ) ) )
 92:        {
 93:            // Copy the bitmap image to the surface.
 94:            BitBlt( hdcTexture, 0, 0, bm.bmWidth, bm.bmHeight, hdcBitmap,
 95:                    0, 0, SRCCOPY );
 96:            pddsTexture->ReleaseDC( hdcTexture );
 97:        }
 98:        DeleteDC( hdcBitmap );
 99:
100:        // Return the newly created texture
101:        return pddsTexture;
102: }
```

Texture dimensions must be a power of two or they will not render and, for all practical purposes, textures should not exceed 256 pixels in width or height. If you look carefully at line 43 of this listing, you'll notice that some hardware also requires textures to be square. DirectX does not force you to use textures with power of two dimensions, but I've never seen it render an odd-sized texture.

Note that we set the surface capabilities as DDSCAPS_TEXTURE, which tells DirectDraw we'll be using this surface for texture mapping operations. Also note we use the DDSD_TEXTURESTAGE flag; because we cleared the surface description object before filling it, the texture's stage will be zero. If you load, for example, an illumination map, you would want to set the dwTextureStage field to 1 so that DirectX knows you'll be using the texture on stage one.

Also note the DDSCAPS2_TEXTUREMANAGE capability. Most hardware will require the texture to reside in video memory when being rendered. A large 3D scene will likely use many textures whose combined footprint exceeds the video memory capacity. When you

13

use the DirectX texture management capability, you let DirectX decide where the texture resides—in system or video memory. DirectX will store the image in system memory and swap it to video when you associate it with the device for rendering. You might want to consider implementing your own texture management, but I recommend being thoughtful about the order in which you render things and letting DirectX handle the details of getting the textures where they need to be.

Notice how we use the standard `BitBlt` function to draw the bitmap to a device context we get from the DirectDraw surface. Remember, all functions that work on a device context will work on a DirectDraw surface, even TrueType font drawing.

This function also asks the device to `EnumTextureFormats`, which calls the `TextureSearchCallback` shown in Listing 13.6. For our sample application, we simply look for the first 16-bit format that comes along, and we skip advanced formats such as bump maps, luminance maps, and so on. You'll usually use 16-bit formats but might sometimes use other formats. For example, if you stretch a texture over a large area, a 32-bit format will greatly reduce color banding because, like the z-buffer, the colors are finer grained.

LISTING 13.6   Selecting a Texture Format

```
 1: static HRESULT CALLBACK TextureSearchCallback( DDPIXELFORMAT* pddpf,
 2:                                                 VOID* param )
 3: {
 4:     // Note: Return with DDENUMRET_OK to continue enumerating more formats.
 5:
 6:     // Skip advanced modes
 7:     if( pddpf->dwFlags & (DDPF_LUMINANCE¦DDPF_BUMPLUMINANCE¦DDPF_BUMPDUDV) )
 8:         return DDENUMRET_OK;
 9:
10:     // Skip any FourCC formats
11:     if( pddpf->dwFourCC != 0 )
12:         return DDENUMRET_OK;
13:
14:     // Skip alpha modes
15:     if( pddpf->dwFlags&DDPF_ALPHAPIXELS )
16:         return DDENUMRET_OK;
17:
18:     // We only want 16-bit formats, so skip all others
19:     if( pddpf->dwRGBBitCount != 16 )
20:         return DDENUMRET_OK;
21:
22:     // We found a good match. Copy the current pixel format to our output
23:     // parameter
24:     memcpy( (DDPIXELFORMAT*)param, pddpf, sizeof(DDPIXELFORMAT) );
25:
```

```
26:     // Return with DDENUMRET_CANCEL to end enumeration.
27:     return DDENUMRET_CANCEL;
28: }
```

Prepare Geometry

Recall from "The Syntax for a D3DLVERTEX Structure" in Hour 12 that each vertex can also include texture mapping values, which are commonly referred to as uv coordinates.

Take a look at Figure 13.1. In effect, the u identifies the relative location within the x or horizontal dimension of bitmap, and the v identifies the relative location within the y or vertical dimension of the bitmap. It is relative because uv values will always be interpreted (truncated) to fall between 0 and 1. In other words, if you set a u to 1.5, it is the same as 0.5. Hence, a u of 0.5 would associate the vertex containing the value to the middle of the associated texture in the bitmap's x (horizontal) dimension. If the map is 256 pixels wide, a u of 0.5 is pixel 128; if the map is only 128 pixels wide, the same u would indicate pixel 64.

FIGURE 13.1

Mapping a 2D image to a 3D object.

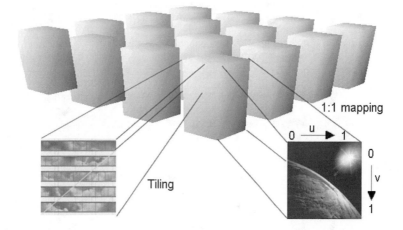

If you were hanging a picture on a wall, you would not want the picture to repeat. A simple arrangement is a rectangle with a u from 0 to 1 as you go left to right, and a v of 0 to 1 as you go top to bottom. However, if you must cover a large area, you'll want to tile the texture by using uv values larger than 1. Because the uv values wrap, the texture simply repeats, or tiles (at least with normal settings—you can use render states to change how the device manages out-of-range uv values). Tiling is useful, but your map's left edge must match the right edge, and the top edge must match the bottom or you'll have another one of those "ugh" situations.

13

We'll build on Hour 12's project by adding uv values to the existing cube vertices. We're already using a standard vertex format that includes fields for u and v values, so we'll just give them values that will map a building texture on them, as shown in Listing 13.7.

LISTING 13.7   Revised Cube Constructor Function

```
 1: CCube::CCube(D3DVECTOR origin,D3DVECTOR size,float R,float G,float B)
 2: {
 3:     // allocate the vertex array
 4:
 5:     verts=new D3DLVERTEX[8];
 6:
 7:     // calculate far corner of the cube
 8:
 9:     D3DVECTOR extent=origin+size;
10:
11:     // calculate highlight, midtone, and shadow colors
12:
13:     D3DCOLOR clr[8];
14:     float luma[8]={0.7f,1.0f,0.5f,0.8f,0.15f,0.45f,0.35f,0.65f};
15:     for (int i=0;i<8;i++)
16:         clr[i]=D3DRGB(R*luma[i],G*luma[i],B*luma[i]);
17:
18:     // Set up the 8 corners of the cube...
19:     verts[0]=D3DLVERTEX(D3DVECTOR(origin.x,origin.y,origin.z),clr[0],0,
20:     // ...this time setting UV coords as well
21:         0.0f,0.0f);
22:     verts[1]=D3DLVERTEX(D3DVECTOR(origin.x,extent.y,origin.z),clr[1],0,
23:         0.0f,2.0f);
24:     verts[2]=D3DLVERTEX(D3DVECTOR(extent.x,origin.y,origin.z),clr[2],0,
25:         1.0f,0.0f);
26:     verts[3]=D3DLVERTEX(D3DVECTOR(extent.x,extent.y,origin.z),clr[3],0,
27:         1.0f,2.0f);
28:     verts[4]=D3DLVERTEX(D3DVECTOR(extent.x,origin.y,extent.z),clr[4],0,
29:         2.0f,0.0f);
30:     verts[5]=D3DLVERTEX(D3DVECTOR(extent.x,extent.y,extent.z),clr[5],0,
31:         2.0f,2.0f);
32:     verts[6]=D3DLVERTEX(D3DVECTOR(origin.x,origin.y,extent.z),clr[6],0,
33:         1.0f,0.0f);
34:     verts[7]=D3DLVERTEX(D3DVECTOR(origin.x,extent.y,extent.z),clr[7],0,
35:         1.0f,2.0f);
36: }
```

Set Up the Device and Render

The example largely separates device setup and rendering because it is so simple that we can set the device up and render to our heart's content. The larger and more complex your scenes become, and the more special effects you set out to implement, the more you'll need to consolidate device setup and rendering. In other words, the render function for a particular object will want to ensure that at least the lighting, z-buffer, and alpha settings are where they need to be for this object (or part of an object!).

DirectX7 includes a new feature, called state blocks, that re-enforces the concept that device settings will vary from object to object during the rendering of a given scene. A state block is like a macro; you record the device state settings into the state block, and then you can set the device in one swoop rather than make several SetRenderState() calls. What I do is just build the object using the appropriate setup calls, and then record and switch to the state block during optimization. Look in Direct3D Immediate Mode Essentials in the DirectX help for more on state blocks.

For now, let's set our scene's render states when we set the projection matrix. Each call to the device in Listing 13.8 is worthy of mention. First, remember that the depth of the viewport is defined by the projection matrix; in this case we're setting the near plane to 10.0f and the far plane to 2000.0f.

LISTING 13.8   Projection Matrix and Render States

```
 1:  // Projection matrix.
 2:  D3DMATRIX proj_m;
 3:
 4:  // Set projection matrix.
 5:  D3DUtil_SetProjectionMatrix(proj_m, 0.8f, 1.333f, 10.0f, 2000.0f);
 6:  lpDevice->SetTransform(D3DTRANSFORMSTATE_PROJECTION,&proj_m);
 7:  // Disable Direct3D lighting, since we will provide our own
 8:  lpDevice->SetRenderState(D3DRENDERSTATE_LIGHTING,FALSE);
 9:
10:  // Set linear (nice) filtering.
11:  lpDevice->SetTextureStageState(0,D3DTSS_MAGFILTER,D3DTFG_LINEAR);
12:
13:  // Enable z-buffering.
14:  lpDevice->SetRenderState(D3DRENDERSTATE_ZENABLE,D3DZB_TRUE);
15:  // return success to caller
```

After the projection matrix is set, turn lighting off because in this case we're stating light as a diffuse color in the vertices. This is the color variable calculated in Listing 13.7 and included in the vertex data. I suspect the render function you write for each object will ensure the lights are on or off to suit their needs. By the way, the order in which you do these setup calls is a matter of preference; I can't think of any cases where it really matters, as long as they're all set before you DrawPrimitive(). If your job or application involves rendering with Direct3D, I recommend you carefully study the DirectX Help Essentials and Reference regarding SetRenderState().

The next call in Listing 13.8, SetTextureStageState(), is another function worthy of deeper studies. Remember Direct3D enables you to layer textures in stages and render them at one time if, of course, the hardware supports it. Each stage has several types of state that you set essentially like setting the device itself. By setting texture stage states, you control how color will be blended when rendered. In this case, we're asking for some filtering during the mapping so that the rendered image doesn't look blocky or pixellated.

Don't be lulled into thinking texture stages involve only textures. In reality, it is the focal point of controlling color blending. I simply don't have the time to elaborate on this fully here, so I'll whet your appetite with another example. Consider a space ship with one of those shield gizmos that just got hit by a weapon. Say you want the visual to change color to indicate shield strength, as a feedback to the player, and that it plays a little bitmap animation over time. In Direct3D, you could do this by using a grayscale map (or sequence), and then feeding the diffuse color into the vertices. Listing 13.9 shows a partial setup.

LISTING 13.9 Modulation Example

```
 1:  lpDevice->SetRenderState(D3DRENDERSTATE_SPECULARENABLE,FALSE);
 2:  lpDevice->SetRenderState(D3DRENDERSTATE_LIGHTING,FALSE);
 3:
 4:  lpDevice->SetRenderState(D3DRENDERSTATE_ALPHABLENDENABLE,TRUE);
 5:  lpDevice->SetRenderState(D3DRENDERSTATE_SRCBLEND,D3DBLEND_SRCCOLOR);
 6:  lpDevice->SetRenderState(D3DRENDERSTATE_DESTBLEND,D3DBLEND_INVSRCCOLOR);
 7:
 8:  lpDevice->SetTexture(0,pShieldTex);
 9:  lpDevice->SetTextureStageState(0,D3DTSS_COLORARG1,D3DTA_TEXTURE);
10:  lpDevice->SetTextureStageState(0,D3DTSS_COLORARG2,D3DTA_DIFFUSE);
11:  lpDevice->SetTextureStageState(0,D3DTSS_COLOROP,D3DTOP_MODULATE);
```

Note I've turned speculars and lighting off (shields are self-illuminated). Because the shield map will be mostly black and we want that transparent, we'll turn on alpha blending then set the source and destination blend factors for the alpha operation. Note these are device states. For the texture, we associate the shield map with the device, set the color arguments to ensure they are where we need them, and then set the color operation for texture stage 0 to modulate. Modulate is a multiply operation, so the dark areas of the map stay dark and the light areas of the map multiply the diffuse color; in other words, the map sets intensity and opacity and the diffuse color contained in the vertices sets the color.

Let's get back to Earth here and look at an example we can fit in a 24-hour course. The example renders pretty much the same as in Hour 12, so Listing 13.10 shows only the context of the changes. Remember we attached a z-buffer, so we want to be sure and tell the device to clear it (the z-buffer) when we `Clear()` the device. The only other change here is setting the texture to the device's texture stage 0.

LISTING 13.10   Render the Geometry

```
 1:    D3DMATRIX view_matrix;
 2:    D3DUtil_SetViewMatrix(view_matrix,
 3:                          view_loc,
 4:                          D3DVECTOR(0.0f,0.0f,0.0f),
 5:                          D3DVECTOR(0.0f,1.0f,0.0f));
 6:    lpDevice->SetTransform(D3DTRANSFORMSTATE_VIEW,&view_matrix);
 7:
 8:    // Clear the viewport. This time remembering to clear the z-buffer also
 9:    lpDevice->Clear(0,NULL,D3DCLEAR_ZBUFFER¦D3DCLEAR_TARGET,0,1.0f,0);
10:
11:  // Set texture as active
12:  lpDevice->SetTexture( 0, lpTexture);
13:
14:  // Start the scene render
15:  if( SUCCEEDED( lpDevice->BeginScene() ) ) {
16:    // Loop through the cubes and draw
17:    for (int i=0;i<NUM_ROWS;i++)
18:      for (int j=0;j<NUM_COLUMNS;j++)
19:        if (cubes[i][j]) cubes[i][j]->draw(lpDevice);
20:
21:    // end the scene
22:    lpDevice->EndScene();
23:    }
```

Summary

In this hour you learned how to set up and use a z-buffer, when and when not to use a z-buffer, and how to texture map your scene for added detail and realism. You also applied this knowledge to a sample application, building on your knowledge from previous hours.

13

Q&A

Q Assigning texture uv coordinates is complicated. Is there a better way?

A Yes. Later in this book, you'll learn how to import models created with 3D graphics packages, which include uv data.

Q Because we weren't using the uv coordinates in Hour 12, wasn't it wasteful to include them in the vertex structure and pass them to the device?

A Because Direct3D lets you specify the structure of the vertex data you are rendering, you will probably define and use your own structures more often than not. And yes, passing uv's you aren't using is a waste and will decrease performance.

Q Must the uv mapping for each stage of a multitexture render be the same?

A No. You can include up to eight sets of uv coordinates in the vertex, and then select which set a given stage is using via the `SetTextureStageState()` function.

Workshop

The workshop will enable you to test yourself on what you have learned in this hour and get you thinking about how to apply this knowledge in a real life application. The answers to the quiz are in Appendix A, "Answers."

Quiz

1. What is the purpose of the z-buffer?
2. When would you want to use a larger bit depth z-buffer?
3. How do you define the domain of the z-buffer?
4. Are there occasions when you would want to disable the z-buffer?
5. If so, how do you control whether the z-buffer is enabled?
6. What are uv coordinates?
7. Identify the minimum preparation required in Direct3D to render a texture mapped object.

Exercise

Using the sample project, experiment with different maps and different device and texture stage state settings and observe how it affects the rendered buildings.

HOUR 14

Adding Realism Through Lighting

To bring depth and realism to your 3D application, you can use Direct3D lighting. In this hour, you will learn the following:

- How to create lights in Direct3D.
- What the three different types of lights in Direct3D are.
- How to activate the Direct3D lighting pipeline.
- How to animate lights in your scene.

Creating a Light

Traditionally, Direct3D programmers have been wary of using the Direct3D lighting pipeline because it is very slow in some cases. However, several video cards now support the Direct3D lighting pipeline in hardware, which means Direct3D lighting will be very fast! In addition, using the Direct3D lighting pipeline is an easy way to add realism to your application with minimal effort. Finally, even if the Direct3D pipeline isn't supported directly by the hardware, the software pipeline is adequate for many applications.

Creating a new light is easy. All you have to do is call the
`IDirect3Ddevice7::SetLight()` method, telling the function which light you are creating, and passing the function a structure filled with information about the light you want to create.

The Syntax for `IDirect3Ddevice7::SetLight ()`

▼ SYNTAX

```
HRESULTS SetLight(
    DWORD dwIndex,
    LPD3DLIGHT7 lpD3DLight7
);
```

The `SetLight()` function creates a new light according to the `LPD3DLIGHT7` structure. On success, this function returns `D3D_OK`.

Parameters:

`dwIndex`	The zero-based index of the light. If a light already exists at the specified index, it is replaced.
`lpD3DLight7`	A structure filled with the properties of the light that should be created.

▲

The hardest part about creating a new light is filling in the `LPD3DLIGHT7` structure. To understand all the fields of this structure, you must first understand the different types of lights that Direct3D implements.

Types of Light

Direct3D implements three different kinds of lights: point lights, spotlights, and parallel, or directional, lights. All three types of lights share certain properties, and some properties are specific to certain types of lights.

A property that every light shares is light color. Direct3D breaks the color of each light into three separate components: diffuse, specular, and ambient. These three components approximate lighting that occurs in the real world. In the real world, light travels from a source and is reflected and absorbed by objects that it touches. To describe the general level of light in a scene, you can set the ambient color of a light. Ambient light is light that has been reflected so many times that it is impossible to tell which direction it is coming from. Diffuse light is light that comes from a certain direction, and thus diffuse light is brightest when it hits a surface straight on. Specular light can be thought of as the light that makes an object shiny.

Light color, as well as the rest of the light properties, are specified in the `D3DLIGHT7` structure as follows:

The Syntax for the D3DLIGHT7 Structure

▼ SYNTAX

```
typedef struct _D3DLIGHT7 {
    D3DLIGHTTYPE    dltType;
    D3DCOLORVALUE   dcvDiffuse;
    D3DCOLORVALUE   dcvSpecular;
    D3DCOLORVALUE   dcvAmbient;
    D3DVECTOR       dvPosition;
    D3DVECTOR       dvDirection;
    D3DVALUE        dvRange;
    D3DVALUE        dvFalloff;
    D3DVALUE        dvAttenuation0;
    D3DVALUE        dvAttenuation1;
    D3DVALUE        dvAttenuation2;
    D3DVALUE        dvTheta;
    D3DVALUE        dvPhi;
} D3DLIGHT7, *LPD3DLIGHT7;
```

The *type* element specifies the type of light (point, spot, or directional). The *diffuse*, *specular*, and *ambient* elements specify the color of the light. The rest of the elements depend on the type of light being created, and they will be discussed in the next sections.

Point Lights

A point light is a light that is similar to a light bulb. A point light radiates light outward from a certain point in all directions. For an illustrated example of a point light, see Figure 14.1.

FIGURE 14.1

A diagram of a point light.

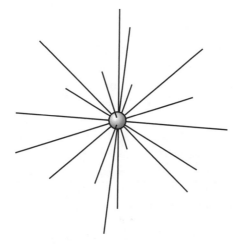

14

Point lights have definite position, and thus they must define the *position* element, but because a point light emits light in every direction, it is not necessary to specify the *direction* element. The *range* element specifies the maximum range over which the light can have an effect, and the *attenuation* elements specify how the intensity of the light changes with distance. Specifically, the `dvAttenuation0` element specifies the constant attenuation, the `dvAttenuation1` element specifies the linear attenuation, and the `dvAttenuation2` element specifies the quadratic attenuation. The rest of the elements aren't used with point lights, so you don't need to specify them.

Spotlights

You can think of a spotlight as a flashlight. A spotlight emits rays of light in the shape of a cone. For an illustrated example of a spotlight, see Figure 14.2.

FIGURE 14.2
A diagram of a spotlight.

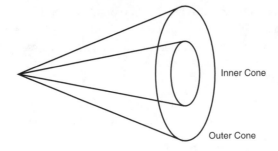

Inner Cone

Outer Cone

Spotlights also have definite position, so you must specify the *position* element. In addition, you must also specify the *direction* element to tell Direct3D where the light is pointing. The *range* element tells Direct3D the maximum range of the spotlight, and the *attenuation* elements specify how the intensity of the spotlight will change over distance. Spotlights also have a few other unique properties. First, the *falloff* element is used to describe the light intensity change from the bright inner cone of the spotlight to the edges of the spotlight. You must specify the size of the angle of the inner cone of the spotlight by setting the *theta* element to an angle (in radians). Likewise, you must specify the size of the angle of the outer cone of the spotlight by setting the *phi* element.

The *theta* element must be between 0 and the value of the *phi* element. The *phi* element must be between 0 and pi.

Directional Lights

A directional light is a light that is so far away that all its rays hit the scene parallel. The sun is a good example of a parallel light because it is so far away from earth that nearly all the rays that reach earth from the sun are parallel. For an illustrated example of a parallel light, see Figure 14.3.

FIGURE **14.3**

A diagram of a directional light.

You can think of a directional light as a point light sitting at a point an infinite distance away from the scene. Because a directional light sits at a point an infinite distance away, it is not necessary to specify the *position* element when you create a directional light. However, you must specify the *direction* element. None of the other elements in the D3DLIGHT7 structure affect a directional light, so you don't need to bother setting them when you are creating a directional light.

Adding Lighting to Our Project

Each object in your scene can also have diffuse, specular, and ambient color components. For objects, these values are called materials because they describe how a surface reflects incoming light. You can make a material shiny by increasing the specular component of its material, or you can make it brighter by increasing the diffuse component of its material.

The CCube object used in the sample application now has a new public data member—a D3DMATERIAL7 structure. In addition, the CCube object now has three new functions to set each material component. Listing 14.1 shows the three new functions.

LISTING **14.1** The New CCube Functions That Handle Materials

```
1: void CCube::SetMaterialDiffuse(  float diffuseR,  float diffuseG,
   ➥float diffuseB,
2:                                  float diffuseA  )
3: {
4:     // Set the RGBA for diffuse reflection
```

continues

14

LISTING 14.1   continued

```
 5:        material.dcvDiffuse.r = (D3DVALUE) diffuseR;
 6:        material.dcvDiffuse.g = (D3DVALUE) diffuseG;
 7:        material.dcvDiffuse.b = (D3DVALUE) diffuseB;
 8:        material.dcvDiffuse.a = (D3DVALUE) diffuseA;
 9: }
10:
11: void CCube::SetMaterialAmbient( float ambientR,  float ambientG,
    ➥float ambientB,
12:                                         float ambientA  )
13: {
14:    // Set the RGBA for ambient reflection.
15:        material.dcvAmbient.r = (D3DVALUE)  ambientR;
16:        material.dcvAmbient.g = (D3DVALUE)  ambientB;
17:        material.dcvAmbient.b = (D3DVALUE)  ambientG;
18:        material.dcvAmbient.a = (D3DVALUE)  ambientA;
19:
20: }
21:
22: void CCube::SetMaterialSpecular( float specularR, float specularG,
    ➥float specularB,
23:                                         float specularA, float specularPower )
24: {
25:    // Set the RGBA and the sharpness of the specular highlight
26:        material.dcvSpecular.r = (D3DVALUE) specularR;
27:        material.dcvSpecular.g = (D3DVALUE) specularG;
28:        material.dcvSpecular.b = (D3DVALUE) specularB;
29:        material.dcvSpecular.a = (D3DVALUE) specularA;
30:        material.dvPower = (float) specularPower;
31: }
```

When you are ready to render your new object, you must tell Direct3D the material of the object. You can call the `IDirect3Ddevice7::SetMaterial()` function to set the material that Direct3D should use. In the sample application, you simply set the material before each cube is drawn. Listing 14.2 shows the new `CCube::draw()` function.

LISTING 14.2   The New `CCube::draw()` Function

```
1: void CCube::draw(LPDIRECT3DDEVICE7 device)
2: {
3:        // Set RenderState to reflect the cube's material
4:        device->SetMaterial( &material );
5:
```

```
 6:       // Draw
 7:       device->DrawIndexedPrimitive( D3DPT_TRIANGLELIST, D3DFVF_VERTEX,
 8:                                     verts, CUBE_VERTEX_COUNT,
 9:                                     cube_index, CUBE_INDEX_COUNT,
10:                                     0);
11: };
```

Generally, the color values that you specify for materials and lights in your scene should have values between 0.0 and 1.0. However, there are special cases when you might specify a value out of this range. For example, you could define a light with negative color values to pull light away from the scene. Or, you might want an extremely bright light, and thus enter values higher than 1.0. It all depends on the situation. You should experiment with many different color values to get the best results.

Direct3D combines the material value of an object with the incoming light values to determine the color of the pixel it should place on the screen. As mentioned before, the diffuse and specular components depend on the direction an object is facing. How does Direct3D know which direction our object is facing? We have to tell Direct3D which direction our object is facing by providing a *vertex normal* (a vector pointing in the appropriate direction) for each vertex in our scene. During lighting calculations, the angles between the vertex normals, the direction of the light, and the direction from the vertices to the viewer are used to determine how light will affect the color of each vertex. Determining a vertex normal isn't always clear for complex geometric objects, however it is easier to determine vertex normals for simple geometric objects. For example, the vertex normals on a box should point away from the face of the box we are rendering, and the vertex normals of a sphere should point away from the center of the sphere. For more information about vertex normals and the mathematics behind Direct3D lighting, you should consult the Direct3D SDK documentation. Figure 14.4 is an illustrated example of vertex normals.

Adding vertex normals to the application is easy. Each building can be thought of as a box, and the vertex normals for a box should point away from the face of the box that is being rendered. Because a box has six faces, you must define six different vertex normals. When you then create your vertices, you pass the appropriate vertex normal to the D3DVERTEX constructor. Listing 14.3 shows how the sample application creates vertex normals for the CCube() object.

14

FIGURE **14.4**

Some diagrams of vertex normals.

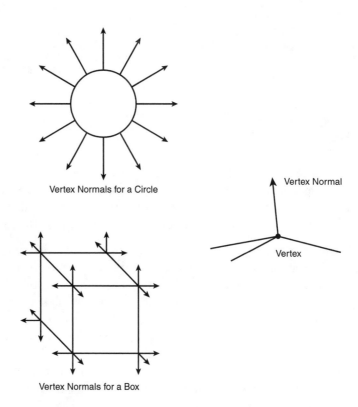

Vertex Normals for a Circle

Vertex Normal

Vertex

Vertex Normals for a Box

LISTING **14.3**   The New CCube() Constructor

```
 1: CCube::CCube(D3DVECTOR origin,D3DVECTOR size,float R,float G,float B)
 2: {
 3:     // Zero out the material information
 4:     ZeroMemory( &material, sizeof(material) );
 5:
 6:     // allocate the vertex array
 7:     verts=new D3DVERTEX[CUBE_VERTEX_COUNT];
 8:
 9:     // calculate far corner of the cube
10:     D3DVECTOR extent=origin+size;
11:
12:     // Original 3d points
13:     D3DVECTOR vec0(origin.x,origin.y,origin.z);
14:     D3DVECTOR vec1(origin.x,extent.y,origin.z);
15:     D3DVECTOR vec2(extent.x,origin.y,origin.z);
16:     D3DVECTOR vec3(extent.x,extent.y,origin.z);
17:     D3DVECTOR vec4(extent.x,origin.y,extent.z);
18:     D3DVECTOR vec5(extent.x,extent.y,extent.z);
19:     D3DVECTOR vec6(origin.x,origin.y,extent.z);
```

```
20:        D3DVECTOR vec7(origin.x,extent.y,extent.z);
21:
22:        // Define the normals for the cube
23:        D3DVECTOR normal0( 0.0f, 0.0f,-1.0f ); // Front face
24:        D3DVECTOR normal1( 1.0f, 0.0f, 0.0f ); // Right face
25:        D3DVECTOR normal2( 0.0f, 0.0f, 1.0f ); // Back face
26:        D3DVECTOR normal3(-1.0f, 0.0f, 0.0f ); // Left face
27:        D3DVECTOR normal4( 0.0f, 1.0f, 0.0f ); // Top face
28:        D3DVECTOR normal5( 0.0f,-1.0f, 0.0f ); // Bottom face
29:
30:        D3DVALUE u0,u1,u2,u3,u4,u5,u6,u7;
31:        D3DVALUE v0,v1,v2,v3,v4,v5,v6,v7;
32:
33:        u0 = 0.0f; v0 = 0.0f;
34:        u1 = 0.0f; v1 = 2.0f;
35:        u2 = 1.0f; v2 = 0.0f;
36:        u3 = 1.0f; v3 = 2.0f;
37:        u4 = 2.0f; v4 = 0.0f;
38:        u5 = 2.0f; v5 = 2.0f;
39:        u6 = 1.0f; v6 = 0.0f;
40:        u7 = 1.0f; v7 = 2.0f;
41:
42:        // Set up the 8 corners of the cube, this time setting up
43:        // vertex normals as well.
44:        //    Note: First vector is position.    Second vector is normal.
45:
46:        // front face
47:        verts[0]=D3DVERTEX( vec0, normal0, u0, v0 );
48:        verts[1]=D3DVERTEX( vec1, normal0, u1, v1 );
49:        verts[2]=D3DVERTEX( vec2, normal0, u2, v2 );
50:        verts[3]=D3DVERTEX( vec3, normal0, u3, v3 );
51:
52:        // right
53:        verts[4]=D3DVERTEX( vec2, normal1, u2, v2 );
54:        verts[5]=D3DVERTEX( vec3, normal1, u3, v3 );
55:        verts[6]=D3DVERTEX( vec4, normal1, u4, v4 );
56:        verts[7]=D3DVERTEX( vec5, normal1, u5, v5 );
57:
58:        //  back face
59:        verts[ 8]=D3DVERTEX( vec4, normal2, u4, v4 );
60:        verts[ 9]=D3DVERTEX( vec5, normal2, u5, v5 );
61:        verts[10]=D3DVERTEX( vec6, normal2, u6, v6 );
62:        verts[11]=D3DVERTEX( vec7, normal2, u7, v7 );
63:
64:        // left face
65:        verts[12]=D3DVERTEX( vec6, normal3, u6, v6 );
66:        verts[13]=D3DVERTEX( vec7, normal3, u7, v7 );
67:        verts[14]=D3DVERTEX( vec0, normal3, u0, v0 );
```

14

continues

LISTING **14.3** continued

```
68:        verts[15]=D3DVERTEX( vec1, normal3, u1, v1 );
69:
70:        // top face
71:        verts[16]=D3DVERTEX( vec1, normal4, u1, v1 );
72:        verts[17]=D3DVERTEX( vec7, normal4, u7, v7 );
73:        verts[18]=D3DVERTEX( vec3, normal4, u3, v3 );
74:        verts[19]=D3DVERTEX( vec5, normal4, u5, v5 );
75:
76:        // bottom face
77:        verts[20]=D3DVERTEX( vec6, normal5, u6, v6 );
78:        verts[21]=D3DVERTEX( vec0, normal5, u0, v0 );
79:        verts[22]=D3DVERTEX( vec4, normal5, u4, v4 );
80:        verts[23]=D3DVERTEX( vec2, normal5, u2, v2 );
81: }
```

As you shall see, adding lighting to your application usually isn't that hard. After you
have changed the code to use vertex normals and materials, there are just a few simple
steps to actually implementing lighting in your application. First, you must create the
lights. After that, you must activate the Direct3D lighting pipeline. While the application
is running, you might want to animate the lights, and finally, you might need to remove
and delete the lights that were used by your application.

The application for this hour is the same basic application that was used in Hour 13,
"Adding Textures and Z-Buffers to the Scene." When you run the application, you should
see a block of texture mapped buildings in a dim ambient light. The application has three
lights, but none of them are enabled by default. To enable or disable a light, simply press
the '1', '2', or '3' key on your keyboard. The '1' key is linked to the point light, the '2'
key is linked to the spotlight, and the '3' key is linked to the directional light. When you
enable a light, you will see that the light is moving and changing.

Creating the Light

You have already seen the syntax for the SetLight() function and the D3DLIGHT7 structure. Now it's time for some real-world application. As mentioned before, there are three
types of lights in Direct3D: point lights, spotlights, and directional lights. The sample
application creates each type of these lights. Listing 14.4 shows the code used to create a
point light.

LISTING 14.4 Creating a Point Light

```
 1: float      lightElevation          = 200.0f;
 2:
 3:     ////////////////////////////////////////
 4:     // Light 0 — Initialize the structure.
 5:     ZeroMemory(&light0, sizeof(D3DLIGHT7));
 6:
 7:
 8:     // Position the light above the cubes in the scene
 9:     //   Note: Lights use world space coordinates
10:     light0.dvPosition.x    = 0.0f;
11:     light0.dvPosition.y  = lightElevation;
12:     light0.dvPosition.z  = 0.0f;
13:
14:     // Set up for a mostly red point light.
15:     light0.dltType        = D3DLIGHT_POINT;
16:     light0.dcvDiffuse.r  = 0.8f;
17:     light0.dcvDiffuse.g  = 0.2f;
18:     light0.dcvDiffuse.b  = 0.2f;
19:     light0.dcvAmbient.r  = 0.0f;
20:     light0.dcvAmbient.g  = 0.0f;
21:     light0.dcvAmbient.b  = 0.0f;
22:     light0.dcvSpecular.r = 1.0f;
23:     light0.dcvSpecular.g = 1.0f;
24:     light0.dcvSpecular.b = 1.0f;
25:
26:     // Don't attenuate.
27:     light0.dvAttenuation0 = 1.0f;
28:     light0.dvRange          = D3DLIGHT_RANGE_MAX;
29:
30:     // Set the light in d3d
31:     lpDevice->SetLight(0, &light0);
```

Because a point light emanates light in all directions, there is no need to specify a direction vector for a point light (however it won't hurt if you do specify a direction vector). The attenuation, range, and light colors were picked specifically for this application. Don't be afraid to experiment with different values until you find something that looks appropriate. Remember that Direct3D lighting is only an approximation of the real world, and thus lighting the scene in your application will probably entail more experimentation than other parts of your application. Listing 14.5 shows how the sample application creates a spotlight.

14

LISTING 14.5 Creating a Spotlight

```
 1:    /////////////////////////////////////////
 2:    // Now on to light1 — spotlight
 3:    ZeroMemory(&light1, sizeof(D3DLIGHT7));
 4:
 5:    light1.dvPosition.x  = 0.0f;
 6:    light1.dvPosition.y  = lightElevation;
 7:    light1.dvPosition.z  = 0.0f;
 8:
 9:    // Set up for a mostly green spot light.
10:    light1.dltType       = D3DLIGHT_SPOT;
11:    light1.dcvDiffuse.r  = 0.2f;
12:    light1.dcvDiffuse.g  = 0.8f;
13:    light1.dcvDiffuse.b  = 0.2f;
14:    light1.dcvAmbient.r  = 0.0f;
15:    light1.dcvAmbient.g  = 0.0f;
16:    light1.dcvAmbient.b  = 0.0f;
17:    light1.dcvSpecular.r = 1.0f;
18:    light1.dcvSpecular.g = 1.0f;
19:    light1.dcvSpecular.b = 1.0f;
20:
21:    // Don't attenuate.
22:    light1.dvRange             = D3DLIGHT_RANGE_MAX;
23:
24:
25:    light1.dvDirection    = D3DVECTOR( 0,-1, 0); // point
       ➥directly downward (in the -y direction)
26:    light1.dvFalloff      = 1.0f;             // linear falloff
27:    light1.dvTheta        = 3.14f/ 3.0f;      // inner ring
       ➥( 1/3 *PI radians)
28:    light1.dvPhi          = 2*3.14f /3.0f;    // outer ring
       ➥( 2/3 *PI radians)
29:    light1.dvAttenuation0 = 1.0f;          // Doesn't attenuate but still
30:                                           // limited by range  (falloff)
31:
32:    // Set the light in d3d
33:    lpDevice->SetLight(1, &light1 );
```

Sometimes it can be very tricky to get spotlights to look correct in your application. If you have enabled a spotlight, but you don't see it anywhere, you might try a few helpful debugging techniques. Usually the direction vector you have specified for the spotlight is wrong, but it's hard to guess randomly what the correct direction vector should be. Instead, it's often helpful to make the spotlight big and bright. Usually this causes the spotlight to light something in your scene, allowing you to fix the direction vector. To make your spotlight bigger and brighter, you should increase the spotlight's range, lower the spotlight's falloff and attenuation, increase the spotlight's phi angle, and increase the spotlight's diffuse color. If you are still having trouble, render a sphere at the spotlight's position in your scene, and you should be able to see which face of the sphere is lit.

Directional lights are probably the easiest to create, and they are also the best performing lights in Direct3D. If you find your application running too slowly after adding lighting, keep in mind that directional lights are the fastest, followed by point lights, and finally spotlights. Listing 14.6 shows the code to create a directional light.

LISTING 14.6 Creating a Directional Light

```
1:    ////////////////////////////////////////
2:    // Now on to light2 — directional
3:    ZeroMemory(&light2, sizeof(D3DLIGHT7));
4:
5:    // Note Position is not used in directional lighting
6:    // just the Direction of the light
7:    light2.dvDirection.x  = 0.0f;
8:    light2.dvDirection.y  = -1.0f;
9:    light2.dvDirection.z  = 0.0f;
10:
11:   // Set up for a mostly blue directional light
12:   light2.dltType       = D3DLIGHT_DIRECTIONAL;
13:   light2.dcvDiffuse.r  = 0.2f;
14:   light2.dcvDiffuse.g  = 0.2f;
15:   light2.dcvDiffuse.b  = 0.8f;
16:   light2.dcvAmbient.r  = 0.0f;
17:   light2.dcvAmbient.g  = 0.0f;
18:   light2.dcvAmbient.b  = 0.0f;
19:   light2.dcvSpecular.r = 1.0f;
20:   light2.dcvSpecular.g = 1.0f;
21:   light2.dcvSpecular.b = 1.0f;
22:
23:   // Set the light in d3d
24:   lpDevice->SetLight(2, &light2 );
```

Activating the Lighting Pipeline

Simply creating lights doesn't automatically make them appear in your scene. In addition to enabling each light individually, you must also enable the entire Direct3D lighting pipeline. You can enable the Direct3D lighting pipeline by calling `IDirect3DDevice7::SetRenderState()`, passing `D3DRENDERSTATE_LIGHTING` as the first parameter, and `TRUE` as the second parameter. Listing 14.7 shows the sample code.

14

LISTING 14.7   Enabling the Lighting Pipeline

```
// Enable Direct3D lighting.
lpDevice->SetRenderState(D3DRENDERSTATE_LIGHTING, TRUE);
```

 If you are using vertex buffers in your application, enabling the lighting pipeline is slightly different. When you call the `IDirect3DVertexBuffer7::ProcessVertices()` or `IDirect3DVertexBuffer7::ProcessVerticesStrided()` function, you must include the `D3DVOP_LIGHT` flag.

In some cases, you might find that you only want to enable or disable one of the lights in your application. The 1, 2, and 3 keys toggle the individual lights in the sample application on or off. To enable or disable a certain light, you must call the `IDirect3DVertexBuffer7::LightEnable()` function. Listing 14.8 shows the sample code to toggle a specific light on or off.

LISTING 14.8   Toggling a Specific Light

```
 1: void toggle_light( int light_number )
 2: {
 3:     BOOL on;
 4:
 5:     // Is the light enabled/on ?
 6:     lpDevice->GetLightEnable(light_number, &on);
 7:
 8:     // If it is, disable it, otherwise turn it on
 9:     if (on)
10:         lpDevice->LightEnable(light_number, FALSE);
11:     else
12:         lpDevice->LightEnable(light_number, TRUE);
13: }
```

Animating Lights in the Scene

To animate the lights in your scene, you simply need to update their position and/or direction and then re-render the scene. The sample application moves the lights in a circular pattern above the texture-mapped buildings. In the case of the directional light, the sample application changes the directional light's direction vector. In addition, there is a timer to make sure that the lights aren't moving too fast. Listing 14.9 shows the code used by the application to update light position and direction.

LISTING 14.9   Animating the Lights in the Scene

```
 1: void move_lights()
 2: {
 3:    ////////////////////////////////////////
 4:    // constants for the function
 5:    //
 6:    // radius of the circular path the light follows
 7:    const  D3DVALUE radius      = 150.0f;
 8:    // change in angle in radians per second ( approx. PI/4 -> 1/8 turn )
 9:    const  D3DVALUE rads_sec    = 3.14f /4.0f;
10:
11:    // current angle in radians for light0  (base at 0 radians)
12:    static D3DVALUE angle0      = 0;
13:    // current angle in radians for light1  (base 1/3 of the
       ➥way 2/3*pi radians)
14:    static D3DVALUE angle1      = 2*3.14f /3.0f;
15:    // current angle in radians for light2  (base 2/3 of the
       ➥way 4/3*pi radians)
16:    static D3DVALUE angle2      = 4*3.14f /3.0f;
17:    static DWORD    last_time   = timeGetTime();    // last time
       ➥we moved light
18:
19:    //
20:    //    Calcluate angle change -   (# of millisecs / 1000 ) * radians
       ➥per second = radians
21:    //
22:    DWORD    current_time = timeGetTime();
23:    D3DVALUE angle_delta  = ( (current_time - last_time) / 1000.0f )
       ➥*rads_sec;
24:
25:    // Add angle for next frame for each of the light angles
26:    angle0   += angle_delta;
27:    angle1   += angle_delta;
28:    angle2   += angle_delta;
29:
30:    D3DLIGHT7 light;
31:
32:    //
33:    // Calculate new position based on polar (x', y')  = ( r*cos(theta),
       ➥r*sin(theta) )
34:    // Do it for each light - Equally space the lights around the circle
35:    //
36:    lpDevice->GetLight( 0, &light );
37:    light.dvPosition.x = radius * (D3DVALUE) cos( angle0 );
38:    light.dvPosition.z = radius * (D3DVALUE) sin( angle0 );
39:    light.dvPosition.y = lightElevation;
```

continues

14

LISTING 14.9 continued

```
40:    lpDevice->SetLight( 0, &light );   // Set/Change the lights state
41:
42:    lpDevice->GetLight( 1, &light );
43:    light.dvPosition.x = radius * (D3DVALUE) cos( angle1 );
44:    light.dvPosition.z = radius * (D3DVALUE) sin( angle1 );
45:    light.dvPosition.y = lightElevation;
46:    lpDevice->SetLight( 1, &light );     // Set/Change the lights state
47:
48:    ////////////////////////////////////////////
49:    // The direction vector is moved not the position vector for directional
     ➥lights
50:    lpDevice->GetLight( 2, &light );
51:
52:    // Multiply by -1 to get the correct direction vector
53:    //    - All 3 lights will be equally spaced around the circle
54:
55:    light.dvDirection.x = -1 * (D3DVALUE) cos( angle2 );
56:    light.dvDirection.z = -1 * (D3DVALUE) sin( angle2 );
57:    light.dvDirection.y = 0;  //Always aim through y=0 regardless of x and z
58:    lpDevice->SetLight(2, &light);   // Set/Change the lights state
59:
60:    last_time    = current_time;  // store the time for the next pass
61:    }
```

Removing the Lights

If you want to turn the lighting pipeline off completely, you can call
`IDirect3DDevice7::SetRenderState()`, passing `D3DRENDERSTATE_LIGHTING` as the first
parameter, and `FALSE` as the second parameter. As mentioned before, you can also disable
a certain light by calling the `IDirect3DVertexBuffer7::LightEnable()` function.

Summary

Lighting is a great way to bring more realism to your application. In addition, as more
and more video cards implement the Direct3D lighting pipeline in hardware, it will be
advantageous to use Direct3D lighting. You now know the basics of materials, vertex
normals, and the different types of Direct3D lights, which will allow you to easily add
lighting to your application.

Q&A

Q **Why don't I see any shadows in my scene when I use Direct3D lighting?**

A Because of performance concerns, shadows are not implemented in the Direct3D lighting pipeline. Various techniques can be used to create shadows (such as the stencil buffer). For more information about implementing shadows into your application, you should first consult the Direct3D SDK documentation.

Q **Why do the three different types of light all perform differently?**

A Each type of light in Direct3D has been optimized for the special case it presents. Directional lighting is fastest because there are no calculations dealing with range, attenuation, or position and because the direction is constant. A positional light is slightly slower because it has to take into account the attenuation and range of the light. Finally, the spotlight is slowest because it has to perform calculations with every single element of the D3DLIGHT7 structure.

Workshop

The Workshop is designed to help you anticipate possible questions, review what you've learned, and get you thinking about how to put your knowledge into practice. The answers to the quiz are in Appendix A, "Answers."

Quiz

1. What are the three types of lights implemented by the Direct3D lighting pipeline?
2. How do you enable/disable the Direct3D lighting pipeline?
3. How do you enable/disable a specific light in Direct3D?
4. How do you create a light in Direct3D?
5. What is ambient light?
6. What is diffuse light?
7. What is specular light?
8. What is a vertex normal, and what is it used for?
9. What do the *theta* and *phi* elements of the D3DLIGHT7 structure specify, and what are their valid ranges?
10. What are the three different attenuation factors?

14

Exercises

1. Experiment with the color values of the lights and the material values of the objects in the sample application. Set the diffuse, ambient, and specular components of the lights equal to white light (red = 1.0, green = 1.0, blue = 1.0) and try different material values. Then set the diffuse, ambient, and specular material values equal to white and change the values of the lights. Before you run the application again, try to guess what the results will be.

2. Experiment with the different variables of each light (range, direction, attenuation, and so on). Try to predict the changes you will see in the application before you run it.

PART VI

Direct3D Immediate Mode

Hour

HOUR 15

Importing 3D Objects and Animations Into the Scene

Up until now, the 3D objects that you have created in your application have been rather simple. In this hour, you will be introduced to a new method of creating and using 3D objects in your application, no matter how complex they might be. In this hour, you will learn the following:

- The different 3D modeling packages and file formats.
- The specifics of the Direct3D X file format.
- How to read and use Direct3D X files in your application.
- How to use the CONV3DS utility to create Direct3D X files.

An Overview of 3D Modeling Packages

3D Studio, Lightwave, Maya—you have probably heard the names of these professional 3D modeling packages before. In recent years, there have been more and more 3D modeling applications to choose from. Which 3D modeling package is best is irrelevant to the discussion here. The important thing to know is that just about every 3D modeling application out there has its own proprietary 3D file format. Luckily, most 3D modeling packages also support 3D Studio's .3ds file format. The 3D Studio format doesn't pose a problem to you because a utility is included with the DirectX 7 SDK that will allow you to convert 3D Studio files to Direct3D X files. Direct3D X files are easy to use in your application, and they will allow you to build scenes filled with complex 3D objects easily.

The Direct3D X File Format

Now it's time to get into the Direct3D X file specifics. Direct3D X files are template driven. You can think of each template as a different section of the file that describes a particular part of a 3D model. For example, there are templates to store vertex coordinates, vertex colors, vertex normals, materials, texture coordinates, and so on. The Direct3D X file format can be either text-based or binary-based. The examples given in this hour will use text-based X files because they are easy to read. However, if performance and file size are considerations, you will probably want to create binary X files.

Sometimes the easiest way to learn the structure of a file is to look at it. Listing 15.1 is a simple Direct3D X file. Don't worry if you don't understand any of it yet; each part of the file will be dissected and explained later in the hour.

LISTING 15.1 A Sample Direct3D X File

```
 1: xof 0302txt 0064
 2:
 3: Header {
 4:   1;
 5:   0;
 6:   1;
 7: }
 8:
 9: // Create a blue square:
10: //   Will require:  4 vertices
11: //                  2 triangles
12: //                  blue material
13:
14: // the blue material:
```

```
15: //  r = 0.0, g = 0.0, b = 1.0, a = 1.0
16: Material BlueMaterial {
17:    0.0;0.0;1.0;1.0;;   // face/triangle color
18:    1.0;                // power
19:    0.0;0.0;0.0;;       // specular color
20:    0.0;0.0;0.0;;       // emissive color
21: }
22:
23: //  the square mesh:
24: Mesh Square {
25:    4;                  // number of vertices
26:    1.0;1.0;0.0;,       //  vertex 0
27:    -1.0;1.0;0.0;,      //  vertex 1
28:    -1.0;-1.0;0.0;,     //  vertex 2
29:    1.0;-1.0;0.0;;      //  vertex 3
30:
31:    2;                  // number of triangles
32:    3;0,1,2;,           //  triangle 0
33:    3;0,2,3;;           //  triangle 1
34:
35:    //  now, provide material information:
36: MeshMaterialList {
37:    1;        // 1 material used
38:    2;        // 2 triangles
39:    0,        // triangle 0 uses material 0
40:    0;;       // triangle 1 uses material 0
41:    {BlueMaterial}  //  material 0: the blue material
42: }
43:
44: MeshNormals {
45:    1;              //  all vertices have same normal
46:    0.0;0.0;1.0;,
47:
48:    2;              //  2 faces to define normals for
49:    3;0,0,0;,
50:    3;0,0,0;
51: }
52:
53: }  //  end of mesh
```

At the beginning of every Direct3D X file is a file header. The header contains four different fields:

- A 4-byte "magic number" (the value xof).
- A 4-byte version number of the file.
- A 4-byte format type of the file; txt for a text file, bin for a binary file, tzip for a compressed text file, and bzip for a compressed binary file.

- A 4-byte value indicating the size of floats. This value can be 0064 for 64-bit floats or it can be 0032 for 32-bit floats.

You can add comments to every line of a Direct3D X file. Comments are preceded with double-slashes (// C++ style comment) or the number sign (# comments go here). Comments are useful because they will remind you what each template is for, and they will allow others to understand the overall structure of the file easily. As with commenting your code, it's rarely the case that you will have too many comments!

Everything after the file header is a template. A template tells the program how to interpret the data that it reads from the file. Each template is composed of four general parts. First, each template must have a unique name. The name might consist of alphanumeric characters and/or the underscore character, however it can't start with a number. Second, each template has a universally unique identifier (often referred to as a UUID) that must be surrounded by angle brackets. Third, the template will have a list of member data types. A set of primitive data types (shown in Listing 15.2) can be used, however you can also use other templates in this section as well. Finally, the last part of a template is the template restrictions. Depending on the restrictions defined in a template, the template is considered to be open, closed, or restricted. The restrictions determine what data types can be included in the rest of the template. Open templates can include any other data type, closed templates can't include any other data types, and restricted templates can only include certain listed data types. To indicate an open template, you add three periods enclosed in brackets ([...]) to the end of your template. To indicate a restricted template, you add a list of data types, optionally followed by their UUIDs, enclosed in square brackets. To indicate a closed template, no extra syntax is required. Several templates are already defined for Direct3D X files. Listing 15.3 shows a set of sample templates that are already defined by Direct3D.

LISTING 15.2 Primitive Data Types

```
1: Data Type:          Size:
2: WORD                16 bits
3: DWORD               32 bits
4: FLOAT               IEEE float
5: DOUBLE              64 bits
6: CHAR                8 bits
7: UCHAR               8 bits
8: BYTE                8 bits
9: STRING              NULL-terminated string
```

LISTING 15.3   Sample Templates

```
 1: //  The ColorRGB Template: (a closed template)
 2:
 3: template ColorRGB {
 4:     <D3E16E81-7835-11cf-8F52-0040333594A3>
 5:     FLOAT red;
 6:     FLOAT green;
 7:     FLOAT blue;
 8:     //  declare it a closed template (no extra syntax)
 9: }
10:
11: //  The MeshMaterialList Template: (a restricted template)
12:
13: template MeshMaterialList {
14:     <F6F23F42-7686-11cf-8F52-0040333594A3>
15:     DWORD nMaterials;
16:     DWORD nFaceIndexes;
17:     array DWORD faceIndexes[nFaceIndexes];
18:     [Material]    //  declare it a restricted template
19: }
20:
21: // The Material Template: (an open template)
22:
23: template Material {
24:     <3D82AB4D-62DA-11cf-AB39-0020AF71E433>
25:     ColorRGBA faceColor;
26:     FLOAT power;
27:     ColorRGB specularColor;
28:     ColorRGB emissiveColor;
29:     [...]    // declare it an open template
30: }
```

The templates declared in Listing 15.3 should look familiar because all these templates were used in Listing 15.1. As you can see in Listing 15.3, a template can contain any combination of primitive data types or other templates in its member list. The specifics on each primitive data type available are shown in Listing 15.2.

You can create an array of any data type by adding the keyword array in front of the data type and by specifying the array size in square brackets immediately following the data type name. Listing 15.3 has a simple example of using an array. In the MeshMaterialList template, there is an array of DWORDs. You specify multidimensional arrays in a Direct3D X file the same way you specify multidimensional arrays in C/C++.

A special template, called the header template, should be included in every Direct3D X file. It can be used to store any type of application-specific data that you want. The header has a flags member. Only the first bit of the flags member is defined. If the first bit is on, the data following the header template will be read as text. If the first bit is off, the data following the header template will be read as binary. You can have multiple header templates in your X file to switch between binary and text reading modes. Listing 15.4 shows the template specification for the header template.

LISTING **15.4**   The Header Template

```
1: template Header {
2:    <3D82AB43-62DA-11cf-AB39-0020AF71E433>
3:    WORD major;   // application-specific data
4:    WORD minor;   // application-specific data
5:    DWORD flags;  // flags
6: }
```

Before you are exposed to the rest of the major templates you will be working with, it is time for a more complex example. Don't worry if things seem overwhelming right now; the following sections will explain everything. Listing 15.5 is a more complex example of a Direct3D X file.

LISTING **15.5**   A Sample Direct3D X File

```
 1: xof 0302txt 0064
 2:
 3: Header {
 4:  1;
 5:  0;
 6:  1;
 7: }
 8:
 9: //  Create a texture-mapped cube
10: //   Will require:  8 vertices
11: //                  6 faces
12: //                  white material
13: //                  texture
14:
15: //  the white material, with some texture:
16: //  r = 1.0, g = 1.0, b = 1.0, a = 1.0
17: Material WhiteMaterial {
18:    1.0;1.0;1.0;1.0;;  // face/triangle color
19:    1.0;               // specular power
20:    0.0;0.0;0.0;;      // specular color
21:    0.0;0.0;0.0;;      // emissive color
22:
23:    TextureFileName {
24:        "SomeTexture.ppm";
25:    }
```

15

```
26: }
27:
28: //  the cube mesh:
29: Mesh Cube {
30:    8;              // number of vertices
31:    1.0;1.0;1.0;,    //  vertex 0
32:    1.0;1.0;-1.0;,   //  vertex 1
33:    1.0;-1.0;-1.0;,  //  vertex 2
34:    1.0;-1.0;1.0;,   //  vertex 3
35:    -1.0;1.0;1.0;,   //  vertex 4
36:    -1.0;1.0;-1.0;,  //  vertex 5
37:    -1.0;-1.0;-1.0;, //  vertex 6
38:    -1.0;-1.0;1.0;,  //  vertex 7
39:
40:    6;              // number of faces
41:    4;0,1,2,3;,     //  face 0
42:    4;3,2,6,7;;     //  face 1
43:    4;7,6,5,4;,     //  face 2
44:    4;4,5,1,0;;     //  face 3
45:    4;5,6,2,1;,     //  face 4
46:    4;0,3,7,4;;     //  face 5
47:
48:    //  now, provide material information:
49: MeshMaterialList {
50:    1;       // 1 material used
51:    6;       // 6 faces
52:    0,       // face 0 uses material 0
53:    0,       // face 1 uses material 0
54:    0,       // face 2 uses material 0
55:    0,       // face 3 uses material 0
56:    0,       // face 4 uses material 0
57:    0;;      // face 5 uses material 0
58:    {BlueMaterial} //  material 0: the blue material
59: }
60:
61: MeshNormals {
62:    6;              //  6 normals, one for each face
63:    1.0;0.0;0.0;,    //  normal 0
64:    0.0;-1.0;0.0;,   //  normal 1
65:    -1.0;0.0;0.0;,   //  normal 2
66:    0.0;1.0;0.0;,    //  normal 3
67:    0.0;0.0;-1.0;,   //  normal 4
68:    0.0;0.0;1.0;;    //  normal 5
69:
70:    6;              //  6 faces to define normals for
71:    4;0,0,0;,   // face 0 uses normal 0
72:    4;1,1,1;,   // face 1 uses normal 1
73:    4;2,2,2;,   // face 2 uses normal 2
74:    4;3,3,3;,   // face 3 uses normal 3
75:    4;4,4,4;,   // face 4 uses normal 4
```

continues

LISTING **15.5**   continued

```
76:   4;5,5,5;   // face 5 uses normal 5
77: }
78:
79: MeshTextureCoords {
80:   8;        // 8 texture coordinates, one for each vertex
81:   1.0;1.0;  // vertex 0
82:   0.0;1.0;  // vertex 1
83:   0.0;0.0;  // vertex 2
84:   1.0;0.0;  // vertex 3
85:   1.0;0.0;  // vertex 4
86:   0.0;0.0;  // vertex 5
87:   0.0;1.0;  // vertex 6
88:   1.0;1.0;; // vertex 7
89: }
90:
91: }  //  end of mesh
```

Now it's time to look more closely at the templates being used by the samples. As mentioned before, Direct3D defines several default templates for your use in Direct3D X files. All the examples in this hour will use these predefined templates.

Vertex Storage

When you need to store vertices of a 3D object, you will almost always be storing them in a mesh template. An exception is that you might store a commonly used vertex in a Vector template. Then you can reference this vertex by typing in the vector's name instead of typing out the x, y, and z coordinates. Listing 15.6 has the Direct3D specification for the Vector, MeshFace, and Mesh templates.

LISTING **15.6**   The Vector, MeshFace, and Mesh Templates

```
1: template Vector {
2:     <3D82AB5E-62DA-11cf-AB39-0020AF71E433>
3:     FLOAT x;
4:     FLOAT y;
5:     FLOAT z;
6: }
7:
8: template MeshFace {
9:     <3D82AB5F-62DA-11cf-AB39-0020AF71E433>
10:    DWORD NumFaceVertexIndices;
11:    array DWORD faceVertexIndices[NumFaceVertexIndices];
12: }
13:
14: template Mesh {
```

15

```
15:    <3D82AB44-62DA-11cf-AB39-0020AF71E433>
16:    DWORD NumVertices;
17:    array Vector vertices[NumVertices];
18:    DWORD NumFaces;
19:    array MeshFace faces[NumFaces];
20:    [...]
21: }
```

As you can see, the mesh template is an open template and the vector template is a closed template. The vector template is closed because no other information needs to be associated with a vector. All you need is the vector coordinates, nothing more. However, in the case of the mesh template, more information might be associated with a certain mesh object. For example, in most cases, you will want to specify vertex normals and materials for each mesh.

The first DWORD in the mesh, called NumVertices, specifies the number of vertices in the mesh. Following that, there is an array of Vectors. Each vector specifies a vertex in the mesh. After that, a DWORD called NumFaces exists. NumFaces is the number of faces the mesh has. Next, there is an array of MeshFaces. A MeshFace contains information about a single face of a 3D model—a single triangle, for example. Each MeshFace is composed of a DWORD specifying the number of vertices the MeshFace will reference and an array of DWORDs specifying the specific vertex indices.

Vertex Colors

A Mesh isn't very interesting until you add some color to it. The best way to add color is by using the Material template. That way the 3D object will look correct if the Direct3D lighting pipeline is used. To add materials to your existing Mesh template, you must add a MeshMaterialList template to the end of your Mesh. As you know, each material is composed of several colors. Thus, it isn't surprising to know that the Material template uses the ColorRGBA and the ColorRGB templates. Listing 15.7 shows the definitions of the ColorRGBA, ColorRGB, Material, and MeshMaterialList templates.

LISTING 15.7 The ColorRGBA, ColorRGB, Material, and MeshMaterialList
Templates

```
1: template ColorRGBA {
2:    <35FF44E0-6C7C-11cf-8F52-0040333594A3>
3:    FLOAT red;
4:    FLOAT green;
5:    FLOAT blue;
6:    FLOAT alpha;
```

continues

LISTING **15.7**   continued

```
 7: }
 8:
 9: template ColorRGB {
10:     <D3E16E81-7835-11cf-8F52-0040333594A3>
11:     FLOAT red;
12:     FLOAT green;
13:     FLOAT blue;
14: }
15:
16: template Material {
17:     <3D82AB4D-62DA-11cf-AB39-0020AF71E433>
18:     ColorRGBA faceColor;
19:     FLOAT power;
20:     ColorRGB specularColor;
21:     ColorRGB emissiveColor;
22:     [...]
23: }
24:
25: template MeshMaterialList {
26:     <F6F23F42-7686-11cf-8F52-0040333594A3>
27:     DWORD NumMaterials;
28:     DWORD NumFaceIndexes;
29:     array DWORD faceIndexes[NumFaceIndexes];
30:     [Material]
31: }
```

This should be straightforward now. The only difference between the ColorRGBA and the ColorRGB templates is the alpha component in the ColorRGBA template. The Material template uses the ColorRGBA template to specify the face color and ColorRGB templates to specify the specular and emissive colors of the material. A MeshMaterialList simply assigns a material to each face index. Notice that the MeshMaterialList is a restricted template. It only allows Material templates to be included.

Vertex Normals

Any time you are performing lighting calculations, you will need a list of vertex normals included in your Mesh template. The MeshNormals template builds on other templates already mentioned. Listing 15.8 shows the definition for the MeshNormals template.

LISTING **15.8**   The MeshNormals Template

```
1: template MeshNormals {
2:     <F6F23F43-7686-11cf-8F52-0040333594A3>
3:     DWORD NumNormals;
```

```
4:     array Vector normals[NumNormals];
5:     DWORD NumFaceNormals;
6:     array MeshFace faceNormals[NumFaceNormals];
7: }
```

The first part of the template is the number of normals and an array of those normals. The second part of the template is the number of face normals and an array of indices to the normals for each face. In most cases, NumFaceNormals will be equal to the number of faces defined in the mesh. The MeshNormals template is useful because it allows you to specify multiple normals for the same vertex. In the case of a cube, each vertex has three different normals (a different normal for each face of the cube the vertex defines). Because six faces are on a cube, you will have a total of six different normals. Rather than repeating each vertex three times, defining a different normal for each (as done in earlier hours), you can simply define the eight vertices and six normals, and the MeshNormals template will take care of the rest. As you can guess, this is more efficient, and it uses up less space.

Texture Maps

When you create a new Material template, you can optionally specify a TextureFileName template. This will associate a texture with a material. To add texture coordinates to your mesh, you use the MeshTextureCoords template. The MeshTextureCoords template uses the Coords2d template, which you haven't seen yet. All of these are rather simple templates. Listing 15.9 shows the definitions for each.

LISTING 15.9   The Coords2d, TextureFileName, and MeshTextureCoords Templates

```
 1: template Coords2d {
 2:     <F6F23F44-7686-11cf-8F52-0040333594A3>
 3:     FLOAT u;
 4:     FLOAT v;
 5: }
 6:
 7: template TextureFileName {
 8:     <A42790E1-7810-11cf-8F52-0040333594A3>
 9:     STRING fileName;
10: }
11:
12: template MeshTextureCoords {
13:     <F6F23F40-7686-11cf-8F52-0040333594A3>
14:     DWORD NumTextureCoords;
15:     array Coords2d textureCoords[NumTextureCoords];
16: }
```

Use of these templates is very straightforward. The `TextureFileName` template is simply the string containing the filename of the file to be loaded. `MeshTextureCoords` consists of a `NumTextureCoords` variable; usually this will be the same as the number of vertices in the mesh, and an array of `Coords2d`, which are the u-v texture coordinates.

Frame Hierarchy

You haven't seen any examples of the `Frame` template yet. The word frame denotes a frame of reference for meshes. All the objects in a frame are optional, however most of the time you will provide a 4×4 matrix, followed by a list of meshes. The 4×4 matrix specifies the transform that will be applied to all the meshes and frames listed below it. You can imagine the case where the model is a car. Instead of modeling the entire car as a single mesh, you could break the model into a car body and a single car wheel. Then, you would have to draw the wheel at the four different spots it could be on the car. Using frames, this becomes an easy task. The base frame would contain the base transformation matrix, the mesh of the car body, and four other frames, one for each wheel. These "wheel frames" would contain a transformation matrix that would place the wheel in the appropriate spot relative to the car. The new templates associated with frames that you haven't seen yet are the `Matrix4x4` template, the `FrameTransformMatrix` template, and the `Frame` template. Listing 15.10 shows the definitions of each.

LISTING 15.10 The `Matrix4x4`, `FrameTransformMatrix`, and `Frame` Templates

```
 1: template Matrix4x4 {
 2:    <F6F23F45-7686-11cf-8F52-0040333594A3>
 3:    array FLOAT matrix[16];
 4: }
 5:
 6: template FrameTransformMatrix {
 7:    <F6F23F41-7686-11cf-8F52-0040333594A3>
 8:    Matrix4x4 frameMatrix;
 9: }
10:
11: template Frame {
12:    <3D82AB46-62DA-11cf-AB39-0020AF71E433>
13:    [...]
14: }
```

The definitions are straightforward, but they don't make the usage of the templates very clear. Listing 15.11 is a short example that demonstrates the car example previously mentioned.

LISTING 15.11   A Simple Example of Using Frames

```
 1: // Assume the following are already defined:
 2: //   Meshes: CarBody, CarWheel
 3: //   FrameTransformationMatrix:  CarBodyTrans, Wheel1Trans,
 4: //                    Wheel2Trans, Wheel3Trans, Wheel4Trans
 5:
 6: Frame CarBodyFrame {
 7:     {CarBodyTrans}
 8:     {CarBody}
 9:
10:     Frame Wheel1Frame {
11:         {Wheel1Trans}
12:         {CarWheel}
13:     }
14:
15:     Frame Wheel2Frame {
16:         {Wheel2Trans}
17:         {CarWheel}
18:     }
19:
20:     Frame Wheel3Frame {
21:         {Wheel3Trans}
22:         {CarWheel}
23:     }
24:
25:     Frame Wheel4Frame {
26:         {Wheel4Trans}
27:         {CarWheel}
28:     }
29: }
```

Note that the transformation matrix for each wheel will rotate and move the wheel to its appropriate position. In addition, the transformation matrix for either the car body or the car wheel could scale the car to be any size. This can be a very powerful tool.

Animation Paths

Many templates are designed to set up animations for your 3D object. The first three templates you will have to familiarize yourself with are the FloatKeys, TimedFloatKeys, and AnimationKey templates. The FloatKeys template is simply a template that stores an array of floating-point values and the size of the array. The floating-point values will be used to define rotations, positions, and scaling changes. The TimedFloatKeys template is simply a FloatKeys template with an added time variable. An AnimationKey holds an array of TimedFloatKeys, the size of the array, and a keyType variable. The keyType variable is a DWORD that can take on the integer value of 0, 1, or 2. This value specifies whether the animation should perform a rotation, scale, or position change, respectively. Listing 15.12 shows the definitions for these templates.

LISTING 15.12 The FloatKeys, TimedFloatKeys, and AnimationKey Templates

```
 1: template FloatKeys {
 2:    <F406B180-7B3B-11cf-8F52-0040333594A3>
 3:    DWORD NumValues;
 4:    array FLOAT values[NumValues];
 5: }
 6:
 7: template TimedFloatKeys {
 8:    <10DD46A8-775B-11cf-8F52-0040333594A3>
 9:    DWORD Time;
10:    FloatKeys tfkeys;
11: }
12:
13: template AnimationKey {
14:    <10DD46A8-775B-11cf-8F52-0040333594A3>
15:    DWORD keyType;
16:    DWORD NumKeys;
17:    array TimedFloatKeys keys[NumKeys];
18: }
```

You will use three more important templates when creating animations for 3D objects. They are the AnimationOptions template, the Animation template, and the AnimationSet template. Listing 15.13 shows their definitions.

LISTING 15.13 The AnimationOptions, Animation, and AnimationSet Templates

```
 1: template AnimationOptions {
 2:    <E2BF56C0-840F-11cf-8F52-0040333594A3>
 3:    DWORD openclosed;
 4:    DWORD positionquality;
 5: }
 6:
 7: template Animation {
 8:    <3D82AB4F-62DA-11cf-AB39-0020AF71E433>
 9:    [...]
10: }
11:
12: template AnimationSet {
13:    <3D82AB50-62DA-11cf-AB39-0020AF71E433>
14:    [Animation]
15: }
```

The AnimationOptions template relates directly to the D3DANIMATIONOPTIONS structure. The openclosed variable should be set to 0 for a closed animation or 1 for an open animation. A closed animation will play continually, jumping from the last frame to the first frame after it has completed the animation. An open animation plays once and then stops. The positionquality variable should be set to 0 to specify positioning using splines or 1 to specify linear positioning.

The Animation template is an open template without any required member variables. It should contain a reference to a frame that the animation will be performed on. For use with Direct3D retained mode, you can add an AnimationKey template and an AnimationOptions template to define an animation. The AnimationSet template is a restricted template that simply holds sets of Animation objects.

How do all these templates work together? Listing 15.14 shows a simple example of an animation.

LISTING 15.14   A Sample Animation

```
 1: //  assume CarFrame is the frame containing our car
 2:
 3: AnimationSet CarAnimationSet0 {
 4:    Animation CarDrivingForward {
 5:      {CarFrame}
 6:
 7:      AnimationOptions {
 8:        1;
 9:        1;
10:      }
11:
12:      AnimationKey {
13:        2;             // 2 = modify cars position
14:        5;             // 5 different keys
15:        100; 3; 0.0, 0.0,  0.0;;,
16:        200; 3; 0.0, 0.0, 10.0;;,
17:        300; 3; 0.0, 0.0, 30.0;;,
18:        400; 3; 0.0, 0.0, 70.0;;,
19:        500; 3; 0.0, 0.0, 150.0;;;
20:      }
21:    }
22: }
```

You now know most of the important templates that Direct3D retained mode will recognize and use. Knowing this, you will be able to understand most X files easily.

Converting 3D Studio Files: The CONV3DS Utility

Creating Direct3D X files can be a huge task. The examples you have seen so far are extremely simple. When you create 3D models using a 3D modeling package, they are usually extremely complex. The good news is that a utility is included with Direct3D that will allow you to convert 3D Studio files into Direct3D X files. The name of this utility is CONV3DS. You will find it included with the DirectX 7 SDK.

In most cases, you will simply be able to run the CONV3DS utility by typing `CONV3DS filename.3ds`, where `filename` is the name of the 3D Studio file you want to convert. This will produce an X file named filename.X. A useful way to check newly created X files is to run the program Direct3D RM Viewer. The Direct3D RM Viewer is an application that will allow you to view any X file that you like. The Direct3D RM Viewer is also included with the DirectX 7 SDK.

For a complete reference to the CONV3DS utility, you should refer to the DirectX 7 SDK documentation and the CONV3DS.txt file, a text document that is also included with the DirectX 7 SDK.

Reading the X File Format

Included with the DirectX 7 SDK, however not well documented, is an object that will make it very easy for you to load X files into your application. The object is defined in the file d3dfile.h, and the corresponding implementation of the object is in the file d3dfile.cpp. The object is called `CD3DFile`, and it will provide you with a great reference on the low-level reading of a Direct3D X file as well as making it very easy for you to get X files into your application quickly.

Three specific public functions are in the `CD3DFile` object that will be used in the sample application in this hour. The first function is `CD3DFile::Load()`. The `Load()` function takes one argument: the name (a string) of the X file that you want to load. The second function is used to scale the geometry loaded by the X files to fit the scene. The function `CD3DFile::Scale()` takes a single argument, a floating point variable that it will use to scale the geometry of the X file. The last function that the sample application uses is the `CD3DFile::Render()` function. This function also has one argument, a `LPDIRECT3DDE-VICE7` object, which it will render the X file to. Listing 15.15 shows an example of these three functions in action.

LISTING 15.15   Loading and Rendering a Direct3D X File

```
 1: // . . .
 2:
 3: CD3DFile* car = NULL;
 4:
 5: car = new CD3DFile();
 6:
 7: //  load the file:
 8: if ( FAILED( car->Load("car.x") ) )
 9: {
10:     // handle error
11: }
12: else
13: {
14:     //  make the car twice as big
15:     car->Scale(2.0);
16:
17:     //  render the car to gLPDevice
18:     car->Render(gLPDevice);
19:
20: }
```

Of course, the code in your application will probably look much different, but this should give you the basic idea of how to use the functions.

Adding Vehicles to Our Application

Now it is finally time to tie everything you've learned in this hour together. The sample application in this hour builds on the sample application from Hour 14, "Adding Realism Through Lighting." In addition to the block of buildings, you will be able to see a helicopter circling the rooftops and a car that is parked near the base of one of the buildings. The rotating blue directional light from Hour 14 was replaced with a stationary white directional light to allow you to see the models better.

Reading the Model

As mentioned before, we let the CD3DFile object do the work and load the X files into the application for us. The application has a new object for the helicopter. This object holds a pointer to a CD3DFile object, and it contains information about the helicopter, such as position, angle, and velocity. Because the car is stationary, the file is simply loaded and rendered during the render loop. Listing 15.16 shows the code used in the sample application to read in the files.

LISTING **15.16**   Reading a Direct3D X File

```
 1:    // load the car model
 2:
 3:    lpXFileCar=new CD3DFile();
 4:    if( FAILED( lpXFileCar->Load("car.x"))){
 5:
 6:      // Set error string.
 7:      ErrStr=Err_LoadingXFile;
 8:
 9:      return FALSE;
10:
11:      } else {
12:      lpXFileCar->Scale(5.0f);
13:    };
14:
15:    // load the helicopter model
16:
17:    lpXFileHelo=new CD3DFile();
18:    if( FAILED( lpXFileHelo->Load("heli.x"))){
19:
20:      // Set error string.
21:      ErrStr=Err_LoadingXFile;
22:
23:      return FALSE;
24:
25:      } else {
26:      lpXFileHelo->Scale(5.0f);
27:    };
28:
29:    // create helicopter object
30:    chopper=new CHelicopter(D3DVECTOR(0,250,0),
31:                            D3DVECTOR(0.0f,0.0f,0.0f),
32:                            lpXFileHelo);
33:
34: //  . . .
```

Setting Up the Hierarchy

Because two new objects are in the application, you must be careful where you place them or else they will intersect with other objects in the world. You want to render each object with respect to the rest of the scene. To render the car with respect to the rest of the scene, you will perform an additional transformation on the car. The same principle applies to the helicopter. In the case of the sample application, things have been kept simple. Because the car is stationary, there is simply a translation to place it in the appropriate position. The helicopter, on the other hand, is slightly more complex. The helicopter is flying around the rooftops of the buildings. Instead of a simple translation, the helicopter body also needs to be rotated on its central axis. Otherwise, it would appear that the helicopter wasn't really flying at all. Because the car and helicopter modify the world transformation matrix before they are rendered, they must restore the original matrix after they are rendered.

This hierarchical model is working on many other levels in the application. If you have examined the car and helicopter X files, you will notice that each object is split into its component pieces. For example, the car separates the body from the lights and the wheels. Each of these component pieces of the car and helicopter might also perform some additional transformation so that they are rendered in the appropriate place. It all goes back to the use of Frame templates. Each frame can provide a transformation matrix that is applied to the current transformation matrix. In this way, each object is rendered with respect to all the matrix transformations applied before it. This is an important concept to understand. Listing 15.17 shows the code used in the sample application that is used to set up the world transformation matrix for the helicopter.

LISTING 15.17   Placing the Helicopter in the Scene: The
CHelicopter::calc_move() Function

```
 1: D3DMATRIX CHelicopter::calc_move(float delt)
 2: {
 3:    cur_ang.x=-pitch*4.5f;
 4:    cur_ang.y+=steer*delt*0.05f;
 5:    cur_ang.z=-steer*0.01f;
 6:
 7:    cur_pos.y+=lift*delt*12.0f;
 8:    cur_pos.x+=sin(cur_ang.y)*-cur_ang.x*75.0f*delt;
 9:    cur_pos.z+=cos(cur_ang.y)*-cur_ang.x*75.0f*delt;
10:
11:    // calculate a decay factor based on time
12:    float decay=1.0f-delt*0.2f;
13:
14:    // decay the speed and control positions gradually back towards zero
15:    lift*=decay;
16:    pitch*=decay;
17:    steer*=decay;
18:
19:    // settle towards clear and level flight
20:    cur_ang.x*=decay;
21:    cur_ang.z*=decay;
22:
23:    // set up rotations and combine into view transform matrix
24:    D3DMATRIX matTrans,matRotateY,matRotateZ,matRotateX,view;
25:
26:    D3DUtil_SetTranslateMatrix(matTrans,cur_pos.x,cur_pos.y,cur_pos.z);
27:
```

continues

LISTING **15.17**   continued

```
28:     D3DUtil_SetRotateXMatrix( matRotateX,cur_ang.x);
29:     D3DUtil_SetRotateYMatrix( matRotateY,cur_ang.y);
30:     D3DUtil_SetRotateZMatrix( matRotateZ,cur_ang.z);
31:
32:     D3DMath_MatrixMultiply(view,matRotateY,matTrans);
33:     D3DMath_MatrixMultiply(view,matRotateZ,view);
34:     D3DMath_MatrixMultiply(view,matRotateX,view);
35:
36:     // return view matrix
37:     return view;
38: }
```

Adding the Object to the Scene

After the world matrix has been changed to take into account the position of the object,
the object needs to be rendered. After an object is rendered, the proper world transformation matrix needs to be restored. All this takes place in the render_frame() function and
the CHelicopter::draw() function. Listing 15.18 shows the code snippets from the sample application.

LISTING **15.18**   Rendering the Car and Helicopter

```
 1: void render_frame(float elapsed)
 2: {
 3:   // . . .
 4:
 5:   if (chopper)
 6:     chopper->draw(lpDevice,elapsed);
 7:
 8:   D3DMATRIX world;
 9:   if (lpXFileCar) {
10:   // just translate the car to the appropriate position in the world.
11:     D3DUtil_SetTranslateMatrix(world,0,10,-120);
12:     lpDevice->SetTransform(D3DTRANSFORMSTATE_WORLD,&world);
13:     lpXFileCar->Render(lpDevice);
14:     D3DUtil_SetIdentityMatrix(world);
15:     lpDevice->SetTransform(D3DTRANSFORMSTATE_WORLD,&world);
16:
17:   // . . .
18: }
19:
20: void CHelicopter::draw(LPDIRECT3DDEVICE7 dev,float delt)
21: {
22:
23:   // . . .
24:
25:   if (meshPtr) {
```

```
26:    world=calc_move(delt);
27:    lpDevice->SetTransform(D3DTRANSFORMSTATE_WORLD,&world);
28:    meshPtr->Render(lpDevice);
29:    D3DUtil_SetIdentityMatrix(world);
30:    lpDevice->SetTransform(D3DTRANSFORMSTATE_WORLD,&world);
31:    }
32:
33:    //  . . .
34: }
```

Cleaning Up

Cleanup is a breeze. You simply need to delete the CHelicopter object and the two
CD3DFile objects. Listing 15.19 shows the Cleanup() function used by the sample application.

LISTING **15.19**   The New Cleanup() Function

```
1: void Cleanup()
2: {
3:     // unload animated object classes
4:     SafeDelete(chopper);
5:
6:     // unload 3D models
7:     SafeDelete(lpXFileCar);
8:     SafeDelete(lpXFileHelo);
9:
10:    // de-allocate block objects
11:
12:    for (int i=0;i<NUM_ROWS;i++)
13:        for (int j=0;j<NUM_COLUMNS;j++)
14:            SafeDelete(cubes[i][j]);
15:
16:    // release 3D interfaces
17:
18:    SafeRelease(lpDevice);
19:    SafeRelease(lpD3D);
20:
21:    // release DirectDraw interfaces
22:
23:    SafeRelease(lpDDSPrimary);
24:    SafeRelease(lpDD);
25:
26:    // display error if one thrown
27:
28:    if (ErrStr) {
29:        MessageBox(NULL, ErrStr, szCaption, MB_OK);
30:        ErrStr=NULL;
31:    }
32: }
```

Summary

The Direct3D X file will finally allow you to easily import complex 3D objects into your application. In this hour, you have learned about the Direct3D X file structure, you have learned how to create Direct3D X files, and you have seen how to use them in your application. The Direct3D X file should allow you to easily enhance the look and feel of your Direct3D application in the future.

Q&A

Q Where can I find a full list of all the templates that Direct3D defines?

A The major templates you should know were all covered in this hour. However, if you need another reference or a complete list, the best place to look for it is in the DirectX 7 SDK documentation. In fact, you should familiarize yourself well with the DirectX 7 SDK documentation because it is a great starting point for most DirectX questions.

Q How do I convert a text-based X file into a binary-based X file?

A In addition to the CONV3DS utility, two other useful utilities are included with the DirectX 7 SDK. The first is called CONVX, and it can usually be found in the same directory as CONV3DS. CONVX will convert X files to and from binary or text format. The second utility, CONVXOF, will convert files from the XOF format to the Direct3D X file format. For more information, including a full list of options, simply run the two different executables from the MS-DOS command prompt.

Workshop

The Workshop is designed to help you anticipate possible questions, review what you've learned, and get you thinking about how to put your knowledge into practice. The answers to the quiz are in Appendix A, "Answers."

Quiz

1. What is the name of the "special" template that can contain application-specific information?

2. What are the three different types of template restrictions?

3. What utility can you use to convert 3D Studio files into the Direct3D X file format?

4. Which type of Direct3D X file format is better: text or binary?

5. What is the name of the template that is used to store vertices?

Exercises

1. Open the car.x and heli.x files included with the sample application. Notice their structure and format. Experiment with the files by making a few changes. Open the files with the Direct3D RM Viewer.

2. Adjust the size of the buildings and the car and the helicopter. Try adding a few large triangles to represent the ground in the scene. Try to create a new X file that models the ground and add it to the application.

Hour **16**

Modeling a Complex World—Applying Physics and Object Hierarchies

Hopefully, by now, you've given some thought to the possibility that although it might be neat to render or display 3D objects in a game, those objects must somehow interact and react in order to seem real to a player. You have to somehow develop a way for all the objects and the world that you'll create for a player to seem believable, and in a sense, realistic.

To accomplish this, it will be helpful for you to spend some time learning about a few concepts that go a little above just working with any DirectX API. It's time to work out some algorithms and code that don't deal directly with any DirectX interface, but that do allow you to model your 3D objects and space to provide a realistic feel to your user. We will use Direct3D to help put some of this object behavior onscreen.

In this hour, you will learn about modeling object interaction in 3D space. You will learn about kinematics and motion dynamics, as well as collision detection. You will also get an idea on how to model object "behavior," at least in terms of how objects react and affect each other in 3D space.

We'll also discuss object hierarchies, and how important it is to use this concept when developing your game. Object hierarchies will be important after you learn about matrices and how to apply transformations and rotation algorithms to many vertices of an object at once.

We'll cover a lot of ground in the next hour, so be prepared to visit this hour again. Unlike most of the other hours in this book, we'll cover many concepts and some hairy algorithms over and above using the DirectX API. Do not fear; we'll also get a chance to use some of Direct3D.

 It is important to note, at this point, that many of the algorithms you will learn in the next hour involve some basic calculus, mathematics, and linear algebra. If you are a bit rusty on those subjects, it might be helpful to dig out a calculus textbook to refresh yourself. It's not critical that you follow all the math involved in the following hour, as long as you follow the concepts and take a good look at the code involved.

Reactions and Effects: Defining Real-World Relationships

Isaac Newton's Third Law of Motion states, "For every action, there is an equal and opposite reaction." If we stick to some very basic rules in physics, such as this one, it might be helpful to our study of how objects should behave in a game. What Newton was talking about in this rule is that how an object interacts with other objects should cause some sort of reaction from those other objects. It might be a minimal reaction, or it might result in some very sophisticated calculations attempting to model real-world physics.

As video hardware progresses and lightens the processing burden of the CPU for rendering 3D animations, we will have more processing time to account for real-world physics. We're going to take a look at some of those physics in the next hour, but it will certainly behoove you to take a look at some math and physics textbooks to improve your knowledge of physics models. As you progress as a game programmer, you should be able to push yourself and increase the complexities at which your programs operate. As time goes on, the amount of real-world physics that 3D games incorporate will increase, and you'll have to increase your knowledge of those physics systems if you want your programs to be state-of-the-art. Our examples for this hour are simple, but you'll certainly want to take this lesson as a starting point.

At this point, it's also important to realize that what you'll learn during the rest of this hour involves dynamic motion. It is much simpler to describe objects in a 3D world if those objects are static; that is, they do not move or rotate. Of course, by moving our objects around in 3D space, as you'll soon learn how to do, we increase the overall complexity of our project. We now have to concern ourselves with complex systems that use linear algebra, calculus, and physics to give our objects very real properties and motion. It is the dynamic nature of these objects that increases the complexity of the project.

16

NEW TERM   In our 3D world, there are actually three different spaces, which represent the differences between the points of origin. Initially, when we create our object, we describe our object in 3D terms using an origin of (0, 0, 0). This is called *model space*, and means that everything at this point in time is assuming that the origin of 0 exists on some vertex of our object. After our object is defined, we'll have to transform all the vertices to *world space*, where the origin of (0, 0, 0) might not be at the same spot as our object's origin. Finally, when we are about to render our world, we must transform all our coordinates to *user space*, wherein the camera and user's view are different in origin than our world. All these transformations have to be calculated easily; luckily, Direct3D does this for us, as you'll learn in a little bit.

To make the dynamics of our object interaction more interesting for the user, it is necessary to assign some additional properties to our objects, besides just the sum of their vertices and any textures we use on their surfaces. We must be able to develop some solutions using algebra and calculus to model real-world physics, and those solutions will involve things such as mass and velocity. As we work out some of the algorithms we'll apply to the movements of our objects, we'll use those additional properties as parameters to help solve our equations. As you decide just how much physics you're going to apply to your dynamic objects, you'll need to define additional properties and assign them to those objects.

Motion Dynamics

NEW TERM   Motion dynamics refers to the physics of motion. Motion dynamics is comprised mainly of two different fields of study: kinematics and kinetics. You might have heard the term kinematics before and not really have been sure what it meant. *Kinematics* is, quite simply, the study of object motion without regard to the forces applied to those objects to create that motion. Put another way, it's the study of how objects move over time, without any regard to what will actually make them move.

NEW TERM   The flip side of our study of motion dynamics is *kinetics*, which is the study of forces at work on an object or body. Kinetics involves looking at how forces and torque work on various parts of an object to create motion. For now, we're not interested in studying forces, so we'll limit our study to the kinematics side of the equation.

Forward Kinematics

NEW TERM   If you visualize a human skeleton for a moment, you can see that it's actually made up of a hierarchy of joints, lines, and points. "The arm bone's connected to the elbow bone…" and so on. If we track where all the points in this hierarchical scheme may be at a given time, we are looking at *forward kinematics*, sometimes called *direct kinematics*. It is important to realize that forward kinematics takes into account the fact that when calculating an object's or point's location in space, we must also take into account all the other connected objects and their positions and orientations.

For example, if we move our skeleton's arm perpendicular to its body, move its lower arm straight into the air, and finally, bend the wrist and finger bones up, we now have (in our mind's eye) a skeleton standing and waving hello. All the calculations and movements we performed moved forward from the root of the object—the body—throughout the hierarchy of bones. It is important to realize that the moment we move the upper arm bone, we are also moving the elbow joint, lower arm bone, wrist joint, and hand bones along with it. That's forward kinematics. It's called forward kinematics because you start from a root object, and work *forward* throughout the hierarchy.

Pivot Points and Other Kinematics Features

NEW TERM   The study of kinematics involves looking at all the possible ways to change an object's orientation or position. The number of ways an object's orientation can be changed are called the *degrees of freedom*. Those degrees of freedom (DOF) are actually determined by the type of joint used between points. A simple, prismatic joint can be seen in the piston in Figure 16.1. This joint allows translational freedom in only one degree: linearly.

FIGURE 16.1

One degree of transla-tional freedom.

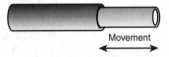

Movement

Another type of joint, called a revolute joint, also allows rotational movement in one direction. This type of joint can be seen in Figure 16.2. Most of the objects in our 3D world will have six degrees of freedom: three angular degrees and three linear degrees. An example of this is shown in Figure 16.3. By looking at this figure, you can see that a given object can move along three different axes, as well as rotate about those same axes.

FIGURE **16.2**
One degree of orbital freedom.

FIGURE **16.3**
Six degrees of freedom.

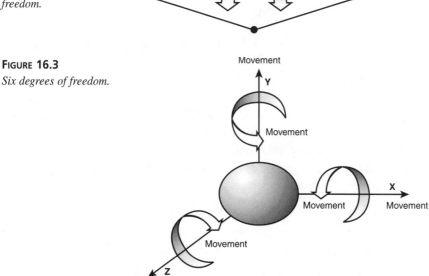

Obviously, the more degrees of freedom we have, the more complex our solution. Therefore, it is important to limit the degrees of freedom where possible—this will translate into fewer necessary calculations in your programs, and, consequently, fewer processing cycles.

NEW TERM Generally speaking, there are two types of solutions for solving for kinematics algorithms: closed form solutions and numerical solutions. *Closed form solutions* involve noniterative calculations, and can be computed rather quickly. Closed form solutions can typically be used if all the joints in a system are revolute or prismatic, and have six degrees of freedom. *Numerical solutions*, which involve iterative calculations, are more costly to compute, and must be used when your system is too complex to use closed form solutions.

An example of a numerical solution is a Euler integrator. This solution basically calculates the integral over some quantum of time for a vector. It's a general-purpose function that you can use to calculate a value over time. You would use something like a Euler integrator when no easy (or quick) closed form solution exists.

One other point to ponder here is whether we're looking at rigid-body or soft-body dynamics. A rigid body, as you might expect, refers to an object that does not change shape or structure. On the other hand, a soft body can change shape and, therefore, increase the complexity of our physics system. Until now, and for the rest of this hour, we've been referring to rigid-body dynamics. Because of the introductory nature of this book, and the limited time we have in this hour, we can't cover the extra solutions needed for soft-body dynamics. I'll leave that as an exercise for you to work on.

Inverse Kinematics

NEW TERM It will become necessary, during game play, to take one end part of our hierarchical skeleton and move it to a point in space—say, our skeleton's hand. This end point is often called the *end effector*. You must come up with a way to calculate all positions and orientations of the connected objects, all the way back through our object hierarchy to the root object. This is called *inverse kinematics*, and this term essentially describes the opposite of forward kinematics. Instead of taking a base part of an object hierarchy and working out to the leaf nodes of our hierarchical tree, we start at the leaf nodes and work back to the root object.

Object Hierarchies

As we talk about kinematics and its definition in terms of motion dynamics, we should look at how we define a system of related objects. In kinematics, at least, objects are usually connected to each other with joints. Therefore, a set of objects connected by using joints represents a larger, more complex object. Very often, that complex object is some sort of figure or machine, although it might not always be so.

NEW TERM What we must do is define objects in terms of frames. A *frame* is essentially an object, or part of an object, that can be transformed independent of other frames it might be connected to.

A frame, in our example, can be composed of meshes of vertices or other child frames. To apply forward kinematics, we apply a transform to a frame and all its child frames, recursively. To apply inverse kinematics, we start with a child frame or end effector, and apply a transformation to it, as well as to its parent frame (and the parent frame's other children), recursively.

These transformations are performed for one of two reasons. First, we might be trying to move an end effector to a new position (and orientation), and will need to move all the connected objects and joints back to the root of our object hierarchy. Alternatively, we might just be interested in moving one part of our object hierarchy, not at the end of the hierarchy, and will need to appropriately move all the connected objects.

NEW TERM As we solve for inverse kinematic motions, it might be useful to simulate *damping*, which is constraining the motion of root or parent objects. Damping is done so that in moving a child node to a point in space, we don't move just one node that is close to the root. In other words, when we calculate our transformations for each joint, we move a little at a time, from the root or parent on down to the child, so that the total movement seems more natural. Damping essentially means making more joints move to create a kinematic motion, instead of just the one or two joints closest to the root. The more damping we use, the more constrained each movement along the joint hierarchy will be.

16

Using Matrices to Combine Motions

So how do we apply transformations to any given vertex or vector? Because either type of value consists of a set of values (three in Direct 3D, to be precise), we will use matrices and the matrix math we learned about in Hour 10, "Introduction to 3D Concepts." As you might recall from that hour, a number of helper functions are available to help us with matrix math. Two additional helper functions are also available to perform the functions you will learn about in just a minute: `DotProduct()` and `CrossProduct()`.

Before we expand our working knowledge of matrices and matrix algebra, and how to use it on our rigid-body system, we must first clear up one thing. There are, essentially, two systems used to describe 3D graphics: left-handed and right-handed. These two systems are shown in Figure 16.4. The arrows in Figure 16.4 indicate positive values; so, in considering the right-handed coordinate system, you can see that positive z-values appear to go *into* the computer screen, which seems intuitive. We're going to use this system because it makes sense to do so. Keep in mind that some graphics books might use either system, and often use the left-handed system, in fact. It is also important to remember when each system is used because when transforming points for the viewpoint actually uses the left-handed notation, that fact will have to be taken into account.

FIGURE **16.4**

Left-handed versus right-handed axes.

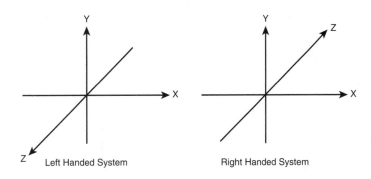

Left Handed System   Right Handed System

Another important consideration to keep in mind is that positive rotations about any axis are counterclockwise. Conversely, negative rotations about an axis are clockwise. We can see what this looks like in Figure 16.5.

FIGURE 16.5

Positive rotation in a right-handed system.

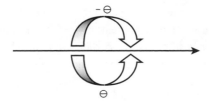

In terms of 3D, you've normally defined things in terms of points and vectors. Let's take just a minute to make sure you understand the exact definitions of these two concepts:

- *Points* represent a position in space using a set of x, y, and z values.
- *Vectors* represent direction and length, and are actually the difference between two points. They are also usually represented as a set of x, y, and z values.

The Direct3D interface supports vectors (of course), and represents them with the D3DVECTOR structure. This structure is very simple, as you might remember:

```
typedef struct _D3DVECTOR {
    union {
        D3DVALUE x;
        D3DVALUE dvX;
    };
    union {
        D3DVALUE y;
        D3DVALUE dvY;
    };
    union {
        D3DVALUE z;
        D3DVALUE dvZ;
    };
} D3DVECTOR, *LPD3DVECTOR;
```

It is important to note that D3DVECTOR structures can be used to represent either points or vectors, as you can tell from the unioned members.

Let's take a look at some basic vector equations that will be important later in this hour. First, vector addition and subtraction are very straightforward. Adding two vectors, v and u, looks like this:

$$u + v = [(u_x + v_x) \ (u_y + v_y) \ (y_z + v_z)]$$

Subtracting two vectors, as you might suspect, is also very straightforward:

$$u - v = [(u_x - v_x)\ (u_y - v_y)\ (u_z - v_z)]$$

NEW TERM | There are two types of vector equations that might seem strange at first. These equations are the dot product and the cross product, which is sometimes called the *vector product*. A *dot product* is an operation on two unit vectors that produces a value that represents the relationship of those two vectors. That relationship is actually the cosine of the angle between the two vectors. A dot product is written using a little dot symbol, and shouldn't be confused with multiplication, which is usually written with either no symbol or a small x, but never with a dot. A dot product can be written as

$$u{\bullet}v = u_x v_x + u_y v_y + u_z v_z$$

In simple terms, the dot product is the sum of the x's product, the y's product, and the z's product of the two vectors. Some additional properties of the dot product are

$$u{\bullet}0 = 0$$

$$u{\bullet}v = v{\bullet}u$$

The cross product looks like a strange function at first, but it is useful. The cross product can be written as

$$uXv = [\ u_y v_z {-} u_z v_y\ \ u_z v_x {-} u_x v_z\ \ u_x v_y {-} u_y v_x\ ]$$

Although this might seem trivial, here are the functions to calculate these two algorithms:

```
double dDotProduct(D3DVECTOR *u, D3DVECTOR *v)
{
    return ((u->x * v->x) + (u->y * v->y) + (u->z * v->z));
}

void CrossProduct(D3DVECTOR *v, D3DVECTOR *v, D3DVECTOR *result)
{
    result->x = (u->y * v->z) - (u->z * v->y);
    result->y = (u->z * v->x) - (u->x * v->z);
    result->z = (u->x * v->y) - (u->y * v->x);
}
```

For now, just get a good grip on how to calculate these two functions. We'll use them shortly as part of our collision detection geometry, as well as in our physics.

There are three conventional ways to represent rotations of an object around axes: matrices, quaternions, and Euler angles. These are summarized as follows:

- Matrices use a set of rows and columns to represent rotations or translations of an object.

- Quaternions normally use a notation such as [w, v], where w is a scalar, and v = (x, y, z). The x, y, and z values represent a vector. The scalar value represents the angle of rotation around the object's central axis.

- Euler angles normally use a notation such as (θ, χ, ϕ), where θ is the rotation (in degrees) about the x-axis, χ is the rotation about the y-axis, and ϕ is the rotation about the z-axis.

We'll discuss how to use matrices and the matrix math you learned in Hour 10 for the rest of this hour. This type of representation is the easiest to understand, and should be enough to get you started. You should be able to find a lot of material in recent books and magazines that discusses performing some of the same algorithms you will learn shortly, but with other systems, such as quaternions. Many of the basic equations you'll learn are the same from representation to representation, and basically the only difference is in how you compute those equations. It is important to note that Direct3D uses quaternions to represent rotation in some of its methods, so it might be helpful to take a look at quaternions at some later date. I'll leave this as an exercise for later.

> If you follow the exercise suggestions at the end of this chapter and try to delve into other computer graphics books or math texts, you will find many conventions for naming things. It might be helpful to try to follow and learn the different ways that notions in physics and dynamics are denoted—it will make things easier to follow. I'll try to explain some of the popular conventions used for the rest of the hour. Just try to spend a minute or two making sure you understand what those conventions are.

NEW TERM   One last important point you should be aware of is what is called a normal. A *normal* to a plane is a line perpendicular to that plane. A normal can be calculated by computing the cross product of three points in that plane. Given three points— A, B, and C—you can calculate the normal to the plane that those three points represent.

N = AB X BC.

If the cross product is 0, the points are collinear, and don't, in fact, define a plane.

Object Interaction

Objects react to each other, and these reactions can be as discrete and finite as having gravitational (or even magnetic) pull, or as simple as following some simple physics rules for when they collide. The complexity at which we consider these reactions will determine how realistic our game will be. The more physical properties of reactions we simulate in our game, the more calculations must be performed. This can have a direct impact on the speed at which our game appears to play. If we take into consideration all the physics involved as objects interact with each other, such as friction, angular momentum, gravity, and so on, we'll probably spend too much time processing all that information. You must find a balance.

Devising algorithms and functions for these physics is an area of great interest in the academic world, and a very hot area in the game development community. For obvious reasons, researchers are always investigating new ways to determine the physical nature and functions of force and movement. Also for obvious reasons, game developers are interested in devising ways to implement those models and observations in games.

What you will find, however, is that there isn't much to go on for existing models, at least in a practical sense, for modeling physics in your game. At the very least, you can probably model such simple physics as gravity and friction. What makes object interaction tougher for you as a programmer is deciding where the balance is, and applying some of the math involved. Let's take a look at some of the basics of object interaction.

Collision Detection

NEW TERM   *Collision detection* simply means detecting when a coordinate of any point on one of two objects is the same as any point on the other. In other words, it is the detection of when two objects actually touch.

Your first thought might be that this will be a monumental task if we must calculate all the points for a given object with all the points of any other object. This, of course, won't be useful because it is computationally too expensive. Instead, we'll perform all our collision detection in two steps.

In our first step, we'll use what's called a *bounding box* to get an easy-to-compute idea of whether our objects even have a chance to collide. To do this, we calculate an imaginary box around our object, and use some simple math to determine whether we have an intersection with any other box. An example of a bounding box can be seen in Figure 16.6.

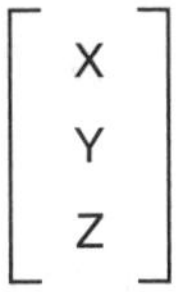

FIGURE **16.6**
The box bounding an object.

$$\begin{bmatrix} X \\ Y \\ Z \end{bmatrix}$$

What happens as we rotate our object around different axes? Well, if we simply calculate our bounding box as a box that surrounds the maximum and minimum x, y, and z values for an object, we end up with Figure 16.7. This type of bounding box is called an *axis-aligned bounding box* (AABB). This means our box expands and shrinks as our object rotates, and is always aligned with the world axis. Besides, we'll always have to calculate our bounding box after any rotation of our object.

FIGURE 16.7

An axis aligned bounding box.

$$\begin{bmatrix} X_X & X_Y & X_Z & X_H \\ Y_X & Y_Y & Y_Z & Y_H \\ Z_X & Z_Y & Z_Z & Z_H \\ H_X & H_Y & H_Z & H_H \end{bmatrix}$$

There is a better way to calculate our bounding box, called an *oriented bounding box* (OBB). An OBB is a bounding box that we calculated first in object space before any rotation. Any time we change our object's orientation by rotation, we also change the OBB's rotation. An example of an OBB that has been rotated to match an object can be seen in Figure 16.8.

FIGURE 16.8

An oriented bounding box.

$$L = \sqrt{(V \cdot V)}$$

So, to see whether two bounding boxes are touching or are intersecting at some point, we could simply use

```
BOOL BoxesTouch(D3DRMBOX *box1, D3DRMBOX *box2)
{
    BOOL fHaveTouched = FALSE;
    if ( ((box1->min.x <= box2.max.y) &&
          (box1->min.y <= box2.max.y) &&
          (box1->min.z <= box2->max.z)) ||
         ((box1->max.x >= box2->min.x) &&
          (box1->max.y >= box2->min.y) &&
          (box1->max.z >= box2->min.z)))
    fHaveTouched = TRUE;
    return fHaveTouched;
}
```

Of course, this only tells us whether our bounding boxes have touched. The reason we're using bounding boxes, however, is because it's relatively quick to test for the *likelihood* that two objects have touched. Also, we can even eliminate checking for collisions unless there's at least a possibility that two objects have collided.

What we could do now, of course, is test for an actual collision. As it turns out, there's a simple rule to follow that makes this fairly easy: Two objects are not touching if a plane separates them that neither object touches. So, to find that plane, we start by examining all the faces of one of the objects. Each face, of course, exists in a plane. We simply examine all the faces of one of our objects, and inspect each vertex, or even just the closest vertex, of the possibly colliding object and see whether that vertex touched the plane.

After we've iterated through all the faces and haven't found a separating plane, we have to look at all the edges in that object. If we combine an edge of one object with a vertex of another object, we have a possible separating plane that we must look at. When we've examined all the faces and edge-vertex combinations and can't find a separating plane, we have found a collision.

At any point in this testing, if we find a plane in which all the vertices of the colliding object are on the far side of the colliding plane (or derived plane), we're done and we don't have a collision.

So how do we find out whether all the vertices are on the far side of a (possibly) separating plane? Well, we have to find a normal to the plane first, and we can do that by calculating the cross product of two vertices on the plane.

NEW TERM   An alternative to calculating a box that surrounds your object, and keeping it object oriented, is to use collision spheres. *Collision spheres* work in essentially the same way as bounding boxes, except that you simply calculate and track the center point of each object and a radius. If the distance between the centers of two objects is less than the sum of the radii of those two objects, the bounding spheres encapsulating both objects have collided. You can then continue on as before, by trying to find the exact point (or face or edge) at which the objects collided. This method has the advantage of being slightly faster, in that you have to track only the center point of an object as it moves (or changes direction) in world space. The radius of the sphere doesn't change as the object moves because it is simply a scalar value representing length.

Object Reactions

After objects collide, it might be helpful to present some sort of simple reaction, such as a visual animation or a sound to indicate simple touching. This can be taken one step farther, to actually modeling a physical collision with forces and such.

Sound is covered in another hour, so we won't go into the obvious here. However, it would be interesting to look at how to model a simple reflection or deflection of two objects.

First, let's examine what happens when an object collides with an immovable plane. To make sure we have two bodies actually colliding (versus going away from each other), we take the dot product of the colliding object's velocity vector with the normal to the collision plane of the collide object. Take a look at Figure 16.9 to see what our collision looks like. Given this diagram, our dot product is V•N.

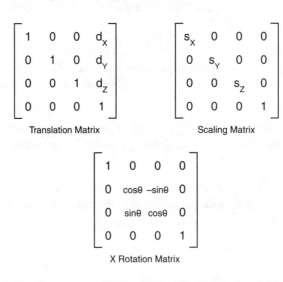

If this dot product value is less than zero, the two bodies are indeed in the act of colliding, and we must create a reaction vector. To do that, we create two more vectors: the motion parallel and the tangential to the normal of collision. The new vector, V', can be solved for by

$V_n = (N \cdot V)N$

$V_t = V - V_n$

$V' = V_t - K_r V_n$

The normal of collision is actually the normal to the plane. K_r represents the coefficient of restitution. By setting K_r to 1, you cause a deflection of an object off another object that results in no loss of force. A value of 0 causes a total loss of force, and the colliding object simply loses all momentum and appears to stick to the plane.

NEW TERM   The *coefficient of restitution* is the amount of force dissipated in a collision. It can be imagined as the elasticity of the collision.

Now that we know what happens when an object collides with an immovable plane, let's take a look at what happens when two objects, each with its own mass and force, collide with each other. In Figure 16.10, we can see two objects colliding at some point P.

FIGURE 16.10

Two objects colliding.

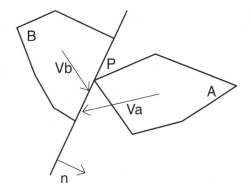

The tricky part is that to model our collision perfectly, we would have to consider the fact that the two objects would take some time to actually collide. In our simple scenario, however, we don't want to deal with computing a collision over some very small quantum of time; we would like to calculate the resulting vectors for the objects immediately at the point of contact. The resulting force from such an impact is called the *impulse*, from Newton's Law of Restitution for Instantaneous Collision with No Friction, and implies that we are calculating an instantaneous collision. A few of the algorithms from that theorem are in Figure 16.11.

FIGURE 16.11

Algorithms for instantaneous collision.

$$V_2^A = V_1^A + \frac{j}{M^A}\,n$$

$$V_2^B = V_1^B - \frac{j}{M^B}\,n$$

$$j = \frac{-(1+e)\,v_1^{AB} \cdot n}{n \cdot n \left(\frac{1}{M^A} + \frac{1}{M^B} \right)}$$

We're concerned with solving for the resulting vectors for each object, V_2^A and V_2^B. After we've obtained the impulse and solved for both the resulting vectors, we've successfully bounced our objects off each other. Of course, these algorithms do not take into account other forces, such as friction, as stated in the earlier discussion.

Adding Collision Detection to Our Application

Let's take a look at some basic functions over the next few minutes, which will provide the basis for our simplified model of real-world physics. Remember that we are, of course, approximating only *some* of the physics involved in object interaction. We're only looking toward simple object-to-object collision detection and reaction, and we are using only one force acting on an object: gravity.

Let's start by creating an object that will hold our mass, momentum, current velocity, and current angle. This class will also provide a few helper functions to make collision detection and reaction easy. The interface for this basic object class looks like this:

```
class CObj
{
public:
    CObj* next;
    float oneOverM;
    CBSphereCollection boundSphereColl;
    CObj();
    virtual ~CObj();
    virtual void set_pitch(float val);
    virtual void set_steer(float val);
    virtual void set_lift(float val);
    virtual D3DMATRIX calc_move(float delt);
    virtual void calc_forces();
    virtual BOOL find_collisions();
    virtual int check_for_collisions(CObj &target);
    virtual void react(CObj &target);

    D3DVECTOR cur_ang;        // current rotational angle
    D3DVECTOR vel_ang;        // velocity of rotation

    D3DVECTOR cur_pos;        // current position
    D3DVECTOR vel_pos;        // current velocity

    float lift;
    float pitch;
    float steer;
};
```

We'll create two objects for testing purposes, CHelicopter and CScene, both of which derive from our CObj. The helicopter represents a flying helicopter in a virtual city, and the CScene object represents the visual viewport of the user, who is free to move about the world. Both classes override the virtual calc_move() function because each object moves in a slightly different way.

The vertex definition of our main object, a helicopter, is stored in the Direct3D .x file format. Our helicopter is actually made up of several smaller objects (rotors, cockpit, and so on), each of which is defined as a vertex mesh. We will use some of the code from the DirectX 7 SDK to load our .x file, and to enumerate through the vertex mesh. You can find a copy of the utility code (written by Microsoft) in the D3DIM directory, as well as in the sample code for this hour.

The sample code, which will suit our purpose for now, defines two C++ classes: CD3DFile and CD3DFileObject. CD3DFile contains functions for loading .x files and for parsing them. It also contains the function EnumObjects(). This function, to which we provide a callback function (like most of DirectX's enum functions), enables us to iterate through the object hierarchy.

Defining Object Bounds

We also want a collision sphere–type object to use when we're calculating collision detection and reaction. The collision sphere simply holds the center and radius for a particular object.

```
class CBoundingSphere
{
public:
    CBoundingSphere* last;
    void transform_center(D3DVECTOR &pos);
    void SetSphere(D3DVECTOR &cent, float rad);
    float radius;
    D3DVECTOR center;
    CBoundingSphere();
    CBoundingSphere(D3DVECTOR &cent, float rad);
    virtual ~CBoundingSphere();
    CBoundingSphere*    next;
};
```

As well, let's create a collection of collision spheres (CBoundingSphere objects). We'll create the collection when we initially create an object, and use it to define, fairly narrowly, whether an object really is colliding. For obvious reasons, just using a root object around our entire object isn't very accurate, so we'll create spheres around our child objects as well.

```
class CBSphereCollection
{
public:
    void transform_centers(D3DVECTOR &pos);
    void AddSphere(D3DVECTOR &center, float radius);
    void BuildCollection(CD3DFile *lpMesh);
    CBoundingSphere rootSphere;
    int numSpheres;
    CBSphereCollection();
    virtual ~CBSphereCollection();
protected:
    static BOOL CalcFileObjBoundingSphere(CD3DFileObject* pObject,
                          D3DMATRIX* pmat,
                          VOID* pContext);
};
```

We provide such a callback function to the file object representing our object, lpMesh.
BuildCollection() is called with this object, and it, in turn, calls EnumObjects(),
which allows us to look at all the vertices of a particular subobject and calculate our
bounding spheres. We will track a sphere encompassing our entire object hierarchy, and
store that as a root sphere. We'll also then add a sphere for each triangle in our object
hierarchy. Let's look at that callback function:

```
BOOL CBSphereCollection::CalcFileObjBoundingSphere( CD3DFileObject* pObject,
                          D3DMATRIX* pmat,
                          VOID* pContext )
{
    CBSphereCollection *cbscol = (CBSphereCollection*)pContext;

    D3DVECTOR    center;
    FLOAT        radius;

    D3DVERTEX* pVertices;
    DWORD      dwNumVertices;

    if( SUCCEEDED( pObject->GetMeshGeometry( &pVertices, &dwNumVertices,
                                    NULL, NULL ) ) )
    {
        if (dwNumVertices == 0)
        {
            // return without processing objects without meshes
            return FALSE;
        }
        FLOAT cx= 0.0f;
        FLOAT cy= 0.0f;
        FLOAT cz= 0.0f;
        for( DWORD i=0; i<dwNumVertices; i++ )
        {
            FLOAT x = pVertices[i].x;
            FLOAT y = pVertices[i].y;
```

```
            FLOAT z = pVertices[i].z;


            // Center
            cx += x*pmat->_11 + y*pmat->_21 + z*pmat->_31 + pmat->_41;
            cy += x*pmat->_12 + y*pmat->_22 + z*pmat->_32 + pmat->_42;
            cz += x*pmat->_13 + y*pmat->_23 + z*pmat->_33 + pmat->_43;



        }
        // Calculate the center
        center.x = cx / (FLOAT) dwNumVertices;
        center.y = cy / (FLOAT) dwNumVertices;
        center.z = cz / (FLOAT) dwNumVertices;
        for( i=0; i<dwNumVertices; i++ )
        {
            FLOAT x = pVertices[i].x;
            FLOAT y = pVertices[i].y;
            FLOAT z = pVertices[i].z;


            // Radius
    FLOAT mx=(x*pmat->_11 + y*pmat->_21 + z*pmat->_31 + pmat->_41) - center.x;
    FLOAT my=(x*pmat->_12 + y*pmat->_22 + z*pmat->_32 + pmat->_42) - center.y;
    FLOAT mz=(x*pmat->_13 + y*pmat->_23 + z*pmat->_33 + pmat->_43) - center.z;

            // Store the largest r (radius) for any point in the mesh
            // as our root sphere
            radius = sqrtf( mx*mx + my*my + mz*mz );
            if( radius > cbscol->rootSphere.radius)
                cbscol->rootSphere.radius = radius;
        }

    }

    cbscol->AddSphere(center, radius);


    // Keep enumerating file objects
    return FALSE;
}
```

While calculating the movement for each object, we'll also be calculating the downward force of gravity, if the global flag g_UseGravity is set to TRUE. To our basic CObj, we'll add a helper function, calc_forces(), which we'll use to calculate any external forces on an object, aside from its own velocity. For now, it's just gravity, so

```
void CObj::calc_forces()
{
```

```
    // if we're using gravity in our world,
    // calculate its effects based on our mass
    if (g_UseGravity && oneOverM != 0)
    {
        vel_pos.x += (g_Gravity.x / oneOverM);
        vel_pos.y += (g_Gravity.y / oneOverM);
        vel_pos.z += (g_Gravity.z / oneOverM);
    }
}
```

Testing for Collisions

As time elapses in the game, each object within our game will have its calc_move()
function called. This function will then, in turn, call calc_forces(), and move the entire
object based on its current velocity. After we move the object, we can simply perform a
check, on an object-by-object basis, to see whether we've hit or bumped anything:

```
int CBSphereCollection::touches(CBSphereCollection &sphereCollection)
{
    // first, check the other object's root sphere against ours...
    D3DVECTOR distance;
    distance = sphereCollection.rootSphere.center - rootSphere.center;
    if (Magnitude(distance) >
                (sphereCollection.rootSphere.radius + rootSphere.radius))
    {
        // there's no chance for collision, bounding spheres don't touch
        return 0;
    }   // ok, let's iterate through each collection..

    CBoundingSphere *mine = rootSphere.next;
    CBoundingSphere *theirs = sphereCollection.rootSphere.next;
    for (;mine;mine=mine->next)
    {
        for (;theirs;theirs=theirs->next)
        {
            if (mine->touches(theirs))
            {
                // we've touched
                return 1;
            }
        }
    }
    return 0;

}
```

Our touches() function for the individual sphere looks much the same:

```
BOOL CBoundingSphere::touches(CBoundingSphere *other)
{
```

```
D3DVECTOR distance;
distance = other->center - center;
if (Magnitude(distance) <= (other->radius + radius))
{
    // there's no chance for collision, bounding spheres don't touch
    return TRUE;
}
return FALSE;
}
```

We return an int from the first function instead of a BOOL because we might later want to provide more information about how the objects are colliding. The latter function just tells us whether two individual spheres are colliding. We quit from the first function as soon as we get a collision, and at that point, we'll have to decide how to react.

Animating Reaction Vectors

Collision reaction can be quite complicated and mathematically intensive. If you're implementing a flight simulator for testing operational flight programs or for accident investigation, then you should dig deep into vector mechanics. Fortunately, games can be more forgiving, that is, it is okay to fake it. Here's a simple example of that:

```
void CPObject::ResolveCollision( CPObject &other, CPPlane &plane)
{
    float           VdotN;
    D3DVECTOR       Vn,Vt;
    // Solve for Vn
    VdotN = D3DRMVectorDotProduct( &plane.vNormal, &other.vVelocity);
    D3DRMVectorScale( &plane.vNormal, VdotN, &Vn);
    // Solve for Vt
    D3DRMVectorSubtract(&other->vVelocity, Vn, &Vt);
    // Scale Vn by Elasticity Coefficient
    D3DRMVectorScale(&Vn, &Vn, fKr);  // fKr is our coefficient of restitution
    // Calculate Vt - KtVn
    D3DRMVectorSubtract(vVelocity, &Vt, &Vn);
}
```

Note that although we have our own functions for calculating the vector arithmetic, we use the Direct3D helper functions. There are actually quite a number of helper functions to support vector arithmetic.

We're performing a very simple reflection collision here. We can vary the amount of force absorbed in the collision by varying our fKr variable, but that won't go far in modeling real-world physics.

Summary

In this hour, you learned about object hierarchies and how to use matrices, combined with those hierarchies, to apply object transformations to complex objects. You learned about kinematics and inverse kinematics, and how to calculate object orientations by using simple algorithms.

You also learned about collision detection and reaction, and how to model physical behaviors on objects while considering forces and dynamics. Armed with this knowledge, you are able to apply a physical model to your game world to simulate real-world physics.

Q&A

Q You said that having fewer than six degrees of freedom can decrease the number of calculations that must be performed. Won't I always want six degrees of freedom?

A For some of the objects you are modeling, perhaps. Some objects may have much less. Consider a person walking on the ground. If that person never gains the ability to fly, he will never have any translation freedom on the y-axis; therefore, he will have fewer than six degrees, for sure.

Q When performing tests for object collision, is it necessary to test all objects against each other?

A Not necessarily. Although I didn't cover it (there are only so many minutes in an hour), you can actually perform some additional calculations on your objects after every quantum of movement that will help narrow your search. Keeping track of the distances between objects will perhaps help you narrow it down, although you might have to perform some square roots, which might be costly. Investigate the many possible algorithms for collision detection, many of which use space partitioning.

Q Do I really have to use all the physics calculations discussed today? There seems to be an awful lot of calculations involved. Doesn't Direct3D take care of any of the details?

A Of course you don't have to use all the physics calculations we discussed. You only have to provide those physics and solutions to model more than just basic object movement. Direct3D provides many nonmember functions to help you calculate most of the matrix math. This will allow you to at least move and scale your objects. You'll have to use the trigonometry and calculus functions to model real-world behaviors only when your game design requires it.

Workshop

The Workshop is designed to help you anticipate possible questions, review what you've learned, and begin thinking ahead to put your knowledge into practice. The answers to the quiz are in Appendix A, "Answers."

Quiz

1. Given that vector **a** = [7 3 9] and vector **b** = [8 2 4], calculate the dot product and cross product for the two vectors.

2. What are the difference between kinematics, kinetics, and inverse kinematics?

3. What is the difference between an AABB and an OBB?

Exercises

1. Take a look at the SIGGRAPH proceedings; they deal with computer graphics and animations and are very informative. You might also want to check out some books on physics, geometry, and calculus to brush up or improve your knowledge of the math involved in modeling 3D animations.

2. Take a look at quaternions, and try to apply the physics and math you've just learned using them. Rewrite some of the functions provided here to use quaternions instead of the matrices we've used.

3. The sample code doesn't provide true collision detection; it stops just short by using collision spheres. Add the code necessary to find the faces (planes) of each object, and implement the algorithm described earlier in the hour.

16

HOUR 17

Introducing DirectInput—Getting User Input

DirectInput is the component of DirectX that is used to read input devices such as the keyboard, the mouse, joysticks, and flight yokes. Unlike the message-based approach to handling the keyboard and mouse in traditional Win32 programming, DirectInput provides a high-performance means of obtaining input from the keyboard and mouse, which results in much better response. Additionally, DirectInput is extensible enough to support very advanced input devices such as flight yokes and joysticks with multiple axes.

DirectInput is structured as a suite of COM objects, which is similar to other parts of DirectX that you've already learned about. This hour introduces you to DirectInput and shows you how to put it to work handling user input from the keyboard, the mouse, and joysticks.

In this hour, you will learn

- What DirectInput has to offer
- About the main objects used in DirectInput
- How to set up DirectInput to read from input devices
- How to read user input from the keyboard
- How to read user input from the mouse
- How to read user input from joysticks

DirectInput Basics

Prior to DirectX, all user input in Windows was retrieved via the Win32 API. Although Win32 offers full support for reading input from the keyboard and mouse, and limited support for joysticks, it proved to be less than adequate for the high-performance input needs of gaming. Let's face it, even a slight lag between moving the joystick left and your character in a game actually moving left could be the difference between life and death. Microsoft saw the need to provide a low-latency alternative to user input with DirectX to go along with the high-performance graphics, sound, and networking features they had already developed.

DirectInput was created for precisely this purpose: to provide a means of obtaining user input from devices with an extremely low latency. Just in case you've forgotten what latency means, in this case it refers to the delay between interacting with an input device (moving the joystick left) and the game responding to the interaction (moving your character left). Obviously, a lower latency results in games feeling much more responsive, which is critical in a time where gamers have come to expect hair-trigger responsiveness in games.

In case you're curious about how DirectInput can offer significantly increased performance over the Win32 approach to user input, let me assure you that nothing magical is involved. DirectInput simply skirts the layered approach of the Win32 API and communicates directly with input device drivers.

DirectInput isn't all about responsiveness, however. Another shortcoming of the Win32 API is that it has limited support for joysticks and no support for more advanced input devices such as flight yokes, steering wheels, joysticks with more than two axes, or force-feedback joysticks. DirectInput addresses this shortcoming by offering an extensible interface that is designed to support advanced input devices currently available, along with those that have yet to be dreamed up. So, when you finish building that virtual reality Twister mat in your garage, you can rest easy knowing that game programmers will be able to support it via DirectInput.

Inside DirectInput

I mentioned in the introduction to this lesson that DirectInput is structured as a set of COM objects, which by now should come as no surprise to you. Following are the COM objects that comprise DirectInput:

- DirectInput
- DirectInputDevice
- DirectInputEffect

The DirectInput object is at the heart of DirectInput and serves as the primary interface to DirectInput. More importantly, the DirectInput object acts as an input device manager that enables you to enumerate and access devices for use with DirectInput. Speaking of input devices, the DirectInputDevice object represents an input device within DirectInput. So, if a user with a couple of extra arms is playing a game that uses the keyboard, the mouse, a joystick, and a steering wheel, four DirectInputDevice objects would be at work behind the scenes.

NEW TERM   The last DirectInput object is DirectInputEffect, which represents a force-feedback effect on an input device that supports force feedback. *Force feedback* is a tactile response to something in a game that typically involves a set of motors mounted inside a special joystick. An example of a force feedback effect is a jarring blow from an opponent in a fighting game, which involves the joystick shaking as you receive the hit. Another example is the tightening of steering in a force-feedback steering wheel as you round a corner in a driving game. Microsoft's SideWinder Force Feedback Pro joystick was one of the first joysticks to support force feedback. You learn about this and other force-feedback input devices in the next hour.

Because force feedback is a specialized and somewhat complex user input topic, I wanted to give it an hour of its own. So, you learn about force feedback in the next hour. The remainder of this hour is devoted to using DirectInput to handle input from the keyboard, mouse, and traditional joysticks.

17

The DirectInput Object

The DirectInput object forms the basis of DirectInput and provides a means of detecting and accessing available input devices. You will typically create a DirectInput object and then use it to create DirectInputDevice objects. Most of the real work of using DirectInput involves the DirectInputDevice object, which you learn about in a moment. However, you must first go through the DirectInput object because it is responsible for managing input devices.

You create a DirectInput object by calling the global `DirectInputCreate()` function, which returns a pointer to an `IDirectInput` interface:

```
HRESULT WINAPI DirectInputCreate(HINSTANCE hinst, DWORD dwVersion,
  LPDIRECTINPUT* lplpDirectInput, LPUNKNOWN punkOuter);
```

The first parameter to `DirectInputCreate()`, `hInst`, is an instance handle for the application or DLL that is creating the DirectInput object. The second parameter, `dwVersion`, is the desired version number for DirectInput, which assists in backward compatibility. You will typically pass `DIRECTINPUT_VERSION` as this parameter, as opposed to a specific version number. The third parameter, `lplpDirectInput`, is a pointer to a DirectInput object pointer. This parameter is set to the DirectInput object pointer after successful creation and serves as the basis for performing future DirectInput operations, such as enumerating and creating input devices. The final parameter to `DirectInputCreate()` is `pUnkOuter`, which might be used to support COM aggregation, but is typically set to `NULL`. If the DirectInput object is successfully created, `DirectInputCreate()` will return `DI_OK`.

After successfully creating a DirectInput object, you can start accessing input devices. DirectInput objects are manipulated through the `IDirectInput` COM interface. The `IDirectInput` interface methods are used to get and set DirectInput object attributes, as well as to create DirectInputDevice objects. Following are some of the more commonly used methods in the `IDirectInput` interface, some of which you will use later in the lesson when you put DirectInput to work in a real application:

- `Initialize()`
- `CreateDevice()`
- `EnumDevices()`
- `GetDeviceStatus()`
- `RunControlPanel()`
- `Release()`

The `Initialize()` method is called to initialize a DirectInput object. You will probably never need to call this method directly because it is called by the `DirectInputCreate()` function when you first create a DirectInput object.

Perhaps the most commonly used method in the `IDirectInput` interface is `CreateDevice()`, which is called to create a DirectInputDevice object based on an attached physical input device. Although it is generally safe to assume that all users have a keyboard and mouse, it isn't a good idea to make the same assumption regarding joysticks and other types of optional input devices. For this reason, you can't just call `CreateDevice()` to create joystick device objects as you do keyboard and mouse devices objects. Instead, you must first call `EnumDevices()` to determine which devices are attached to the system. When you know what optional devices are available, if any, you then create DirectInputDevice objects for them using `CreateDevice()`.

NEW TERM An *attached device* is a device that is installed and physically connected to the system.

> Keep in mind that it is possible for a user to have multiple joysticks or none at all. Also, understand that I'm using the term "joystick" loosely in this discussion. You will use the same enumeration approach to find all input devices beyond the standard keyboard and mouse, including joysticks, steering wheels, flight yokes, and so on.

You might want to query for a specific input device at some point in a game or multimedia application. You can call the `GetDeviceStatus()` method to determine whether a specific device is attached to the system. You might also want to give the user the option to modify the control panel settings for a device, or possibly even install new devices. The `RunControlPanel()` method runs the Windows Control Panel, which allows the user to alter configuration settings for input devices or install new devices.

The last method mentioned in the `IDirectInput` interface is `Release()`. I hope you have a hunch as to the purpose of this method. Give up? OK, the `Release()` method is called to release the DirectInput object. This is an important cleanup operation you must perform when you're finished using DirectInput. You'll also want to unacquire and release any devices that you've created using the DirectInput object. You learn about the methods used to do this in the next section.

The DirectInputDevice Object

The DirectInputDevice object represents a physical input device that is attached to the system. You create DirectInputDevice objects by calling the `CreateDevice()` method on a DirectInput object. DirectInputDevice objects adhere to the IDirectInputDevice COM interface, which contains a host of methods for manipulating input devices. Following are the most commonly used methods in the IDirectInputDevice interface:

- `Initialize()`
- `SetDataFormat()`
- `SetCooperativeLevel()`
- `Acquire()`
- `GetDeviceState()`
- `GetDeviceData()`
- `GetCapabilities()`
- `GetProperty()`
- `SetProperty()`
- `SetEventNotification()`
- `Unacquire()`
- `Release()`

The `Initialize()` method is called to initialize a DirectInputDevice object. Similar to its counterpart in the `IDirectInput` interface, this method is rarely called directly because it is called by the `CreateDevice()` method when you first create a DirectInputDevice object.

After creating a DirectInputDevice object, the next step is to set its data format, which is accomplished with a call to the `SetDataFormat()` method. An application can establish a custom data format, or it can use one of the standard DirectInput device data formats: `c_dfDIKeyboard`, `c_dfDIMouse`, `c_dfDIJoystick`, or `c_dfDIJoystick2`. With the data format established, you then set the behavior of the device by calling `SetCooperativeLevel()`. `SetCooperativeLevel()` determines to what degree an application allows an input device to be shared with other applications.

The last step in preparing a DirectInputDevice to receive data is acquiring the device by calling the `Acquire()` method. After a device is acquired, you can call the `GetDeviceState()` and `GetDeviceData()` methods to get information about how the user has interacted with the device. Which method you use is determined by whether you want the input to be buffered or unbuffered. You learn more about these two approaches to input when you learn about handling keyboard input later in the hour.

You can retrieve the capabilities of an input device by calling the `GetCapabilities()` method. You can also get and set individual device properties by calling the `GetProperty()` and `SetProperty()` methods, respectively. Another interesting method is `SetEventNotification()`, which is used to establish an event that is to be set when the device state changes. This method is useful when receiving buffered input from a device, such as the mouse.

The last two methods mentioned are `Unacquire()` and `Release()`, which are both used to clean up a DirectInputDevice object. It is important to call `Unacquire()` and then `Release()` for every DirectInput device that you've acquired in a given DirectInput session. This device cleanup should always precede the call to `Release()` on the DirectInput object.

DirectInput Housekeeping

You've now gotten a glimpse at the objects and methods used with DirectInput, but you've yet to see them come together in real code. The remainder of this hour shows you how to put DirectInput to work handling input from the keyboard, mouse, and traditional joysticks. Before you get into the specifics of each device, however, let's go over some general DirectInput housekeeping code that will apply to all devices.

Starting Up DirectInput

First, let's take a look at some code that shows how to use the `DirectInputCreate()` function to create a DirectInput object:

```
LPDIRECTINPUT lpDI;

if (DirectInputCreate(hinst, DIRECTINPUT_VERSION, &lpDI, NULL) != DI_OK)
    return FALSE;
```

This code is pretty straightforward; it calls the `DirectInputCreate()` function to create a DirectInput object. This object can then be used to enumerate and create input devices. The steps to creating and using different input devices are similar regardless of the device. Following are the general steps involved in creating and initializing any DirectInput device:

1. Enumerate the attached devices with a call to the `EnumDevices()` method on the DirectInput object.

2. Create the DirectInputDevice object with a call to the `CreateDevice()` method on the DirectInput object.

3. Set the device's data format with a call to the `SetDataFormat()` method.

4. Set the device's behavior with a call to the `SetCooperativeLevel()` method.

5. Acquire the device with a call to the `Acquire()` method.

For standard devices such as the keyboard and mouse, you can skip the first step. This is because of the fact that there aren't likely to be any systems out there with more than one keyboard or mouse. Besides, anyone that is enough of a power user to need more than one keyboard or mouse is bound to figure out a way to make them work with your game!

You'll work through the specific code for each of these steps on different devices in a moment. For now, just think in terms of the logical steps required to get your hands on a device.

Cleaning Up DirectInput

Just as there is an established series of events that must take place in order to initialize DirectInput and access devices, there is also a complementary cleanup process. You'll be glad to know that cleaning up after DirectInput is actually far easier than initializing it. Following are the steps required to clean up a DirectInput session:

1. Unacquire all previously acquired devices by calling the `Unacquire()` method on each.

2. Release all previously created devices by calling the `Release()` method on each.

3. Release the DirectInput object by calling the `Release()` method on it.

Following is code to perform these steps and clean up after DirectInput:

```
if (lpDIDevice)
{
    lpDIDevice->Unacquire();
    lpDIDevice->Release();
    lpDIDevice = NULL;
}
SafeRelease(lpDI);
```

This code assumes that the DirectInput and DirectInputDevice object pointers are named `lpDI` and `lpDIDevice`, respectively. Of course, you might have multiple device pointers active in a given game, in which case you would be responsible for unacquiring and releasing all of them. If you recall, the `SafeRelease()` macro has been used throughout the book to safely release a DirectX object and null its pointer:

```
#define SafeRelease(x) if (x) { x->Release(); x=NULL;}
```

Many of the methods used to initialize and manipulate DirectInput devices are capable of failing; in which case they return a value other than `DI_OK`. It's important to clean up any DirectInput objects that you've created or acquired when a failure occurs. For example, if you successfully create a device but then fail to acquire it, you must release the device if you don't plan to immediately try to acquire it again. I don't always show extensive error-handling code throughout the hour in order to keep the code easier to follow, but keep in mind that it is important to always clean up after DirectInput, even when something doesn't go as planned.

Handling Keyboard Input

Handling keyboard input is relatively straightforward using DirectInput. Because the keyboard is a standard device, you don't have to hassle with enumerating the devices; you can just assume that there is one system keyboard. Following is code to create a keyboard device using the `CreateDevice()` method on a DirectInput object:

```
LPDIRECTINPUTDEVICE pKeyboard;
HRESULT             hr;
hr = lpDI->CreateDevice(GUID_SysKeyboard, &pKeyboard, NULL);
```

The first parameter to this method is the global identifier of the device to be created. In the case of the system keyboard, you can use the predefined `GUID_SysKeyboard` global identifier. The second parameter is a pointer to a DirectInputDevice pointer, which is filled in with the newly created device pointer. The last parameter is used to support COM aggregation, but is typically set to `NULL`. If the DirectInputDevice object is successfully created, `CreateDevice()` will return `DI_OK`.

Now that you've created a keyboard device, you're ready to set the data format for the device. Fortunately, because the keyboard is a standard device, there is a predefined global variable, `c_dfDIKeyboard`, that specifies the data format for the keyboard. Following is code to set the data format for the keyboard device:

```
hr = pKeyboard->SetDataFormat(&c_dfDIKeyboard);
```

With the data format established, you're ready to set the keyboard behavior with a call to `SetCooperativeLevel()`. It's important to point out that DirectInput doesn't allow exclusive access to the keyboard, which probably wouldn't be a good idea even if it did. So, you should always set the keyboard's cooperative level to non-exclusive, as the following code demonstrates:

```
hr = pKeyboard->SetCooperativeLevel(hwnd, DISCL_FOREGROUND |
    DISCL_NONEXCLUSIVE);
```

Notice that a window handle is passed as the first parameter to this method. This is necessary because the cooperative level establishes how devices are shared among applications, and the application window is the basis for this sharing. So, be sure to pass a handle to the main application window as the first parameter to `SetCooperativeLevel()`.

17

If you recall from the earlier discussion of starting up a DirectInput device, the only remaining step for preparing the keyboard is to acquire it. Following is code that acquires the keyboard:

```
pKeyboard->Acquire();
```

Nothing too complicated there! You're now ready to begin handling keyboard input, which I'm sure you're more than ready to do. Before we get into the code of inputting data from the keyboard, let's establish the ground rules for keyboard input handling.

It's important to understand that the keyboard provides absolute information. Unlike the mouse, which provides relative information about its movement, the keyboard always tells you exactly what is going on with its state. To better understand this, think of the keys on your keyboard as a big set of Boolean values. At any given moment, some keys might be pressed (on) and some keys might not (off). The key point is that you can always ascertain the exact state of the keyboard at any given time. The mouse, on the other hand, provides you with relative information such as how far it was moved in a given direction. For this reason, you'll handle mouse input a little differently later in the lesson.

Getting back to the keyboard—because it provides you with absolute input information, it's sufficient for you to just peek at its state to handle input from it. You do this by calling the GetDeviceState() method. Following is code to read the state of the keyboard:

```
char buffer[256];
hr = pKeyboard->GetDeviceState(sizeof(buffer),(LPVOID)&buffer);
```

A buffer of 256 characters is used as the storage medium for the state of the keyboard. The GetDeviceState() method fills the buffer with the current state of the keyboard. As you might be thinking, this buffer isn't of much use unless you can extract state information about specific keys. Fortunately, DirectInput provides defined key constants that specify the index of each key in the keyboard state array. For each key in the keyboard state array, the most significant bit reflects whether the key is pushed or not. You can easily check the bit by performing a bitwise AND on the key value with the hexadecimal value 0x80. This task is made easier with a simple macro:

```
#define KEYDOWN(buf, key) (buf[key] & 0x80)
```

Following is an example of using this macro to determine whether the user has pressed the left or right arrow keys:

```
if (KEYDOWN(buffer, DIK_LEFT))
    // move left
if (KEYDOWN(buffer, DIK_RIGHT))
    // move right
```

Table 17.1 lists some of the most commonly used DirectInput key constants for gaming.

TABLE 17.1 Commonly Used DirectInput Key Constants

Key Constant	Key Represented
DIK_UP	Up Arrow
DIK_DOWN	Down Arrow
DIK_LEFT	Left Arrow
DIK_RIGHT	Right Arrow
DIK_RETURN	Enter
DIK_TAB	Tab
DIK_LSHIFT	Left Shift
DIK_RSHIFT	Right Shift
DIK_LCONTROL	Left Control
DIK_RCONTROL	Right Control
DIK_SPACE	Space Bar
DIK_INSERT	Insert
DIK_DELETE	Delete
DIK_HOME	Home
DIK_END	End
DIK_PRIOR	Page Up
DIK_NEXT	Page Down
DIK_ESCAPE	Escape

17

All the DirectInput keyboard constants are defined in the DirectInput header file, DInput.h. Refer to this file for information on other key constants.

As you learned earlier, cleaning up after a DirectInput device simply involves unacquiring and then releasing the device. Following is code to perform this task for the keyboard:

```
pKeyboard->Unacquire();
pKeyboard->Release();
pKeyboard = NULL;
```

Keep in mind that you must also release the DirectInput object after cleaning up the device if you're finished with the DirectInput session.

The Hour 17 sample application included on the CD-ROM demonstrates how to add DirectInput keyboard support to a real application. The Hour 17 example is the cityscape application that you developed earlier in the book with DirectInput keyboard support added. The application was using traditional keyboard messaging to allow the user to move left and right using the arrow keys.

Handling Mouse Input

Similar to the keyboard, the mouse is a standard device that is expected to be available on all systems. Consequently, it is safe to assume that there is a single system mouse, and forgo enumerating mouse devices. Following is code to create a mouse device using the `CreateDevice()` method on a DirectInput object:

```
LPDIRECTINPUTDEVICE pMouse;
HRESULT             hr;
hr = lpDI->CreateDevice(GUID_SysMouse, &pMouse, NULL);
```

Notice that the predefined `GUID_SysMouse` global identifier is used to specify the system mouse as the device of choice. The second parameter is a pointer to a DirectInputDevice pointer, which is filled in with the newly created mouse device pointer.

Similar to the keyboard, there is a predefined global variable, `c_dfDIMouse`, that specifies the data format for the mouse. Following is code to set the data format for the mouse device:

```
hr = pMouse->SetDataFormat(&c_dfDIMouse);
```

With the data format established, you're ready to set the mouse behavior with a call to `SetCooperativeLevel()`. Unlike the keyboard, you can set the mouse's cooperative level to exclusive, at least as long as the application is in the foreground. The following code demonstrates how to set the mouse's cooperative level:

```
hr = pMouse->SetCooperativeLevel(hwnd, DISCL_FOREGROUND |
    DISCL_EXCLUSIVE);
```

Again, it is necessary to pass the application's main window handle as the first parameter to this method.

If you recall from the earlier keyboard discussion, I mentioned that it was necessary to buffer mouse input because it provides relative input information. It's now time to explore exactly how this buffering is accomplished. Buffered input involves establishing a memory buffer that receives mouse events as they are generated. You then extract the input information from the buffer to handle the specific mouse event. Following is code that creates an event and associates it with the mouse device:

```
hevtMouse = CreateEvent(0, 0, 0, 0);
hr = pMouse->SetEventNotification(hevtMouse);
```

The Win32 `CreateEvent()` function creates an event that is capable of being signaled. In this case, the signaling is established by passing the event into the `SetEventNotification()` method. This results in the event being signaled any time new input data is available for the mouse. This input data must be stored somewhere, which is where the buffer comes into play.

Every input device has a buffer that can be used to store buffered input data. Before you can use an input device's buffer, however, you must set its size. This is accomplished by setting the `DIPROP_BUFFERSIZE` property of the device. To set this property, you must first fill out a `DIPROPDWORD` header structure. The following code demonstrates acceptable values for this structure:

```
DIPROPDWORD dipdw =
{
    {
        sizeof(DIPROPDWORD),
        sizeof(DIPROPHEADER),
        0,
        DIPH_DEVICE,
    },
    32
};
```

The only significant value of this structure is the last one, 32, which sets the number of items capable of being stored in the buffer. You could certainly make the buffer huge and reduce the chances of it overflowing, but in practice this can result in unwanted lag with the mouse responsiveness. A setting of 32 appears to be a reasonable middle ground. To actually set the buffer size, you call the `SetProperty()` method and pass in the appropriate value, as the following code shows:

```
hr = pMouse->SetProperty(DIPROP_BUFFERSIZE, &dipdw.diph);
```

The size of the buffer is measured in items of data for the particular device, not in bytes.

Now you're ready to acquire the mouse and get down to business. Acquiring the mouse is no different than acquiring the keyboard, as the following code demonstrates:

```
pMouse->Acquire();
```

The last step in handling mouse input is actually retrieving mouse data. You have two options here:

1. Wait for Windows to notify you of mouse events, and then retrieve mouse data.

2. Poll for mouse data in the main game loop.

Your selection of one of these options is determined by the role of the mouse in your particular game. In general, games that wait on the mouse before doing anything will use the first approach. At the other end of the spectrum are high-speed games where things are taking place independent of the mouse, which require the latter approach. So, if you were creating a 3D Solitaire card game, you'd probably go with the first approach. On the other hand, if you were creating a Virtual Death Match Wrestling game, you'd need to poll for mouse data.

I'm going to focus on polling for mouse data because the vast majority of games will use that approach. Keep in mind that all the polling code you're about to see must be placed in the main game loop of your game. The first step to polling for mouse data involves creating a DIDEVICEOBJECTDATA structure that will be used to hold each piece of mouse data as it arrives:

```
DIDEVICEOBJECTDATA data;
memset(&data, 0, sizeof(DIDEVICEOBJECTDATA));
```

The next step is to create a loop that iterates through all the available mouse data that has accumulated in the buffer (see Listing 17.1).

LISTING 17.1 A Loop That Iterates Through Available Mouse Input Data

```
 1: BOOL  bDone = FALSE;
 2: DWORD dwNumElements = 1;
 3: int   iDX = 0, iDY = 0;
 4: BOOL  buttonDown[2];
 5:
 6: while (!bDone)
 7: {
 8:     // Obtain input data from the mouse
 9:     if (pMouse->GetDeviceData(sizeof(DIDEVICEOBJECTDATA), &data,
10:         &dwNumElements, 0) == DIERR_INPUTLOST)
11:     {
12:         // Reacquire the mouse and try again
13:         if (pMouse->Acquire() == DI_OK)
```

```
14:                    hr = pMouse->GetDeviceData(sizeof(DIDEVICEOBJECTDATA), &data,
15:                        &dwNumElements, 0);
16:     }
17:
18:     // Respond to the mouse input
19:     switch(data.dwOfs)
20:     {
21:     case DIMOFS_X:
22:         iDX += data.dwData;
23:         break;
24:
25:     case DIMOFS_Y:
26:         iDY += data.dwData;
27:         break;
28:
29:     case DIMOFS_BUTTON0:
30:         if (data.dwData & 0x80)
31:             buttonDown[0] = TRUE;
32:         else
33:             buttonDown[0] = FALSE;
34:         break;
35:
36:     case DIMOFS_BUTTON1:
37:         if (data.dwData & 0x80)
38:             buttonDown[1] = TRUE;
39:         else
40:             buttonDown[1] = FALSE;
41:         break;
42:     }
43:
44:     if (dwNumElements == 0)
45:         bDone = TRUE;
46: }
```

This code demonstrates how to extract mouse data from the buffer. It's important to understand that you aren't guaranteed to get buffer data in any particular order, which is why it is necessary to use a switch statement to determine the data type. The GetDeviceData() method is called to retrieve a single element of mouse data. If this method fails, a single attempt is made to reacquire the mouse and try again. The type of the data is then determined, which can be an X or Y mouse movement or a mouse button press. The iDX and iDY variables are used to store the relative change in mouse position in the X and Y directions. The buttonDown array keeps track of the state of the buttons on a two-button mouse. You would probably want to make all these variables global in the context of a real game.

Handling Joystick Input

The final topic in this hour is handling joystick input. You've come a long way in learning how to use DirectInput, so I think you'll find that working with the joystick isn't too
difficult. The main difference in working with joysticks is that you must enumerate the
joystick devices to determine whether a joystick is attached. The EnumDevices() method
of the IDirectInput interface accomplishes this task:

```
HRESULT EnumDevices(DWORD dwDevType, LPDIENUMCALLBACK lpCallback,
    LPVOID pvRef, DWORD dwFlags);
```

The first parameter specifies the device type to be enumerated, which in this case should
be set to DIDEVTYPE_JOYSTICK. The second parameter is a pointer to a callback function
that will be called for each device enumerated. You will have to create this function and
pass a pointer to it as this parameter; more on this in a moment. The third parameter to
EnumDevices() is a 32-bit application-specific parameter that allows you to pass any
information that you want accessible from the callback function. You will usually pass a
pointer to the DirectInput object as this parameter. The last parameter to EnumDevices()
is a flag that indicates the scope of the enumeration. Table 17.2 contains a list of these
flags along with their usage.

TABLE 17.2   Flags Used to Indicate the Scope of Enumerated Devices

Flag	Devices Enumerated
DIEDFL_ALLDEVICES	All installed devices (default)
DIEDFL_ATTACHEDONLY	Only attached and installed devices
DIEDFL_FORCEFEEDBACK	Only force feedback devices
DIEDFL_INCLUDEALIASES	Devices that are aliases for other devices
DIEDFL_INCLUDEPHANTOMS	Phantom (placeholder) devices

You can combine these flags to enumerate different groups of devices. For example,
combining DIEDFL_ATTACHEDONLY and DIEDFL_FORCEFEEDBACK will enumerate only
attached devices that support force feedback. To enumerate standard joysticks, you
should just use the DIEDFL_ATTACHEDONLY flag. Following is an example of a call to
EnumDevices() that enumerates standard joysticks:

```
lpDI->EnumDevices(DIDEVTYPE_JOYSTICK, EnumJoystickProc, pdi,
    DIEDFL_ATTACHEDONLY);
```

Of course, this call won't result in anything useful until you write the
EnumJoystickProc() callback function. Listing 17.2 contains a suitable callback function that creates a joystick device based on the first attached joystick that is enumerated.

LISTING 17.2 The `EnumJoystickProc()` Callback Function that Is Called to Enumerate Joysticks

```
 1: BOOL FAR PASCAL EnumJoystickProc(LPCDIDEVICEINSTANCE pdinst, LPVOID pvRef)
 2: {
 3:     LPDIRECTINPUT pdi = pvRef;
 4:
 5:     // Create the joystick device
 6:     if (pdi->CreateDevice(&pdinst->guidInstance, &pJoystick,
     ➥ NULL) != DI_OK)
 7:         return DIENUM_CONTINUE;
 8:
 9:     // Obtain an IDirectInput2 interface for the device
10:     if (pJoystick->QueryInterface(IID_IDirectInputDevice2,
11:         (LPVOID*)&pJoystick) != DI_OK)
12:     {
13:         pJoystick->Release();
14:         return DIENUM_CONTINUE;
15:     }
16:
17:     // Set the joystick data format
18:     if (pJoystick->SetDataFormat(&c_dfDIJoystick) != DI_OK)
19:     {
20:         pJoystick->Release();
21:         return DIENUM_CONTINUE;
22:     }
23:
24:     // Set the cooperative level
25:     if (pJoystick->SetCooperativeLevel(hwnd,
     ➥ DISCL_NONEXCLUSIVE | DISCL_FOREGROUND) != DI_OK)
26:     {
27:         pJoystick->Release();
28:         return DIENUM_CONTINUE;
29:     }
30:
31:     // Set the X range
32:     DIPROPRANGE diprg;
33:     diprg.diph.dwSize       = sizeof(diprg);
34:     diprg.diph.dwHeaderSize = sizeof(diprg.diph);
35:     diprg.diph.dwObj        = DIJOFS_X;
36:     diprg.diph.dwHow        = DIPH_BYOFFSET;
37:     diprg.lMin              = -1000;
38:     diprg.lMax              = +1000;
39:     if (pJoystick->SetProperty(pdev, DIPROP_RANGE, &diprg.diph) != DI_OK)
40:     {
41:         pJoystick->Release();
42:         return DIENUM_CONTINUE;
43:     }
44:
45:     // Set the Y range
```

continues

17

LISTING **17.2**   continued

```
46:        diprg.diph.dwObj        = DIJOFS_Y;
47:        if (pJoystick->SetProperty(pdev, DIPROP_RANGE, &diprg.diph) != DI_OK)
48:        {
49:            pJoystick->Release();
50:            return DIENUM_CONTINUE;
51:        }
52:
53:        Set the X dead zone
54:        DIPROPDWORD dipdw;
55:        dipdw.diph.dwSize       = sizeof(dipdw);
56:        dipdw.diph.dwHeaderSize = sizeof(dipdw.diph);
57:        dipdw.diph.dwObj        = DIJOFS_X;
58:        dipdw.diph.dwHow        = DIPH_BYOFFSET;
59:        dipdw.dwData            = 100;
60:        if (pJoystick->SetProperty(DIPROP_DEADZONE, &dipdw.diph) != DI_OK)
61:        {
62:            pJoystick->Release();
63:            return DIENUM_CONTINUE;
64:        }
65:
66:        Set the Y dead zone
67:        dipdw.diph.dwObj        = DIJOFS_Y;
68:        if (pJoystick->SetProperty(DIPROP_DEADZONE, &dipdw.diph) != DI_OK)
69:        {
70:            pJoystick->Release();
71:            return DIENUM_CONTINUE;
72:        }
73:
74:        return DIENUM_STOP;
75: }
```

If the device creation fails, the function returns DIENUM_CONTINUE, which results in the continuation of the enumeration process. The idea is that you want to keep enumerating joysticks until you successfully create and initialize one. If the creation goes as planned, DIENUM_STOP is returned, which ends the enumeration process. The pJoystick variable should be global so that you have access to it beyond the EnumJoystickProc() function.

Another interesting change in dealing with joysticks, as opposed to the keyboard and mouse, is obtaining a different interface for interacting with a joystick device. This is necessary because the IDirectInputDevice2 interface supports the Poll() method, which is very useful for polling joysticks for input. The QueryInterface() method is called to obtain an IDirectInputDevice2 interface pointer, which is stored in the same pJoystick variable.

The data format of the joystick is then set to the predefined global c_dfDIJoystick. After setting the data format, the cooperative level is set with a call to SetCooperativeLevel().

The final step in preparing the newly created joystick device is to set its properties. Joystick properties include the range and dead zone for the X and Y axes. The range dictates the minimum and maximum values associated with the joystick's movement along a given axis. For example, if you set the minimum and maximum values for the X axis to 1000 and -1000, respectively, moving the joystick all the way to the left will result in a value of -1000. Likewise, moving the joystick all the way to the right will result in a value of 1000. And finally, leaving the joystick centered results in a value of 0.

The dead zone for a joystick is the range of movement that you don't want to qualify as input. You can think of the dead zone as an enlarged center position for the joystick, which means that with a dead zone you can move the joystick slightly, and it is still considered centered. Establishing a dead zone helps to keep joysticks from feeling too jittery when you barely move them. Figure 17.1 illustrates the relationship between the range and dead zone of a joystick.

FIGURE 17.1

The relationship between the range and dead zone of a joystick.

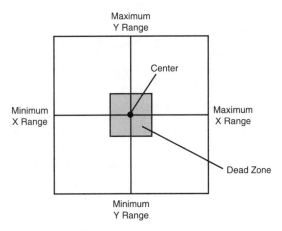

The EnumJoystickProc() callback function uses the SetProperty() method to set the range property for the joystick to -1000 and 1000 for both the X and Y axes. It also establishes a dead zone of 100 for both axes using a similar approach; this means that you will have to move the joystick at least one tenth of its full range for it to register as valid input.

You can breathe a sigh of relief because you're finally ready to learn how to read data from a joystick. Listing 17.3 contains an example of code that polls the joystick and handles its input data; this code would need to be placed in the main game loop.

LISTING 17.3   Code That Polls the Joystick and Handles Its Input Data

```
 1: int    iX = 0, iY = 0;
 2: BOOL   buttonDown[DI_MAX_BUTTONS];
 3: DIJOYSTATE state;
 4:
 5: // Poll for new data
 6: hr = pJoystick->Poll();
 7:
 8: // Obtain input data from the joystick
 9: if (pJoystick->GetDeviceState(sizeof(DIJOYSTATE),
    ➥ &state) == DIERR_INPUTLOST)
10: {
11:     // Reacquire the joystick and try again
12:     if (pJoystick->Acquire() == DI_OK)
13:         pJoystick->GetDeviceState(sizeof(DIJOYSTATE), &state);
14: }
15:
16: // Respond to the joystick input
17: iX = state.lX;
18: iY = state.lY;
19: for (int i = 0; i < DI_MAX_BUTTONS)
20: {
21:     if (state.rgbButtons[i] & 0x80)
22:         buttonDown[i] = TRUE;
23:     else
24:         buttonDown[1] = FALSE;
25: }
```

The Poll() method is first called to poll the joystick for new data. This is necessary so that the next call to GetDeviceState() has the latest joystick input data. If the call to GetDeviceState() fails, an attempt is made to reacquire the joystick and try again. The joystick data is then obtained from the DIJOYSTATE structure, which contains information such as the absolute joystick positions along each axis and the button states. The iX and iY variables are used to store the joystick positions in the X and Y directions. The buttonDown array keeps track of the state of the buttons on the joystick. You would probably want to make all of these variables global in the context of a real game.

I realize that I've skirted the issue of using the joystick data within the context of a working game. In reality, how you use device input data of any type is entirely dependent on the specifics of a given game. Consequently, there is no catch-all solution that I can show you. However, knowing how to retrieve input data from various devices should be enough to get you going in supporting a wide range of devices in your own games.

Summary

This hour introduces you to DirectInput, the component of DirectX that is used to read input devices such as the keyboard, the mouse, joysticks, and flight yokes. You began the hour by learning some basics about DirectInput, such as why it is necessary and what benefits it offers over the Win32 approach to handling device input. You then dug into the DirectInput architecture and explored the different COM objects that comprise DirectInput. I deliberately avoided covering the DirectInputEffect object, which applies to force feedback devices; you tackle this in the next hour.

After laying the groundwork for DirectInput, the hour then guided you through the practical details of retrieving data from devices via DirectInput. More specifically, you learned how to retrieve input data from the keyboard, the mouse, and joysticks. Although it takes a little work to set up DirectInput and interact with DirectInput devices, the payoff is significant in terms of providing a very responsive feel to your games.

Q&A

Q I'm still a little fuzzy as to why the cooperative levels vary between different input devices. What gives?

A First, let's recap that the cooperative level of a device indicates two things. The first thing is whether the device is available when the application is only in the foreground or in both the foreground and background. It's relatively obvious that the keyboard and mouse should only support a foreground cooperative level because you wouldn't want a background application stealing mouse movements or keystrokes. The second thing the cooperative level dictates is whether a device is acquired exclusively by an application. The keyboard cannot be set to an exclusive cooperative level because Windows itself requires certain keystrokes (Ctrl+Alt+Delete, Alt+Tab, and so on) to work regardless of what an application is up to.

Q What is different about joysticks that requires you to poll for joystick input using the `Poll()` method?

A Unlike most keyboards and mice, some joysticks don't generate hardware interrupts, which are required in order for the `GetDeviceState()` method to return valid input data. More specifically, analog joysticks are typically the joysticks that must be polled. Keep in mind that it doesn't hurt anything to call the `Poll()` method on any device; it will just do nothing if the device doesn't require polling. You can determine whether a device requires polling by calling the `GetCapabilities()` method and checking the `DIDEVCAPS` structure for the `DIDC_POLLEDDATAFORMAT` flag.

Workshop

The Workshop is designed to help you anticipate possible questions, review what you've learned, and begin thinking ahead to put your knowledge into practice. The answers to the quiz are in Appendix A, "Answers."

Quiz

1. With respect to DirectInput, what does the term "low latency" mean?
2. How does DirectInput offer improved performance over the Win32 API approach to handling device input?
3. What COM object acts as an input device manager that allows you to enumerate and access devices for use with DirectInput?
4. What global function must you call to create a DirectInput object?
5. Why do you typically never need to call the `Initialize()` method to initialize a DirectInput object?
6. What is an attached device?
7. Why can't you just call `CreateDevice()` to create joystick device objects as you do keyboard and mouse devices objects?
8. What method do you call to determine to what degree an application allows an input device to be shared with other applications?
9. What method must you call to obtain unbuffered input data from a device?
10. What must you do to properly clean up a DirectInput session?
11. Does reading the keyboard with DirectInput inhibit normal Windows keystroke messages?

Exercises

1. Modify the cityscape application from earlier in the book so that it uses DirectInput to input data from the mouse. The application's view should move left and right based on the user dragging the mouse left and right.
2. Modify the cityscape application so that it uses DirectInput to input data from a joystick. The application's view should move left and right based on the user moving the joystick left and right.

HOUR 18

Getting Through to the User—Force Feedback

In the previous hour, I touched on the fact that DirectInput supports force feedback, which is a technology that enables you to provide tactile feedback to a user through an input device. Now that you have a solid understanding of DirectInput and how it is used to obtain input from various devices, it's time to explore force feedback and how it works.

This hour introduces you to the force feedback features in DirectInput and discusses some of the ways in which force feedback effects are used. You also learn about the COM object that implements force feedback, along with the practical details of how to use force feedback in your own games. By the end of this hour, you'll have the skills necessary to shake and rattle game players with force feedback and have them begging for more!

In this hour, you will learn

- The basics of the force feedback technology
- How DirectInput supports force feedback
- How to enumerate and create force feedback effects
- How to use force feedback in games

Understanding Force Feedback

Although I love driving games, I've complained for years about how difficult it is to really have control in driving games without feeling the tightness of the steering wheel. Driving involves issuing responses to very subtle changes in steering wheel pressure, which is reflective of the amount of control you have over the car. If you've ever driven in icy conditions, you know what I'm talking about.

Up until the past few years, driving games have had a hard time conveying realism because they had no way of injecting feedback into steering wheels. Arcade game manufacturers were the first to address this need, which resulted in a variety of coin-op driving games that used force feedback to make the driving experience more realistic. However, the mechanics involved made it difficult to scale the technology to video games at home. Until now!

Innovative input device design coupled with DirectInput has finally ushered in force feedback to the PC world. Microsoft was the first to bring a product to market with the SideWinder Force Feedback Pro joystick. Other manufacturers have since followed suit with their own joysticks. Even more recently, several different force feedback steering wheels have cropped up, which finally allow me to have my cake and eat it too while playing driving games in the comfort of my own home.

Force feedback devices have opened up all kinds of new opportunities for game developers. You can now add kick to guns in shoot-em-up games, jar the player with a punch in fighting games, rattle the player when an explosion goes off, or even simulate a chainsaw with force feedback. Microsoft had a really cool in-store display for the SideWinder Force Feedback Pro joystick that even demonstrated a light saber force feedback effect.

Force Feedback Lingo

NEW TERM Before you get into the specifics of how DirectInput supports force feedback, you need to learn some basics about force feedback terminology. Let's start with the basic element of force feedback: the effect. A force feedback *effect* is an instance of force feedback that involves a push or resistance. The push or resistance associated with an effect is called the *force* of the effect. The *magnitude* of a force is the strength of the force, which increases in a linear fashion. In other words, a force of 1,000 is twice as powerful as a force of 500. The maximum force magnitude for a DirectInput device is 10,000. You can alter the magnitude of a force by applying a gain, which adjusts the magnitude to make it weaker.

NEW TERM *Gain* is the degree to which a force magnitude is weakened.

NEW TERM The *direction* of a force indicates the direction from which the force is acting. So, a southeast force originates from the southeast and acts in the direction of northwest. An easier way to think of this is to associate the direction of a force with the direction you would have to push the joystick to resist the force. A negative force magnitude indicates that a force is acting in the opposite direction.

NEW TERM Every effect has a *duration*, which determines how long the effect is to last. The duration of effects is measured in microseconds.

NEW TERM Some effects are periodic, which means they repeat according to a certain pattern or cycle. Periodic effects have a period that indicates the duration of a single cycle. Varying the period of a periodic effect can dramatically alter the feel of the effect. Periodic effects also have a *phase* associated with them, which is the point in the wave where playback begins. If you're having a hard time visualizing the period and phase of a periodic effect, check out Figure 18.1.

FIGURE 18.1

The relationship between the period, phase, and magnitude of a periodic effect.

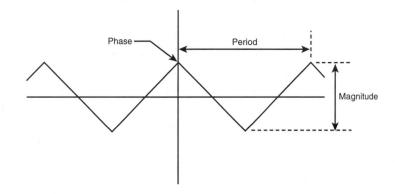

NEW TERM *Period* is the duration of a single cycle of a periodic effect, measured in microseconds.

NEW TERM You can alter an effect by applying an *envelope*, which is a set of values used to alter the shape of the effect. More specifically, an envelope consists of an attack value and a fade value, which alter the magnitude of the beginning and end of an effect's force. There is a duration associated with attack and fade that determines how long the magnitude approaches or moves away from the sustain value. *Sustain* is the basic magnitude of the force in the absence of an attack or fade. Figure 18.2 illustrates how attack and fade can be used to alter a constant force effect.

FIGURE **18.2**

A constant force effect altered by attack and fade.

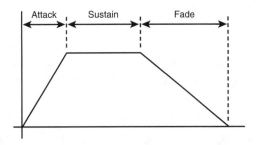

NEW TERM   *Attack* is the period at the beginning of an effect when the force magnitude is approaching its sustain level.

NEW TERM   *Fade* is the period at the end of an effect when the force magnitude is moving away from its sustain level.

NEW TERM   *Sustain* is the period in an effect when the basic force magnitude is attained (after the attack and before the fade).

Types of Effects

In learning some of the force feedback terminology, you've touched on some of the different types of force feedback effects supported by DirectInput. DirectInput supports a wide range of effects that can be used to convey different things to the user. The effects are divided into basic categories that describe the general characteristics of the effects:

- Constant force
- Ramp force
- Periodic effect
- Condition

Constant forces are the simplest effects and include effects that produce a constant (steady) force in a given direction. Constant effects are useful for producing effects such as punches and hits, as well as some types of resistance effects.

Ramp forces include effects that produce a force that steadily increases or decreases. Ramp forces are similar to constant forces except that the magnitude of the force is steadily changing, whereas the magnitude of a constant force doesn't change. Ramp forces can be used to produce effects that fade in and out. For example, you might use a ramp force to communicate the increased resistance felt as a character walks into water.

Periodic effects are very different from constant and ramp forces because they vary in magnitude according to a periodic wave pattern, such as a sine wave. Periodic effects are useful for producing effects such as vibrations.

Conditions are effects that are only produced in response to user input. A good example of a condition is the spring effect that attempts to restore a joystick to its center position; the effect is applied only when the user moves the joystick out of center.

Although these effect types paint the broad picture of effect support in DirectInput, you have a lot of flexibility when it comes to altering effects. You can also create completely custom effects if you find that the built-in DirectInput effects don't suit your needs. Also, some force feedback devices might include native effects that you can use in lieu of a DirectInput effect.

Peeking Inside DirectInput

I mentioned earlier that force feedback is implemented as a part of DirectInput. Although this is logical because force feedback is associated with input devices, when you think about it, force feedback is really a type of output. I'm not trying to confuse you, I just want you to understand the role of force feedback in DirectX. It's certainly strange to think of a joystick or steering wheel as an output device, but when it comes to force feedback, that's exactly what it is. You'll find that using force feedback effects is conceptually similar to playing sounds. In other words, you'll use DirectInput to play force feedback effects on an input device much as you use DirectSound to play sounds on a sound device.

Now that I've completely confused the issue, let's take a look at how force feedback is implemented in DirectInput. You'll be glad to know that force feedback is built upon the same DirectInput objects that you learned about in the previous hour. In fact, you can add force feedback support to an existing DirectInput application by learning about one additional DirectInput object, DirectInputEffect. Of course, DirectInputEffect is a COM object, and its role is to encapsulate a force feedback effect for a given input device.

You create DirectInputEffect objects by calling the `CreateEffect()` method on a DirectInputDevice2 object. DirectInputEffect objects adhere to the `IDirectInputEffect`

18

COM interface, which contains methods for controlling the playback of effects. Following are the most commonly used methods in the `IDirectInputEffect` interface:

- `Initialize()`
- `Start()`
- `Stop()`
- `Download()`
- `Unload()`
- `SetParameters()`
- `GetEffectStatus()`
- `Release()`

The `Initialize()` method is called to initialize a DirectInputEffect object. Similar to its counterparts in the `IDirectInput` and `IDirectInputDevice` interfaces, this method is rarely called directly because it is called by the `CreateEffect()` method when you first create a DirectInputEffect object. The majority of the work involved in using effects takes place during effect creation, when you must set up a variety of data structures to establish the parameters of the effect to be created. You learn more about creating effects a little later in the lesson.

After you've created a DirectInputEffect object, you can begin playing the effect on an input device. The `Start()` method starts playing an effect. It's important to understand that effects must be downloaded into the memory of a force feedback device. If an effect has not been downloaded or has been modified since being downloaded, the `Start()` method will cause the effect to be downloaded before it is played. To stop playing an effect, you can call the `Stop()` method.

The `Download()` and `Unload()` methods are used to manually download and unload effects to and from a device. It typically isn't necessary to call these methods directly because they are automatically called by other DirectInputEffect methods whenever it is appropriate.

You can dynamically alter an effect by calling the `SetParameters()` method. This method accepts a `DIEFFECT` structure that contains information about an effect, as well as a series of flags that indicate which part of the effect is to be altered. Table 18.1 lists some of the more commonly used flags associated with the `SetParameters()` method.

TABLE 18.1   Flags Commonly Used with the `SetParameters()` Method

Flag	Usage
DIEP_AXES	Sets the axes of the effect
DIEP_DIRECTION	Sets the direction of the effect
DIEP_DURATION	Sets the duration of the effect
DIEP_ENVELOPE	Sets the envelope of the effect
DIEP_GAIN	Sets the gain of the effect
DIEP_TRIGGERBUTTON	Sets the trigger button for the effect
DIEP_TRIGGERDELAY	Sets the trigger delay for the effect
DIEP_TRIGGERREPEATINTERVAL	Sets the trigger repeat interval for the effect
DIEP_NODOWNLOAD	Suppresses the automatic downloading of the effect
DIEP_START	Starts the effect after the parameters are set

The `GetEffectStatus()` method is used to get the status of an effect. Values returned by this method can be `DIEGES_PLAYING`, `DIEGES_EMULATED`, or `0`. `DIEGES_PLAYING` indicates that the effect is playing, whereas `DIEGES_EMULATED` indicates that the effect is emulated. A value of `0` indicates that the effect isn't playing or emulated.

As with all DirectX COM objects, it is necessary to release a DirectInputEffect object after you're finished with it. The `Release()` method handles this task. This cleanup should always precede the call to `Release()` on the `DirectInput` object.

Putting Force Feedback to Work

You'll be glad to know that using force feedback doesn't involve too much extra work beyond that of supporting a traditional joystick. Consequently, the initialization of a force feedback device closely resembles that of a traditional input device. Following are the main steps involved in creating and initializing a force feedback device:

1. Enumerate the attached force feedback devices with a call to the `EnumDevices()` method on the `DirectInput` object.

2. Create the `DirectInputDevice` object with a call to the `CreateDevice()` method on the `DirectInput` object.

3. Obtain a pointer to an `IDirectInputDevice2` interface with a call to the `QueryInterface()` method.

4. Set the device's data format with a call to the `SetDataFormat()` method.

5. Set the device's behavior with a call to the `SetCooperativeLevel()` method.

6. Enumerate the available force feedback effects with a call to the `EnumEffects()` method in the `IDirectInputDevice2` interface.

7. Create DirectInputEffect objects with calls to the `CreateEffect()` method in the `IDirectInputDevice2` interface.

8. Acquire the device with a call to the `Acquire()` method.

You might notice that a few steps here are different from working with a traditional input device, such as a basic joystick. First, the device enumeration must take into account that you're looking specifically for force feedback devices. This is how you would be able to tell whether the user can take advantage of force feedback features. If no force feedback devices are found, you could simply fall back on traditional input device support.

The next big change in working with force feedback devices is enumerating the available force feedback effects. This step isn't strictly required, especially if you are planning on using basic effects such as constant forces. Instead of enumerating effects and using the global identifier returned by the callback function, you can use one of the following predefined effect identifiers:

- `GUID_ConstantForce`
- `GUID_RampForce`
- `GUID_Square`
- `GUID_Sine`
- `GUID_Triangle`
- `GUID_SawtoothUp`
- `GUID_SawtoothDown`
- `GUID_Spring`
- `GUID_Damper`
- `GUID_Inertia`
- `GUID_Friction`

Of course, it's still a good idea to enumerate the available effects even if you use one of the predefined effects. This is because not all force feedback devices are guaranteed to support all of these effects. Granted, it's a safe bet that simple effects such as `GUID_ConstantForce` will be available, but the safe and sure approach is to always enumerate effects.

After you've successfully enumerated an effect and obtained its global identifier (or selected a predefined global effect identifier), you are ready to create the effect as a DirectInputEffect object. You call the `CreateEffect()` method to accomplish this task, but there are a handful of structures that you'll need to initialize properly before doing so. We'll get into the details of these structures in a moment. For now, I just want to focus on the big picture.

Speaking of the big picture, when an effect is successfully created, you're ready to play it on a device. Playing an effect is as simple as calling the `Start()` method on the effect. Now you have an idea how force feedback is implemented in a game. Let's move on to the specifics of how to accomplish this stuff in code.

Enumerating and Creating Force Feedback Devices

Just as you learned how to enumerate traditional joysticks in the previous hour, you must also enumerate force feedback devices. The reason is because you can't just assume that every user has shelled out the money to buy a fancy force feedback joystick or steering wheel. Remember, the keyboard and mouse are the only two input devices that you can make assumptions about being available; everything else must be enumerated.

Following is code that gets the enumeration process started for force feedback devices:

```
lpDI->EnumDevices(DIDEVTYPE_JOYSTICK, EnumFFJoystickProc, lpDI,
    DIEDFL_FORCEFEEDBACK | DIEDFL_ATTACHEDONLY);
```

This call is similar to the one that enumerates traditional joysticks. In fact, the only change is the addition of the `DIEDFL_FORCEFEEDBACK` flag, which indicates that only force feedback devices are to be enumerated. Of course, the key to enumeration working is providing a suitable callback function. Listing 18.1 contains the `EnumFFJoystickProc()` callback function, which creates a force feedback joystick device based on the first attached device that is enumerated.

LISTING 18.1 The `EnumFFJoystickProc()` Callback Function That Is Called to Enumerate Force Feedback Joysticks

```
 1: BOOL FAR PASCAL EnumFFJoystickProc(LPCDIDEVICEINSTANCE pdinst,
    ➥ LPVOID pvRef)
 2: {
 3:     LPDIRECTINPUTDEVICE pDevice;
 4:     LPDIRECTINPUT pdi = (LPDIRECTINPUT)pvRef;
 5:
 6:     // Create the joystick device
 7:     if (pdi->CreateDevice(pdinst->guidInstance, &pDevice, NULL) != DI_OK)
 8:         return DIENUM_CONTINUE;
 9:
10:     // Obtain an IDirectInput2 interface for the device
11:     if (pDevice->QueryInterface(IID_IDirectInputDevice2,
12:         (LPVOID*)&pFFJoystick) != DI_OK)
13:     {
```

continues

18

LISTING 18.1 continued

```
14:         pDevice->Release();
15:         return DIENUM_CONTINUE;
16:     }
17:     pDevice->Release();
18:
19:     // Set the joystick data format
20:     if (pFFJoystick->SetDataFormat(&c_dfDIJoystick) != DI_OK)
21:     {
22:         pFFJoystick->Release();
23:         return DIENUM_CONTINUE;
24:     }
25:
26:     // Set the cooperative level
27:     if (pFFJoystick->SetCooperativeLevel(hWnd,
    ➥ DISCL_EXCLUSIVE | DISCL_FOREGROUND) != DI_OK)
28:     {
29:         pFFJoystick->Release();
30:         return DIENUM_CONTINUE;
31:     }
32:
33:     // Set the X range
34:     DIPROPRANGE diprg;
35:     diprg.diph.dwSize       = sizeof(diprg);
36:     diprg.diph.dwHeaderSize = sizeof(diprg.diph);
37:     diprg.diph.dwObj        = DIJOFS_X;
38:     diprg.diph.dwHow        = DIPH_BYOFFSET;
39:     diprg.lMin              = -1000;
40:     diprg.lMax              = +1000;
41:     if (pFFJoystick->SetProperty(DIPROP_RANGE, &diprg.diph) != DI_OK)
42:     {
43:         pFFJoystick->Release();
44:         return DIENUM_CONTINUE;
45:     }
46:
47:     // Set the Y range
48:     diprg.diph.dwObj        = DIJOFS_Y;
49:     if (pFFJoystick->SetProperty(DIPROP_RANGE, &diprg.diph) != DI_OK)
50:     {
51:         pFFJoystick->Release();
52:         return DIENUM_CONTINUE;
53:     }
54:
55:     // Turn off auto center
56:     DIPROPDWORD DIPropAutoCenter;
57:     DIPropAutoCenter.diph.dwSize = sizeof(DIPROPDWORD);
58:     DIPropAutoCenter.diph.dwHeaderSize = sizeof(DIPROPHEADER);
59:     DIPropAutoCenter.diph.dwObj = 0;
60:     DIPropAutoCenter.diph.dwHow = DIPH_DEVICE;
61:     DIPropAutoCenter.dwData = DIPROPAUTOCENTER_OFF;
62:     if (pFFJoystick->SetProperty(DIPROP_AUTOCENTER,
```

```
             ➥ &DIPropAutoCenter.diph) != DI_OK)
63:      {
64:          pFFJoystick->Release();
65:          return DIENUM_CONTINUE;
66:      }
67:
68:      return DIENUM_STOP;
69: }
```

This callback function is similar in many ways to the joystick enumeration function you learned about in the previous hour. One notable change is that the cooperative level of the joystick is set to exclusive, which is a requirement of all force feedback devices. The other big change is the addition of code to turn off the auto center feature. Auto center is a feature that involves the motors of a force feedback device automatically trying to restore the joystick to the center position. Auto center basically emulates the feel of a traditional joystick by simulating centering springs, but it can get in the way of other force feedback effects. In most cases, you'll want to turn off auto center.

At this point, you've successfully enumerated and created a force feedback device that is ready to both communicate user input and play force feedback effects. The next step is to enumerate force feedback effects to see what effects you're capable of playing.

Enumerating Force Feedback Effects

As you might suspect, the process of enumerating force feedback effects is similar to that of enumerating input devices. More specifically, you must create a callback function that is called in response to each enumerated effect. To get the enumeration process started, you must first call the EnumEffects() method using the IDirectInputDevice2 interface on an input device. Following is the syntax for this method:

```
HRESULT EnumEffects(LPDIENUMEFFECTSCALLBACK lpCallback, LPVOID pvRef,
    DWORD dwEffType);
```

The first parameter, lpCallback, is a pointer to the enumeration callback function. The second parameter, pvRef, is a pointer to application-specific data that is passed into the callback function. The last parameter, dwEffType, is a flag that determines what kinds of effects are enumerated. Valid values for this flag include

- DIEFT_ALL
- DIEFT_CONSTANTFORCE
- DIEFT_RAMPFORCE
- DIEFT_PERIODIC
- DIEFT_CONDITION

18

- `DIEFT_FFATTACK`

- `DIEFT_FFFADE`

- `DIEFT_SATURATION`

- `DIEFT_DEADBAND`

- `DIEFT_POSNEGCOEFFICIENTS`

- `DIEFT_POSNEGSATURATION`

- `DIEFT_CUSTOMFORCE`

- `DIEFT_HARDWARE`

You'll probably recognize the first few flags because they indicate the basic effect types you learned about earlier in the hour. You can combine any of the flags listed to enumerate a range of force feedback devices. Following is an example of calling the `EnumEffects()` method to enumerate constant force effects:

```
GUID guidEffect;
pFFJoystick->EnumEffects((LPDIENUMEFFECTSCALLBACK)EnumEffectProc, &guidEffect,
    DIEFT_CONSTANTFORCE);
```

This code establishes the callback function as `EnumEffectProc()`, which you will learn about in a moment. It also passes in the address of a global effect identifier, `guidEffect`, which will eventually contain the enumerated effect. The flag `DIEFT_CONSTANTFORCE` is used to indicate that only constant force effects are to be enumerated.

The work of obtaining a global effect identifier is left up to the enumeration callback function, `EnumEffectProc()`. Listing 18.2 contains the code for this function.

LISTING 18.2 The `EnumEffectProc()` Callback Function That Is Called to Enumerate Force Feedback Effects

```
 1: BOOL CALLBACK EnumEffectProc(LPCDIEFFECTINFO pei, LPVOID pv)
 2: {
 3:     GUID* pguidEffect = NULL;
 4:
 5:     if(pv)
 6:     {
 7:         // Set the global effect identifier
 8:         pguidEffect = (GUID*)pv;
 9:         *pguidEffect = pei->guid;
10:
11:         // Stop enumerating
12:         return DIENUM_STOP;
13:     }
14:
15:     // Keep enumerating
16:     return DIENUM_CONTINUE;
17: }
```

The `EnumEffectProc()` callback function in Listing 18.2 presents a fairly simplistic approach to enumerating effects because it grabs the first effect and quits. You could add additional logic to dig into the `DIEFFECTINFO` structure pointed to by the `pei` parameter and determine more about each enumerated effect. For now, let's assume that the first enumerated constant force effect is acceptable. That way we can move on to creating the actual effect object.

Creating Force Feedback Effects

After you've determined that a particular force feedback effect is available, you're ready to create the actual effect. Force feedback effects are relatively complex to allow for lots of flexibility. For this reason, there are a variety of different data structures that you must initialize in order to create an effect. Following are the structures involved in creating an effect:

- An array of axes for the effect
- An array of direction values for the effect
- A type-specific structure such as `DICONSTANTFORCE`, `DIRAMPFORCE`, `DIPERIODIC`, or `DICONDITION`
- A `DIENVELOPE` structure for defining the effect's envelope (optional)
- A `DIEFFECT` structure that pulls together the other data structures

The first two data structures are very closely related because the number of axes of an effect determines the number of dimensions of the direction. For example, an effect acting along the X and Y axes will require a direction that consists of X and Y components, assuming that you're expressing the direction in terms of Cartesian coordinates. The real point I'm getting at is that the number of elements in the direction array must match the number of elements in the axes array, even if you don't end up using all the elements. Why would you not use all the elements?

The answer has to do with the fact that you can express the direction of an effect in one of three ways:

- Cartesian coordinates
- Polar coordinates
- Spherical coordinates

Cartesian coordinates consist of simple XYZ components. However, because they are being used solely for establishing a direction, the magnitudes of the values don't really matter. For example, the following direction arrays all refer to a two-dimensional effect originating in the up, or north, direction:

```
LONG lDirection1[2] = { 0, -1 };
LONG lDirection2[2] = { 0, -4 };
LONG lDirection3[2] = { 0, -27 };
```

18

Keep in mind that the Y-axis increases down, which means that a negative Y direction indicates an upward direction.

Although Cartesian coordinates are perfectly acceptable for describing effect directions, I prefer polar coordinates. Polar coordinates involve a single value that indicates a directional angle measured clockwise from the up (north) direction, which lies at 0 degrees. So, a two-dimensional direction originating from the east direction would have the following polar coordinates:

```
LONG lDirection[2] = { 90 * DI_DEGREES, 0 };
```

Notice that the DI_DEGREES constant is used to properly convert the degrees for use with DirectInput, which expects degrees to be entered in hundredths of degrees. The DI_DEGREES constant makes the code a little easier to read. You might also be curious about the second array element, 0. If you recall, I said that the number of elements in the direction array must match the number of elements in the axes array. Because the first element is all that matters when dealing with polar coordinates, you can just set the second element to 0.

Your other option in establishing effect direction is to use spherical coordinates. Spherical coordinates are really only useful for describing three-dimensional directions, which as of yet aren't supported in any force feedback devices. So, let's skip the details of them and move on.

Now that I've hopefully convinced you to use polar coordinates to define directions, let's see some code for both the axes and direction arrays together. The following code establishes a two-dimensional effect acting from the northwest direction:

```
DWORD dwAxes[2] = { DIJOFS_X, DIJOFS_Y };
LONG  lDirection[2] = { 315 * DI_DEGREES, 0 };
```

The next step in creating an effect is to fill out a type-specific structure with details about the effect. In the case of a constant force effect, this involves filling out a DICONSTANT-FORCE structure. Fortunately, the DICONSTANTFORCE structure contains only one member, lMagnitude, which specifies the magnitude of the force. Following is code to set the magnitude of a constant force to the maximum allowable force:

```
DICONSTANTFORCE diConstantForce;
diConstantForce.lMagnitude = DI_FFNOMINALMAX;
```

The magnitude of constant force effects ranges from -10000 to +10000. The DI_FFNOMINALMAX predefined constant is set to +10000. A negative force magnitude acts in the opposite direction of the force, whereas a magnitude of 0 results in no force.

The last structure to set up for an effect is the DIEFFECT structure, which pulls together all the other effect data. This structure is where you indicate the type of coordinates used to specify the direction of the effect (DIEFF_CARTESIAN, DIEFF_POLAR, or DIEFF_SPHERICAL). You also set the duration of the effect, in microseconds, along with the gain of the effect, if any. Additionally, you can set the effect so that it is triggered automatically off one of the joystick fire buttons. Following is sample code to fill out a DIEFFECT structure for a simple constant force effect:

```
DIEFFECT diEffect;
diEffect.dwSize = sizeof(DIEFFECT);
diEffect.dwFlags = DIEFF_POLAR | DIEFF_OBJECTOFFSETS;
diEffect.dwDuration = 4 * DI_SECONDS;
diEffect.dwSamplePeriod = 0;
diEffect.dwGain = DI_FFNOMINALMAX;
diEffect.dwTriggerButton = DIEB_NOTRIGGER;
diEffect.dwTriggerRepeatInterval = 0;
diEffect.cAxes = 2;
diEffect.rgdwAxes = dwAxes;
diEffect.rglDirection = lDirection;
diEffect.lpEnvelope = NULL;
diEffect.cbTypeSpecificParams = sizeof(DICONSTANTFORCE);
diEffect.lpvTypeSpecificParams = &diConstantForce;
```

Notice that the coordinate type is set to polar, and the duration of the effect is set to 4 seconds. The gain of the effect is set to the maximum, which results in the effect playing at the full magnitude that was set in the DICONSTANTFORCE structure. A lower gain results in the force's magnitude being lessened. The effect is set so that it doesn't trigger off of a joystick fire button thanks to the DIEB_NOTRIGGER flag. Keep in mind that you can still play the effect in response to the fire button; you'll just have to do it yourself. The trigger repeat interval is used to set the repeat delay for triggered effects when a fire button is held down; in this case it doesn't apply.

The number of axes for the effect is set to 2, which indicates the lengths of both the axes and direction arrays. These arrays are then set to DIEFFECT structure members. This example doesn't use an envelope, so the lpEnvelope member is set to NULL. Finally, the DICONSTANTFORCE structure is set to the appropriate DIEFFECT member, which finishes up the preparation of the effect for creation.

Creating the effect is then as simple as calling the CreateEffect() method, like this:

```
pFFJoystick->CreateEffect(GUID_ConstantForce, &diEffect, &pConstForce, NULL);
```

The first parameter is either the global identifier returned from effect enumeration or one of the predefined global effect identifiers. The second parameter is the address of the DIEFFECT structure you just created. The third parameter is the address of the effect object to be created. And finally, the last parameter is for COM aggregation and is typically passed as NULL.

18

To put everything into perspective, Listing 18.3 contains a complete listing of the code involved in creating a simple constant force effect.

LISTING 18.3   Code to Create a Simple Constant Force Effect Originating from the West Direction

```
 1: DWORD    dwAxes[2] = { DIJOFS_X, DIJOFS_Y };
 2: LONG     lDirection[2] = { 270 * DI_DEGREES, 0 };
 3:
 4: DICONSTANTFORCE diConstantForce;
 5: diConstantForce.lMagnitude = DI_FFNOMINALMAX;
 6:
 7: DIEFFECT diEffect;
 8: diEffect.dwSize = sizeof(DIEFFECT);
 9: diEffect.dwFlags = DIEFF_POLAR | DIEFF_OBJECTOFFSETS;
10: diEffect.dwDuration = 0.5 * DI_SECONDS;
11: diEffect.dwSamplePeriod = 0;
12: diEffect.dwGain = DI_FFNOMINALMAX;
13: diEffect.dwTriggerButton = DIEB_NOTRIGGER;
14: diEffect.dwTriggerRepeatInterval = 0;
15: diEffect.cAxes = 2;
16: diEffect.rgdwAxes = dwAxes;
17: diEffect.rglDirection = lDirection;
18: diEffect.lpEnvelope = NULL;
19: diEffect.cbTypeSpecificParams = sizeof(DICONSTANTFORCE);
20: diEffect.lpvTypeSpecificParams = &diConstantForce;
21:
22: LPDIRECTINPUTEFFECT pConstForce;
23: pFFJoystick->CreateEffect(GUID_ConstantForce, &diEffect,
    ➥ &pConstForce, NULL);
```

Playing Force Feedback Effects

You'll be glad to know that the main work involved in supporting force feedback is creating the effects. Playing an effect is the easy part, as the following code demonstrates:

```
pConstForce->Start(1, 0);
```

The two parameters to the Start() method are the number of iterations for the effect and a flag indicating how the effect is to be played, respectively. In this example, the effect is played once, as evident by passing 1 as the number of iterations. You can also pass INFINITE for this value to play the effect repeatedly until it is explicitly stopped. The second parameter can use either of the flags DIES_SOLO and DIES_DOWNLOAD, or both. The DIES_SOLO flag indicates that any other effects being played should be stopped in order to play the specified effect. The DIES_DOWNLOAD flag indicates that the effect should not automatically be downloaded into the input device to be played. Passing 0 for the second parameter to Start() results in neither of these flags taking effect.

> One caveat to using INFINITE as the first parameter to Start() is that any envelope defined for the effect will be applied over and over each time the effect is played. This might be the desired result, but in some cases it might not. If you don't want this result, you can still repeat the effect by setting the dwDuration member of the DIEFFECT structure to INFINITE.

To stop an effect, you call the Stop() method, like this:

```
pConstForce->Stop();
```

Altering Force Feedback Effects

It is fairly common to alter an effect after creating it. For example, you might want to change the magnitude of a constant force in response to something that occurred in a game. DirectInput provides a straightforward approach for altering effect properties via the SetParameters() method. The SetParameters() method allows you to alter the properties of an effect using the same structures you worked with when initially creating the effect.

Earlier in the hour, you learned about some of the different flags used with the SetParameters() method. Following is an example of setting the magnitude of a constant force effect using the SetParameters() method:

```
diConstantForce.lMagnitude = DI_FFNOMINALMAX / 2;
pConstForce->SetParameters(&diEffect, DIEP_TYPESPECIFICPARAMS);
```

This code sets the magnitude of a constant force effect to half of its maximum value. Notice that this code requires you to keep around the original structures used to create the effect. You could also create and initialize new structures, but it's a lot easier to reuse the old ones. So, if you plan on altering an effect after creation, you might as well make the effect creation structures global variables.

Force Feedback Effect Recipes

To finish up the hour, I want to provide you with a couple of recipes for force feedback effects that you might find handy. Because you already have the knowledge to enumerate and create effects, I'm going to focus on the specific properties that comprise these effects.

First is an explosion effect, which is a periodic effect that makes the joystick shake for a second. This effect uses an envelope to fade out over the entire duration of the effect. Keep in mind that you will need to enumerate periodic effects in order to obtain a global identifier that will work with this effect. Listing 18.4 contains the code that describes the effect.

LISTING 18.4 Code That Describes an Explosion Force Feedback Effect

```
1: DWORD    dwAxes[1] = {DIJOFS_X};
2: LONG     lDirection[1] = {0};
3:
4: DIENVELOPE diEnvelope;
5: diEnvelope.dwSize = sizeof(DIENVELOPE);
6: diEnvelope.dwAttackLevel = 0;
7: diEnvelope.dwAttackTime = 0;
8: diEnvelope.dwFadeLevel = 0;
9: diEnvelope.dwFadeTime = 1.0 * DI_SECONDS;
10:
11: DIPERIODIC diPeriodic;
12: diPeriodic.dwMagnitude = DI_FFNOMINALMAX;
13: diPeriodic.lOffset = 0;
14: diPeriodic.dwPhase = 0;
15: diPeriodic.dwPeriod = 0.1 * DI_SECONDS;
16:
17: DIEFFECT diEffect;
18: diEffect.dwSize = sizeof(DIEFFECT);
19: diEffect.dwFlags = DIEFF_OBJECTOFFSETS | DIEFF_CARTESIAN;
20: diEffect.dwDuration = 1.0 * DI_SECONDS;
21: diEffect.dwSamplePeriod = 0;
22: diEffect.dwGain = DI_FFNOMINALMAX;
23: diEffect.dwTriggerButton = DIEB_NOTRIGGER;
24: diEffect.dwTriggerRepeatInterval = 0;
25: diEffect.cAxes = 1;
26: diEffect.rgdwAxes = dwAxes;
27: diEffect.rglDirection = lDirection;
28: diEffect.lpEnvelope = &diEnvelope;
29: diEffect.cbTypeSpecificParams = sizeof(DIPERIODIC);
30: diEffect.lpvTypeSpecificParams = &diPeriodic;
```

Another useful effect is a gunfire effect that quickly shakes the joystick in response to a gun being fired. Listing 18.5 contains the code for this effect.

LISTING 18.5 Code That Describes a Gunfire Force Feedback Effect

```
1: DWORD    dwAxes[1] = {DIJOFS_Y};
2: LONG     lDirection[1] = {1};
3:
4: DICONSTANTFORCE diConstantForce;
5: diConstantForce.lMagnitude = DI_FFNOMINALMAX;
6:
7: DIEFFECT diEffect;
8: diEffect.dwSize = sizeof(DIEFFECT);
9: diEffect.dwFlags = DIEFF_CARTESIAN | DIEFF_OBJECTOFFSETS;
10: diEffect.dwDuration = 0.02 * DI_SECONDS;
11: diEffect.dwSamplePeriod = 0;
```

```
12: diEffect.dwGain = DI_FFNOMINALMAX;
13: diEffect.dwTriggerButton = DIEB_NOTRIGGER;
14: diEffect.dwTriggerRepeatInterval = 0;
15: diEffect.cAxes = 1;
16: diEffect.rgdwAxes = dwAxes;
17: diEffect.rglDirection = lDirection;
18: diEffect.lpEnvelope = NULL;
19: diEffect.cbTypeSpecificParams = sizeof(DICONSTANTFORCE);
20: diEffect.lpvTypeSpecificParams = &diConstantForce;
```

Because the gunfire effect acts in a single direction to simulate a gun "kicking" at you, I decided to demonstrate how to use Cartesian coordinates.

By studying these two effects, you should be able to come up with some interesting effects of your own. This is certainly a situation in which exploring different values can be extremely interesting.

Summary

This hour continues the previous hour's coverage of DirectInput, by introducing you to the force feedback features of DirectInput. You began the hour by learning some of the basic terminology associated with force feedback programming, along with some key concepts necessary to move forward and implement force feedback in games. From there, you peeked inside the DirectInputEffect COM object and studied some of the methods it supports for creating and playing force feedback effects.

You then spent the remainder of the hour learning the ins and outs of creating and using force feedback effects. It was hopefully comforting for you to learn that force feedback doesn't change much in the way input devices are handled by DirectInput; it really is an additional feature that you can support if you so desire. The hour ends by showing you a couple of force feedback effect "recipes" that you can try out in your own games.

Q&A

Q Is it possible to alter the magnitude of all forces on a given device?

A Yes. In addition to using gain to alter the magnitude of individual forces, you can also use gain to alter the magnitude of all forces played on a given device. You set the gain for an entire device by calling the `SetProperty()` method on the device and including `DIEP_GAIN` in the flags parameter.

18

Q How does DirectInput support device-specific force feedback effects?

A DirectInput supports device-specific force feedback effects in much the same way as it supports standard effects. The main difference is that the hardware device vendor is responsible for providing a global identifier for the effect, as well as a custom structure for the type-specific parameters of the effect. After you have the global identifier and the type-specific structure, you can proceed with initializing and creating the effect just as you would any other effect.

Q I've noticed an I-FORCE logo on many DirectX games. Are these games using DirectInput?

A Yes. I-FORCE is an after-market SDK that abstracts DirectInput force effect creation, storage, retrieval, and real-time control by treating force effects in a way similar to sounds or other resources.

Workshop

The Workshop is designed to help you anticipate possible questions, review what you've learned, and begin thinking ahead to put your knowledge into practice. The answers to the quiz are in Appendix A, "Answers."

Quiz

1. What is the force of a force feedback effect?
2. What is the magnitude of a force?
3. How does gain impact an effect?
4. What specific direction does the direction of a force indicate?
5. What is a periodic effect?
6. What is an envelope?
7. What is the sustain of an effect?
8. What is the attack of an effect?
9. What is the fade of an effect?
10. What are the four basic types of force feedback effects?

Exercises

1. Modify the cityscape application from the previous hour so that it supports force feedback. More specifically, add a gunshot constant force effect that quickly jars the joystick each time the main fire button is pressed. You'll also want to play a gunshot sound to make the effect more realistic.

2. Modify the cityscape application so that a rumbling effect is played whenever the taxi drives by. You will need to use a periodic effect to accomplish this.

HOUR 19

3D Sound—From Panning to Doppler Effects

In Hour 6, "DirectSound—Adding Ambience and Sound Effects to Your Game," I introduced you to DirectSound, and you learned how to create DirectSound buffers and manage such important tasks as low-latency sound mixing and playback. You saw, in some detail, the mechanics of the DirectSound API and how you use the methods DirectSound supports to add realistic (low-latency) sound effects to your game.

This hour takes you a step further. Hour 6 was intentionally vague regarding the fascinating realm of 3D sound. After all, it's one thing to hear an opponent, but it's quite another to hear the opponent in 3D space! I mentioned the 3D aspects of DirectSound casually, but I didn't really get into the meat of 3D sound and the interfaces necessary to pull it off.

In this hour, you will learn

- The physics of sound and how we perceive sound
- How DirectSound supports 3D sound simulation
- How to create and use 3D sound buffers and listeners
- How to use 3D sound in games

Introduction to 3D Sound

I fondly recall some of the earliest computer games I owned, dating back to my Apple II days. *Sound*, at least at that time, consisted of bleeps and dings created by successive reads to the Apple's speaker port. The more often you read the port, the more often the speaker would emit a tiny sound. If you varied the rate at which you read the speaker port, you were rewarded with a varyingly pitched sound.

The early days of the PC weren't much better, but soon dedicated sound hardware was introduced and better sounds and music emanated from the PC's speaker, and later, stereo speakers. Even so, the sounds were still two dimensional—flat and lifeless.

Today, there is a wealth of ongoing research studying spatial sound and how humans perceive sound. True, much of the research isn't directed at game programming in particular, but I see no reason why game programmers can't take advantage of innovations in 3D sound generation to enhance their user's gaming experience, even with only two speakers. Microsoft must feel the same as I do because they have put together a formidable 3D sound package, and as you'll soon see, using it isn't hard to do at all. After you understand some basic terms and concepts, adding 3D sound effects is easy!

The Physics of Sound

What is sound? In a nutshell, sound is nothing more than moving air. The air around us is compressed and expanded by pressure waves. (That's why there is no sound in space, no matter what *Star Wars* would have you believe!) In the real world, then, sound is created when things vibrate. When an object vibrates, the air around it ebbs and flows at the same rate as the object's oscillation, at least in close proximity to the object. The faster the object moves, the faster the air moves. If the object vibrates more forcefully, so does the air.

With this simplistic understanding, here are some key terms and illustrations to help you understand sound in 3D.

NEW TERM   *Spatial sound* is another reference to sound in three dimensions.

Pitch is the frequency of the pressure wave's oscillation. The faster the oscillation, the higher the pitch (frequency). Conversely, the slower the oscillation, the lower the pitch.

NEW TERM *Volume* is the relative strength of the pressure wave. Waves with higher energy levels are louder, whereas waves with less energy are quieter.

NEW TERM *Rolloff* is the reduction in volume because of increased distance from the vibrating object. Air *attentuates* pressure waves over distance, which is to say sound can't travel forever at the same intensity (volume).

NEW TERM *Doppler shift* is the effect of increasing and decreasing pitch as the vibrating object moves past the listener. In effect, if the object is moving towards you, the object's velocity is added to the sound frequency, causing an increase in pitch. You similarly hear a decrease in pitch as the object travels away from you because the velocity of the object is subtracted from the sound frequency. I'll also refer to this as *Doppler effect*.

Figure 19.1 tries to show the relationship between the density of sound pressure waves and pitch. The higher the wave frequency, the higher the pitch. Figure 19.1 also tries to indicate rolloff. The person close to the car hears the horn quite loudly, whereas the more distant person hears a quieter horn, if they can hear it at all.

FIGURE 19.1

Sound waves, pitch (frequency), and rolloff.

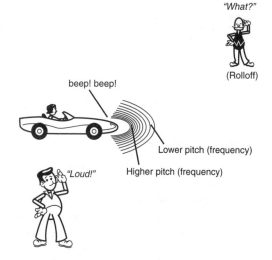

"What?"

(Rolloff)

beep! beep!

Lower pitch (frequency)

"Loud!" Higher pitch (frequency)

19

The Doppler effect is really about frequency shifting. That is, if you were stationary and the car approached you at a high rate of speed and honked, the sound you would hear would be of a higher pitch than if the car were stationary near you. Similarly, if the car were driving away at a high rate of speed and honked, you would hear a lower pitch than if the car were simply parked nearby. It isn't that the car's horn changed its sound, but rather that you, as the listener, perceive the sound differently because of the *motion* of the car. Figure 19.2 tries to show you this effect visually. Note that nothing I've said indicates that the listener must be stationary. In fact, it's often the case that the sound's source and the listener are *both* in motion, thus complicating matters!

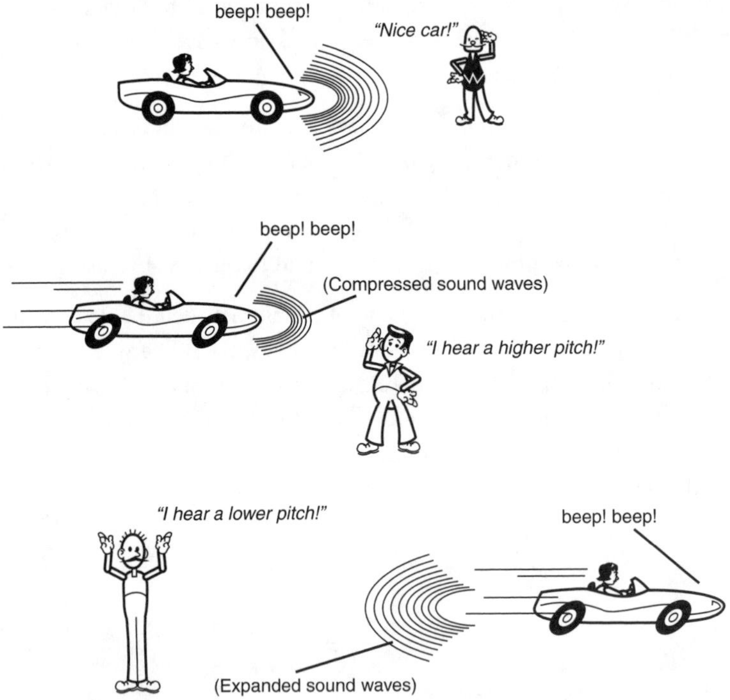

FIGURE 19.2
The Doppler effect.

How We Perceive Sound

You probably noticed I used the word *perceive* in that last paragraph. Sound, and any sense really, is all about perception. The Doppler effect is only evident for the stationary person, if you refer back to my idealized scenario in Figure 19.2. The person driving the car will hear essentially the same horn sound in every case. But we perceive more than frequency shifts—we also perceive direction, as well as volume (sound intensity or rolloff) and can apply many filters (and I'm not referring to "selective hearing", which my children sometimes employ). Our sense of hearing is somewhat akin to our stereoscopic sight. We have two eyes not only for redundancy, but also to perceive depth. In a similar manner, we have two ears to perceive spatial sounds. If a bee flies behind us while we're blindfolded, we still know the bee is behind us.

Though the actual human auditory perception model is much more complicated than what I will discuss here, there are four main factors that influence our perception of a sound's origin:

- Rolloff
- Intensity difference
- Intensity delay
- Muffling

I discussed *rolloff* earlier in the hour. But to recap, the closer you are to a sound's source, the louder the sound will be. You sense an object's distance by internally processing rolloff.

Intensity difference helps you discern from which direction a sound's origin is placed. If an object making a sound is to your left, the sound pressure wave will hit your left ear with slightly more intensity that it will strike your right ear. Your ears are nominally capable of sensing very small differences in sound pressure.

Just as you are able to sense differences in sound intensity, you are able also to sense differences in sound timing. Using my previous example, the sound would strike your left ear slightly before it would strike your right ear. Your brain interprets this *intensity delay* to also help place an object's origin in 3D space.

Finally, your ears are designed to focus your listening attention to sounds emanating from in front of your current spatial position. Clearly, though, sounds can come from somewhere behind you. To help you decide if the sound comes from in front or behind you, your ears *muffle* sounds from behind. Your brain then interprets muffled sounds as originating from behind you.

Your brain interprets all these incoming cues and applies to them a mathematical transformation using a formula known as the *head-related transfer function*. Of course, your transfer function is likely very different from my own because our heads are not shaped the same, our ears are not located in the same places on our heads, and so on. But the process we go through to interpret the sound and its location is very similar.

19

The single most important cue you can provide your user, however, is to make sure that the visual object you are rendering holds a spatial location similar to the spatial location of the sound you are generating at the time. If your spaceship moves to the left at such-and-such a velocity, your sound cues must closely match the motion of the spaceship.

The four factors I just mentioned are the major design factors behind DirectSound3D. You have to make sure that your visual objects are tied adequately to your aural ones. And nobody can help you if your head-related transfer function only processes polkas! In any case, before you begin writing DirectSound3D code, I'll briefly touch on the architectural differences between 2D and 3D DirectSound.

The Architecture of DirectSound3D

You examined DirectSound in some detail in Hour 6, and I even briefly described there the interfaces you'll be using here. So the basic architecture of DirectSound3D is very much the same as the 2D version. You're still using DirectSound.

The major difference is DirectSound3D doesn't use `IDirectSoundBuffer`. Instead, because you will be applying several dynamic sound filters to your sound buffer, DirectSound3D employs the `IDirectSound3DBuffer` interface. Essentially, the `IDirectSound3DBuffer` interface allows you to set additional parameters related to your sound's spatial location and tone. The other main difference is DirectSound3D adds the notion of a *listener*. It is the listener's perception of the sound that counts the most when using spatial sound. For this, DirectSound3D uses the `IDirectSound3DListener` interface. It is through these interfaces that you will adjust the sound parameters to truly make the sounds move in space, at least as far as your users are concerned. I'll discuss each of these interfaces and how you use them in the next section.

DirectSound 3D Components

As I've mentioned, spatial sounds require both a sound source, simulated by the sound buffer, and a sound sink. The specialized 3D sound buffer, `IDirectSound3Dbuffer`, enables you to provide a motion cue to your sound source and filter the aural signatures of the sounds DirectSound will generate. The sound sink, which is ultimately your user, is represented in DirectSound3D by `IDirectSound3DListener`. `IDirectSound3DListener` is used to apply Doppler Shift and rolloff, just as if the listener were truly in the simulation. I'll begin by describing `IDirectSound3DBuffer`, and then I'll discuss `IDirectSound3DListener`.

DirectSound 3D Buffers

Because you are using a variation of DirectSound, all that you learned from Hour 6 applies here. You create your DirectSound object in the same manner and query for its various interfaces just as you did before. However, to obtain an `IDirectSound3DBuffer` versus an `IDirectSoundBuffer` interface, you must create your sound buffer slightly differently. Before I show how this is done, take a look at the methods `IDirectSound3DBuffer` provides:

- GetAllParameters()
- SetAllParameters()
- GetMaxDistance()
- GetMinDistance()
- SetMaxDistance()
- SetMinDistance()
- GetMode()
- SetMode()
- GetPosition()
- SetPosition()
- GetConeAngles()
- GetConeOrientation()
- GetConeOutsideVolume()
- SetConeAngles()
- SetConeOrientation()
- SetConeOutsideVolume()
- GetVelocity()
- SetVelocity()
- AddRef()
- QueryInterface()
- Release()

19

As you can see, IDirectSound3DBuffer is very different from IDirectSoundBuffer. The good news is IDirectSound3Dbuffer inherits the capabilities of IDirectSoundBuffer, and so all the things you could do with a sound buffer in 2D you can also do in 3D. IDirectSound3DBuffer enhances the capabilities of sound buffer management rather than replaces the functionality you've come to expect. Knowing this, it's time to see how you create a 3D sound buffer.

Creating the Buffers

As you saw in Hour 6, you use the DirectSound API method CreateSoundBuffer() to obtain a new sound buffer (and you'll require a new sound buffer for every sound you intend to generate). To reiterate, though, here is the method signature:

```
HRESULT CreateSoundBuffer(LPCDSBUFFERDESC lpcDSBufferDesc,
    LPLPDIRECTSOUNDBUFFER lplpDirectSoundBuffer, IUnknown FAR * pUnkOuter);
```

So far, there's no difference. The trick is to add a parameter to the DSBUFFERDESC structure before you make the CreateSoundBuffer() call. As you know, you set the dwFlags attribute to tailor the capabilities of the buffer you are requesting. In this case, you add the DSBCAPS_CTRL3D flag and specify a 3D processing algorithm. This code would initialize the DSBUFFERDESC structure for 3D sound:

```
DSBUFFERDESC dsbd;
ZeroMemory(&dsbd, sizeof(DSBUFFERDESC));
dsbd.dwSize       = sizeof(DSBUFFERDESC);
dsbd.dwFlags      = DSBCAPS_STATIC |
                    DSBCAPS_CTRL3D |
                    DSBCAPS_CTRLFREQUENCY |
                    DSBCAPS_CTRLVOLUME |
                    DSBCAPS_CTRLPAN;
dsbd.dwBufferBytes = dwSoundSize; // set on a per-sound basis
dsbd.lpwfxFormat   = dwSoundFormat; // set on a per-sound basis
dsbdDesc.guid3DAlgorithm = GUID_NULL; // or DS3DALG _DEFAULT
```

In this case, you're asking for a static 3D sound buffer with volume, panning, and frequency control capability that will use the default 2-speaker virtualization algorithm. After you initialize this structure and pass it to CreateSoundBuffer(), you simply query for IDirectSound3DBuffer:

```
// Note pDSB is returned from CreateSoundBuffer()
LPDIRECTSOUND3DBUFFER pDS3DB = NULL;
pDSB->QueryInterface(IID_IDirectSound3DBuffer, (LPVOID*)&pDS3DB;
```

Now you have both an IDirectSoundBuffer and an IDirectSound3DBuffer interface pointer with which you can manipulate your sound's characteristics. Knowing this, it's time to examine the capabilities of IDirectSound3DBuffer more closely.

If you're using DirectX 7 but want compatibility with DirectX 6.1, you should use the DSBUFFERDESC1 structure to create your sound buffers. DirectX 6.1 has no concept of 2-speaker virtualization.

DirectX 7.0 has eliminated the DSBCAPS_CTRLDEFAULT buffer flag, which was formerly available in DirectX 6.1. Instead, you should use the individual flags DSBCAPS_CTRL3D, DSBCAPS_CTRLFREQUENCY, DSBCAPS_CTRLPAN, and DSBCAPS_CTRLVOLUME.

Establishing Sound Characteristics

Sounds have characteristics just as visual objects do. That is, a visual object might appear to be green with scales (and chasing you!). Well, a sound might be directional and be emitted from a moving source (the green monster is growling at you). In this section, I want to concentrate on sound parameter *batch mode processing* and the concept of *directional sound*. In a later section, you'll examine the buffer's *processing mode*, which is related to how DirectSound3D actually applies the filters to the buffer to create differing effects.

You'll often find it the case when programming for low-latency, as you do when writing game code, that setting individual parameters can be costly. That is, if you have some arbitrary object that requires five parameters to be established prior to using the object, you would normally have to make five separate method calls to initialize the object for use. If setting a parameter is expensive (from the object's processing perspective), it makes sense to change parameters rarely. It's best if you can pack as much parameter modification into a single call.

Enter batch parameter processing. By using `IDirectSound3DBuffer::GetAllParameters()` and `IDirectSound3DBuffer::SetAllParameters()`, you can effectively set any 3D sound buffer parameter entirely at once. These two methods use the `DS3DBUFFER` DirectSound3D structure, defined as such:

```
typedef struct {
    DWORD       dwSize;
    D3DVECTOR   vPosition;
    D3DVECTOR   vVelocity;
    DWORD       dwInsideConeAngle;
    DWORD       dwOutsideConeAngle;
    D3DVECTOR   vConeOrientation;
    LONG        lConeOutsideVolume;
    D3DVALUE    flMinDistance;
    D3DVALUE    flMaxDistance;
    DWORD       dwMode;
} DS3DBUFFER, *LPDS3DBUFFER;
```

When you establish new parameters, you also have the option of specifying when they should be applied. You might choose to have them applied immediately, or you might defer their effects until a later time. These constants are used to tell DirectSound3D when to apply the changes:

- `DS3D_DEFERRED`
- `DS3D_IMMEDIATE`

19

Note if you use `DS3D_DEFERRED`, you must call the `IDirectSound3DListener::`
`CommitDeferredSettings()` method to have the changes applied. All deferred settings
will be enacted at that time. The advantage to deferring the change in settings is you can
defer the lengthy recalculations that will likely take place as a result of the parameter
change. You will generally want to have more control over lengthy calculations than less!

I'll leave the positional and velocity parameter values for the next section. Instead, I'll
now concentrate on directional sound. Some sound sources are *omnidirectional*. That is,
they emanate sound in all directions at once, like an explosion. Other sounds, though,
have a directional component, such as spoken voice. When you speak, your voice is
directed from your mouth towards the listener. True, others nearby will hear your voice,
but the bulk of the sound energy travels in a line from your mouth to your listener's ear.

You can imagine directional sound travelling as if it were in a conic section. Sound
energy within the conic section is not attenuated (rolloff is not applied). Sound energy
outside this cone is attenuated (its energy is decreased) until no energy remains and the
sound is not heard. DirectSound3D provides for this effect by allowing you to set each
of two conic sections. The first section, the *inner cone*, has no attenuation applied. The
inner cone is contained by an *outer cone*, outside of which no sound is heard. Between
the two conic sections, the sound is attenuated. Figure 19.3 depicts this.

FIGURE 19.3
*Directed sound and
inner and outer cones.*

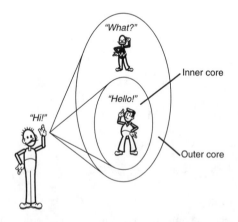

When you create a DirectSound3D sound buffer, all sounds are omnidirectional. In
effect, the inner cone and outer cone emanate 360 degrees and are essentially the same
cone. If your application requires a more directed sound, you might change the default
conic section values and apply directed sound qualities to your sound buffer. To do this,
you can either use the batch parameter processing methods I mentioned earlier, or you
could use the targeted parameter methods `IDirectSound3DBuffer::GetConeXXXX()`
and `IDirectSound3DBuffer::SetConeXXXX()`, where *XXXX* represents the particular
parameter in question.

Setting Buffer Location and Velocity

You might or might not require directed sound, but if you're programming 3D sound, you surely will want to establish the sound's location and velocity. If both the object and the listener are in motion, you'll probably want to set the buffer processing mode to DS3DMODE_HEADRELATIVE to make your calculations somewhat simpler. You'll see this a bit later in the hour. For now, it's time to address a sound's location and velocity.

Setting the sound's position and velocity is a simple matter. You either establish them using the batch parameter processing methods I described earlier, or you call the individual methods IDirectSound3DBuffer::Get/SetVelocity() and IDirectSound3DBuffer::Get/SetPosition(). What makes things interesting is the value passed to these methods is a vector quantity. That is, you must provide enough spatial information to properly place the sound in 3D space and describe its motion. You might remember that I introduced the D3DVECTOR structure in Hour 10, "Introduction to 3D Objects," and discussed the reasoning behind the use of vectors in 3D space. That same reasoning applies in this case as well.

When you work with the sound's positional value, the vector you are dealing with represents the location of the sound's object in either absolute world coordinates (from the origin) or as a relative displacement from the listener. The processing mode you select determines this. As with all parameters, when you set a new position, you supply not only the vector, but you also must tell DirectSound3D when to apply the modification (as I discussed earlier).

The sound's velocity is actually used to calculate the appropriate Doppler shift relative to the given listener. This is an important point—the velocity value *is not* used to move the buffer in 3D space! The value you set here is used for Doppler calculations only.

> Setting the buffer's velocity affects the Doppler Shift calculations *only*. The buffer *is not* moved! To move the buffer in 3D space, you simply adjust the positional value according to your object's equations of motion.

The value you supply for distance units is assumed to be in meters. If you're interested in working with other values, such as feet, you must calculate the appropriate conversion value and provide that to the IDirectSound3DListener::SetDistanceFactor() method. Note, however, that internally DirectSound3D will still use meters as the unit of measurement. It will merely apply your conversion factor as required to properly calculate the sound's location in 3D space.

Now that you have a 3D sound buffer and know how to manipulate its parameters, it's time you were introduced to the listener. *Something* ought to hear your sounds after all this work!

DirectSound 3D Listener

If a tree falls in the woods, does it make a sound? If you're there to hear it, it sure does. And that's the point—without someone to hear the sound, who cares (except for the tree, of course)? That's where the DirectSound3D *listener* comes in. The DirectSound3D listener acts as your user's avatar in your game. Through the listener object, you place your user within your 3D realm and manipulate the acoustics to enhance the realism of the play. I'll now go over the IDirectSound3DListener interface and describe how you use it to achieve stellar audio effects.

Creating the Listener

DirectSound by itself has no concept of a listener—you merely play sounds and control sound timing. So when you enter the 3D world, you have more work to do. And so it is with creating the listener. All I have discussed regarding DirectSound and the enhancements IDirectSound3DBuffer makes still apply. But in this case, you have the additional tasks of creating another DirectX object and managing its lifetime.

Creating the listener is a simple matter, however. After you have created your primary sound buffer using IDirectSound::CreateSoundBuffer(), you query for the listener. Here is an example:

```
DSBUFFERDESC dsbd;
ZeroMemory( &dsbd, sizeof(DSBUFFERDESC) );
dsbd.dwSize  = sizeof(DSBUFFERDESC);
dsbd.dwFlags = DSBCAPS_CTRL3D¦DSBCAPS_PRIMARYBUFFER;

// pDS is a LPDIRECTSOUND pointer created earlier
LPDIRECTSOUNDBUFFER pdsbPrimary = NULL;
if( FAILED(pDS->CreateSoundBuffer(&dsbd, &pdsbPrimary, NULL)) )
    return E_FAIL;

LPDIRECTSOUND3DLISTENER pdslListener = NULL;
if( FAILED(pdsbPrimary->QueryInterface(IID_IDirectSound3DListener,
                                (LPVOID*)&pdslListener)) )
    return E_FAIL;
```

The thing to note here is the primary sound buffer is created using the same DSBCAPS_CTRL3D flag you saw earlier. If you forget this, you won't obtain a listener interface. Assuming that you do have a listener interface, I'll now list the methods the interface provides, and then I'll discuss how you use them. Here are the IDirectSound3DListener methods:

- GetAllParameters()

- SetAllParameters()

- CommitDeferredSettings()

- GetDistanceFactor()

- SetDistanceFactor()

- GetDopplerFactor()

- SetDopplerFactor()

- GetOrientation()

- SetOrientation()

- GetPosition()

- SetPosition()

- GetRolloffFactor()

- SetRolloffFactor()

- GetVelocity()

- SetVelocity()

- AddRef()

- QueryInterface()

- Release()

As you see, you have methods similar to those of IDirectSound3DBuffer, in that you have batch parameter processing capability, or you can set individual parameters at will, depending on your needs at the time. You can also see the IDirectSound3Dlistener::CommitDeferredSettings() method I mentioned for processing all your stored batch parameters.

Doppler and Rolloff Settings

The reason you've gone to the trouble you have to provide for spatial sounds in your game is you want to enhance the realism for your user when he plays. This is directly coupled with the physics of sound I covered earlier. In our daily lives, we use many aural cues to position sounds within our perception of reality. Computers, however, have to create those sounds using, at best, stereophonic equipment. To *simulate* 3D sounds, DirectSound3D provides sound filtering capabilities, the primary of which are for Doppler effects and rolloff. This is your big chance!

Now that you have an IDirectSound3Dlistener DirectSound3D object, you can begin to apply real-world effects. As I discuss Doppler effects and rolloff, remember that Doppler effects simulate *motion*, whereas rolloff simulates *distance*.

19

First, I will discuss Doppler effects. Given a sound object/listener pair, DirectSound3D will automatically calculate for you the Doppler effect present between the pair when either or both have velocities established. You are free to change the manner in which the Doppler shift is calculated by using the IDirectSound3Dlistener::Get/SetDoppler Factor() methods (or by dealing them in a batch). Note that Doppler effects are cumulative. That is, if either or both of the pair is moving, DirectSound3D will adjust the Doppler effect heard by the listener automatically. Any global additions (or subtractions) you make by setting a new Doppler factor will be taken into account when the parameter is changed.

The trick to all this is to determine how your objects are moving and set their respective DirectSound3D velocities accordingly. I discussed the buffer's velocity setting earlier, and I'll address the listener's velocity setting in the next section. Without motion, there is no Doppler effect! How the sound will be perceived depends on how you move these objects. Changing the overall Doppler setting can enhance or retard the Doppler effect globally.

The Doppler value you use will range between these values:

- DS3D_MINDOPPLERFACTOR
- DS3D_MAXDOPPLERFACTOR

DS3D_MINDOPPLERFACTOR is currently defined to be 0.0, whereas DS3D_MAXDOPPLERFACTOR is currently defined to be 10.0. Using a value of DS3D_MINDOPPLERFACTOR indicates no Doppler effects will be calculated. A value of 1.0, defined as DS3D_DEFAULTDOPPLERFACTOR, indicates real-world Doppler shifts are to be used. Any value greater than DS3D_DEFAULT-DOPPLERFACTOR (up to DS3D_MAXDOPPLERFACTOR) compounds the Doppler effect. If you set the Doppler factor setting to DS3D_MAXDOPPLERFACTOR, what you are requesting is that you want 10 times the Doppler effect to be heard than would be heard in a real-world scenario.

So much for Doppler effects. I'll now turn to discussing rolloff. You adjust the rolloff factor to indicate relative distance between the object generating the sound and the listener. Dealing with rolloff is very much like dealing with the Doppler effects. DirectSound3D will calculate for you the nominal rolloff based on object positions, but you're free to adjust that by setting a new rolloff factor value using the batch methods or by using IDirectSound3Dlistener::Get/SetRolloffFactor(). And, like Doppler effects, rolloff has a predefined range and default setting. The range values are defined in this manner:

- DS3D_MINROLLOFFFACTOR
- DS3D_MAXROLLOFFFACTOR

You use these values in the same manner as Doppler effects, and the default value DS3D_DEFAULTROLLOFFFACTOR is the same numerical value (1.0). Rolloff values of less than 1.0 (but greater than 0.0) indicate the sound will carry abnormally further than in a real-world setting. A rolloff factor of greater than 1.0 means that the sounds will be muted in a much shorter distance than in the real world. And remember, the setting you use here is a multiplicative factor, so a setting of DS3D_MAXROLLOFFFACTOR would mean the rolloff is ten times more severe than you would find in the real world.

Setting Listener Position and Velocity

You've already seen how to change the sound buffer's position and velocity, and it might not be surprising to find the listener reacts in the very same fashion. You're always free to set the parameters in a batch scenario, or you can use the individual methods designed for each parameter. Regarding position, you would use IDirectSound3Dlistener::Get/SetPosition(). For velocity, you would use IDirectSound3Dlistener::Get/SetVelocity(). And like the sound buffer, the velocity term doesn't refer to the motion of the listener but rather to the velocity used to calculate the Doppler effect. To simulate the motion of the listener, you continuously set the position value according to the equations of motion you've defined for your listener object.

As with the buffer, setting the listener's velocity affects the Doppler shift calculations *only*. The listener itself *is not* moved! To move the listener in 3D space, you adjust the positional value according to your object's equations of motion.

19

The positional and velocity values are initially set to be in meters and meters per second, respectively. You might remember that I mentioned the IDirectSound3DListener::SetDistanceFactor() method when I discussed these parameters regarding sound buffers. To reiterate, you can easily change the distance factor by supplying a new conversion value (from meters to feet, for example). You might find this handy in some situations.

The major difference between the sound buffer object and the listener is the listener has an *orientation*. Orientation refers to how the listener's head is canted, either up or down, as shown in Figure 19.4. When you hear sounds, the sound pressure levels will be greater if you look directly towards the sound's source than if you are looking 90 degrees above it. DirectSound3D takes this into account when making its filter calculations.

FIGURE 19.4

DirectSound3D orientation and vectors (initial setting).

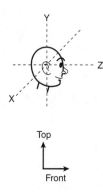

Orientation is established in terms of two vectors, the *top vector* and the *front vector*. If the listener is oriented normally, the top vector points upwards and the front vector points out of the front of their face. In this case, the top vector would be (0.0, 1.0, 0.0)—all y-axis. Similarly, the front vector defaults to (0.0, 0.0, 1.0), or all z-axis. If the listener's head tilted back 45 degrees, both the top and front vectors would change accordingly. The top and front vectors would change in terms of the YZ plane (this assumes that the listener's head doesn't also turn as it tilts, which would introduce an X term). The new top vector would be

(0.0, sin(45), -cos(45))

The new front vector would then become

(0.0, sin(45), cos(45))

Figure 19.5 should help clarify my calculations.

FIGURE 19.5

45 degree canted orientation and resulting vectors.

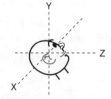

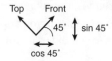

When you have your orientation vector, you use the `IDirectSound3Dlistener::Get/SetOrientation()` methods to put it into effect. Note the vectors must be orthogonal; that is, they must form a right angle to each other. If you miscalculate one or the other, DirectSound3D will adjust the front vector to be orthogonal with the top vector—the top vector takes priority.

Processing 3DSound

I elected to defer discussion of the processing mode until this point because it is important to understand the basics of both the DirectSound3D buffer and listener objects when dealing with mode settings. As it happens, you have the capability to set the buffer's sound *processing mode*. That is, you can turn off 3D sound entirely, control the sound via the listener object (and have the buffer update its parameters accordingly for you), or manipulate the buffer parameters yourself. The `IDirectSound3DBuffer::GetMode()` and `IDirectSound3DBuffer::SetMode()` methods use a single parameter from this list:

- `DS3DMODE_DISABLE`
- `DS3DMODE_HEADRELATIVE`
- `DS3DMODE_NORMAL`

`DS3DMODE_DISABLE` simply does as it claims—3D sound processing is disabled. `DS3DMODE_HEADRELATIVE` puts DirectSound3D into a mode in which you are able to maneuver the listener and have DirectSound3D automatically update the parameters for the buffer. This enables the buffer's absolute sound parameters to be automatically set, based on listener parameters, so that the relative settings between the sound object and the listener are constant. And `DS3DMODE_NORMAL` simply sets the processing mode to require you to manage both the object's and the listener's parameters, respectively, using absolute coordinate values.

The reason the processing mode is so important is the calculations involved with placing the sound object and the listener, as well as determining their velocities (for Doppler effects, anyway), can be quite involved. DirectSound3D makes you an offer you can't easily refuse! DirectSound3D will manage the calculations for the sound object for you, if you want. This is a good deal because it saves you time and processor cycles. True, the calculations still must be made to determine the relative velocities between the objects, but those calculations will be made using optimized DirectSound3D code rather than code *you* had to write and test. That's a bargain, believe me.

Adding DirectSound 3D to Your Application

In this section, you will learn how to add 3D sound to the application you've been building along the way. As you remember from previous work, the siren sound seemed to go from left to right (or right to left) and would fade in the distance. You simulated this effect by panning (the movement) and by controlling the volume (less volume at distant points). When you add 3D effects, none of this is necessary. In the 3D case, DirectSound3D handles the rolloff for you, which replaces the volume work you did, and the apparent motion of the sound is handled by setting the buffer's 3D position, which eliminates the panning. I'll begin by creating the listener object.

Creating the Listener

Listener creation is really a three-step process. You first create a primary sound buffer; then you query the resulting buffer for the listener; and finally, you initialize the listener. To help with these three steps, I created two rather simple helper functions, create_3dlistener() and init_3deffects().

create_3dlistener(), shown in Listing 19.1, creates the primary sound buffer and queries it for the IDirectSound3DListener interface, very much as you saw earlier in the chapter.

LISTING 19.1   Code That Creates a 3D Listener Object

```
 1: //------ Function to create the 3D listener interface ------//
 2:
 3: BOOL create_3dlistener()
 4: {
 5:     // Setup the DS buffer description
 6:     DSBUFFERDESC dsbdDesc;
 7:     ZeroMemory(&dsbdDesc, sizeof(DSBUFFERDESC));
 8:     dsbdDesc.dwSize = sizeof(DSBUFFERDESC);
 9:     dsbdDesc.dwFlags = DSBCAPS_PRIMARYBUFFER | DSBCAPS_CTRL3D;
10:     dsbdDesc.guid3DAlgorithm = DS3DALG_DEFAULT;
11:
12:     // Create the DS buffer
13:     if (lpDS->CreateSoundBuffer(&dsbdDesc,
14:         &lpDSPrimary, NULL) != DS_OK)
15:     {
16:         ErrStr = Err_CreateBuff;
17:         return FALSE;
18:     }
19:
20:     if (lpDSPrimary->QueryInterface(IID_IDirectSound3DListener,
21:                               (LPVOID*)&lpDS3DListener) !=
22:         DS_OK)
23:     {
24:         ErrStr = Err_Create3DList;
25:         return FALSE;
26:     }
27:
28:     return TRUE;
29: }
```

If any part of this fails, the FALSE return value will cause the application to terminate with an appropriate error message shown in a message box. After I call create_3dlistener(), I call the second helper function, init_3deffects(). init_3deffects() is shown in Listing 19.2.

LISTING 19.2 Code That Initializes the 3D Objects

```
 1: //------ Function to initialize the 3D objects -----//
 2:
 3: BOOL init_3deffects()
 4: {
 5:     // First, the listener
 6:     DS3DLISTENER dsListenerParms;
 7:     ZeroMemory(&dsListenerParms, sizeof(DS3DLISTENER));
 8:     dsListenerParms.dwSize = sizeof(DS3DLISTENER);
 9:
10:     // Retrieve current parameters for later modification
11:     if ( FAILED(lpDS3DListener->GetAllParameters(&dsListenerParms)) )
12:     {
13:         ErrStr = Err_Create3DParm;
14:         return FALSE;
15:     }
16:
17:     // Modify the current parameters
18:     dsListenerParms.flDopplerFactor = DS3D_DEFAULTDOPPLERFACTOR;
19:     dsListenerParms.flRolloffFactor = DS3D_DEFAULTROLLOFFFACTOR;
20:     if ( FAILED(lpDS3DListener->SetAllParameters(&dsListenerParms,
                                            DS3D_IMMEDIATE)) )
21:     {
22:         ErrStr = Err_Create3DList;
23:         return FALSE;
24:     }
25:
26:     // Then, the buffer
27:     DS3DBUFFER dsBufferParms;
28:     ZeroMemory(&dsBufferParms, sizeof(DS3DBUFFER));
29:     dsBufferParms.dwSize = sizeof(DS3DBUFFER);
30:
31:     // Retrieve current parameters for later modification
32:     if ( FAILED(lpDS3DBSiren->GetAllParameters(&dsBufferParms)) )
33:     {
34:         ErrStr = Err_Create3DParm;
35:         return FALSE;
36:     }
37:
38:     // Modify the current parameters
39:     dsBufferParms.flMinDistance = DS3D_DEFAULTMINDISTANCE;
40:     dsBufferParms.flMaxDistance = DS3D_DEFAULTMAXDISTANCE;
41:     dsBufferParms.dwMode = DS3DMODE_HEADRELATIVE;
```

19

continues

LISTING **19.2**   continued

```
42:     if ( FAILED(lpDS3DBSiren->SetAllParameters(&dsBufferParms,
                                                   DS3D_IMMEDIATE)) )
43:     {
44:         ErrStr = Err_Create3DBuff;
45:         return FALSE;
46:     }
47:
48:     return TRUE;
49: }
```

As you see, `init_3deffects()` also initializes the buffer, the creation of which you'll
see in an upcoming section. When these functions do their job, you're ready for 3D
sound!

Loading Sounds

Loading the sound data is nearly the same as before. The main difference is you must
supply the 2-speaker virtualization algorithm identifier I mentioned previously. This
applies to the `DSBUFFERDESC` structure created in `load_sounds()`, which should be
changed to this:

```
// Setup the DS buffer description
DSBUFFERDESC  dsbdDesc;
ZeroMemory(&dsbdDesc, sizeof(DSBUFFERDESC));
dsbdDesc.dwSize = sizeof(DSBUFFERDESC);
dsbdDesc.dwFlags = DSBCAPS_STATIC |
                   DSBCAPS_CTRL3D |
                   DSBCAPS_CTRLFREQUENCY |
                   DSBCAPS_CTRLPAN |
                   DSBCAPS_CTRLVOLUME;
dsbdDesc.dwBufferBytes = dwDataLen;
dsbdDesc.lpwfxFormat = &wfFormat;
dsbdDesc.guid3DAlgorithm = GUID_NULL;
```

Because you're using secondary sound buffers, you must provide `GUID_NULL` as the
algorithm's identifier.

Creating the 3D Buffer

Because the helper function approach worked so well for creating the 3D listener object,
I used the same approach for creating the 3D sound buffer, which will be used to contain
the siren sound. `create_3dbuffer()` very simply queries the siren's `IDirectSoundBuffer`
interface for the `IDirectSound3DBuffer` interface and returns `TRUE` if it was successful.
See Listing 19.3 for the details.

Listing 19.3   Code That Creates the 3D Buffer Object

```
 1: //------ Function to create the 3D buffer ------//
 2:
 3: BOOL create_3dbuffer()
 4: {
 5:     if (lpDSBSounds[0]->QueryInterface(IID_IDirectSound3DBuffer,
 6:                              (LPVOID*)&lpDS3DBSiren) !=
 7:         DS_OK)
 8:     {
 9:         ErrStr = Err_Create3DBuff;
10:         return FALSE;
11:     }
12:
13:     return TRUE;
14: }
```

Note that I had to add an additional global IDirectSound3DBuffer interface pointer variable (lpDS3DBSiren) to contain the 3D buffer's interface pointer. If this function fails, as with the 3D listener, the application will terminate and an error message will be displayed.

Animating Sound Effects

The animation of the siren sound effect is handled by changing the sound buffer's position and updating its velocity, as I described earlier in the hour. If the siren is playing, I check its current position. If it's out of bounds, I turn the siren off. However, if it's in bounds, I add a small positional increment and call IDirectSound3Dbuffer:: SetPosition(), as you see in Listing 19.4. I set the velocity depending on the direction the object is travelling. If the object started on one side of the listener and has not passed the listener, the velocity is set to one value (-25.0 in this case). After the object passes the listener, another velocity value is set (2.5). This provides for a great Doppler effect.

LISTING 19.4   Code That Animates the Siren Sound Effect

```
1: // If siren sound is playing, see if we should stop it
2: lpDSBSounds[0]->GetStatus(&dwStatus);
3: if (dwStatus & DSBSTATUS_LOOPING)
4: {
5:     // Give it some distance for rolloff
6:     if ((lSirenPos < -200000) || (lSirenPos > 200000))
7:         lpDSBSounds[0]->Stop();
8:     else
9:     {
```

19

continues

LISTING 19.4 continued

```
10:         // Bump our position
11:         lSirenPos += lSirenPosInc;
12:
13:         // Change velocity (left to right or right to left)
14:         lpDS3DBSiren->SetVelocity((lSirenPos*lStart) > 0 ? -25.0 : 2.5,
                                      1.5, 0.0, DS3D_IMMEDIATE);
15:
16:         // Set new position
17:         lpDS3DBSiren->SetPosition((double)lSirenPos/10000.0,
                                      1.5, 0.0, DS3D_IMMEDIATE);
18:     }
19: }
```

That's all there is to it. DirectSound3D manages the rest!

Release Interfaces

Releasing the DirectSound3D interfaces when the application terminates is handled
in the same manner in which all the other DirectX interfaces are released. You call
Cleanup() when you receive the WM_DESTROY Windows message. In this case, though, I
added the release code for the 3D interfaces. The enhanced Cleanup() function is shown
in Listing 19.5.

LISTING 19.5 Code That Releases All the DirectX Objects

```
 1: //------ Cleanup Function to Release Objects ------//
 2:
 3: #define SafeRelease(x) if (x) { x->Release(); x=NULL;}
 4:
 5: void Cleanup()
 6: {
 7:     // release loaded image surfaces
 8:
 9:     SafeRelease(back1_surf);
10:     SafeRelease(back2_surf);
11:     SafeRelease(int_surf);
12:     SafeRelease(ground_surf);
13:     SafeRelease(light_surf);
14:     SafeRelease(taxi_surf);
15:
16:     // release DirectDraw interfaces
17:
18:     SafeRelease(lpDDSPrimary);
19:     SafeRelease(lpDD);
20:
21:     // release DirectSound3D interfaces
22:
```

```
23:        SafeRelease(lpDS3DBSiren);
24:        SafeRelease(lpDS3DListener);
25:
26:        // release sound buffer interfaces
27:
28:        for ( int i = 0; i < NUMSOUNDS; i++ )
29:        {
30:            SafeRelease(lpDSBSounds[i])
31:        }
32:
33:        // release DirectSound interfaces
34:
35:        SafeRelease(lpDSPrimary);
36:        SafeRelease(lpDS);
37:
38:        // release DirectInput interfaces
39:
40:        if (pKeyboard)
41:        {
42:            pKeyboard->Unacquire();
43:            pKeyboard->Release();
44:            pKeyboard = NULL;
45:        }
46:        SafeRelease(lpDI);
47:
48:        // display error if one thrown
49:
50:        if (ErrStr) {
51:            MessageBox(NULL, ErrStr, szCaption, MB_OK);
52:            ErrStr=NULL;
53:        }
54: }
```

19

I bolded the relevant code to make the changes easier for you to see.

Summary

Now that you've finished this hour, load your favorite game and give it a spin. But this time, turn off your computer's sound and play. Not quite as exciting, is it? It isn't enough to have a compelling visual system, even if it is as rich as many of today's top games are. As a game player, you simply must have the aural inputs to make the game interesting and fun to play. With this hour, I've taken you a step further into increasing the reality your users will enjoy when they play your creation. You've learned how to add basic sounds in Hour 6 and inter-active music streams in Hour 8, "DirectMusic—Interactive Music," and with this hour you cap off your sound generation skills toolbox by adding the third dimension to your work. The good news is this is something that will set your product apart from most of today's game offerings. Try these techniques and technologies—I think you'll be pleased.

Q&A

Q **Sometimes when I try my game on different computers, it crashes. When I ran the same game in a debugging configuration, I found it crashed when I tried to create a sound buffer (the crash resulted in an access violation, error 0xC0000005). Why is this so?**

A The DirectSound driver you are using doesn't support 3D. Either you are using Windows NT, there is no driver present, or the driver you selected isn't the best driver available to the system (and you should enumerate the drivers and select another). This should be considered a bug in DirectSound and taken into account in your game code (perhaps by using exception handling code where appropriate).

Workshop

The Workshop is designed to help you anticipate possible questions, review what you've learned, and begin thinking ahead to put your knowledge into practice. The answers to the quiz are in Appendix A, "Answers."

Quiz

1. How is sound created?
2. What five factors influence our perception of sound?
3. Which of the five factors you listed is most critical?
4. Why process DirectSound3D parameter changes in a batch (if possible)?
5. True or false: Setting the sound buffer's velocity changes its spatial location.
6. True or false: You create the listener object using a secondary sound buffer object.
7. What is rolloff?
8. What is Doppler shift?
9. Must the orientation vectors be at 90 degrees to each other?
10. Can you request DirectSound3D to manage the relative velocities between the sound buffer and the listener?

Exercises

1. Adjust the Doppler and rolloff values in the sample application. See what happens when you use values for each that are greater than the default values.
2. Try creating directed sounds by creating the inner and outer conic sections. See how the sound is affected as you move from the inner to the outer cone; then outside the outer cone.

PART VII

DirectPlay

Hour

Hour 20

Putting Your Game on the Net—Writing Multiplayer Titles

Up until now, you have learned how to add DirectX features to a game or application to make it playable by one person or by one person playing against the computer, perhaps. Most computer games have followed this paradigm for quite some time. But, also for some time now, Microsoft has provided the capability to add multiplayer features to a game with the DirectPlay portion of DirectX. Currently in its fourth version, DirectPlay provides an API for you, as game programmer, to add the capability for your game to be played by more than one human player at a time (and perhaps even by more than one computer opponent as well).

The DirectPlay API provides functions through a COM object interface, `IDirectPlay4`, that enable you to manage game sessions, groups, and players. You can use these functions to allow your game to look for other players and games on a network or the Internet, create a player object representing the player in a game, and send game play data between computers. The DirectPlay API provides some very high-level functions to make it easy for you to manage your game or player, as well as a few low-level functions intended for you to use to send data specific to your game to other players.

DirectPlay supports no specific hardware like the Direct3D, DirectDraw, or DirectSound portions do. DirectPlay will, however, allow your game to take advantage of any network or modem hardware a player's computer might have. The DirectPlay architecture is really "network agnostic"—a game written using DirectPlay can run over two computers wired directly together, one or more computers on a LAN, or even the Internet. DirectPlay can even be played over different network protocols, so there is no requirement that a user's computer must have a specific protocol, say TCP/IP, to run your game. In fact, DirectPlay is designed to let the user decide which protocol or network type connection to use when the game is running, giving you the freedom to focus on worrying about what type of data your game needs to run instead of what type of network to code for to carry that data.

During this hour, you will explore the DirectPlay API, as well as learn about different ways to develop a multiplayer game. Specifically, during this hour, you will learn

- How to establish DirectPlay communications
- About DirectPlay service providers
- How to manage games, players, groups, and game data
- How to manage game state information
- Approaches to minimize network traffic for faster response times

DirectPlay Architecture

DirectPlay, as an API, only provides the interface for you to use to exchange data between computers and manage games and players. As such, it is a useful tool for you to use to add multiplayer capabilities to your game. You will still, however, have to make some choices in how your game is structured—DirectPlay only provides the capabilities. It's up to you to decide what kind of data your game will use, and how it will use the data over the network.

DirectPlay supports two types of game communication models: client-server and peer-to-peer. Both models have distinct advantages and disadvantages compared to each other, and the models differ in how game "state" information is stored or transmitted to each game program.

In the client/server mode, as you might have guessed, a server is responsible for relaying game data and state information between participating computers, as well as storing that state information. This centralized management of such data means that a client only really needs to worry about relaying and receiving data from one computer—the server, and not with any of its "neighbors." In addition, the server computer can provide security for a game, so players will be required to have an account and provide passwords to participate in playing a game. This can be useful if you wanted to charge money for a game because the game can only be played if you have a valid account on a server and that account is paid for by the player. An example of a client/server type of DirectPlay game looks like Figure 20.1.

FIGURE 20.1

DirectPlay in a client/server configuration.

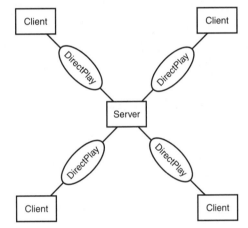

In contrast, a peer-to-peer DirectPlay game will require that each client maintain state information about itself as well as for every other player and object in a game. The game client also must know what information to share with its neighbors, as well as with whom to share it. Because a player's state information changes throughout the game, the changed information must be sent to all the other players participating in that game. A sample peer-to-peer type of DirectPlay game can be seen in Figure 20.2.

20

FIGURE 20.2

DirectPlay in a peer-to-peer configuration.

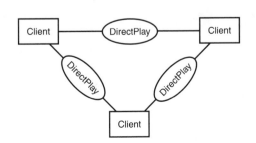

Peer-to-peer games require no additional hardware support, and the capability for any game client to be a host can be written into every game client. In other words, only one piece of software is written—the game. The disadvantage to peer-to-peer games is that the amount of information to be shared among all the players can possibly overwhelm a computer or network between the players. A client/server based game, however, can be used when the player count is high because only one computer needs to have all the state information, and most of the data traffic flows from client to server.

For the rest of this hour, I will cover the basics of creating a game using the peer-to-peer model. Developing a client/server based game would require some additional development idioms that can't be covered well in the short hour we have here. The API is the same for both types of games, so you'll have an idea of how to use DirectPlay in either model.

NEW TERM The *game state* is the type of game data that describes a player's status at any point in the game. State information usually includes such data as location, health, and direction.

DirectPlay, as you might expect from previous hours, relies upon a COM interface, named `IDirectPlay4`. This interface houses functions that are related to five main areas:

- Initialization
- Game session management
- Player/group management
- Message management
- Game data transfer

I will go into these specific areas in a few minutes, but in the meantime, it might be helpful to look at the entire `IDirectPlay4` interface. The `IDirectPlay4` interface has the followingfunctions:

- `AddGroupToGroup()`
- `AddPlayerToGroup()`
- `CancelMessage()`
- `CancelPriority()`
- `Close()`
- `CreateGroup()`
- `CreateGroupInGroup()`
- `CreatePlayer()`
- `DeleteGroupFromGroup()`

- DeletePlayerFromGroup()
- DestroyGroup()
- DestroyPlayer()
- EnumConnections()
- EnumGroupPlayers()
- EnumGroups()
- EnumGroupsInGroup()
- EnumPlayers()
- EnumSessions()
- GetCaps()
- GetGroupConnectionSettings()
- GetGroupData()
- GetGroupFlags()
- GetGroupName()
- GetGroupOwner()
- GetGroupParent()
- GetMessageCount()
- GetMessageQueue()
- GetPlayerAccount()
- GetPlayerAddress()
- GetPlayerCaps()
- GetPlayerData()
- GetPlayerFlags()
- GetPlayerName()
- GetSessionDesc()
- Initialize()
- InitializeConnection()
- Open()
- Receive()
- SecureOpen()
- Send()
- SendChatMessage()
- SendEx()

20

- SetGroupConnectionSettings()
- SetGroupData()
- SetGroupName()
- SetGroupOwner()
- SetPlayerData()
- SetPlayerName()
- SetSessionDesc()
- StartSession()
- AddRef()
- QueryInterface()
- Release()

The last three functions, as you should already be aware, are inherited from the IUnknown interface that every COM-based object inherits from. I won't cover them further. The rest of the functions will be dealt with in groups throughout the rest of this hour.

The IDirectPlay4 interface, and its companion, the IDirectPlayLobby3 interface that you will learn about next hour, supports the notion of using a Unicode or ANSI system. By asking for a specific type of interface—IDirectPlay4 for Unicode, or IDirectPlay4A for ANSI—you will be able to use either multibyte Unicode strings or single byte ANSI strings. The functions are exactly the same for both interfaces, as are the parameters passed to those functions. The only difference in the two interfaces is what type of strings are used in the structures passed to and from functions. As I detail the various structures used as parameters to the IDirectPlay4 interface, you will see that all the string-based members of those structures are actually of a union type. The union member used will depend on which interface is being used, and you will see that the ANSI types of those strings will end in 'A'. The Unicode strings will have no trailing character. An example of such a structure is DPNAME, whose prototype follows:

```
typedef struct {
    DWORD dwSize;
    DWORD dwFlags;
    union {
        LPWSTR lpszShortName;
        LPSTR  lpszShortNameA;
    };
    union {
        LPWSTR lpszLongName;
        LPSTR  lpszLongNameA;
    };
} DPNAME, FAR *LPDPNAME;
```

This particular structure is used to name specific entities in DirectPlay, such as a player or group. Notice that the string for a short and long name in this structure is actually part of a union. If you use the IDirectPlay4 interface, you would use the lpszShortName and lpszLongName members. If you were instead using the ANSI interface IDirectPlay4A, you would use the lpszShortNameA and lpszLongNameA union members. For the rest of this hour, we will use the Unicode interface, IDirectPlay4. It might be helpful for you to use conditional directives in your code, around every place you might set or retrieve a string, like so:

```
DPNAME dpName;
dpName.dwSize = sizeof(DPNAME);
#ifdef UNICODE
dpName.lpszShortName = _tcsdup(strShortName);
dpName.lpszLongName = _tcsdup(strLongName);
#else
dpName.lpszShortNameA = _tcsdup(strShortName);
dpName.lpszLongNameA = _tcsdup(strLongName);
#endif
```

This will allow you to simply create a new Visual C++ target for either ANSI or Unicode, with which you can define UNICODE to 0 or 1, respectively. Then, all that will be required for your game to support either standard is a recompile to the correct target.

To start working with the IDirectPlay4 interface, it would be helpful to understand the notion of a DirectPlay session. Essentially, a session indicates a specific instance of a game. That is to say, a session represents a game or a round of a game. A session can be created by a player or server and later be joined by other players interested in getting involved with the current game.

A session is usually created by the first person who wants to host a game. In the client/server mode, the session is created by the server, in which case the server might require new players to provide authentication to join the session. This is called a secure session, and it is an optional way for the server to create a session. To provide this authentication, the server is required to be running on Windows NT.

NEW TERM A *secure session* is a type of session that will require users to provide a valid username and password to join.

DirectPlay treats the first computer or server to create a session as the *session host*. It is possible to also require other players joining a session to provide a password. The session host can require this password by setting the lpszPassword string in the DPSESSION-DESC2 structure passed to IDirectPlay4::Open(). You will learn about this function and the DPSESSIONDESC2 structure in a few minutes. It is important to note that any session

20

host can create a password-protected session. This differs from a secure session, where a player must provide accurate username and password information.

NEW TERM The *session host* is the first computer that creates a session.

Creating a DirectPlay Object

Before we create our DirectPlay object, it is important for you to know about GUIDs. GUIDs are basically 128-bit values used to uniquely identify an item. In DirectPlay's case, GUIDs are used to identify DirectPlay applications, service providers, and sessions, among other things. One thing that your application must have is a GUID identifying it uniquely from other DirectPlay applications. You can obtain this GUID programmatically with a call to CoCreateGuid(), which has the following prototype:

```
HRESULT CoCreateGuid(
  GUID  *pguid  //Pointer to the GUID on return
);
```

This call will return a pointer to a GUID structure, which you should store in your application somewhere, perhaps as a const static variable. This GUID should only be generated once, so if you don't mind cutting and pasting, you can also use the command line utility uuidgen.exe, which will also generate a GUID. Either way, after you have obtained the GUID that will represent your specific DirectPlay application, you can store it using the DEFINE_GUID macro, defined in afxdisp.h, like so:

```
// {CA761230-ED42-11CE-BACD-00AA0057B223}
DEFINE_GUID(MY_APPLICATION_GUID,
0xca761230, 0xed42, 0x11ce, 0xba, 0xcd, 0x0, 0xaa, 0x0, 0x57, 0xb2,
0x23);
```

To obtain an instance of an IDirectPlay4 interface, we use the now familiar CoCreateInstance() function:

```
LPDIRECTPLAY4 pDP = NULL;
HRESULT hr;
hr = CoCreateInstance( CLSID_DirectPlay, NULL, CLSCTX_INPROC_SERVER,
➥ IID_IDirectPlay4, (VOID**)&pDP );
if( FAILED(hr) )
    return hr;
```

Choosing a Network Connection

In previous hours, you learned the concept of a HAL—an abstraction of the DirectX API from the underlying hardware. DirectPlay does not support a HAL, per se, but does support something very similar to it: *Service Providers*. A service provider is a library that interfaces DirectPlay to a specific type of communications medium. All service providers provide a consistent interface to DirectPlay, despite the underlying hardware. You will never have to interface to a Service Provider yourself—DirectPlay takes care of it for you. As seen in Figure 20.3, the specifics of the service provider are mostly hidden from the DirectPlay application.

FIGURE 20.3

DirectPlay hides service provider specifics.

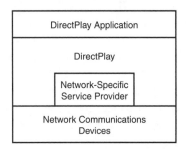

| DirectPlay Application |
| DirectPlay |
| Network-Specific Service Provider |
| Network Communications Devices |

NEW TERM   *Service providers* furnish network-specific communications services for DirectPlay. They abstract the details of the network transport from game communications.

Four providers are installed by default with DirectPlay:

- TCP/IP
- IPX
- Modem-to-modem
- Serial link

The first two providers: TCP/IP and IPX, allow DirectPlay to communicate over a network connection, meaning two or more computers can communicate with each other. The last two: modem-to-modem and serial link, typically support only two players. It would be possible, however, to host a multiplayer game with these last two providers if one of the computers was a server with multiple communications devices (although this would involve using the client/server model) .

As I said earlier, you do not need to concern yourself with what type of service provider a user will choose when your game runs; or, more specifically, what type of communications hardware a user might have. DirectPlay will allow the user to pick the connection type when he runs your game, initially.

The `IDirectPlay4::EnumConnections()` is used to obtain a list of all the registered service providers available for DirectPlay to use. Again, this list will probably include the standard four mentioned previously. The prototype for this function looks like this:

20

```
HRESULT EnumConnections(
  LPCGUID lpguidApplication,
  LPDPENUMCONNECTIONSCALLBACK lpEnumCallback,
  LPVOID lpContext,
  DWORD dwFlags
);
```

lpguidApplication should be set to NULL, to indicate that we are looking for all possible communication providers accessible on this computer. If we had associated a GUID for our application with a specific set of providers, only that limited set will be returned. The lpEnumCallback is a pointer to our DPENUMCONNECTIONSCALLBACK function. This is a callback function, which I will talk about shortly. lpContext is a pointer to a user-defined value, which will be passed as a parameter to our callback function. The last parameter, dwFlags, should be set to DPCONNECTION_DIRECTPLAY, which indicates that we are interested in only DirectPlay service providers. If we were interested in locating lobby service providers, we would instead set dwFlags to DPCONNECTION_DIRECTPLAYLOBBY. DirectPlay lobbies are covered in the next hour.

A callback function is a function that will be called by DirectPlay on your behalf, once for each item in a list. This concept is used by DirectPlay in several places, including enumerating sessions, players, groups, and service providers. You can spot those functions that will use a callback by the leading *Enum* in the function name.

What happens when you call one of these *Enum* functions is DirectPlay will, internally, loop through a list, calling your callback function once for each item in the list. Each of the *Enum* functions allows you to pass a user-defined value, which will, in turn, be passed on every call to your callback function. For example, this value might represent a window handle, and your callback function could use this handle and the rest of the data provided by DirectPlay's call to it to populate a window control. An example of a DPENUMCONNECTIONSCALLBACK function is in Listing 20.1.

LISTING 20.1   A Connection Callback Function

```
 1: BOOL FAR PASCAL EnumConnectionsCallback( const GUID* pSPGUID,
    ➥ VOID* lpConnection,
 2:                          DWORD dwConnectionSize, const DPNAME* lpName,
 3:                          DWORD dwFlags, VOID* lpContext )
 4: {
 5:     HWND    hWnd = (HWND)lpContext;
        ➥ // This was passed as the lpContext variable
 6:     LRESULT lIndex;
 7:     GUID*   lpGuid;
 8:     // Store service provider name in a combo box
 9:     lIndex = SendDlgItemMessage( hWnd, IDC_SPCOMBO, CB_ADDSTRING, 0,
10:                          (LPARAM)pName->lpszShortNameA );
```

```
11:    if( lIndex == LB_ERR )
12:        return TRUE;
13:    // Make space for service provider GUID
14:    lpGuid = (GUID*)GlobalAllocPtr( GHND, sizeof(GUID) );
15:    if( lpGuid == NULL )
16:        return TRUE;
17:    // Store pointer to GUID in combo box
18:    *lpGuid = *lpSPGUID;
19:    SendDlgItemMessage( hWnd, IDC_SPCOMBO, CB_SETITEMDATA, (WPARAM)lIndex,
20:                        (LPARAM)lpGuid );
21:    return TRUE;
22: }
```

It is important to note that this function returns a value of true, as do the rest of the DirectPlay callback functions you will provide. Returning a value of false will cause DirectPlay to stop calling your function, and you will not receive the rest of whatever list you are trying to receive. The preceding function assumes that even despite an error from the Win32 function calls, DirectPlay can still continue to call this function for other instances of service providers.

It is important to know that the first two parameters passed to our callback function are a GUID representing the service provider and a pointer to a *DirectPlay Address* buffer. This buffer contains information specific to each service provider to complete the connection. For the modem-to-modem provider, this address will signify a telephone number to dial. For the TCP/IP provider, it will contain the Internet address to connect to. These addresses are usually entered by the user, but might also come from a DirectPlay lobby, as you will learn next hour.

NEW TERM   *DirectPlay addresses* are compound structures composed of GUIDs representing service providers and address types. They also contain data specific to a service provider that indicates an address or network location to establish a connection to.

For now, you can simply store this extra buffer data and use it in a call to InitializeConnection(), which connects the computer to other computers using DirectPlay. The InitializeConnection() function has the following prototype:

```
HRESULT InitializeConnection(
  LPVOID lpConnection,
  DWORD dwFlags
);
```

The first parameter is a pointer to the DirectPlay address, indicating where the computer should connect. Again, this data will come from either a call to EnumConnections() or from a lobby. A DirectPlay address consists of several smaller structures of data, beginning with the GUID of the service provider that DirectPlay uses to connect with. The dwFlags is currently unused, and should be set to 0.

20

Joining a Session

When it comes time to join a session, a simple call to `IDirectPlay4::Open()` will do the trick. The prototype for this function looks like the following:

```
HRESULT Open(
  LPDPSESSIONDESC2 lpsd,
  DWORD dwFlags
);
```

`lpsd` is a pointer to a `DPSESSIONDESC2` structure, which I will get to in a second. `dwFlags` can be set to either `DPOPEN_CREATE` or `DPOPEN_JOIN`, depending on whether you want to create a session from scratch or to join an existing session, respectively. If you are interested in dispensing with any connection boxes that DirectPlay might display while the connection is progressing, you can also `OR` the value `DPOPEN_RETURNSTATUS` with `dwFlags`, and DirectPlay will return control back to you immediately, with a value of `DPERR_CONNECTING` as the result. You can then continue to call the `Open()` function until you receive a value of `DP_OK`, or any other value, indicating success or failure, respectively.

The `DPSESSIONDESC2` structure looks like this:

```
typedef struct {
    DWORD dwSize;
    DWORD dwFlags;
    GUID  guidInstance;
    GUID  guidApplication;
    DWORD dwMaxPlayers;
    DWORD dwCurrentPlayers;
    union  {
        LPWSTR lpszSessionName;
        LPSTR  lpszSessionNameA;
    };
    union  {
        LPWSTR lpszPassword;
        LPSTR  lpszPasswordA;
    };
    DWORD dwReserved1;
    DWORD dwReserved2;
    DWORD dwUser1;
    DWORD dwUser2;
    DWORD dwUser3;
    DWORD dwUser4;
} DPSESSIONDESC2, FAR *LPDPSESSIONDESC2;
```

The `guidApplication` value should be set to the GUID that you created for your game. This signifies to DirectPlay which type of game client can join or create this game. The `dwMaxPlayers` indicates the maximum number of players who can join this session, and dwCurrentPlayers indicates the current number of participating players. As with most of the structures used as parameters to IDirectPlay4 functions, the dwSize value should be set to the size of the structure, like so:

```
DPSESSIONDESC2 dpSession;
DpSession.dwSize = sizeof(dpSession);
```

For the dwFlags parameter, many flags are possible. These vary how the session is treated or constructed. Keep in mind that to use more than one flag at a time, you simply bitwise OR them (using the c-style || operator). Let's look at some of the possible values for this parameter:

- DPSESSION_CLIENTSERVER: If this is set, the session will use the client/server architecture. If not, this will be a peer-to-peer session.
- DPSESSION_JOINDISABLED: This prevents any other players from using Open() (or SecureOpen()) to join this session.
- DPSESSION_MIGRATEHOST: With this flag set, the session host duties might be taken over by another computer in the session if the session host exits. This is a way to ensure that the game session will continue, even if the first hosting computer leaves for any reason. This flag cannot be used in combination with DPSESSION_CLIENTSERVER.
- DPSESSION_NEWPLAYERSDISABLED: This is similar to DPSESSION_JOINDISABLED, but also prevents clients from creating new player objects via CreatePlayer().
- DPSESSION_PASSWORDREQUIRED: This flag specifies that the session is password protected, and any clients wanting to join must supply the password when calling Open().
- DPSESSION_PRIVATE: This indicates that this session is normally hidden and won't show up in calls to EnumSessions(), unless a password is supplied to that function.
- DPSESSION_SECURESERVER: This indicates that the session is being hosted by a secure server and any clients must use SecureOpen() to join this session. They must also fill out the DPCREDENTIALS structure with a valid username, password, and domain.

20

To create or join a *secure session*, we use the SecureOpen() function, which is similar to Open(). The SecureOpen() function requires two additional parameters as you can see here:

```
HRESULT SecureOpen(
  LPCDPSESSIONDESC2 lpsd,
  DWORD dwFlags,
  LPCDPSECURITYDESC lpSecurity,
  LPCDPCREDENTIALS lpCredentials
);
```

The first two parameters are used exactly as in Open(). The last two are filled out with additional security information. The lpSecurity parameter is a pointer to a DPSECURITY structure, and the lpCredentials parameter is a pointer to a DPCREDENTIALS structure. The prototypes for these two structures look like this:

```
typedef struct {
    DWORD  dwSize;
    DWORD  dwFlags;
    union {
        LPWSTR  lpszSSPIProvider;
        LPSTR   lpszSSPIProviderA;
    };
    union {
        LPWSTR  lpszCAPIProvider;
        LPSTR   lpszCAPIProviderA;
    };
    DWORD  dwCAPIProviderType;
    DWORD  dwEncryptionAlgorithm;
} DPSECURITYDESC, FAR *LPDPSECURITYDESC;

typedef struct {
    DWORD  dwSize;
    DWORD  dwFlags;
    union {
        LPWSTR lpszUsername;
        LPSTR  lpszUsernameA;
    };
    union {
        LPWSTR lpszPassword;
        LPSTR  lpszPasswordA;
    };
    union {
        LPWSTR lpszDomain;
        LPSTR  lpszDomainA;
    };
} DPCREDENTIALS, FAR *LPDPCREDENTIALS;
```

The dwSize member of each structureshould be set to the size of the respective structure. The dwFlags of both structures should be set to 0 because they are currently not used. For most purposes, you can set the lpszSSPIProvider and lpszCAPIProvider members of the DPCREDENTIALS structure to NULL and the dwCAPIProviderType and dwEncryptionAlgorithm values to 0. For the DPCREDENTIALS structure, set the lpszUserName, lpszPassword, and lpszDomain values to the appropriate username, password, and NT domain name in which the user has an account.

NEW TERM   A *secure session* is a session hosted by a computer that can provide user authentication and data encryption. Currently, this is only supported by a Windows NT computer.

Of course, if we aren't going to create our own session, but want to find out what sessions are currently in progress, we can use the EnumSessions() function, providing it with a pointer to a callback function. The prototype for EnumSessions() is as follows:

```
HRESULT EnumSessions(
  LPDPSESSIONDESC2 lpsd,
  DWORD dwTimeout,
  LPDPENUMSESSIONSCALLBACK2 lpEnumSessionsCallback2,
  LPVOID lpContext,
  DWORD dwFlags
);
```

The lpEnumSessionsCallback2 parameter is a pointer to our DPENUMSESSIONSCALLBACK2 type function. If we are looking for specific types of sessions, we can create a DPSES-SIONDESC2 structure, fill out a few elements in that structure, and pass a pointer to that as lpsd. Only sessions matching the values in our lpsd structure will be enumerated. We can, of course, pass anything we want to lpContext because that will be passed to our callback function each time.

Communicating with Players

The purpose of establishing the network session is so the application can access node-to-node communications. DirectPlay facilitates this application-level messaging and message routing through abstractions for players and groups. These objects have identity, and you can establish relationships among them to control the flow of message traffic.

Players and Groups

Now that we've picked our service provider and listed all the possible game sessions for our user to choose a specific one, it's time to let our player enter the game. After the game calls Open() or SecureOpen() to join a game (or create one), the player must then create a DirectPlay player object to represent that user in the game. You can do this with a call to CreatePlayer(). Every user will need at least one player to represent him in a game session. This player object is used by DirectPlay to direct its communication. Each player is represented by a DPID, and this ID value is used to signify a DirectPlay message's destination. CreatePlayer() has the following prototype:

```
HRESULT CreatePlayer(
  LPDPID lpidPlayer,
  LPDPNAME lpPlayerName,
  HANDLE hEvent,
  LPVOID lpData,
  DWORD dwDataSize,
  DWORD dwFlags
);
```

20

The lpidPlayer value is filled in by DirectPlay after our player is created. You should fill in a DPNAME structure, passing it as a parameter to lpPlayerName. The hEvent parameter specifies a HANDLE to a Win32 Event structure, which can be created by a call to the Win32 function CreateEvent(). If you want to associate any game specific data with this player, you can pass a pointer to it via lpData and set the dwDataSize to the size of that data. This custom data can represent any player specific data you want, above and beyond any information DirectPlay natively maintains about your player. Finally, the dwFlags parameter can be set to either 0 or

- DPLAYER_SERVERPLAYER—Indicates that the player is the server player for a client/server type of game.
- DPLAYER_SPECATOR—Indicates that this player won't be involved in any actual game play, but will, instead, participate in the game session as a spectator.

The hEvent structure is important because it can be used as a signal to your program that a DirectPlay message has arrived at the player's computer. You can use the Win32 functions WaitForSingleObject() or WaitForMultipleObjects() to wait for the event handle hEvent to be set to a signaled state by DirectPlay. When DirectPlay signals that event handle, you can be assured that a call to the message Receive() function will return with a message. Normally, you would want to create a separate thread in your application that will wait on this event handle to be signaled and will process messages after a call to Receive().

In a client/server type of DirectPlay session, the server must create a player representing the server. It will have the ID of DPID_SERVERPLAYER. Of course, there can only be one player in a session with this ID. The server creates this player by specifying the flag DPPLAYER_SERVERPLAYER in the dwFlags parameter passed to CreatePlayer().

Players can become part of groups, and groups can even become members of other groups. You can use this notion to target groups of players for a specific reason and allow DirectPlay to only send messages based on a player's group membership. You can use the CreateGroup() and CreateGroupInGroup() functions to create new groups, and AddPlayerToGroup() and AddGroupToGroup() functions to add existing players and groups to groups, respectively.

Using the DirectPlay Send() function, which allows us to send DirectPlay messages, it would be possible for us to send any type of message to players A and B, as seen in Figure 20.4. To do this, we would actually send the message to Group A—DirectPlay will automatically see to it that our message is sent to both players. Similarly, sending a message to group B will result in both players C and D receiving that message.

FIGURE 20.4

A DirectPlay grouping example.

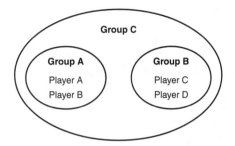

There can be many reasons to use this notion of grouping, but the most obvious might be to direct your messages based on game geography. You can group players together based on either their physical location (same room, same state, and so on), or their virtual game geography. Of course, players who want to band together to form "sides" in a game can also be grouped together using DirectPlay groups.

The CreateGroup() function is similar to CreatePlayer(), in that it takes a parameter to a DPNAME structure, which provides, among other things, the group's name. The CreateGroup() can also assign an arbitrary data value to a group, which can be seen on any computer joined to the session the group is in. Of course, as with CreatePlayer(), a DPID value is returned indicating the ID representing this group. The CreateGroup() has the following prototype:

```
HRESULT CreateGroup(
  LPDPID lpidGroup,
  LPDPNAME lpGroupName,
  LPVOID lpData,
  DWORD dwDataSize,
  DWORD dwFlags
);
```

The CreateGroupInGroup() function takes one extra parameter: the ID of the group that will contain the new group to be created.

The AddPlayerToGroup() and AddGroupToGroup() are very similar. Both take a first parameter, of type DPID, which indicates to which parent group a player or group is to be added. For the second parameter, the first function takes a DPID representing the player to add, and the second function, AddGroupToGroup(), takes a DPID representing the group to add. Those two functions look like this:

```
HRESULT AddPlayerToGroup(
  DPID idGroup,
```

20

```
    DPID idPlayer
);
HRESULT AddGroupToGroup(
  DPID idParentGroup,
  DPID idGroup
);
```

It is possible, when creating groups, to create a *staging group*. A staging group is a DirectPlay group, created with the DPGROUP_STAGINGAREA flag set, that allows you to gather players together before actually starting game play. If your game needs to gather players in this manner, you can wait to actually start the game until StartSession() is called. Calling this function will cause all game clients to receive a DPMSG_STARTSESSION message. The prototype for this function is as follows:

```
HRESULT StartSession(
  DWORD dwFlags,
  DPID idGroup
);
```

The parameter dwFlags is currently unused, and should be set to 0. The idGroup parameter will be set to the group used to stage players before the game starts.

NEW TERM A *staging group* is a DirectPlay group used to gather players before a session starts. Use in conjunction with StartSession() to wait for enough players to join a session before it begins.

DirectPlay Messages

Two types of messages are sent by DirectPlay applications during a session: system messages and user messages. *System messages* are used by DirectPlay to indicate changes in the session (including session creation itself), and are usually processed internally by DirectPlay. *User messages* are messages that the DirectPlay application uses for its own data, and can be any user-defined type. You can send your own user messages using the Send() function, which we have already mentioned. The Send() function looks like the following:

```
HRESULT Send(
  DPID idFrom,
  DPID idTo,
  DWORD dwFlags,
  LPVOID lpData,
  DWORD dwDataSize
);
```

The idFrom parameter indicates the sending player, whereas the idTo parameter indicates the destination of the message. To send the message to all players in a session, regardless of group, use the value DPID_ALLPLAYERS. If the message is a system message, the idFrom value will be set to DPID_SYSMSG. The dwFlags value indicates how the message should be sent, and it can be set to one or more of the following:

- DPSEND_ENCRYPTED—Indicates that the message should be encrypted and only be set if the DPSEND_GUARANTEED flag is also set. To use encryption, the session must also be secure, which means that it must have been created by a call to SecureOpen().

- DPSEND_GUARANTEED—Indicates that a message is guaranteed to be delivered to its target. By default, a message is sent with no guarantee of delivery. I will talk about guaranteed messaging in the next section.

- DPSEND_SIGNED—This flag signs the message with a digital signature. Like encryption, this type of message can be used only in a secure session.

Dealing with Network Latency

A large part of a game's playability is related to its "responsiveness." Responsiveness is a measure of how long it takes the game to display a response to a user's input. An example of poor responsiveness in multiplayer games would be when the user presses the Fire button on a joystick, and he doesn't see the missile launch for many seconds later. Obviously, the quicker the apparent reaction time to a user's input event, the more responsive the game feels. The largest factor affecting a game's responsiveness is latency, a term you learned about in Hour 6, "DirectSound—Adding Ambience and Sound Effects to Your Game." Although in that hour the term was used to describe the amount of time between when a sound is applied programmatically, and when the user actually hears the sound. In network terms, latency is used to describe the amount of time that it takes data to travel across a network or communications link.

Network latency might be influenced by the amount of data currently on the user's network, or by any path that data might take traveling between two computers. Obviously, physical factors can influence latency: because data is ultimately transmitted as electronic signals over some sort of wire, those signals are limited by the speed of light. If an Internet-based connection were established between two computers located on opposite sides of the earth, any network traffic must pass thousands of miles, perhaps bouncing off of satellites and through radio waves, as well as over land-based wire. All that traffic will be limited by the speed of light, no matter what other factors are involved; and there are many.

The networks that make up the Internet (and indeed, even some local networks) consist of many routing devices. Each time a network packet must pass through a routing device, a small delay is introduced into the overall time taken to deliver that packet. In the

20

simplest sense, the fewer routers, or "hops," in routing terms, that a network packet of data must pass through the lower the latency. Not only will a router slow a packet down simply by routing it, but also it might have to split a packet up into smaller packets for delivery. The time needed to re-assemble all these smaller packets into the original, larger packet that was sent by the originating computer also introduces delays.

Another large factor in network latency is dropped or mangled packets. At the lowest level, the network or communication device is responsible for making sure that a received packet is whole and error-free. If the network for some reason drops a packet, or a packet is received with errors, a re-transmittal of the original packet might be required. Whether this occurs automatically for you (that is, transparently by DirectPlay) will depend on whether you are using DirectPlay's guaranteed messaging features. If you are using that feature, every time DirectPlay has to retransmit a message (resulting in retransmittal of the network packets), a longer delay will be introduced. If you do not take advantage of DirectPlay's guaranteed deliver feature, you will have to deal with dropped or bad messages yourself. Of course, without guaranteed deliver, you will never know that a message never reached its destination, or was otherwise corrupted, so you will have to deal with this in some fashion or other.

The last biggest factor affecting network latency is the bandwidth of a communications device, and the buffers used by the operating system for that communications device. As you transmit more and more data for your game, you increase your chances for over-whelming another computer's capability to receive your data. Low bandwidth communications, like a modem-to-modem connection, have a relatively small amount of capability for transmitting data. This means that if you are trying to send too much data at once, you will have to wait until the modem has finished signaling your data and sending it across the wire before you can send more.

And even if you have a very fast local network, a slow computer might have trouble dealing with all the game data that it is receiving, and might fall behind in trying to deal with it all. Most low-level communications drivers use buffers to store data coming in from a communications device, and unless the CPU retrieves that data from them and frees the buffer for further storage, that device will become essentially useless and either start dropping network packets or telling other computers to stop sending packets. This situation will correct itself as the CPU catches up, and empties the buffers; but, in the meantime, data is lying around in buffers getting old.

DirectPlay offers many features and capabilities to help you deal with network latency. Decreasing network latency will help improve responsiveness, and improving responsiveness will make your game more playable.

Deterministic/Non-Deterministic Data

One way to deal with network latency is to remove the need to worry about dropped packets or at least for having to transmit more data than is needed. The less data you have to transmit, the more likely it is to be delivered, and delivered on time. One way of reducing the amount of data you will transmit over the wire is by deciding whether data is deterministic.

NEW TERM *Deterministic data* simply means data that can be computed or guessed from previous data (also called "dead reckoning"). An example of deterministic data would be calculating a competitor's ship's current screen position from its previous position, heading, and velocity. It might be wise, using this formula, for you to only transmit some sort of data through DirectPlay only when a ship's heading or velocity changes. At any point in time, unless those two factors change, you can safely guess where a competing ship might be. Of course, this is only an estimate you are making, so you might want to occasionally have each player's game client transmit her current position, so you can make sure that your guesses are accurate or make corrections.

NEW TERM *Non-deterministic data*, of course, is the opposite of deterministic data—it cannot be calculated with specific information being transmitted between computers. If, in a role playing type of game, a player's character were to "give" an item to another player's character, the specific item to be given must be transmitted as data. The receiving player cannot guess which item is to be received.

Of course, the balance between deciding which data is deterministic versus non-deterministic might require some thought. By categorizing all the possible types of information that must be exchanged between computers into either one of these categories, you will be able to narrow down the information into that which must be transmitted more frequently than the other. Again, even with deterministic data, you will probably have to transmit some game state information occasionally, just so competitor's game clients won't get too out of synch.

Deterministic data refers to a future result, which can be calculated (sometimes roughly) without requiring specific data on hand. This type of result (or value) can be determined by any game program or server without any data being transmitted over the network or exchanged. Non-Deterministic Data, however, cannot be calculated or determined without specific data being transmitted over the network.

Guaranteed Messaging

Along with deciding how much data should be sent and how often, you can also make some decisions on whether data should be sent as "guaranteed" by DirectPlay.

20

Guaranteed messaging implies that every message you send is received by its destination. Of course, as you might suspect, this incurs a penalty in the latency department. If you send every possible DirectPlay message as guaranteed, you could possibly double or even triple your latency. DirectPlay has to wait for the receiving end of a message to transmit back to it that the receiving end has received your message with no errors or no loss of data. If some data is lost or garbled, DirectPlay must re-transmit your message. This is, of course, handled transparently to you, but consider that DirectPlay will try very hard to make sure that what you send is what the receiving end gets.

You do get the choice to decide whether to use guaranteed messaging on a message-by-message basis, so you can reserve this feature for those types of messages that *must* get through, no matter what. A good example of this would be when a player's ship explodes. It might be very important to the rest of the players in a game to know this fact and to deal with it accordingly.

To use guaranteed messaging, you can simply set the DPSEND_GUARANTEED flag in the dwFlags parameter passed to IDirectPlay4::Send() or IDirectPlay4::SendEx(). By setting this flag, you are signifying that for this message, at least, DirectPlay should guarantee that your message is received by its destinations.

Message Management

One last way to control network latency is by using DirectPlay's message management functions: GetMessageQueue(), GetMessageCount(), CancelMessage(), CancelPriority(), and SendEx(). These functions allow you to control and monitor DirectPlay's send and receive queues. As you send DirectPlay messages (using Send() or SendEx()), your data is temporarily stored in a message queue. These messages are stored in the destination's receive message queue until they are retrieved by a DirectPlay application.

The CancelMessage() function allows you to delete a specific message by ID. To obtain this ID, you must send your message using SendEx(), instead of Send(). Using SendEx(), you can obtain the ID of a specific message, which you can later use to cancel that message if it hasn't already been sent. This might come in handy if a player makes a move which might cancel out a previous move, meaning that you can simply cancel the message indicating the first move and ignore sending the second. You could also even take this management a little further (especially, perhaps on slow links like modem-to-modem) and cancel a message indicating a player's state if it hasn't been sent within a certain time and new state data should be transmitted anyway.

CancelPriority() cancels all messages currently pending transmittal by DirectPlay that are within a certain priority range. This introduces the idea that DirectPlay can also prioritize messages by indicating a message's priority in the call to SendEx(). By setting the dwPriority value to an appropriate DWORD value on a call to SendEx(), you can ensure that DirectPlay will try to send messages in order of priority. A value of 0 is the lowest priority, while 65535 is the highest.

The function GetMessageQueue() is used to determine how many messages are in a particular player's send or receive queue. By setting the idFrom and idTo parameters, you can determine how many messages are waiting to be sent to or received from a specific player. By setting dwFlags to either DPMESSAGEQUEUE_SEND or DPMESSAGEQUEUE_RECEIVE, you can specify which queue to look at. GetMessageCount() simply returns the number of messages waiting to be processed in a specific player's receive message queue.

You can use these last two functions to gauge just how well a receiving computer is handling messages. If, for example, the receiving computer were much slower than the sending one, it would be possible for the faster computer to overwhelm the slow computer by sending too much data too fast. You can implement "throttling," which means that you start to delay sending messages, or, maybe even more likely, start discarding low priority messages. This would be easy to do with a single call to CancelPriority(), where you can stop DirectPlay from sending a lot of messages with a given priority (or lower).

Summary

This hour covered a lot of information. You learned how to devise a strategy for dealing with deterministic and non-deterministic data, as well as how to maintain game state information between game clients. You learned about players, sessions, and groups, as well as the management of those objects.

You learned about how to develop strategies for writing games that have high responsiveness over a network, as well as how to handle situations that might arise if your game is played over a slow network.

You also learned about DirectPlay's notion of Service Providers, and how to pick a specific service provider, or let the user choose which one to use. You also learned how to use DirectPlay's callback functions to enumerate game sessions, groups, and players on a network.

We'll continue on with this notion of adding multiplayer capabilities in the next hour, when we discuss DirectPlay lobbies. You'll continue to add functionality to your game to add an additional, "social" experience to your game.

20

Q&A

Q **When setting up a network session, the user must make decisions, such as which service provider to use and perhaps some device-specific parameters like a phone number for a modem or a baud rate on a serial port. How is that interface implemented?**

A You can use the Windows dialog boxes that come with the service providers to do most these things, but that is often ugly, undesirable, and disruptive to a full-screen (immersive) application. Yuck, all of a sudden I'm back in Windows looking at a dialog box! These dialog boxes can be silenced and replaced by your application's user interface, but now your application must assemble the DirectPlay address to create the connection. You should either plan to allow dialog boxes to intrude or implement some of your own user interface to replace them.

Q **You said that, in a client/server configuration, most of the data traffic flows client to server. Because the host has most the data, wouldn't most of the flow be from server to client?**

A It really depends on application, architecture, and the engineering philosophies behind what messages you use to get the job done. If there are many players in distinct areas of a vast virtual world, the server gets incoming data from all the players and must send updates of one to another only when they draw near each other. Hence, over time, the main data flow is client to server. However, if we fill that world with AI agents, the client must display their images using server-sent messages, and the main data flow will be server to client.

Q **Do you have to use event handles to receive player messages?**

A This opens up a very old argument between deterministic and asynchronous solutions to real-time problems. A deterministic application is, in essence, a cyclic activity that manages its own time slicing. That typically means it polls the message queue rather than waits for an event signal. One could argue that polling is inefficient, but another could point out the problem is network latency, not the time it takes to see if any messages are waiting. To answer the question: No, you do not have to use event handles unless your application uses asynchronous threads.

Workshop

The Workshop is designed to help you anticipate possible questions, review what you've learned, and begin thinking ahead to put your knowledge into practice. The answers to the quiz are in Appendix A, "Answers."

Quiz

1. What is a DirectPlay Service Provider? What is an example of one?
2. What two main models of communication are used by DirectPlay?
3. What is a callback function and how is it used?
4. What is meant by deterministic data?
5. How do you create a secure session?
6. How are DirectPlay players and groups identified?
7. What is meant by guaranteed messaging? How do you use it?
8. What is the `DPSESSION_MIGRATEHOST` flag used for in the `DPSESSIONDESC2` structure?
9. How might you send a message to all players in a session?
10. Can an `IDirectPlay4` object be used for more than one session?

Exercises

1. Be sure to check out the *Duel* sample in the DirectX SDK. It is a good example of how to tie different components of DirectX together, as well as how to manage game state information.
2. For a real challenge, experiment with the *Duel* sample to see if you can make it more responsive to player input without impacting network consistency.

20

Hour 21

Game Central—Creating Lobbies

In the previous hour, you learned how to add multi-player capabilities to your game with DirectPlay. In this hour, you will learn how to expand upon your knowledge of DirectPlay, and will learn about DirectPlay lobbies. Besides making it easy for players to find other players for a game, adding support for DirectPlay lobbies in your game will also give players a chance to chat or exchange game strategy before or during games. DirectPlay lobby support adds virtual meeting capabilities to your game.

DirectPlay lobbies are really meant to supplement a DirectPlay enabled game. It isn't necessary that your game support DirectPlay lobbies to be multiplayer capable, but you will find that by adding very little code to your game, you will be able to add support for a DirectPlay lobby, thereby enhancing the gamer's experience. Now, not only will players be able to play interactively with each other, but also they will have a forum to gather together before, during, and after gaming sessions.

This lesson introduces you to the IDirectPlayLobby3 interface, and how to use methods from this interface and the IDirectPlay4 to provide functionality for interaction between players in a multiplayer game. You will build upon the knowledge you gained from the previous hour to add lobby functionality to your game.

In this hour, you will learn

- The concepts of a DirectPlay lobby
- About the IDirectPlayLobby3 interface
- Adding users, groups, and sessions
- To send and receive chat messages from the lobby and game client
- How to use a lobby to automatically launch a DirectPlay application

Introduction to DirectPlay Lobbies

Usually four components exist in a DirectPlay lobby: the lobby server, the game server, the lobby client, and the game client. Sometimes, especially in peer-to-peer games, the game server might not be the same as the lobby server, and it might even be another player's computer. The lobby server is responsible for tracking game data and player account information. The game server, of course, deals with actual game play, and is either a dedicated server, or another player's game client acting as host for a session. The lobby client provides most of the functionality associated with dealing with a lobby, whereas the game client handles all of the actual game play. As you can see in Figure 21.1, all four parts work together to form a lobby.

FIGURE 21.1
DirectPlay lobby block diagram.

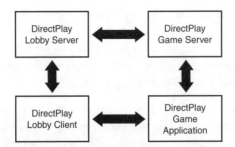

Most of the duties associated with communicating with a lobby server and letting the player interact with the lobby as a whole are handled by the lobby client. The game client, which you are already familiar with from last hour, is not usually running until the game itself begins. The game client is usually launched by the lobby client, although it need not be. You might ask yourself why the game client doesn't run until the game is started, and the answer is very simple: until the game commences, it is the lobby client's job to take care of chatting and player locating responsibilities, as well as to obtain the connection parameters needed for the game. When these are in hand, the lobby client launches the game client, passing to it all that the game client needs to know to start the game.

A DirectPlay lobby is, in the simplest sense, a meeting place for players. In this sense, a lobby could represent a large room in which players can gather. There can be many lobbies for a particular game, or even many lobbies for many games. You might be familiar with this by playing on some of the large, commercial gaming sites on the Internet. You might have noticed, by playing on one of these sites, that for a particular game, lobbies are generally categorized by type of game play. One lobby might target seasoned game players, and one might target beginners. It might be wise to offer the gamer some choice in which type of game to join.

Bringing Players Together Under One Roof

The lobby client would, of course, show these lobbies as choices for a player. When a player has decided which lobby suits his or her taste, he can then join that lobby. Once in the lobby, the player can now begin looking for a particular game to join, or he can simply hang around and chat with others in the same lobby. As you will see in a short while, it is very easy to add inter-player chat capabilities to your game, and the value it will add to your game is great. Let's face it, a lot of the fun in playing games comes from the before and after game chatter that goes on.

Now that the player is in the lobby, he will begin looking for other players to join in on a game with, or simply wait for games to start with random players. A lobby client will show other players in the lobby, as well as all of the games in session or starting. This is usually done graphically, using icons for other players, and perhaps conveying the idea of players sitting around a table to represent a game session.

It is at this point that the player can either start a game session, indicate that he wants to join a game session in progress, or join a session and wait for enough players to join before actually starting the game. As you will see later, it is possible to join a game session without actually starting the game. This makes it possible for a player to join a game and wait for others to join before starting the game, or to even wait for the right amount of people to join (there might be a minimum amount of players needed for a card game, for example).

When a player has found a group of players and a game session to join (or has started one of his own), the actual game can commence. It is at this point that the lobby client can launch the game client. The lobby client continues running, however, right alongside of the game application and can communicate with it for the duration of the game session.

21

Before the game client is actually launched, the lobby client has obtained all the communication parameters needed by the game client. Part of what the lobby is responsible for is keeping track of communication parameters, such as computer addresses and service provider types, as well as an automatic launch of the game application. What this means is that it is possible to bypass all the dialogs normally presented to the user asking for connection information. Those dialogs are not shown because the game client, when it is asking DirectPlay to connect, already knows everything it needs to know about the connection.

Finally, while a player is playing the game, data from the game can be relayed back to the lobby session. This data is sent from the game client to the lobby, and it might just be collected and stored for later use. Data from the game could represent such things as a player's score or perhaps some sort of move or play that the player performed. This data can be sent by the lobby client to the lobby server and stored somewhere, perhaps in a database. This collected data can then be compiled into lists or statistics and perhaps presented on a web page somewhere. A good way to use this data would be to host tournaments, perhaps giving prizes to the top 10 scores in each lobby over a certain period of time.

To write code for a game that implements a DirectPlay lobby, you will be using objects based on both the `IDirectPlayLobby3` and `IDirectPlay4` interfaces. As you will see shortly, the two interfaces go hand-in-hand, and you'll need an instance of both to perform all of the functions a lobby will need.

Because DirectPlay can be written to use a variety of connection schemes, such as client/server and peer to peer and because writing a lobby server is very involved, for the rest of this hour, you will concentrate simply on adding lobby code to a game that already is DirectPlay-able. Writing a full-fledged lobby and game server is usually a large commercial venture, complete with advertising and Web sites geared towards presenting game play data and tournaments. Lobby and game servers usually require logging data to a database over time, which is too large a project to learn in an hour (let alone a day). We will cover the concepts and goals of a lobby server next, though, so you'll have an idea of how your game might work on a larger scale—not just on a modem between you and your buddy.

A full-fledged lobby client will be written using the Lobby Provider SDK from Microsoft. The presentation of the lobby concept to a user could easily be handled by a combination of Web browsing and a lobby client (perhaps an ActiveX component), or just by a sophisticated, standalone lobby client. For more information on how to write your own sophisticated lobby client or server, you should contact Microsoft for more information on the lobby provider kit.

NEW TERM A *lobby provider* is a client component (DLL) supplied by the developer of a lobby server. It implements communication functions with the lobby server as requested by DirectPlay.

> Don't be discouraged by the fact that we won't be covering how to write a
> large-scale lobby server or sophisticated lobby client. The DirectX SDK
> includes a test lobby server, which should be more than adequate to test
> your game with. If you are successful at writing a game with DirectPlay fea-
> tures built-in, you can always consider having the game hosted on a large-
> scale game hosting site. One of the benefits of using the DirectPlay
> architecture and supporting DirectPlay lobbies is that if you write the API
> correctly, your game should be hostable on almost any of the game hosting
> sites. I'll leave that as something for you to look into.

The Game Server

The lobby server will most likely be database driven and should be very scalable because
the idea is to get a large amount of players together—the more the merrier. It will also
most likely be tied to the Web, somehow. As you look at the large commercial ventures,
you will see that they tie a large amount of information together, such as tournament and
game info, and present it on a Web site. They also track your player information and
store that in a database as well.

As mentioned previously, the lobby server might or might not be the same as the game
server, and they might not even be running on the same computer, nor even located close
to each other physically. It is possible for a lobby server to be running on the Internet
somewhere, perhaps in conjunction with a Web site, and for the actual game session to
be hosted via some dialup service. Remember that it is the lobby client's responsibility to
obtain the game connection information from the server and to send that information to
the game client. The lobby client could connect to the Internet via the DirectPlay TCP/IP
service provider, but the game session could be played over the DirectPlay modem service provider. This might be likely if the game play was to take place over a proprietary
low-latency network.

Making a DirectPlay Application Lobbyable

When a user decides to join a session in-progress or start a new game when all players
have joined, the DirectPlay Lobby interface, `IDirectPlayLobby3`, enables you to launch
the actual game program automatically. The capability for DirectPlay (via the lobby
interface) to launch your application means that your application is lobby-aware.

NEW TERM   A *lobby-aware application* is a DirectPlay application capable of being launched
by a lobby and is capable of obtaining its connection parameters from a DirectPlay
lobby.

21

For a DirectPlay game to connect to other clients or servers running on other computers, it must use a network connection. Without lobby support, this is usually accomplished by asking the user for connection parameters (for example, an Internet address for a TCP/IP type of connection). The user fills in a dialog box presented by DirectPlay with the parameters needed for DirectPlay to successfully complete the connection.

A DirectPlay game can also get its connection information from a lobby because a lobby would have specific information on a game session, including connection parameters. To make a game "lobbyable," a small amount of code change is needed to an already DirectPlay enabled game to accommodate this. A DirectPlay enabled game can also include the code necessary to provide a lobby interface internally, thereby also taking advantage of obtaining connection parameters from the lobby. Thus, there are three possible ways in which a DirectPlay game can be written. They are as follows:

- Stand-Alone—This type of client does not know about lobbies, nor how to use them.
- Lobby-Aware—This type of client can be launched by an external lobby and is aware of how to obtain information about the game session (including connection settings) from the lobby that launched it.
- Self-Lobbied—This type of game contains code to provide lobby client functions internally, so it does not require an external client to launch it.

It is the last two types of game that you will now learn how to build. The first type, Stand-Alone, you already know how to build from the last hour. With very little change to the code of a Stand-Alone type of game, you will be able to write games that are Lobby-Aware or Self-Lobbied.

The IDirectPlayLobby Interface

The IDirectPlayLobby3 interface is, like the rest of DirectX, based on COM. It has the following list of methods:

- Connect()
- ConnectEx()
- CreateAddress()
- CreateCompoundAddress()
- EnumAddress()
- EnumAddressTypes()
- EnumLocalApplications()
- GetConnectionSettings()

- ReceiveLobbyMessage()
- RegisterApplication()
- RunApplication()
- SendLobbyMessage()
- SetConnectionSettings()
- SetLobbyMessageEvent()
- UnregisterApplication()
- WaitForConnectionSettings()
- AddRef()
- QueryInterface()
- Release()

Like the other DirectX interfaces you have already learned about, the last three functions: AddRef(), QueryInterface(), and Release() are inherited from the IUnknown interface.

To begin your foray into lobby client building, you must first obtain a pointer to an IDirectPlayLobby3 interface. You can do this with a call to the COM function CoCreateInstance. An example of doing this is

```
HRESULT hr;
LPDIRECTPLAYLOBBY3A lpDirectPlayLobby3A;
hr = CoCreateInstance( CLSID_DirectPlayLobby, NULL,
    CLSCTX_INPROC_SERVER,
    IID_IDirectPlayLobby3A,
    (LPVOID*)&lpDirectPlayLobby3A);
if ( FAILED(hr) )
  goto FAILURE;
```

You should be familiar with using this function to obtain references to COM objects by now. Notice that we are obtaining an interface for an IDirectPlayLobby3A COM object. This is important because we will be using ANSI strings in the structures that we pass to functions later. If we were going to be passing Unicode strings as members of structures that we will pass to our lobby object's functions, we would instead want to get a reference to an IDirectPlayLobby3 interface. Just like the IDirectPlay4 interface, the IDirectPlayLobby3 interface has both an ANSI and Unicode interface, represented by IDirectPlayLobby3A and IDirectPlayLobby, respectively. For the remainder of this hour, I will refer to this interface as simply IDirectPlayLobby3. You must decide whether to use the ANSI or Unicode version. One of the benefits of using a Unicode interface and Unicode strings is ease of porting your game to other languages besides English.

21

DirectX also provides a helper function for creating `IDirectPlayLobby3` objects—
`DirectPlayLobbyCreate()`. The following is the prototype for this function:

```
HRESULT WINAPI DirectPlayLobbyCreate(LPGUID lpGUIDSP,
                                     LPDIRECTPLAYLOBBY *lplpDPL,
                                     IUnknown *lpUnk,
                                     LPVOID lpData,
                                     DWORD dwDataSize);
```

As you can see, this function returns a pointer to a DirectPlay Lobby via the `LPDIRECT-PLAYLOBBY` type parameter `lplpDPL`. Like most of the other DirectX interfaces, this function takes a pointer to an `IUnknown` interface, which is used for aggregation. Like the other DirectX interfaces, this feature isn't currently supported, so you must pass `NULL`. The `lpData` must currently be set to `NULL`, and the `dwDataSize` should be 0. The `LPGUID` parameter must also be set to `NULL`.

Lobby Support for the Game Client

Your DirectPlay Lobby can help your game client, when you launch it to start a game, by setting most of the information needed by the game client via a call to `SetConnectionSettings()`. The following is the prototype for this function:

```
HRESULT SetConnectionSettings(DWORD dwFlags,
                              DWORD dwAppID,
                              LPDPLCONNECTION lpConn);
```

The `dwFlags` parameter is reserved, and it must be 0. The `dwAppID` parameter is the GUID that represents which game client that these connections will be used by. Keep in mind that it is possible for a lobby client to launch more than one type of game, so this is how it identifies for which type of game it is setting communication parameters. The `lpConn` parameter is a pointer to a `DPLCONNECTION` structure, which looks like the following:

```
typedef struct {
    DWORD            dwSize;
    DWORD            dwFlags;
    LPDPSESSIONDESC2 lpSessionDesc;
    LPDPNAME         lpPlayerName;
    GUID             guidSP;
    LPVOID           lpAddress;
    DWORD            dwAddressSize;
} DPLCONNECTION, FAR *LPDPLCONNECTION;
```

The dwSize parameter should be set to the size of the DPLCONNECTION structure. The dwFlags represents how to open a session, and it should be either DPLCONNECTION_CREATE-SESSION, or DPLCONNECTION_JOINSESSION, which tell the game client to create or join an existing session, respectively. The lpSessionDesc parameter is a pointer to a DPSESSION-DESC2 structure, which I will cover shortly, in the "Creating a Session" section. For now, just know that it indicates information about the session. The player name is represented by the lpPlayerName and is the means by which the lobby client informs the game client on what name to use for the player. The guidSP represents the type of service provider to use (you should recall what these are from the previous hour). The lpAddress and dwAddressSize parameters represent a pointer to the address information and the size of the address information, respectively. These last two parameters also deal with information that the service provider needs, and were covered last hour.

After the lobby client sets the communication parameters via the call to SetConnectionSettings(), the game client, as it first runs, can then call GetConnectionSettings() to obtain all the information needed to finalize the connection to the games session host. The parameter for GetConnectionSettings() is

```
HRESULT GetConnectionSettings(DWORD dwAppID,
                 LPVOID lpData,
                 LPDWORD lpdwDataSize);
```

When called from a lobby client, the dwAppID points to the GUID representing the game client. When called by your game client, it should be set to 0. The lpData parameter is set to a buffer to hold the connection settings, and lpDataSize points to a variable indicating the size of this buffer.

Registering the Game as Lobbyable

DirectPlay must somehow know that your game is lobbyable (so that it might be launched by any type of lobby client), so at some point during the installation of your game, you can use the function RegisterApplication(). The prototype for this function is as follows:

```
HRESULT RegisterApplication(DWORD dwFlags, LPDPAPPLICATIONDESC lpAppDesc);
```

Using this function makes changes to the registry and associates a GUID with your game. This GUID will be used later by the lobby to launch your game at the appropriate time. The GUID used in the DPAPPLICATIONDESC structure passed to this function is important because it is used to identify this application within a session.

A DPAPPLICATIONDESC structure specifies such things as the filename and path to the game client, as well as a name and description. This structure also associates a GUID with your game client. A prototype of that structure can be seen in Listing 21.1.

21

LISTING 21.1   Registration Information Structure

```
 1: typedef struct {
 2:     DWORD dwSize;
 3:     DWORD dwFlags;
 4:     union {
 5:         LPSTR lpszApplicationNameA;
 6:         LPWSTR lpszApplicationName;
 7:     }
 8:     GUID guidApplication;
 9:     union {
10:         LPSTR lpszFileNameA;
11:         LPWSTR lpszFileName;
12:     }
13:     union {
14:         LPSTR lpszCommandLineA;
15:         LPWSTR lpszCommandLine;
16:     } union {
17:         LPSTR lpszPathA;
18:         LPWSTR lpszPath;
19:     } union {
20:         LPSTR lpszCurrentDirectoryA;
21:         LPWSTR lpszCurrentDirectory;
22:     }
23:     LPSTR lpszDescriptionA;
24:     LPWSTR lpszDescriptionW;
25: } DPAPPLICATIONDESC, FAR *LPDPAPPLICATIONDESC;
```

If you look closely at the preceding use of unions, you might begin to realize how the
IDirectPlayLobby3 interface has a dual nature. Because we are currently dealing with
the ANSI version of the interface, we will be setting the strings that end with the capital
'A'. Most of these structure members should be self explanatory. It might be wise to note
that, again, we see the GUID of the game client, this time represented by the
guidApplication member. The dwFlags value is currently not used, and must be 0. You
should also set the dwSize member to the size of the structure (that is, dwSize =
sizeof(DPAPPLICATIONDESC)).

When you are uninstalling an application, you must call the UnregisterApplication()
function. This function removes the game client from the registry.

```
HRESULT UnregisterApplication(DWORD dwFlags, REFGUID guidApplication);
```

As you might have guessed, the guidApplication parameter is the GUID of the game
client as it registered it, and the dwFlags parameter is currently reserved and should be
set to 0.

If a lobby client needs to be able to obtain a list of all the applications that are lobbyable, it can retrieve this with a call to `EnumLocalApplications()`. The prototype for this function is:

```
HRESULT EnumLocalApplications(
            LPDPENUMLOCALAPPLICATIONSCALLBACK lpEnumLocalAppCallback,
            LPVOID lpContext,
            DWORD dwFlags);
```

This function uses the now familiar call-back method of informing the application of all game clients that have been registered as lobbyable. You must pass a pointer to a function with the prototype `LPDPENUMLOCALAPPLICATIONCALLBACK` to this function via the `lpEnumLocalAppCallback` parameter. As you might guess, your call-back function is called repeatedly, once for each application that is registered. A lobby client would probably use this function to populate a list box or combo box on a dialog or form in your lobby client somewhere.

Users, Groups, and Sessions

One of the first things a lobby client will probably do, after connecting with a lobby server and finding a particular game session, is create a DirectPlay player object to represent the user. To do this, you will actually use the `IDirectPlay4` interface function `CreatePlayer()`. This function was covered in the previous hour, so you should be familiar with it already. It is important to remember that a call to this function returns a pointer to a `DPID` structure. This structure will be used later to join groups, and send and receive chat messages, as you will see shortly.

Before a player is created, though, a lobby client will usually call `EnumSessions()` to learn about all the sessions in progress at a particular server. The DirectPlay sessions that you learned how to create in the previous hour will actually represent individual games in progress or about to be started.

After players are joined to a session, using the `Open()` function of the `IDirectPlay4` object, they can join groups within the session. Joining a group would be useful if your game was complex and supported the notion of players grouping together—it wouldn't be so handy, say, in a card game. It is possible, using the `CreateGroup()` and `AddGroupToGroup()` functions, to create a hierarchy of groups so that it might be possible to have large bands of groups, each with their own, smaller bands of players participating in one game session. You might also want to do this to take advantage of the DirectPlay's built-in multicasting support so that you can limit in-game messages to a specific group of players or group of groups. An example of how this might be structured can be seen in Figure 21.2.

21

FIGURE 21.2

DirectPlay grouping example.

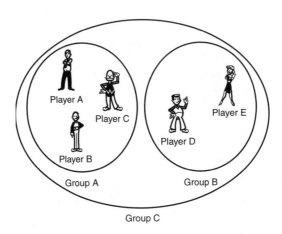

To find out which groups are gathered within a particular session, you can call the EnumGroups() function. It has the following prototype:

```
HRESULT EnumGroups( LPGUID lpguidInstance,
                    LPDPENUMPLAYERSCALLBACK2 lpEnumPlayersCallback2,
                    LPVOID lpContext,
                    DWORD dwFlags );
```

As you might have guessed, the lpEnumPlayersCallback2 parameter should be a pointer to the callback function, which will be called for as many groups as there are currently defined. A lobby client would probably want to do something useful with this function, such as adding the names of the groups passed to you to a combo box or some other list control on a dialog somewhere. The LPDPENUMPLAYERSCALLBACK2 function has the following prototype:

```
BOOL FAR PASCAL EnumPlayersCallback2(
  DPID dpid,
  DWORD dwPlayerType,
  LPCDPNAME lpName,
  DWORD dwFlags,
  LPVOID lpContext);
```

Note that the DPID parameter will indicate the group's ID, and that dwPlayerType will have the value DPPLAYERTYPE_GROUP, which indicates that the values represent a group. The lpContext parameter is set to the value passed by the EnumGroups() function. You can set this to any value you like because it will just simply be passed to your lpEnumPlayersCallback2 function every time.

As you might have guessed, the function, EnumGroupPlayers() takes a similar pointer to a LPDPENUMPLAYERSCALLBACK2 function and sets the value of dwPlayerType to DPPLAY-ERTYPE_PLAYER. It, of course, enumerates a list of players in a particular group for you. The prototype for this function is

```
HRESULT EnumGroupPlayers(
  DPID idGroup,
  LPGUID lpguidInstance,
  LPDPENUMPLAYERSCALLBACK2 lpEnumPlayersCallback2,
  LPVOID lpContext,
  DWORD dwFlags
);
```

You can also call the EnumGroupsInGroup() function to obtain a list of groups within a group. This function has the following prototype:

```
HRESULT EnumGroupsInGroup(
  DPID idGroup,
  LPGUID lpguidInstance,
  LPDPENUMPLAYERSCALLBACK2 lpEnumCallback,
  LPVOID lpContext,
  DWORD dwFlags
);
```

This function uses a similar LPDPENUMPLAYERSCALLBACK2 type of function pointer. This function is very similar to the previous functions, and it iterates through the list of groups within a particular group, represented by idGroup.

After you have decided which session to join and have listed all the groups in each session, it's time to pick a group and add your player to it. To add players to a group, you use the AddPlayerToGroup() function. It has the following prototype:

```
HRESULT AddPlayerToGroup(DPID idGroup, DPID idPlayer);
```

With this call, you can pass the DPID structure representing the group to join, and the DPID structure representing the player that was initially created by the lobby.

Providing Chat Services

The ability to chat is provided by the DirectPlay interface, IDirectPlay4. The two functions, SendChatMessage(), and Receive() are used in combination by the lobby to send and receive chat messages, respectively. The prototype for these two functions are similar:

```
HRESULT SendChatMessage(DPID idFrom, DPID idTo,
                   DWORD dwFlags, LPDPCHAT lpChatMessage);
HRESULT Receive(LPDPID lpidFrom, LPDPID lpidTo,
              DWORD dwFlags, LPVOID lpData, lpdwDataSize);
```

21

The `SendChatMessage` indicates to whom the message is to (`idTo`), and to whom it is from (`idFrom`). To send a message to all players in a game session, you can set the `dwFlags` parameter to the value `DPID_ALLPLAYERS` or use the `EnumPlayers()` function covered previously to get the `DPID` of a specific player to send to. The `lpChatMessage` is a pointer to a `DPCHAT` structure, which looks like the following:

```
typedef struct {
    DWORD dwSize;
    DWORD dwFlags;
    union{
      LPWSTR lpszMessage;
      LPSTR  lpszMessageA;
    };
} DPCHAT, FAR *LPDPCHAT;
```

This structure is fairly simple and should be straightforward. Note that as you might expect, the `dwSize` parameter should be set to the size of a `DPCHAT` structure, and that the `dwFlags` parameter is currently unused and should be set to 0. Set the `lpszMessageA` pointer to your chat message string for an ANSI type of string, and use the `lpszMessage` parameter for a Unicode type of string.

The `Receive()` function is used to receive any type of DirectPlay message, not just chatting messages. The `lpidFrom` parameter will be set to `DPID_SYSMSG` when the message is a chat message, and the `lpData` parameter, which points to a `DPMSG_GENERIC` type of structure; in this case, it will have a `dwType` of `DPMSG_CHAT` (see Listing 21.2).

LISTING 21.2 An Example of Checking for a Chat Type of Message

```
 1: DPID idFrom, idTo;
 2: HRESULT hr;
 3: LPVOID lpvMsgBuffer;
 4: DWORD dwMsgBufferSize;
 5: do
 6: {
 7:     idFrom = 0;
 8:     idTo = 0;
 9:     hr = lpDirectPlayLobby3A->Receive(&idFrom, &idTo,
                    ➥DPRECEIVE_ALL, lpvMsgBuffer, dwMsgBufferSize);
10:     if (hr == DPERR_BUFFERTOOSMALL)
11:     {
12:         if (lpvMsgBuffer)
13:             delete lpvMsgBuffer;
14:         lpvMsgBuffer = (VOID*)(new BYTE[dwMsgBufferSize]);
15:         if (lpvMsgBuffer == NULL)
16:             hr = DPERR_OUTOFMEMORY;
17:     }
18: } while (hr == DPERR_BUFFERTOOSMALL);
19: if ((SUCCEEDED(hr)) &&     (dwMsgBufferSize >= sizeof(DPMSG_GENERIC)))
20: {
```

```
21:     if (idFrom == DPID_SYSMSG)
22:     {
23:         // This must be a system message, let's see what type
24:         if ((LPDPMSG_GENERIC)lpvMsgBuffer->dwType == DPMSG_CHAT))
25:         {
26:             // Ta Da!  It's a chat type of message, so let's deal with it
27:             // Some sort of chat dealing code here
28:         }
29:     }
30: }
```

You should remember when using these functions that although `SendChatMessage()` is specific to sending chat type messages, the `Receive()` function is used to receive *any* type of message, including generic system messages and other game messages.

Creating a Session

When it comes time to create a session, you will need to use a `DPSESSIONDESC2` structure that I alluded to earlier. Let's take a quick look at that structure in Listing 21.3.

LISTING 21.3   The `DPSESSIONDESC2` Structure

```
 1: typedef struct
 2: {
 3:     DWORD   dwSize;
 4:     DWORD   dwFlags;
 5:     GUID    guidInstance;
 6:     GUID    guidApplication;
 7:     DWORD   dwMaxPlayers;
 8:     DWORD   dwCurrentPlayers;
 9:     union
10:     {
11:         LPWSTR   lpszSessionName;
12:         LPSTR    lpszSessionNameA;
13:     };
14:     union
15:     {
16:         LPWSTR   lpszPassword;
17:         LPSTR    lpszPasswordA;
18:     };
19:     DWORD   dwReserved1;
20:     DWORD   dwReserved2;
21:     DWORD   dwUser1;
22:     DWORD   dwUser2;
23:     DWORD   dwUser3;
24:     DWORD   dwUser4;
25: } DPSESSIONDESC2, FAR *LPDPSESSIONDESC2;
```

21

The dwSize value should be set to the size of this structure. The dwFlags member indicates, among other things, whether the game session is client/server (DPSESSION_CLIENTSERVER) or peer-to-peer based (the default). It also indicates whether the session is hosted by a secure server (DPSESSION_SECURESERVER); in which case, you would need to set the lpszPassword value. The guidInstance indicates the GUID for this session and would be returned from a call to Open() or EnumSessions()—more on these functions in a minute. The guidApplication represents the GUID for the game client that is appropriate for this game session. The dwMaxPlayers variable holds the maximum number of players allowed in this session—set this to 0 to indicate no limit. The dwCurrentPlayers represents the number of players currently in this session. The session name is stored in lpszSessionName. As you might have guessed, dwReserved1 and dwReserved2 are reserved and should be set to 0. The last four members represent user-defined variables and can be used by the lobby or game client to represent basically anything that you might want.

You use the Open() function to create or join a lobby session. This function takes a pointer to a DPSESSIONDESC2 structure, as you can see here:

```
HRESULT Open(LPDPSESSIONDESC2 lpsd, DWORD dwFlags);
```

The dwFlags value can be one of DPOPEN_CREATE, DPOPEN_JOIN, or DPOPEN_RETURNSTATUS. The first two either create a new session based on the information on the passed in session description, or join an existing session, respectively. The last possible value is interesting because it allows you to use the Open() function asynchronously. You OR this value in, and it will return a DPERR_CONNECTING error. It will also cause DirectPlay to show any dialog boxes indicating connection status. Instead, you must continue to call Open() until you get a value other than DPERR_CONNECTING, indicating the actual success or failure of the call.

As you will remember from the previous hour, you can use the EnumSessions() function to retrieve a list of sessions currently in progress. You would then follow this with a call to Open(), with the guidSession value set and the dwFlags parameter set to DPOPEN_JOIN when the player has chosen which session to join. It is also important to realize that, although we covered this topic lastly, you must actually open a session before you can create a player or send and receive messages.

When the lobby or game server is ready to finally start the game, it will call StartSession(), which sends a DPMSG_STARTSESSION type of message to the lobby client. This is the signal to the lobby client that it should now launch the game client to start the game. It accomplishes this by calling RunApplication(). The prototype for this function is as follows:

```
HRESULT RunApplication(
    DWORD dwFlags,
    LPDWORD lpdwAppID,
    LPDPLCONNECTION lpConn,
    HANDLE hReceiveEvent
);
```

The dwFlags parameter is currently reserved and should be set to 0. The lpdwAppID parameter is a pointer to a DWORD type variable. This value will be set to an ID identifying the launched application. This will be used later when the lobby and application communicate with each other. The lpConn parameter is a pointer to a structure of type DPLCONNECTION, which you have already seen. By passing this structure this way, the lobby client does not need to call SetConnectionSettings() because DirectPlay will call that function for you.

The hReceiveEvent is a Win32 HANDLE structure, which can be used in combination with the WaitForObject() or WaitForMultipleObjects() Win32 functions. This handle represents a synchronization object, which is set by DirectPlay when there is a message waiting for the lobby to receive, which it can then retrieve with a call to Receive().

Launching a DirectPlay Lobby Application

When the lobby server is ready to start a game session, it launches the game application on each client machine in the session. It then passes each client the connection settings it should use to establish the DirectPlay session. That means the game is lobbyable if it checks for connection settings from the lobby during program initialization, and uses those settings to immediately join the network session.

Making the Game Lobbyable

So now, let's add the code to our game client necessary to make the application lobbyable (see Listing 21.4). You should already have a pointer to an IDirectPlayLobby3 interface, created from our earlier code sample. We can now get down to the business of obtaining the communication parameters needed to make our connection.

LISTING 21.4   Getting DirectPlay Connection Settings from a Lobby

```
 1: hr = lpDirectPlayLobby3A->GetConnectionSettings(0, NULL, &dwSize);
 2: if (DPERR_BUFFERTOOSMALL != hr)
 3:     goto FAILURE;
 4: // Allocate memory for the connection settings.
 5: lpConnectionSettings = (LPDPLCONNECTION)GlobalAllocPtr(GHND, dwSize);
 6: if (NULL == lpConnectionSettings)
 7: {
 8:     hr = DPERR_OUTOFMEMORY;
 9:     goto FAILURE;
10: }
11: // Retrieve the connection settings.
12: hr = lpDirectPlayLobby3A->GetConnectionSettings(0,
                ➥lpConnectionSettings, &dwSize);
13: if FAILED(hr)
14:     goto FAILURE;
```

21

Note that in the preceding call to `GetConnectionSettings()`, you are using the test-set-test method of obtaining data via a buffer that you provide. This method is a way of calling a function initially to obtain the size of a buffer required to retrieve all the data the function will give you. By setting the `dwSize` parameter to `0`, and passing a `NULL` pointer to a buffer, the first call to `GetConnectionSettings()` function will inform you of how large a buffer you will need to obtain all the settings by setting the `dwSize` parameter to the required size value. You can then call `GetConnectionSettings()` again with a buffer allocated to the exact size needed. Remember that a lobby client will have called `SetConnectionSettings()` to set these connections before launching the game client.

Sending and Receiving Lobby Messages

Remember that one of the advantages to having a lobby client to help the game get launched is that the lobby client still runs alongside the game client, sitting quietly on the sidelines to support any communication that isn't essential to game play. Our game client might want to send a player's current score every so often, so it might perform the following:

```
1: DWORD dwGameScore;
2: DWORD dwGameScoreSize = sizeof(GAMESCORE);
3: HRESULT hr;
4: hr = lpDirectPlayLobby3A->SendLobbyMessage(0, 0,
   ➥(LPVOID)&dwGameScore, dwGameScoreSize);
5: if (FAILED(hr))
6:     goto FAILURE;
```

It might be wise to use a custom defined structure as your base type for any game client to lobby client messages, such as:

```
typedef struct {
    DWORD dwSize;
    DWORD dwType;
} CUSTOM_MSGTYPE;
```

This will allow you to check for the size and type of custom message that you will be sending between lobby client and game client. This is the way that DirectPlay treats system messages because their content will vary according to type. This way, with a simple check of the `dwType` value, you can (rather) safely typecast the message to the correct structure type. This would require two typecasts: one to typecast to your generic structure type (to check the `dwType` value), and the other to typecast to the final, correct structure type.

This data will be most useful when you are writing your own lobby provider and client. As I said early in this hour, this data might be key to providing feedback to your players on how they might be doing in relation to one another. Besides the chat messages, which are sent from player to player, these types of messages are really not part of standard game play, but can still be used to enhance the long term value of the game.

Cleanup

Be sure to call `Close()` on the DirectPlay object prior to calling `Release()`. Then, simply call `Release()` on both the DirectPlay and DirectPlayLobby interfaces obtained earlier.

Summary

In this hour, you learned how to create an object based on the `IDirectPlayLobby3` interface and how to use that object along with the DirectPlay object from the previous hour to join lobbies and find game sessions. You learned how to send chat messages back and forth, add users and groups, and send data from the game to the lobby and vice versa.

You also learned how to make a normal DirectPlay game lobbyable, either self-lobbied or launched by an external lobby. Using the DirectPlay object and lobby objects, your game is now multiplayer and very interactive! From what you learned this hour, you should be prepared to market your game to the large online service providers, or even start an online service yourself.

Q&A

Q I'm confused. To register (and unregister) the application, we need an IDirectPlayLobby3 interface. How do we get this as part of setup if we're using, for example, InstallShield? In particular, how do we provide it for uninstall?

A You can write a small console application and run it from the setup after installing DirectX. To unregister, create another console application and run it from the uninstall script before deleting the application files. You can also register with `DirectXRegisterApplication` and unregister with `DirectXUnRegisterApplication`, which have advantages and disadvantages, so you should read up on them in the DirectX documentation before selecting the approach that is best for you.

Q I'm planning to write a client/server based game that will always be launched by a lobby. Where can I learn more about lobby providers?

A To look into writing your own lobby provider, email the DirectX team at Microsoft for more information. They can provide you with a Lobby Provider Kit, which will enable you to write your own Lobby Service Provider.

21

Workshop

The Workshop is designed to help you anticipate possible questions, review what you've learned, and get you thinking about how to put your knowledge into practice. The answers to the quiz are in Appendix A, "Answers."

Quiz

1. How does the game client relay information back to the lobby?

2. How does the lobby pass the connection information needed to a game client?

3. When does the lobby begin running a lobby-aware game, and how does it start it?

4. How does the lobby obtain a list of games that are lobby-aware and that can be launched by a lobby?

5. How do you create an address representing an Internet based server for a game to connect to?

6. What is meant by a "lobby-aware" game?

7. Which client can change information about a session?

Exercises

1. Be sure to check out the DirectPlay samples in the DirectX SDK. Most of the samples are lobby-aware applications, and you can use the test lobby server to get a feel for how a game will respond with a lobby interface. Be sure to read the instructions on how to start the lobby server because you need to make changes to your registry to allow the sample applications to communicate with it.

2. Use the code samples in this and the previous hour to make the cube sample program from Hour 7 network aware. That is, have it create a DirectPlay session using the standard service provider dialogs. You can also use the DirectX SDK samples as a source.

3. Using your networked cube project, have each application broadcast user commands rather than execute them, and execute any commands the application receives from the session.

4. Finally, make your networked cube project lobbyable, register it, and launch it using the DirectX test lobby server.

PART VIII

The DirectMedia SDK

Hour

HOUR **22**

Adding Video with DirectShow

DirectShow is the part of DirectX Media that allows you to playback multi-media streams such as MPEG, AVI and Apple QuickTime from local files or the Internet. DirectShow is accessed via COM in the same way as most other DirectX components.

In this hour, you will learn

- What filters are, how they work, and what filters are available.
- How to stream multimedia from the Internet.
- How to string filters together to perform different playback operations.
- How to playback video-based media to any DirectDraw surface.
- How to playback video-based media with sound.

Introducing DirectShow

DirectShow is not, as the name suggests, a single technology. It's made of several different COM interfaces, all of which support different forms of multimedia playback and capture. DirectShow can do all these things because of a clever technology called filters. The logical definition of a filter is something that performs an operation on some kind of data and produces an altered output. For example, you could have a filter decompress an AVI video file and then pass the data to a render filter, which in turn would draw the decompressed video data onto a DirectDraw surface. This DirectDraw surface could in turn be used to texture map a 3D model of a TV in your Direct3D based game.

An extreme case could also be streaming live satellite video feed from an Internet URL filter, which could then be processed by an AVI compression filter before being rendered by a disk file filter, effectively saving the live video feed as an AVI file.

Filters are managed by an object known as the *filter graph*. The filter graph is what makes the different filters work together to produce the desired output (see Figure 22.1). You simply add filters to the filter graph, and it will make sure the stream data is processed by the appropriate filters, creating the desired output.

FIGURE 22.1
How the filter graph works.

Many different filters are included in the DirectX Media SDK, and you can even create your own. Consult your DirectX Media documentation for information and samples about how to use the different filters.

In this hour, I will only cover using filters to render video streams. No capture or modification filters will be covered because it's beyond the scope of this hour.

In my many years of game programming, I've found that DirectShow is almost exclusively used to render video streams to a DirectDraw surface so that's what I'm going to show you.

Video Playback Capabilities

DirectShow, as mentioned, has many video playback capabilities. Here are a few of the most popular:

- MP3 music. A highly compressed audio stream of high quality.
- MP2 video (including DVD movies).

- MP1 video.

- RealAudio and video.

- AVI video. Microsoft's Audio Video Interleaved format.

- Playback to a full screen DirectDraw surface.

- Playback of most popular Internet audio and video formats via the new Media Player ActiveX control, which can easily be embedded in Web pages and can be made to work with both Internet Explorer and Netscape. (This is covered in the next section.)

Internet Streaming Video Applications

As mentioned before, DirectShow can be made to stream multimedia data from an Internet URL in your COM-based application, or you can embed the Media Player ActiveX control directly inside your Web pages.

In this section, I'll give you a small sample on how to stream and interact with a video clip with sound from inside a Web page.

> When streaming from the Internet, note that the Media Player ActiveX control differs between streaming and nonstreaming formats.
>
> Choosing a 20MB video stream in AVI format would cause Media Player to download the entire file before playing it, and that would probably anger any visitor to your Web site who does not have a 2MB connection.
>
> Some streaming formats:
>
> MPEG-1, MPEG-2, MPEG-3, ASF (Advanced Streaming Format), VOD (Video On Demand), RA (Real Audio) version 4, and RV (Real Video) version 4.
>
> Some nonstreaming formats:
>
> AVI, MOV, MIDI, WAV, SND, and Indeo 5.

Using the Media Player ActiveX control is easy. Listing 22.1 contains the code that will help you use it. (Don't worry about the parameters because I'm going to explain them in a moment.)

LISTING 22.1   Using the Media Player ActiveX Control

```
1: <OBJECT ID="MyMediaPlayer"
2:    classid="CLSID:22D6F312-B0F6-11D0-94AB-0080C74C7E95"
```

continues

LISTING **22.1**   continued

```
 3:  CODEBASE="http://activex.microsoft.com/activex/controls/
     ➥mplayer/en/nsmp2inf.cab#Version=5,1,52,701"
 4:  standby="Loading Microsoft&reg; Windows&reg; Media Player components..."
 5:  type="application/x-oleobject">
 6:  <PARAM NAME="AnimationAtStart" VALUE="0">
 7:  <PARAM NAME="ShowControls" VALUE="0">
 8:  <PARAM NAME="AutoStart" VALUE="0">
 9:  <PARAM NAME="VideoBorderWidth" VALUE="5">
10:  <PARAM NAME="VideoBorderColor" VALUE="255">
11: </OBJECT>
```

And that's it for adding a window capable of showing multimedia content in your Web site. Simply place this piece of code where you want the window to be.

Now for the promised parameter explanation:

The Media Player ActiveX control is placed inside an OBJECT block which must start with <OBJECT ID="XX"> and end with </OBJECT> just like standard HTML tags.

The OBJECT ID is the name you'll use to access the Media Player control from script languages such as VBscript (Visual Basic script) and JScript (JavaScript). This can be any identifier you want (for example: MyMediaPlayer).

Just as DirectX COM objects need a unique identifier, so does the Media Player control. That's the CLASSID parameter.

The CODEBASE parameter is just like the one in Java. It specifies where the code for the specified object is. (The URL where the control is placed.)

STANDBY almost specifies what it does all by itself. It's just the message displayed, when the Control is loading.

TYPE is the type of the embedded object. All kinds of objects can be embedded in Web pages, so they need to specify a type that the browser can use to identify them and execute them properly. In this case it's an application/OLE object, identifying this as an ActiveX control.

Now comes a bunch of <PARAM> tags. The ones used in this example are but a few of the many parameters you can pass the Media Player. See your Direct Media SDK documentation for a more comprehensive list.

```
<PARAM NAME="AnimationAtStart" VALUE="0">
```

Do not show normal controls such as Play, stop, and so on.

```
<PARAM NAME="AutoStart" VALUE="0">
```

Do not auto start the media stream.

```
<PARAM NAME="VideoBorderWidth" VALUE="5">
```

Place a five-pixel border around the control.

```
<PARAM NAME="VideoBorderColor" VALUE="255">
```

Set the border color to RED.

As you can see, we have set the Media Player control to hide its controls and not do anything. We want to control the action ourselves.

I use JavaScript for this example because it runs in Netscape too. (See your DirectXMedia SDK documentation for Visual Basic script examples.)

First we create play, pause, and stop buttons. We also include an about button, so people can get information about the Control and its version.

```
<INPUT TYPE="BUTTON" NAME="PlayBtn"  VALUE="Play" OnClick="PlayStream()">
<INPUT TYPE="BUTTON" Name="PauseBtn" VALUE="Pause" OnClick="PauseStream()">
<INPUT TYPE="BUTTON" NAME="StopBtn"  VALUE="Stop" OnClick="StopStream()">
<INPUT TYPE="BUTTON" NAME="AboutBtn" VALUE="About Player Control" OnClick=
➥"MyMediaPlayer.AboutBox()">
```

What we basically do here is name four buttons and tie a JavaScript function to their OnClick handler.

NEW TERM   An *OnClick handler* performs an action when an HTML object is clicked on. Can be tied to most HTML objects, including Web links and images.

Now on to the JavaScript code: To implement the button's OnClick handlers, look at Listing 22.2.

LISTING 22.2   OnClick Handlers

```
 1: // Start media playback
 2: function PlayStream()
 3: {
 4:     // Set Media Player filename to the value of the MediaFile box.
 5:     MyMediaPlayer.FileName=MediaFile.value;
 6:
 7:     // Start the playback
 8:     MyMediaPlayer.Play();
 9: }
10:
11: // Pause media playback.
12: // If the stream is paused restart it.
```

continues

LISTING 22.2 continued

```
13: function PauseStream()
14: {
15:     // Check if we are paused
16:     if (MyMediaPlayer.PlayState==1)
17:     {
18:       // We are paused. Restart playback.
19:       MyMediaPlayer.Play();
20:     }
21:     else
22:     {
23:       // We are not paused. Pause playback.
24:       MyMediaPlayer.Pause();
25:     }
26: }
27:
28: // Stop streaming and reset to start of title
29: function StopStream()
30: {
31:     // Stop playback
32:     MyMediaPlayer.Stop();
33:
34:     // Set position to 0 (Beginning of stream)
35:     MyMediaPlayer.CurrentPosition = 0;
36: }
```

But how do you stream media from the Internet in a C++ application? That requires a more thorough investigation of the filter graph, which is the topic of the next section.

Graph Filters

As mentioned before, graph filters are modules used together in a sequence to take a media stream, process it, and output it to some form of media or device. Most filters can be categorized as follows:

- Source Filter—Takes media data from a source such as a file, an URL, or a VCR and inserts it into the Filter Graph.
- Transform Filter—Takes the media data, processes it, and then passes it along.
- Rendering Filter—Usually renders the media data to some form of graphical hardware device, but the data could be rendered to a file.

When filters are connected to perform a certain action, it's called a filter graph. Filter graphs are managed by something called the filter graph manager, which abstracts filter graph construction and hides the details of filter graph construction, so let's look at how to use it.

Stringing Filters Together

Filters are assembled into a filter graph and, in turn, are controlled by the filter graph manager. In order for the filter graph to work, filters must be introduced into the graph in the proper order. For example, you add the source filter, the transform filter, and then the render filter. The media stream must also be started and stopped in the correct order.

The filter graph connects filters and controls the media stream. It can also return data to the application, and it can search for supported filters. You can also use the filter graph manager utility provided with the DirectX Media SDK, although that's beyond the scope of this hour.

Filters are connected by something called pins. A *pin* is a connection between two filters and is either of type input or type output. As shown in Figure 22.2, a source filter would typically expose only an output pin because it only passes data on, whereas a transform filter would have input and output pins because it accepts both input from one filter and outputs to another filter.

FIGURE 22.2

Filters and pins.

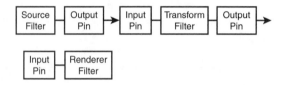

Pins are needed to translate data between filters. Every filter must present data in a unified form, so the pins translate the data to their respective filter's internal data format.

Figure 22.3 shows how a typical filter graph might look.

FIGURE 22.3

A typical filter graph for rendering MPEG video.

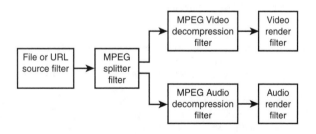

As you can see, filters are very flexible and can be tweaked to provide virtually every possible form of media processing. If it's not enough, you can write your own filters and pins, but that requires making COM components, so it won't be covered here. But don't worry; you are not going to need it for most applications. As a matter of fact, we will not even use filters in our sample DirectShow application. Well, actually we will, but we'll let DirectShow build them for us.

Sample DirectShow Application

The sample DirectShow application I've prepared plays back a full screen video sequence with sound. The video clip is borrowed from the DirectX Media SDK samples. It loops the video stream, and if you task switch, the surfaces will be automatically restored when you switch back.

I've provided a Windows/DirectX class wrapper and stuffed it away in a separate file, so I won't confuse you when going through the playback code and the actual DirectShow class. I've also written a complete DirectShow class wrapper, which can render a multimedia video stream with sound to any DirectDraw surface.

So, you don't even have to read the next section to play video, but you'll learn a lot more if you stick with me through it.

Initializing DirectShow

Initializing DirectShow is not a whole lot different than the rest of the DirectX components. The first thing we need to do is call `CoInitialize(NULL)` to initialize the COM libraries. If we forget this, all calls to `QueryInterface` will fail. Then we need to create a multimedia stream object.

> Note the use of the FAILED macro. It is suggested that with COM, always use the SUCCESS and FAILED macros because a COM object might have multiple error values and 1=TRUE and 0=FALSE is reversed in COM.

```
// Multimedia stream pointer
    IAMMultiMediaStream *pAMStream;

// Create Multimedia stream object
    if (FAILED(CoCreateInstance(CLSID_AMMultiMediaStream, NULL,
                CLSCTX_INPROC_SERVER,
                IID_IAMMultiMediaStream, (void **)&pAMStream)))
    {
        // Show error message
        MessageBox(GetActiveWindow(),"Could not get IAMMultimedia interface!",
        ➥"FATAL ERROR",MB_ICONSTOP¦MB_OK);

        // Return FALSE to let caller know we failed.
        return FALSE;
    }
```

Then we try to initialize the multimedia stream.

22

```
    // Initialize Multimedia stream object
    if (FAILED(pAMStream->Initialize(STREAMTYPE_READ, 0, NULL)))
    {
        // Show error message
        MessageBox(GetActiveWindow(),"Could not setup stream for read!",
                   "FATAL ERROR",MB_ICONSTOP¦MB_OK);

        // Return FALSE to let caller know we failed.
        return FALSE;
    }
```

That's all we need to initialize DirectShow. Next we need to set up the multimedia stream.

Setting Up the Filter

First we add video playback to the Multimedia stream. When MSPID_PrimaryVideo is added, it uses the first parameter as the target surface for video playback. Note that what we actually do here is add the filters, but because we won't need any special abilities, we'll just let DirectShow manage it all for us.

```
// Add primary video stream.
    if (FAILED((pAMStream->AddMediaStream(pDD, &MSPID_PrimaryVideo, 0, NULL))))
    {
        // Show error message
        MessageBox(GetActiveWindow(),"Could add primary video stream!",
                   "FATAL ERROR",MB_ICONSTOP¦MB_OK);

        // Return FALSE to let caller know we failed.
        return FALSE;
    }
```

Now we add a sound renderer to the Multimedia stream. Note the flag AMMSF_ADDDE-FAULTRENDERER. This specifies that we want to output to the default sound renderer. From now on, we don't need to do any more to play sound. It will happen automatically.

```
// Add default sound render to primary video stream,
// so sound will be played back automatically.
if (FAILED(pAMStream->AddMediaStream(NULL, &MSPID_PrimaryAudio,
                                     AMMSF_ADDDEFAULTRENDERER, NULL)))
{
    // Show error message
    MessageBox(GetActiveWindow(),"Could not add default sound render!",
               "FATAL ERROR",MB_ICONSTOP¦MB_OK);

    // Return FALSE to let caller know we failed.
    return FALSE;
}
```

Next we need to convert the filename to UNICODE so the `OpenFile` function will accept it:

```
// Convert filename to UNICODE.
    // Notice the safe way to get the actual size of a string.
    WCHAR wPath[MAX_PATH];
    MultiByteToWideChar(CP_ACP, 0, pFileName, -1, wPath,
                        sizeof(wPath)/sizeof(wPath[0]));
```

It had to come, and here it is. This is where we build the filter graph:

```
// Build the filter graph for our multimedia stream.
if (FAILED((pAMStream->OpenFile(wPath, 0))))
{
    // Show error message
    MessageBox(GetActiveWindow(),"Could not open file!",
               "FATAL ERROR",MB_ICONSTOP|MB_OK);

    // Return FALSE to let caller know we failed.
    return FALSE;
}
```

Setting Up the File Stream

First we assign the multimedia stream pointer to our global pointer, which in this case is a member of our video player class. We also need to increase the reference count for the file.

```
// Assign member to temporary stream pointer.
m_pMMStream = pAMStream;

// Add a reference to the file
pAMStream->AddRef();
```

Now we need to create a stream sample object to be associated with our offscreen DirectDraw surface. To get the stream sample, we need to get the Primary Video Stream interface.

```
// Get media stream interface
    if (FAILED(m_pMMStream->GetMediaStream(MSPID_PrimaryVideo,
            &m_pPrimaryVideoStream)))
    {
        // Show error message
        MessageBox(GetActiveWindow(),
                   "Could not get Primary Video Stream interface!",
                   "FATAL ERROR",MB_ICONSTOP|MB_OK);

        return FALSE;
    }
```

Now that we have the Primary Video Stream interface, we use it to query for the
IdirectDrawMediaStream interface, which we will use to get our stream sample.

```
// Get DirectDraw media stream interface
    if (FAILED(m_pPrimaryVideoStream->QueryInterface(
                            IID_IDirectDrawMediaStream,
                            (void **)&m_pDDStream)))
    {
        // Show error message
        MessageBox(GetActiveWindow(),
                        "Could not get DirectDraw media stream interface!",
                        "FATAL ERROR",MB_ICONSTOP¦MB_OK);

        return FALSE;
    }
```

Now we can get the sample.

```
// Create stream sample
    if (FAILED(m_pDDStream->CreateSample(NULL,NULL,0,&m_pSample)))
    {
        // Show error message
        MessageBox(GetActiveWindow(),"Could not create stream sample!",
                        "FATAL ERROR",MB_ICONSTOP¦MB_OK);

        return FALSE;
    }
```

Each sample obtained its own DirectDraw surface and clipping rectangle. We'll save the
clipping rectangle in the member variable m_rSrcRect because we will need it later for
blitting the video stream to the screen. We also get the DirectDraw surface attached to
the sample.

```
// Get DirectDraw surface interface from Sample.
    if (FAILED(m_pSample->GetSurface(&m_pDDSurface,&m_rSrcRect)))
    {
        // Show error message
        MessageBox(GetActiveWindow(),
            "Could not get IDirectDrawSurface interface from stream sample!",
            "FATAL ERROR",MB_ICONSTOP¦MB_OK);


        return FALSE;
    }
```

We use the sample surface to get a IDirectDrawSurface4 for our video stream, which
we will use to blit to the screen later. Note that the sample and this surface are connected
now. Later when we update the sample, this surface will be updated automatically.

```
// Get DirectDraw surface4 interface
    if (FAILED(m_pDDSurface->QueryInterface(IID_IDirectDrawSurface4,
```

```
                                              (void**)&m_pDDSurface4)))
    {
        // Show error message
        MessageBox(GetActiveWindow(),
                    "Could not get IDirectDrawSurface4 interface!",
                    "FATAL ERROR",MB_ICONSTOP¦MB_OK);


        return FALSE;
    }
```

Then we set a global flag, identifying that the stream is now open.

```
// Ok. Media is open now.
m_bMediaOpen=TRUE;
```

And that's it. Now we are ready to actually draw something.

Streaming the Movie

First we need to start the movie. In the video class provided, I have implemented start and stop functions. For simplicity, I'll list only the function used to start the video playback.

```
// Start video playback
BOOL CDShow::Start()
{
    // Return FALSE if media was not open
    if (!m_bMediaOpen) return FALSE;

    // Set stream position to zero
    m_pMMStream->Seek(0);

    // Set state to playback
    m_pMMStream->SetState(STREAMSTATE_RUN);

    // Set playing to TRUE
    m_bPlaying=TRUE;

    // Everything went ok. Return TRUE.
    return TRUE;
}
```

Note how we set a global member, specifying that the stream is now playing. It will come in handy later, as we'll loop the video when it's done. (See the sample source code.)

Now let's get on with the drawing. Included in the following code snippet is the Draw function of our video playback class. We simply call the Update function of our media sample. Note that we set m_bPlaying to FALSE if it fails because that means the video clip has ended.

Then we simply blit the surface we linked to the sample object, and the video will be drawn. Note that we pass a surface that should receive the media stream and a destination rectangle. If the destination rectangle is larger than the stream, it will be stretched. A typical game video would be 320×240, stretched to 640×480.

```
// Draw video to DirectDraw surface.
BOOL CDShow::Draw(LPDIRECTDRAWSURFACE4 lpDDSurface4, RECT rDestRect)
{
    // Return FALSE if media was not open
    if (!m_bMediaOpen) return FALSE;

    // Update media stream.
    // If it does not return S_OK, we are not playing.
    if (m_pSample->Update(0,NULL,NULL,0)!=S_OK) m_bPlaying=FALSE;

    // Now blit video to specified surface and rect.
    // Restore surface if lost.
    if (lpDDSurface4->Blt(&rDestRect,m_pDDSurface4,
                          &m_rSrcRect,DDBLT_WAIT,NULL)==DDERR_SURFACELOST)
        lpDDSurface4->Restore();

    // Ok. return TRUE.
    return TRUE;
}
```

And that's it. Now all we need is to stop the movie and clean up after ourselves.

Cleanup

Fortunately, cleaning up is easy. Here is the cleanup function:

```
// CleanUp function.
// Called automatically upon object destruction.
void CDShow::CleanUp()
{
    // Reset media open
    m_bMediaOpen=FALSE;

    // Set playing to FALSE
    m_bPlaying=FALSE;

    // Release allocated interfaces
    SAFE_RELEASE(m_pPrimaryVideoStream);
    SAFE_RELEASE(m_pDDStream);
```

```
    SAFE_RELEASE(m_pSample);
    SAFE_RELEASE(m_pDDSurface);
    SAFE_RELEASE(m_pDDSurface4);
    SAFE_RELEASE(m_pMMStream);

    // Uninitialize COM libraries
    CoUninitialize();
}
```

You are probably no stranger to SAFE_RELEASE by now, so I won't go into details of that one. Then we call CoUninitialize(); to unload COM libraries and we're finished. Easy, huh?

Summary

In this hour, you learned about DirectShow, and how to use it to render a video stream to any DirectDraw surface. You also learned a bit about the inner workings of DirectShow and about filters and filter graphs. So to wrap it up, you're now ready to add video to your DirectX based games.

Q&A

Q Can I render DirectShow video streams onto ANY DirectDraw surface?

A Yes. You can render to any DirectDraw surface you want, including Direct3D textures.

Q Will the Media Player ActiveX control work with browsers other than Internet Explorer?

A The Media Player ActiveX control will work in all browsers that support ActiveX controls. That means Internet Explorer, but it's also possible to make it work with Netscape. See your Direct Media SDK documentation on how to do this.

Q If I want to make an animated logo using an AVI video clip, can I use color keying?

A Yes. Simply set the color key of the DirectX Surface of your sample stream object.

Q I noticed you used DirectDrawSurface4 rather than DirectDrawSurface7. Why?

A DirectX Media is a separate SDK that ships with DirectX but lags behind the DirectX SDK itself. In fact, DirectX 7 includes DirectX Media SDK version 6.0, which is as yet unaware of DirectX 7 interfaces.

Q Oh. Is that a problem?

A It depends on what you're doing. For Web pages, it's no problem, but for game applications dedicated to DirectX 7 interfaces (remember, COM ensures you can use the older interfaces) it could cause problems. If you use DirectDraw7 and DirectDrawSurface7, it will compile, link, and run, but you'll get error reports in the debug window, and this could lead to compatibility problems with some hardware or drivers. Some developers choose to avoid this risk by excluding all forms of movie play and using engine cinematics instead.

Workshop

The workshop will enable you to test yourself on what you have learned in this hour and get you thinking about how to apply this knowledge in a real life application. The answers to the quiz are in Appendix A, "Answers."

Quiz

1. What is a DirectShow filter?

2. What is a DirectShow pin?

3. What happens if the destination rectangle of a DirectShow stream is larger than that of the stream itself?

4. Mention a few streaming and nonstreaming DirectShow supported media formats.

5. What would happen if you put a 20MB nonstreaming video on your homepage?

Exercises

1. Modify the cityscape from Hour 17, "Introducing DirectInput—Getting User Input," to display a video billboard on one of the buildings. (Hint: Give one house different textures on each side and let one of them be a video stream.)

2. Make a cool menu for your own game, and let the logo be a color keyed video stream. (Hint: Use any animation program that can save to AVI or MPEG.)

Hour 23

Bring Surfaces to Life with DirectX Transform

by Sam Christiansen and Sylvia Mollerstrom

DirectX Transform is the part of the DirectX Media SDK that lets you animate, blend, and distort two-dimensional images and three-dimensional mesh objects. DirectX Transform helps you write transforms, which are a set of instructions that take zero (or more) graphical or 3D mesh inputs and result in one graphical or 3D mesh output. For example, in this hour, you will learn how to write a Wipe Transform that creates an animated transition between two images. This transform takes two different images as inputs and results in one single output image that is, by varying degrees, a composite of the two input images.

DirectX Transform is a powerful tool that can help you create things like Adobe PhotoShop filters and animated content for Web pages. You can take transforms that you write with DirectX Transform and create the above things without modifying the transforms in any way—part of the beauty of

DirectX Transform is that it does everything for you automatically! To get you started with using and writing transforms, this hour will help you work with DirectX Transform inside of your DirectX application.

In this hour, you will

- Learn about the power of DirectX Transforms
- Learn about the DXSurface object
- Learn how to create special effects using DirectX Transforms
- Learn how to use DirectX Transforms in your application

The Power of DirectX Transform

DirectX Transform is so powerful because it combines two concepts that are normally at opposite ends of the computer experience. Because it comes with many pre-built transforms, it is easy to use if you want to just dabble in it; however, it is also easily extensible so that you can quickly move beyond the basics and into some powerful issues by writing your own transforms. Normally when you want to create smooth transitions between graphics, you have to worry about many details. With DirectX Transform, all these details are taken care of so that you only have to worry about doing exactly what you want!

The following are some of the highlights of DirectX Transform:

- With DirectX Transform, you can use many different file formats (such as .GIF, .JPEG, and .BMP). DirectX Transform automatically converts the images to a version that it can read.
- DirectX Transform is easy to use, yet extensible: it comes with many pre-built transforms, or you can write your own.
- DirectX Transform allows you to easily create transition type transforms. Normally, artists would have to draw every frame of the transition; even if the artist uses a computer, the computer will use up a lot of memory in order to draw each frame of the animation. But, with DirectX Transform, you only need two input surfaces. This saves you both time and space when transitioning.
- DirectX Transform helps you write procedural surfaces. These are surfaces that store functions instead of an array describing each pixel of an image. Because procedural surfaces do not have to store information for each pixel, they let you create naturalistic patterns (like marble or wood), and they use even less space!
- DirectX Transform lets you scale your transforms to hardware. So, you can take advantage of fast hardware to make your transforms look even better.

A Versatile DirectDraw Surface: IDXSurface

The DXSurface is at the heart of DirectX Transform. The DXSurface is an object that usually wraps a DirectDrawSurface object. In other words, at the core of each DXSurface, there is a DirectDrawSurface. The DXSurface takes care of all the details of a DirectDrawSurface, thereby allowing you to concentrate on other things (such as creating transforms). This is great for programmers because it means that they can be more productive. As you will see, DXSurfaces are very easy to work with.

Although we won't use them much, here is a list of the more important functions provided by the IDXSurface interface:

- GetBounds() is used to retrieve the surface's bounding area.
- GetColorKey() is used to retrieve the surface's color key value (the transparent color of the image).
- GetDirectDrawSurface() is used to retrieve a surface's DirectDrawSurface object.
- GetPixelFormat() is used to retrieve the surface's pixel format.
- LockSurface() is used to lock the surface and obtain a pointer to the surface's image data.
- SetColorKey() is used to set a surface's color key.

For many of the things you will want to do with DirectX Transform, you probably won't use any of these functions. For a complete list of all the methods (and their parameters) available in the IDXSurface interface, you should consult the DirectX Media SDK documentation.

Creating a DXSurface

Creating a DXSurface is easy. You can do it in two steps: first, create an IDXSurfaceFactory and then use the factory object to create as many surfaces as you like. Later in this hour, you will go through creating an IDXSurfaceFactory. However, for now, assume that you have already created the IDXSurfaceFactory object. After you have this object, in order to create a new DXSurface, you simply call the IDXSurfaceFactory::CreateSurface() function.

The Syntax for IDXSurfaceFactory::CreateSurface()

```
HRESULT CreateSurface(
    IUnknown *lpDirectDraw,
    const DDSURFACEDESC *lpSurfaceDesc,
    const GUID *lpPixelFormatID,
    const DXBNDS *lpDXBounds,
```

```
▼      DWORD dwFlags,
       IUnknown *lpOuter,
       REFIID riid,
       (void**)lpDXSurface
);
```

Parameters:

lpDirectDraw	Address of the DirectDraw object the factory should use to create the surface. Can be NULL; in which case, the factory's DirectDraw object will be used.
lpSurfaceDesc	Address of a DDSURFACEDESC object that describes the desired surface. Can be NULL.
lpPixelFormatID	Address of the desired pixel format. If NULL, the pixel format of the display will be used.
lpDXBounds	Address of a DXBNDS object containing the desired width, height, and depth of the surface.
dwFlags	Optional creation flags.
lpOuter	Optional IUnknown interface pointer.
riid	Interface of the new surface. This is IID_IDXSurface for a DXSurface object.
lpDXSurface	A pointer to the address of the new DXSurface object.

Don't let all those parameters overwhelm you! For most surfaces, all you need to specify
▲ are the bounds (the width, height, and depth) of the surface.

Reading Graphics from Various File Formats

In most cases, instead of creating an empty surface, you will want to create a surface and
then load an image into it. DirectX Transform lets you do this in one easy step: all you
have to do is call the LoadImage() function.

LoadImage() is a member function of the DXSurfaceFactory object, and it supports most
of the common file formats (.GIF, .JPEG, .BMP, and more). One of the great things
about DirectX Transform is that when you have loaded an image, it is treated like a normal DXSurface, regardless of what file format it was originally.

The Syntax for `IDXSurfaceFactory::LoadImage()`

```
HRESULT LoadImage(
    const LPWSTR wFileName,
    IUnknown *lpDirectDraw,
    const DDSURFACEDESC *lpSurfaceDesc,
    const GUID *lpPixelFormat,
    REFIID riid,
    (void**) lpDXSurface
);
```

23

Parameters:

wFileName	Unicode string containing the file name of the image to load.
lpDirectDraw	Address of the `DirectDraw` object the factory should use to create the surface. Can be `NULL`; in which case, the factory's `DirectDraw` object will be used.
lpSurfaceDesc	Address of a `DDSURFACEDESC` object that describes the desired surface. Can be `NULL`.
lpPixelFormat	Address of the desired pixel format.
riid	Interface of the new surface. This is `IID_IDXSurface` for a `DXSurface` object.
lpDXSurface	A pointer to the address of a `DXSurface` object.

> The first parameter of the `LoadImage()` function is a Unicode string. To convert an ANSI string to a Unicode string, use the `mbstowcs()` function.

Automatic Color Conversion

You have just seen how `DXSurfaces` simplify image loading. Another useful feature incorporated in `DXSurfaces` is color conversion. Regardless of the pixel format of the image you load, the DXSurface will automatically convert it to the appropriate pixel format for you.

The two different pixel formats that `DXSurfaces` use are `ARGB32` and `PMARGB32`. Both of these pixel formats contain alpha, red, green, and blue data. The red, green, and blue data affect the color of the pixel. The alpha value is the measure of a pixel's opacity. If the alpha value is zero, the pixel is clear. If the alpha value is the maximum alpha value, the pixel is opaque. If the alpha value is somewhere in between these two extremes, the pixel would be translucent so that it would allow the pixel beneath it to show through.

The PM in PMARGB32 stands for pre-multiplied. Blending two images together using their alpha values is a mathematically intense operation, so it can take the computer a long time to do. Alpha pre-multiplication is a technique used to speed up the blending process. Using this technique, each pixel's red, green, and blue color components are scaled by the pixel's alpha value. In other words, the red, green, and blue color components are multiplied by the alpha value and then the new values are stored so that the computer does not have to multiply out the components each time. It is not important to know how DirectX Transform does this; however, it is important to remember that surfaces in the PMARGB32 format will provide better performance when you use them in blending operations.

Special Effects: DirectX Transforms

Now that you have learned how to create IDXSurfaces, the next step is to learn how to manipulate them in order to create special effects. The real power of DirectX Transform is that these effects are essentially free. In other words, DirectX Transforms use algorithms to create the animations you see in real time so that you can simply use a single frame and get DirectX Transform to perform the animation for you. This is much more convenient than the old way of spending hours drawing each individual frame of an animation.

To create a DirectX Transform, follow these two steps:

1. Create a Transform Factory
2. Use the Transform Factory to create a DirectX Transform

DirectX Transform extends the idea of a transform to both 2D and 3D. In 2D, the transforms use surfaces. In 3D, the transforms use 3D meshes. In addition, DirectX Transforms can be used to make procedural surfaces.

Creating the Transform Factory

In order to access transforms, you need to create a DirectX Transform Factory. You can think of the factory as an interface that helps you create an object; you ask the factory to create a new object, and the factory creates the object and returns it to you. It probably won't surprise you to hear that you use COM to create the transform factory.

> Before you make any COM calls to create the transform factory, it is impor-
> tant to call the CoInitialize() function. This function will initialize COM so
> that COM function calls can be used by our application.

To create a transform factory, you call the COM function CoCreateInstance(), as
shown in Listing 23.1.

LISTING 23.1   Creating the Transform Factory

```
 1: IDXTransformFactory* lpTransformFactory = NULL;
 2: HRESULT hres;
 3:
 4: CoInitialize(NULL);
 5:
 6: //  create the transform factory:
 7: hres = CoCreateInstance( CLSID_DXTransformFactory,
 8:                          NULL,
 9:                          CLSCTX_INPROC,
10:                          IID_IDXTransformFactory,
11:                          (void**)&lpTransformFactory);
```

The first argument, CLSID_DXTransformFactory, tells COM which class you want to create an instance of. In this case, you want to create a DXTransformFactory. The second
argument is a pointer to an IUnknown object, which is NULL in this case. The third argument, CLSCTX_INPROC, tells COM that you want the execution context to be in-process,
as opposed to local (CLSCTX_LOCAL) or remote (CLSCTX_REMOTE). The next parameter,
IID_IDXTransformFactory, tells COM which interface you want to use; in this case, it is
an IDXTransformFactory. Finally, you pass the address of a pointer to the factory that
will be created (in this case, &lpTransformFactory).

Using the Factory to Access Transforms

When you have created a transform factory, it is easy to use the factory to create transforms. All you have to do is call the CreateTransform() function, and the factory will
create the new transform.

The syntax for **IDXTransformFactory::CreateTransform()**

```
HRESULT CreateTransform(
    IUnknown **Inputs,
    ULONG NumInputs,
    IUnknown **Outputs,
    ULONG NumOutputs,
    IPropertyBag *InitialProp,
    IErrorLog *ErrorLog,
```

▼
```
    REFCLSID TransformCLSID,
    REFIID TransformIID,
    void **Transform
);
```

Parameters:

Inputs	A pointer to an array of inputs (IDXSurfaces, for example). Can be NULL.
NumInputs	The size of the Inputs array. Can be zero.
Outputs	A pointer to an array of outputs. Can be NULL.
NumOutputs	The size of the Outputs array. Can be zero.
InitialProp	A pointer to an object holding desired initial properties of the transform. Can be NULL.
ErrorLog	A pointer to an IErrorLog object. Is optional, and can be NULL.
TransformCLSID	The CLSID of the transform to create.
TransformIID	The interface ID of the transform.
Transform	The address of a pointer to the Transform object that will be created.

> If either NumInputs or NumOutputs is equal to something other than zero, CreateTransform() will automatically set up the transform. Conversely, you can delay the setup until a later time by setting both NumInputs and NumOutputs to zero.

All of these parameters might seem daunting right now. But, don't worry because you will see in the sample application that it is actually very easy to create and use trans-
▲ forms.

2D Transforms

Whether or not you know it, you have probably already seen 2D transforms. 2D transforms are image transforms that operate on two-dimensional surfaces. Some examples of 2D transforms are: fading from one image to another, rotating an image, and scaling an image. As you read earlier, some of these transforms need two input images and others only need one. For example, to rotate or scale an image, we have only one input image (the image that hasn't been rotated or scaled) and one output image (the scaled or rotated image). On the other hand, to fade from one image to another, two input images are combined to create an output image. Figure 23.1 shows an example of the 2D Wipe Transform.

FIGURE **23.1**

*The 2D Wipe
Transform.*

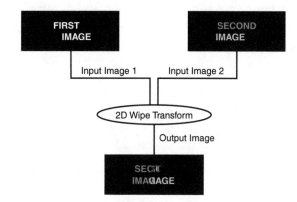

DirectX Transform comes with a set of 2D transforms; however, it also allows you to create your own transforms. The focus here will be on using the transforms already provided by DirectX Transform. For more information about creating your own 2D transforms, a good place to start is the DirectX Transform SDK documentation.

Each transform has certain properties that tell the transform how to run. For example, the rotate transform needs to know how much it should rotate the input image. In order to get at and change these properties, DirectX Transform provides us with two possible interfaces: IDXEffect or a custom interface.

Many transition-type transforms use the IDXEffect interface, which is simple, yet powerful. It was written to provide a common interface to transition-type transforms (transforms like the fade transform, which can be used to animate images) .

IDXEffect has a floating point progress variable (which holds a value between 0.0 and 1.0) that tells the transform the percentage of the transition that has been completed. Using the fade transform as an example, if the progress variable were 0.0, the output would be the first input image. If the progress variable were 1.0, the output would be the second input image. If the progress variable were 0.5, the output would be a combination of the two input images (half of the first and half of the second). IDXEffect defines the following functions:

- get_Capabilities() is used to find out if a transformation is PERIODIC (the transform produces the same output image when the progress variable is equal to 1.0 or 0.0) or MORPH (when the progress variable is 0.0 the output is the first input image, and when the progress variable is 1.0 the output is the second input image).

- get_Duration() is used to get the amount of time recommended for performing the transition.
- get_Progress() is used to find the progress of a transition.
- get_StepResolution() is used to find the smallest significant step size.
- put_Duration() is used to set the amount of time recommended for performing this transition.
- put_Progress() is used to set the progress of a transition.

The IDXEffect interface is not applicable to all transforms. This is because not all transforms produce transitions and because the IDXEffect interface might not unlock all the functionality of a transform. To account for this situation, each transform can also define a custom interface.

The BasicImage transform is an example of a 2D transform that doesn't produce transitions. The BasicImage transform is useful for performing simple image manipulation routines on a surface. In particular, the BasicImage transform can rotate, mirror, or invert an image. For this type of transform, the IDXEffect interface does not make sense. Instead, BasicImage defines a custom interface that allows the user to specify exactly what type of image manipulation she wants performed on the input surface.

At the other end of the spectrum, sometimes, IDXEffect does not provide all the functionality that some transition-type transforms require. For example, there is a 2D transform included with DirectX Transform that takes two input images and produces a "wipe" transition between them (the Wipe Transform). In addition to the IDXEffect interface, the Wipe Transform has a custom interface that allows the user to specify the wipe direction (horizontal or vertical) and a gradient size (the portion of the transform that blends the two images together). In the case of the Wipe Transform, you can choose to ignore the custom interface so that the transform will run with default values; however, the custom interface is there if you want more control over the transform.

More than 40 2D transforms are included in the DirectX Media SDK. For a complete list of 2D transform specifications (including names, CLSIDs, interfaces, and more), you should consult the DirectX Media SDK Documentation.

The sample application in this hour creates a transition using a 2D transform. To see specific implementation details of 2D transforms, refer to the sample application.

Procedural Surfaces

Procedural surfaces are surfaces that are described by a mathematical procedure or function. There are several advantages to using procedural surfaces. First, procedural surfaces use very little space. Instead of storing pixel values in a giant two-dimensional array, the pixel values are calculated, when needed, by a mathematical function. This might seem trivial at first, but a closer look at the numbers reveals what a huge advantage this is. Suppose that you have an image in your application that is 640 by 480 pixels. Assuming that each pixel is 32 bits (4 bytes), our surface will take up $640 \times 480 \times 4 = 1,228,800$ bytes. That's 1.2 megabytes! It wouldn't take many surfaces of this size before a computer runs out of memory.

Procedural surfaces can also use randomness in their functions to produce unique patterns every time they are used. This makes them perfect for use as organic textures like wood or marble. In addition, procedural surfaces are often resolution independent. This means that no matter what resolution you view the surface in, it will still appear sharp and clear (as opposed to getting blocky and pixelated like normal surfaces).

However, procedural surfaces also have some disadvantages. As you read earlier, in a normal DXSurface, the color values for each pixel are stored in a giant two-dimensional array. Because each pixel's value is already known, you can read or write the pixel value at a particular location on the surface. However, in a procedural surface, there is no array, so it has to use a mathematical formula to calculate the pixel value at a particular location. This leads to an important property of procedural surfaces: they are read-only surfaces. That is, you can read pixel values from a procedural surface, but you can't write pixel values to a procedural surface.

Another disadvantage of procedural surfaces that stems from the way pixel information is stored is that looking up pixel values on procedural surfaces is much slower than on DXSurfaces. Looking up a pixel value on a normal DXSurface is fast because all you have to do is look at the particular spot in the array. However, executing a mathematical function to find a pixel value is usually slow in comparison. If the mathematical function is complex and the surface is large, reading pixel values can bring your application to a crawl.

In addition, it's hard to define a mathematical function to describe every type of surface you want. For example, it would be impossible to create a procedural surface with a picture of someone you know on it.

What do procedural surfaces look like? That depends on the mathematical function! A *gradient* is a simple example of a surface that is easy to define as a procedural surface.

Because a gradient is just a blend of colors, its procedural surface might contain two colors—the color on the left side of the surface and the color on the right side of the surface. When a pixel value is read from the surface, the mathematical function finds the average color at the point in question and returns it as the pixel value. Complex procedural surfaces also exist that produce extremely realistic organic patterns such as clouds, marble, or wood.

Two important classes are defined by DirectX Transform in order to simplify the creation of a procedural surface. The first class, `CDXBaseSurface`, serves as the base class for the actual surface object. The second class, `CDXBaseARGBPtr`, provides an interface to the actual mathematical function the procedural surface will use. To create your own procedural surface, you must create two things: a surface object that inherits from `CDXBaseSurface` and a "surface filling" object that inherits from `CDXBaseARGBPtr`.

`CDXBaseSurface` has several virtual functions that you can choose to override; however, you are only required to override three member functions. First, you must override the `CDXBaseSurface::CreateARGBPointer()` function; this function allocates your `CDXBaseARGBPtr` object. Second, you must override the `CDXBaseSurface::DeleteARGBPointer()` function; this function deallocates your `CDXBaseARGBPtr` object. Finally, you must override the `CDXBaseSurface::SurfaceCLSID()` function; this function must return the CLSID of your procedural surface.

`CDXBaseARGBPtr` has only one function you are required to override, the `CDXBaseARGBPtr::FillSamples()` function. This function contains the mathematical function that describes your procedural surface. Listing 23.2 is an example of what your procedural surface objects might look like.

LISTING 23.2   Procedural Surface Objects

```
 1: //  the surface object, which inherits from CDXBaseSurface:
 2:
 3: class MyProceduralSurface : public CDXBaseSurface
 4: {
 5: public:
 6:     MyProceduralSurface();
 7:     ~MyProceduralSurface()
 8:
 9:     const GUID& SurfaceCLSID() { return MyProceduralSurface_CLSID; }
10:
11:     HRESULT CreateARGBPointer(CDXBaseSurface *lpSurface,
                                  CDXBaseARGBPtr **alpARGBPtr)
12:         { (*alpARGBPtr) = new MyProceduralSurfaceARGBPtr(); }
13:
14:     void DeleteARGBPointer(CDXBaseARGBPtr *lpARGBPtr)
```

```
15:           { delete (MyProceduralSurfaceARGBPtr*) lpARGBPtr; }
16: };
17:
18: //  the ARGBPtr object, which inherits from CDXBaseARGBPtr
19:
20: class MyProceduralSurfaceARGBPtr : public CDXBaseARGBPtr
21: {
22: public:
23:     MyProceduralSurfaceARGBPtr(CDXBaseSurface *lpDXBaseSurface);
24:     ~MyProceduralSurfaceARGBPtr();
25:
26:     void FillSamples(const DXPtrFillInfo& lpDXFillInfo);
27: };
```

The DXPtrFillInfo structure is passed to the CDXBaseARGBPtr::FillSamples() function. This structure contains information about where the pixel data generated by your mathematical function should go. Most of the work of your procedural surface takes place in the FillSamples() function.

Procedural surfaces are a huge topic! Now that you know the basics of implementing a procedural surface, you should try to create the actual mathematical functions used by the procedural surface. Experiment with different functions, but start with something simple like the gradient procedural surface that was mentioned previously.

3D Transforms

3D transforms use many of the same ideas that 2D transforms use. In fact, many of the transition-type 3D transforms use the same DXEffect object to control the transition that the 2D transforms use. In general, 2D transforms receive images as input and perform functions on the pixels representing the images to produce an output image. 3D transforms are different because they take a 3D mesh as input and perform functions on the geometry representing the 3D object to produce a new 3D mesh. 3D transforms can also modify the textures applied to a 3D object.

It is important to use consistent conventions when you are working with 3D transforms. The geometry convention for all 3D transforms is the right-handed convention. The right-handed convention states that the positive z-axis points towards the user, the front side of a face is determined by moving around the vertices counterclockwise, and the positive angle of rotation around an axis is determined using the right-hand rule. To use the right-hand rule, make a hitchhiker's fist and simply point your right thumb along the direction of the positive axis in question; your fingers will curl in the direction of a positive angle.

As mentioned previously, most of the 3D transforms included in DirectX Transform take a single mesh as an input and create a single mesh as an output. In particular, 3D transforms use meshes of type Direct3DRMMeshBuilder3. In most cases, we simply want to load a 3D object saved in the X file format. When you have created the IDirect3DRM3 object, you can create a Direct3DRMMeshBuilder3 by calling CreateMeshBuilder(). After that, you can load an X file using the Direct3DRMMeshBuilder3::Load() function. Listing 23.3 shows an example of how it all fits together.

LISTING 23.3   Loading an X File for Use in 3D Transforms

```
 1: BOOL LoadMesh(LPCTSTR FileName)
 2: {
 3:     /****************************
 4:     lpInputD3DMeshBuilder == IDirect3DRMMeshBuidler3
 5:     lpD3DRetainedMode3 == IDirect3DRM3
 6:     ****************************/
 7:
 8:     HRESULT hres;
 9:
10:     //  create the mesh builder
11:
12:     hres = lpD3DRetainedMode3->CreateMeshBuilder(&lpInputD3DMeshBuilder);
13:
14:     if (hres != D3D_OK) return FALSE;
15:
16:     //  load an X file
17:
18:     hres = lpD3DMeshBuilder->Load((void*)FileName,
19:                                    NULL,
20:                                    D3DRMLOAD_FROMFILE,
21:                                    NULL,
22:                                    NULL);
23:
24:     if (hres != D3D_OK) return FALSE;
25:
26:     return TRUE;
27: }
```

3D transforms use all the same methods 2D transforms use. Almost all the 3D transforms included with DirectX Transform take advantage of the IDXEffect interface. This makes the job of creating transitions very easy. When you have loaded a mesh and created the transform, you simply update the progress variable in IDXEffect and render the output object to the viewport. Listing 23.4 shows an example of what that code might look like.

LISTING 23.4   A Sample Transition in 3D

```
 1: // load a mesh into InputD3DMeshBuilder
 2: LoadMesh("MyFile.x");
 3:
 4: // create the 3D explosion transform
 5: g_pTransFact->CreateTransform(NULL,
 6:                                0,
 7:                                NULL,
 8:                                0,
 9:                                NULL,
10:                                NULL,
11:                                CLSID_Explode,
12:                                IID_IDXTransform,
13:                                (void**)&My3DTransform);
14:
15: My3DTransform->QueryInterface(IID_IDXEffect,
16:                               (void**)&lpDXEffect);
17:
18: g_d3drm3->CreateMeshBuilder(&lpOutputD3DMeshBuilder);
19:
20: lpD3DRMFrame3->AddVisual(lpOutputD3DMeshBuilder);
21:
22: // setup the 3D transform
23: My3DTransform->Setup((IUnknown*)lpInputD3DMeshBuilder,
24:                      1,
25:                      (IUnknown*)lpOutputD3DMeshBuilder,
26:                      1,
27:                      0);
28:
29: float progress = 0.0f;
30:
31: while (progress < 1.0f)
32: {
33:     // set the new progress
34:     lpDXEffect->put_Progress(progress);
35:
36:     // execute the transform
37:     My3DTransform->Execute(NULL, NULL, NULL);
38:
39:     // clear the screen and render
40:     lpD3DRMViewport2->Clear(D3DRMCLEAR_ALL);
41:     lpD3DRMViewport2->Render(lpD3DRMFrame3);
42:     lpD3DRMViewport2->Update();
43:     progress += 0.01f;
44: }
```

23

Just a reminder: This short code snippet doesn't fill in all the blanks! You will have to use your knowledge of Direct3D to initialize the Direct3D objects. However, it is nice to see that the actual concepts behind creating a transform and creating a transition are almost the same for both 2D and 3D.

A Sample DirectX Transform Application

The sample application shows off how easy DirectX Transform is to use. The application lets us load two different images (of any supported type) and then it runs the 2D Wipe transition on the two input images.

The sample application is split into several files, but don't let that alarm you. Each file was kept relatively small in order to make it easier for you to change and play with the code. Just changing a few lines will allow you to change the transition and it should be fairly easy to use the DirectX Transform specific files in a Direct3D application.

Here is a description of what each source file contains:

- Hour23.cpp contains the `WinMain()` function, a message handler, a cleanup function, and a bunch of global variables.
- Init.cpp contains two functions. The first function initializes the window, and the second function initializes the `DirectDraw` objects.
- InitDTrans.cpp also contains two functions. The first initializes the DirectX Transform objects. The second function sets up the transform.
- LoadImage.cpp contains a single function that prompts the user to select a file to be loaded into a `DXSurface` object.
- TransformImages.cpp holds the code that performs the transition.

Some of the source code should look familiar because it's from previous hours. However, the application has four essentially new parts. The application creates `DXSurface` objects, loads images into `DXSurface` objects, creates a 2D transform, and animates the 2D transform.

Create DXSurface Objects

A hierarchy of objects must be created before you can actually create `DXSurface` objects. You need a `DXTransformFactory` to create a `DXSurfaceFactory`; when you have a `DXSurfaceFactory`, you can call `DXSurfaceFactory::CreateSurface()` to create a new `DXSurface`.

In the sample app, the `CreateSurface()` function is used to create two different surfaces. First, it is used to create an output surface (the surface that the transform draws its output to) and then it is used to create the primary `DirectDraw` surface. The primary `DirectDraw` surface is the surface that you actually see on your monitor.

Listing 23.5 shows how the `CreateSurface()` function is used in the sample application.

LISTING 23.5   Creating a `DXSurface`

```
 1: //  create a new surface with the factory (our output surface)
 2: hres = lpSurfaceFactory->CreateSurface(    NULL, // pointer to DDraw
 3:                           NULL, // surface description
 4:                           &DDPF_PMARGB32, // pixel format ID
 5:                           &ImageBounds, // bounds
 6:                           0, // flags
 7:                           NULL, // pointer for aggregation
 8:                           IID_IDXSurface, // REFIID
 9:                           (void**)&lpOutputSurface); // our new surface
```

Load the Images

One of the true conveniences of using `DXSurfaces` is the freedom from worrying about image file formats. To load an image, simply call the `IDXSurfaceFactory::LoadImage()` function.

In the application, the hardest part is making sure that the file name we pass is a Unicode string. Listing 23.6 shows how the application uses `LoadImage()`.

LISTING 23.6   Loading an Image with `LoadImage()`

```
 1: // Convert FileName to a unicode string...
 2: mbstowcs(WFileName, FileName, 256);
 3:
 4: //  create a new surface with the factory (our output surface)
 5: hres = lpSurfaceFactory->LoadImage( WFileName, // File Name (LPWSTR)
 6:                           NULL,
 7:                           NULL,
 8:                           NULL,
 9:                           IID_IDXSurface, // REFIID
10:                           (void**)surface); // Surface
```

Create the Transform

When the transform factory has been created, you can create the DXTransform object by calling IDXTransformFactory::CreateTransform(). In the sample application, we create the 2D Wipe Transform. If you wanted to change the transform, all you would have to do is change the CLSID you pass to CreateTransform() (assuming that the transform has the same number of inputs, outputs, and uses the DXEffect interface). Listing 23.7 shows the code the sample application uses to create its transform.

LISTING 23.7   Creating the Transform

```
 1: // create our transform
 2: hres = lpTransformFactory->CreateTransform(
 3:                     NULL, //  inputs
 4:                     0, //  num inputs
 5:                     NULL,  //  outputs
 6:                     0, //  num outputs
 7:                     NULL, //  property flag
 8:                     NULL, //  error log
 9:                     CLSID_DXTWipe, //  CLSID of Effect
10:                     IID_IDXTransform, //  Transform ID
11:                     (void**)&lpTransform); //  Pointer to our Transform
12:
13: if (hres != S_OK)
14: {
15:     ErrStr = Err_CreateTransform;
16:     return FALSE;
17: }
```

Animate the Image Transforms

Before you display the transition, you have to set up your transform. If you entered inputs and outputs in the CreateTransform() call, your transform is already set up. However, if you didn't enter inputs and outputs in the CreatTransform() call, you must call IDXTransform::Setup(). Listing 23.8 shows how the sample application uses the Setup() function.

LISTING 23.8   Setting Up the Transform

```
 1: BOOL SetupTransform()
 2: {
 3:     HRESULT hres;
 4:     IUnknown* in[2];
 5:     IUnknown* out[1];
 6:
```

```
 7:    in[0] = lpSurfaceA;
 8:    in[1] = lpSurfaceB;
 9:
10:    out[0] = lpOutputSurface;
11:
12:    // setup our transform:  2 inputs, 1 output
13:    hres = lpTransform->Setup(in, 2, out, 1, 0);
14:
15:    if (hres != S_OK)
16:    {
17:        ErrStr = Err_TransformSetup;
18:        return FALSE;
19:    }
20:
21:    return TRUE;
22: }
```

23

Now that the transform has been set up, you are finally ready to display the animated transition. Each time you want to draw the next step of the transition, you have to change the progress variable in the DXEffect object. After that, you must call IDXTransform::Execute() to update the output surface. Listing 23.9 shows how it all fits together.

LISTING 23.9   Executing the Transform

```
1: DXVEC TransformPlacement = { DXBT_DISCRETE, 0 };
2:
3: // set new progress before we execute (so a change will take place)
4: lpDXEffect->put_Progress(progress);
5:
6: // execute with the new progress
7: hres = lpTransform->Execute( NULL, //  Request ID (GUID)
8:                  NULL, //  Bounds (DXBNDS)
9:                  &TransformPlacement); //  Placement (DXVEC)
```

Cleanup

When releasing the DirectX Transform objects, it is important to remember the order in which you created them. It is safest to release objects in the opposite order that you created them. Listing 23.10 shows the Cleanup() function used in the sample application.

LISTING 23.10 Cleanup()

```
 1: //---- Cleanup - Cleanup objects, post error message ----//
 2: void Cleanup()
 3: {
 4:     // release transform factory interfaces
 5:     SafeRelease(lpSurfaceA);
 6:     SafeRelease(lpSurfaceB);
 7:     SafeRelease(lpDDSPrimary);
 8:     SafeRelease(lpOutputSurface);
 9:     SafeRelease(lpSurfaceFactory);
10:     SafeRelease(lpTransform);
11:     SafeRelease(lpTransformFactory);
12:
13:     // release DirectDraw interfaces
14:     SafeRelease(lpDD);
15:
16:     //  uninitialize com
17:     CoUninitialize();
18:
19:     // display error if one thrown
20:     if (ErrStr)
21:     {
22:         MessageBox(NULL, ErrStr, szCaption, MB_OK);
23:         ErrStr=NULL;
24:     }
25: }
```

Summary

DirectX Transform is a powerful, easy way to get great special effects in your application. In this hour, you learned about procedural surfaces, 2D and 3D transforms, and the interfaces and objects that are inside of DirectX Transform. You also created your first DirectX Transform application. This is a great starting point for further experimentation.

Q&A

Q Where can I find more information about procedural surfaces, how to create a PhotoShop plug-in, or how to use DirectX Transform on a Web page?

A The Internet is always a great place to start your research. Use your favorite search engine or visit your favorite programming-related Web pages. Also, the DirectX Media SDK Documentation is an excellent place to look for more information about all of the above.

Q Can I chain the output of one 2D transform to the input of another?

A Absolutely! You might be able to create some very interesting transforms this way. However, depending on the transforms, at some point you will reach a limit where the CPU can't handle any more and your application will slow to a crawl.

Workshop

23

The Workshop is designed to help you anticipate possible questions, review what you've learned, and begin thinking ahead to put your knowledge into practice. The answers to the quiz are in Appendix A, "Answers."

Quiz

1. What is the difference between the `PMARGB32` and `ARGB32` pixel formats?

2. What kind of objects do 2D transforms operate on?

3. What kind of objects do 3D transforms operate on?

4. Why is reading pixels from a procedural surface usually slower than reading pixels from a normal surface?

5. Why are procedural surfaces smaller than normal surfaces?

6. What function must you call before you create your `DXTransformFactory` object?

7. What type of string (ANSI or Unicode) does the `DXTransformFactory::LoadImage()` function take?

8. In what order should you release DirectX Transform objects?

9. What type of transform is most likely to take advantage of the `DXEffect` interface?

10. What does the progress variable in the `DXEffect` object stand for?

Exercises

1. Change the 2D transform used in the sample application so it uses the 2D Fade transform (note, the `CLSID` for the Fade transform is `CLSID_DXFade`).

2. After you have changed the 2D transform to the Fade transform, try specifying the pixel format of the images you load. See if performance differs when you specify `PMARGB32` or `ARGB32`.

HOUR **24**

Integrating Media Into Web Pages and Applications with DirectAnimation

by Brian Noyes

The final part of the DirectX Media SDK that we will cover is Direct-
Animation. DirectAnimation is a powerful part of the DirectX Media
libraries that ties together many of the capabilities you have seen so far in
this book and allows you to access them from a high level of abstraction
using interfaces that can be accessed in a variety of languages and ways.

DirectAnimation allows you to integrate many different media types to create complex animations that can be used as Web content, as a media element
of an application, or as a standalone application in its own right. In addition

to being extremely powerful and flexible, DirectAnimation is easy to use because it takes care of most of the gory details of setting up an animation and integrating various types of media for you. It allows you to interact with the DirectAnimation interfaces in your code from a much higher level of abstraction, allowing you to focus on the model or behavior you are trying to represent, instead of the lower-level details of how to represent that behavior.

In this hour, you will learn

- About the capabilities of DirectAnimation
- What interfaces and components make up DirectAnimation
- How to access DirectAnimation capabilities from different programming environments
- How to code a DirectAnimation scene from C++
- How to code a DirectAnimation scene from scripting languages for the Web

DirectAnimation—One API, Many Uses

DirectAnimation is an extremely versatile and capable part of the DirectX libraries. It basically rolls up most of the major capabilities of the underlying DirectX foundation classes into a single set of interfaces that lets you quickly integrate a variety of media types and access and program those interfaces from a number of different languages and development environments. Using DirectAnimation, you can integrate 2D images, 3D geometrics, audio, video, vector graphics, and text into your Web pages or applications using an amazingly small amount of code. DirectAnimation presents itself as a set of ActiveX controls available on your system that you interact with programmatically through interfaces on those controls, just like any other COM component.

You can use DirectAnimation from a variety of languages and development environments, ranging from C++, to Web page scripts, and HTML code. What this means is that not only can you use DirectAnimation to code animations and integrate media into a stand-alone application, but you can also harness the power of DirectAnimation directly from a Web page to create anything ranging from a simple animated element (for example, a spinning 3-D logo), to a portal into a virtual world. DirectAnimation also includes several run-time controls that you can embed on a Web page and simply set properties on to create animations without even using script. If you are coding from C++, you can use DirectAnimation to manage the entire scene of your application or simply to create an animated element of your application, such as a cockpit gauge, a video screen, or a sound track.

If DirectAnimation is capable of all this, you might be wondering why you would ever use the other parts of the DirectX foundation to code things at a lower level. There are two simple answers to that question: performance and control. By working at a higher level of abstraction, you make some sacrifices in managing the performance and priorities of your application because you are handing most of that control over to DirectAnimation itself. Because the primary design consideration for games and simulations is usually performance, you might not be willing to trade an ounce of performance for some additional ease of coding. Also, as mentioned before, DirectAnimation rolls up most of the capabilities of the underlying libraries, but not all. And some of those exceptions happen to be the most powerful and complex capabilities of the individual DirectX classes, which are often the ones you need to use to distinguish your application from a competitor's product. This is just another design decision you will have to face—maximizing performance and capability versus time to market. That extra time you save using DirectAnimation for low-bandwidth parts of your application could be worth it in terms of quicker market presence and cost of development.

So now you should have a high-level understanding of what DirectAnimation is capable of, and how you can access that capability. It is probably still a little fuzzy to you on how this all comes together in code to create the next great game or an award-winning Web site, but we will get there. First, we need to dive a little deeper into the `DirectAnimation` controls and interfaces to understand how you program DirectAnimation and use it to pull discrete media elements together into a purposeful scene or element of your application or Web page.

Scratching the Surface—A Look at the Interfaces

Like other parts of the DirectX libraries, DirectAnimation exposes itself to the programmer as a set of interfaces. Most of the interfaces you will deal with come from one of two main components: the DirectAnimation control or the DirectAnimation Windowed control. The main difference between the two is the way they are presented as an ActiveX control by a host application. The DirectAnimation control is a "windowless" control in ActiveX terminology. Some host applications do not support windowless controls, so the Windowed control is just a different version for those types of containers. There are only minor differences from the programmer's perspective. You can also use the DirectAnimation control by creating an instance of the `IDAView` interface and use the control through that interface and DirectDraw to do the painting of the scene to the screen. We will use the DirectAnimation control in our example, but a sample application is also included that follows the mold of the other examples in this book by using the `IDAView` interface and a DirectDraw surface.

Because DirectAnimation includes so many of the capabilities of the rest of DirectX, but you interact with those capabilities slightly differently in DirectAnimation, we will only be able to scratch the surface of DirectAnimation's diversity in this hour. But we will cover the overall architecture of DirectAnimation and show you some of the basics of programming with DirectAnimation. From there, you should be able to dig deeper on your own, using the examples and documentation in the SDK to learn more.

> There is an incompatibility between the DirectX SDK Debug libraries and DirectAnimation. If you selected the Debug version of the DirectX libraries when you installed the DirectX SDK, many features of DirectAnimation will not work properly. To fix the problem, you will need to re-run the DirectX SDK setup and select the Retail version of the libraries when prompted.

DirectAnimation Architecture

The DirectAnimation architecture is shown in a conceptual format in Figure 24.1. The DirectAnimation control basically derives its capabilities from the rest of the DirectX classes or the Windows operating system (when it uses the GDI for drawing instead of a DirectDraw surface). The DirectAnimation control presents the graphical interface of the animation through either the `IDAView` or `IDAViewerControl` interface. You can choose to use the `IDAViewerControl` (or `IDAViewerControlWindowed` for the windowed version) to create and manipulate the control if you are willing to let it use the GDI to do the drawing and if your application supports hosting an ActiveX control. The `IDAViewerControl` interface takes care of the drawing calls for you. Or you can use the `IDAView` interface and pass a DirectDraw surface to it and manage the updating of the screen yourself.

FIGURE 24.1
DirectAnimation architecture.

Structured Graphics Control	Sprite Control	Path Control	Sequencer Control

DirectAnimation Control

Behavior interfaces

DAStatics interface

DAViewerControl interface	DAView interface

DirectX classes	DirectX Media classes	Windows Services

The basic element of animation in DirectAnimation is a *behavior*. These behaviors are created from interfaces derived from the IDABehavior interface. Behavior classes are defined for all the different types of media that you can integrate in your application, as well as behaviors for data types, events, transformations, and styles.

The IDAStatics interface is a central element of the DirectAnimation API. It has a huge number of methods and properties defined that you can use to create and manipulate behaviors in the DirectAnimation model.

A large number of interfaces are available from DirectAnimation that present the functionality of all the different types of behaviors that can be created. The numbering scheme that DirectAnimation uses on these interfaces is to put the version number of the interface immediately following the IDA part of the interface name (for example, IDA2Statics). Note that there are also a number of interfaces with a 2 or 3 in their name following the basic name of the interface (for example, IDAPoint3). These interfaces represent two or three dimensional versions of a type of object. The last thing to realize is that Microsoft ships the DirectAnimation library as an integral part of Internet Explorer and has included a newer version of danim.dll with Internet Explorer 5 that includes several new interfaces or newer versions of existing interfaces. So the documentation for the DirectX Media SDK might list fewer versions of some interfaces than actually exist on your system.

The DirectAnimation Model

The DirectAnimation programming model centers around the creation and manipulation of behavior objects. To get started, you have to create a DirectAnimation Control and obtain an IDAViewerControl (or IDAView) interface for that control. You can then obtain an IDAStatics interface for that control, which will allow you to start creating behavior objects from the DirectAnimation control. After you have done this initialization, most of DirectAnimation programming is all about behaviors and the interfaces to those behaviors.

Behavior objects can be constructed from other behavior objects, resulting in hierarchies of behaviors that can be used to represent complex real-world objects in very few lines of code. Because there are behaviors for simple data types, such as DANumber objects, you can use these behaviors to represent time varying characteristics of objects as well, and modify those root behaviors at runtime. After you have built up the hierarchy of behaviors that represent some element in your animation, the DirectAnimation model will propagate a change to the underlying behavior through the rest of the dependent behaviors without any further action required on your part.

24

This requires a little different mentality when constructing a model for your application. You have to think ahead and outline the hierarchical dependencies between behaviors so that changes to a root or underlying behavior has the expected result at the higher levels. When you have laid out the interrelationships, you construct the behaviors based on those relationships, start the model running, and let DirectAnimation do the rest. This top down approach takes a little getting used to because other parts of DirectX require you to think from the bottom up.

For example, an aircraft could be constructed of a fuselage behavior and a propeller behavior. The propeller behavior can be constructed with a rotation behavior based on a DANumber behavior that is linked to a throttle control in your game and the 3D object that provides the visual representation. The composite propeller and fuselage behavior can have a translation behavior applied to it representing the movement through the air. That translation behavior can be based on a calculation combining several DANumbers representing airspeed, propeller rotation speed, drag, and so on. You code all these dependencies, and then the only thing you actually modify at runtime is the DANumber representing the throttle setting, and DirectAnimation will do all the calculations to figure out how to modify the containing behaviors, based on the dependencies you describe in code at design time.

Behaviors can also be reactive and interactive. There are event behaviors that can be setup to change other behaviors when the event occurs. Also, events can be defined based on user input, so this provides an interactive element to the behaviors. Each type of behavior will have a number of methods defined on its interface that allows you to perform operations relevant to that behavior type. There are also a number of inherited methods from the IDABehavior interface that will apply to all behaviors. Some methods, such as Transform() are pretty much common to all behaviors, but because the semantics of the transformation is different depending on the type of the behavior, these are individually defined, but have similar signatures.

So basically, the DirectAnimation model is really all about defining behaviors and the relationships between them. After this is done, you start the DirectAnimation control running, and it does the rest. You can still modify the behaviors after it is running by initializing behaviors using the ModifiableBehavior() method of the IDAStatics interface and then using the SwitchTo() method on those behaviors somewhere else in your code (that is, a menu or command handler).

A Versatile Programming Environment

Because the DirectAnimation interfaces include most of their capability through automation compatible interfaces, these interfaces can be accessed and manipulated from any language that supports COM or automation interface programming. You can access the full capabilities of DirectAnimation through normal COM interfaces or automation interfaces through Visual C++, Visual Basic, and Java. But the automation compatible interfaces can also be accessed from scripting languages and other environments that do not support the manipulation of COM interface pointers directly. The most common scripting languages that support this type of interaction are HTML embedded JScript and VBScript.

If you choose to use DirectAnimation from C++, the possibilities open up even more. You can use DirectAnimation to create a standalone application where the Direct-Animation scene takes up the entire window area, or you could simply use Direct-Animation to create media elements that are embedded in your application, either as ActiveX controls or simply programmatic elements of the main application (that is, child windows of the main window). You can also embed DirectAnimation inside other ActiveX controls that you create from Visual C++ and distribute those controls either as elements of an application, as third-party controls, or as Web content ActiveX controls. This also enables you to protect your source code from distribution in the Web environment. If you code your animation in script, anyone is able to copy or modify your code.

Another advantage to using DirectAnimation from C++ is that some interfaces included in DirectAnimation are not accessible from automation environments, and these additional interfaces can make a significant difference in performance and capability. Most notably, by programming DirectAnimation from C++, you can create a DirectDraw surface yourself as shown in earlier parts of this book, pass that surface to the Direct-Animation model, and then control the updating of the surface yourself. By doing this, you can greatly improve performance because the normal DirectAnimation control just uses the GDI to draw to the screen. It gives you better control of the update frequency, and you can have better control of how you react to events and provide hooks into the behaviors that compose a DirectAnimation scene.

Because of the automation and type library support provided by DirectAnimation, there are multiple ways to access the functionality within more powerful languages like Visual C++. Because there are so many variants and we are trying to keep this lesson down to an hour, we will only dive into the shallow end of two of the choices: C++ and scripts.

DirectAnimation Programming in C++

When programming DirectAnimationfrom Visual C++, you have a lot of choices on how you can access and use the capabilities of the library. You can stick to straight C++ COM interface programming, as is required for most other DirectX libraries, or you can take advantage of the type library and automation support and use some of the features of Visual C++ to make your life a little easier. Because of the way you program with

DirectAnimation, getting a little help with all the COM interface management becomes much more important than it is for DirectDraw. DirectDraw has a lot of helper functions defined that hide most of the COM details from you. DirectAnimation does not include similar helper functions, but the code can still be very straightforward and easy to code and understand with a little help from the Visual C++ environment.

The thing about DirectAnimation that causes straight C++ COM programming to get a little painful is that you will be creating and manipulating a ton of interfaces. This makes keeping track of all the reference counting and HRESULT error checking extremely tedious and error prone. That is where wrapper classes come in. You have a number of choices in the Visual C++ environment that can help you out with the interface management. You can use the ActiveX Template Library (ATL) classes: the Components and Controls library to create wrapper classes, or the #import directive to generate smart pointer classes from a type library.

In the sample C++ code we will be covering in detail, we will be using the #import mechanism. We won't go into a great deal of explanation on this, but you will see that it is pretty straightforward to use, and significantly simplifies the code. This will let us focus more on what is going on with DirectAnimation, instead of what is going on with COM.

Using Scripts to Use DirectAnimation on the Web

You can also use scripts in HTML to program DirectAnimation capabilities directly into a Web page. In fact, this is the primary thrust of the DirectAnimation documentation and samples. The process is essentially the same as in C++. You create a DirectAnimation control, get an IDAStatics interface from it, create behaviors and set the model running. The main difference is in the syntax, but the code actually turns out to be very similar to the code you use with the #import mechanism in Visual C++.

Sample DirectAnimation Application in C++

Enough with the theory and abstractions: let's work with some code to show just how powerful and easy DirectAnimation really is. We will put together a simple C++ application containing an animated scene, complete with 3D objects, 2D images, lights, camera, and sound.

We will be taking two departures from previous examples. First, we will be using the #import mechanism to simplify our COM interface handling with DirectAnimation. Second, we will use an MFC AppWizard generated application as our starting point for the code. You don't really need to know or care about MFC to understand this example, but by going that route, we can use the DirectAnimation control easily and not have to code a bunch of Windows and DirectDraw initialization code.

To get started, you will need to run Visual C++ and select New from the File menu. Select the Projects tab, and select MFC AppWizard (exe) from the program options. Enter a location for the project, and enter a project name of DASample, and click OK as shown in Figure 24.2.

FIGURE 24.2

Creating the DASample project.

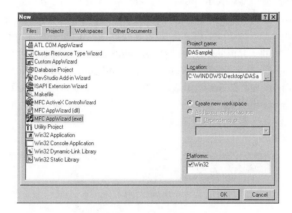

24

In the dialog that follows, select Single Document and press the Finish button. This accepts the rest of the defaults for an MFC SDI application. We will only be making our modifications to the CDASampleView class generated by the AppWizard to avoid getting into much MFC. Some other code will be generated by the wizard for print preview, help support, and other things, but we will just ignore that code.

The reason for going this route is that the MFC CWnd class supports hosting of ActiveX controls with very little code. By using an MFC AppWizard project, everything is already in place to allow us to use this class. We will be embedding a DAViewerControl in the CDASampleView class using this capability. That will allow us to focus just on the DirectAnimation code.

Initializing DirectAnimation

There are basically two ways to get DirectAnimation initialized. Which way you choose depends on whether you are going to let the DirectAnimation control do all the drawing on its own using the GDI, or whether you want to pass it a DirectDraw surface and control updating the screen yourself.

The first route is by far the easiest, and it is the one we will use in our sample application. The main drawback to this approach again is performance—because the control is

using the GDI for drawing the scene, you miss out on all the performance benefits
DirectDraw provides you. We will describe the process required to use DirectDraw at the
end so that you know how to go further on your own, and a separate example project is
included that uses raw COM interfaces and the DirectDraw/DAView approach to show
you how.

We must add a couple of other things before we get down to the DirectAnimation code
so that we have somewhere to put that code. We will add a handler to the `CDASampleView`
class for the Windows `WM_CREATE` message and will put all our DirectAnimation initialization code there to insulate you from the MFC architecture as much as possible in this
example. To add this handler from Visual Studio, you can simply right-click the
`CDASampleView` class in the ClassView pane, and select Add Windows Message Handler
as shown in Figure 24.3. Select the `WM_CREATE` message from the list in the resulting dialog box, and press the Add and Edit button. This plops you into the handler function with
the focus on the line where you should start adding your code.

FIGURE 24.3

*Adding the Windows
message handler.*

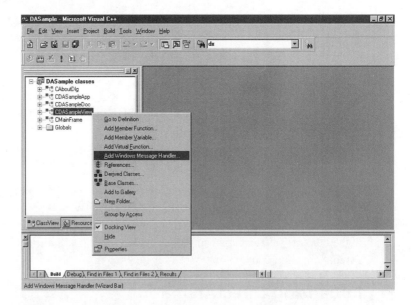

We'll come back to this handler in a moment, but there are a few other initialization
steps to take first. We are going to want a child window to host the DirectAnimation control that won't go out of scope when the `WM_CREATE` handler finishes. To do this, just add
a CWnd member to the `CDASampleView` class with the code in Listing 24.1 as a public
member of the class.

LISTING 24.1   CWnd Member Variable in DASampleView.h

```
1: public:
2:    CWnd m_ctl;
```

We also need to add the DirectAnimation library to our application. If we were going to code straight C++ COM code, we would #include the danim.h file and add the daguid.lib static link libraries to the project link settings. But because we are going to use the #import directive, all we do is add Listing 24.2 to the top of our DASampleView.h file.

LISTING 24.2   #import Declaration in DASampleView.h

```
1: #pragma warning(disable: 4192)
2: #import <danim.dll> rename_namespace( "DAnim" )
3: using namespace DAnim;
```

The #pragma just avoids a bunch of warnings about redefinition exclusions that you don't need to worry about. The #import statement allows the compiler to pull in the type library information out of the danim.dll file and automatically generates smart pointer wrapper classes for the DirectAnimation interfaces for you. The namespace parts just let you use the generated classes and definitions without having to qualify each one with a namespace. After you have added this, you basically have full access to the DirectAnimation interfaces through smart pointer wrapper classes. When you have added this and compile your project, the compiler will generate two files in your output directory: danim.tlh and danim.tli. These files contain the header and implementation code for the classes the compiler finds in the danim.dll type library. You can browse through these files to see the classes generated if desired.

Sometimes the Visual C++ compiler gets ahead of itself while generating the .tlh and .tli files and starts trying to compile using those files before it has fully closed them. This results in a compile error saying `fatal error C1083: Cannot open include file`. All you have to do is try to compile again, and it usually succeeds the second time.

The CWnd::CreateControl() Function

To initialize the DAViewerControl, we will let MFC do a lot of work for us by using the CWnd::CreateControl() function. This function creates an ActiveX control from a CLSID or a ProgID string, and automatically makes the numerous connections required between an ActiveX control and its host container.

```
▼ BOOL CWnd::CreateControl( REFCLSID clsid, LPCTSTR lpszWindowName,
  DWORD dwStyle, const RECT& rect, CWnd* pParentWnd,
  UINT nID, CFile* pPersist = NULL,
  BOOL bStorage = FALSE, BSTR bstrLicKey = NULL );
```

This function returns TRUE on success.

Parameters:

clsid	A reference to a CLSID constant for the control you are creating. An overloaded form of this function takes a ProgID string to identify the desired class.
lpszWindowName	A string indicating the desired name for the new window that will be created for the control. This value can be NULL if the control will not be referenced elsewhere by name.
dwStyle	A style flag indicating how to display the control. WS_VISIBLE is the most likely value here.
rect	A rectangle defining the extents of the control that will be created.
pParentWnd	A CWnd pointer to the parent window that will host the control. This must not be NULL.
nID	A control ID number that can be used to identify or retrieve the control from its parent.

The rest of the parameters can typically be excluded, allowing their default values to be
▲ used.

Listing 24.3 shows the initialization of the DAViewerControl and how to obtain an
IDAViewerControl interface pointer from it.

LISTING 24.3 DAViewerControl Initialization

```
1: RECT rect={0,0,400,300};
2: m_ctl.CreateControl(__uuidof(DAViewerControl),NULL,
   ➥ WS_VISIBLE, rect,this,101);
3: IDAViewerControlPtr pVC = m_ctl.GetControlUnknown();
4: IDAStaticsPtr pS = pVC->MeterLibrary;
```

The `CWnd::CreateControl()` function takes several arguments. We pass it the `CLSID` of the `DAViewerControl` by using the `__uuidof()` function on the `DAViewerControl` identifier. This identifier will be created by the compiler as part of the `#import` operation in the danim.tlh file. We leave the window name `NULL`, make the window visible, give it a desired rectangle in client coordinates, a CWnd pointer to the parent window, and a control ID. You have to initialize the control to a specific rectangle, but you can later resize the control just like any window in response to the `WM_SIZE` message.

The next line of code is the first one that uses the smart pointer classes, so we will explain how this works briefly. You declare a smart pointer class for a given interface by simply appending `ptr` to the end of the interface name. The smart pointer class is derived from the `_com_ptr_t` class, and is declared in the .tlh file generated by the compiler from the `#import` statement. It handles all reference counting on the interface for you, so you don't have to worry about calls to `AddRef()` and `Release()`. When the pointer goes out of scope, it will call `Release()` itself. It has operators defined so that you just use pointer syntax as if it were a pointer of the desired interface type itself. It also has other operators defined to ease your coding, such as the "=" operator. This operator will perform a `QueryInterface()` call for you for the desired interface type. Finally, the last thing they do is allow interface calls to pass a return type other than `HRESULT`, so the coding style is more natural than always having to pass the return value as a pointer argument to the interface method. This also allows you to reassign the result of a method back to an object that is used to call the method, as you will see later. This saves having to declare a bunch of extra temporary objects. If an error occurs in an interface method call, the smart pointer class throws an exception of type `_com_error`, so you should wrap all your code in try/catch blocks to protect it.

So what the third line of code in Listing 24.3 does is assign an `IDAViewerControl` interface pointer to the pVC object. It does this by calling the `CWnd::GetControlUnknown()` function to get an IUnknown pointer for the control we just created, and then performs an implicit `QueryInterface()` for `IDAViewerControl` on that interface.

The last line retrieves an `IDAStatics` interface pointer from the `DAViewerControl` using its `MeterLibrary` property. We could have created the interface directly from COM, but the `MeterLibrary` property both sets the coordinate system and gets us the interface we need next, so it saves a little code.

Two coordinate unit systems are available in DirectAnimation—pixels and meters. Meters are the most straightforward to use because they are display-resolution independent and because even when you specify that you want to use the PixelLibrary, pixel units will only be used when constructing objects. When you make transformations on those objects, meter-based space will still be used. However, there is also an

24

`IDAStatics::Pixel` property that allows you to determine quickly how many meters per pixel there are at the current display resolution, and you can use that to perform calculations for your animation.

The origin of the coordinate system is at the center of the `DAViewerControl`. Even when working in meter space, images will be imported at their natural size based on display resolution and their pixel dimensions. You can apply scaling to them using transformations as discussed later in the "Adding Some Motion" section.

You see here that the smart pointer class also allows you to set and retrieve properties from an interface as if they were member variables of the class. To access properties through a normal COM interface, you have to use `get_XXX()` and `put_XXX()` methods, where XXX is the property you are trying to access.

So after only a few lines of code and a lot of explanation, we have an initialized `DirectAnimation` control as a child window of our view window, and we have an `IDAViewerControl` pointer to that control. We also have an `IDAStatics` interface to use to create behaviors to add to our control. We will be adding a 3D object with a rotation behavior applied to it, importing another 2D image to act as a moving background, importing some sound to run in the background for our scene, and then setting up the camera and lighting for viewing the scene in our window.

Loading 2D Images

The first behavior we will create is a DAImage behavior. DirectAnimation provides multiple methods on the `IDAStatics` interface to import different types of media into the model. Each import method is basically the same. You provide it a path to the media file, and it returns an interface to the type of media behavior you are creating. Listing 24.4 shows how to import an image file, and then tile it so that it fills whatever it is applied to. Other methods on the `IDAImage` interface allow you to perform other operations, such as getting a bounding box for the image or mapping its size to a unit square for use as a texture.

LISTING 24.4   Importing a 2D Image

```
1: _bstr_t mediaBase = GetMediaBase();
2: // Import image
3: IDAImagePtr stars = pS->ImportImage(mediaBase +
   ➥_bstr_t("Image\\stars.jpg"));
4: // Tile for a continuous background
5: stars = stars->Tile();
```

You must pass a fully qualified path to the import methods so that they can find the media file you are asking for. This can be either a path to a file on disk or a URL. Relative pathnames will not work in C++, but will work in script from a Web page. Because we are using some of the sample media files included with the DirectX Media SDK for this example, there is a utility function called GetMediaBase() in the example code that uses a registry key installed by the SDK to locate the sample media folder and place that path in a string variable named mediaBase. Note also that COM methods take BSTR types as arguments for strings. The wrapper classes use a utility class called _bstr_t to ease handling of BSTR's. The Tile() method does just what it says, tiles the image over wherever this image gets applied. In our case, we will be setting it as a background image, which gives it the appearance of an infinite background within our window.

Creating a 3D Object

24

Next we create a DAGeometry behavior. This is the DirectAnimation class used to represent and manipulate 3D objects. To import a 3D object, the object must be defined in a .x file, just like with Direct3D. DirectAnimation will only import simple objects from DirectX files. It cannot import all the elements that Direct3D is capable of handling in a DirectX file, only simple objects defined as a single mesh.

After you have imported the object, you can apply other behaviors to it, including 2D images as textures, transform behaviors to position the object or set it in motion, and many other behaviors you can experiment with on your own. Listing 24.5 shows how to import the .x file and scale it to fit our window.

LISTING 24.5   Importing a 3D Object

```
1: // Import a geometry and scale to fit window
2: IDAGeometryPtr dxGeo = pS->ImportGeometry(mediaBase +
   ➥_bstr_t("Geometry\\dx.x"));
3: IDATransform3Ptr scale = pS->Scale3Uniform(.01);
4: dxGeo = dxGeo->Transform(scale);
```

The IDAStatics::Scale3Uniform() method takes a scale factor and returns an IDATransform3 interface pointer. We then pass this pointer to the IDAGeometry::Transform() method to perform the actual scaling. This method returns a new IDAGeometry interface pointer to the transformed object, and thanks to the assignment operator of smart pointer classes, we just assign this new interface pointer back to our old pointer variable so that we don't have to create explicit intermediate temporary pointers.

Adding Some Motion

Now let's put the "Animation" in our DirectAnimation model. We will add several rotations to our 3D object, and then put a translation motion on our background (see Listing 24.6).

LISTING 24.6 Adding Motion Behaviors

```
 1: // Create a three rotation behaviors and apply to DX
 2: const double PI = 3.14159;
 3: IDATransform3Ptr rotx = pS->Rotate3Rate(pS->XVector3, 2);
 4: IDATransform3Ptr rotz = pS->Rotate3(pS->ZVector3,5*PI/8);
 5: IDATransform3Ptr roty = pS->Rotate3Rate(pS->YVector3,.3);
 6: // Apply rotations - order is important!!!
 7: dxGeo = dxGeo->Transform(rotx);
 8: dxGeo = dxGeo->Transform(rotz);
 9: dxGeo = dxGeo->Transform(roty);
10:
11: // Create a translation behavior and apply to stars
12: stars = stars->Transform(pS->Translate2Rate(.01,0));
```

We create three transformation behaviors, one around each axis, and then apply them to the object one at a time. There are rotation transformation methods that allow you to combine the individual steps by defining the vectors around which they operate, but sometimes it is easier to stay anchored to axes that you are comfortable with. DirectAnimation uses radians for angles, unless you use one of the variants of the methods with "Degrees" in the method name. We use the X, Y, and Z vector properties of the IDAStatics interface to specify the axis of rotation for each transformation. We also create a translation behavior and apply it to the stars background image.

The order in which you apply transformations to a behavior is important. For example, if you apply a rotation before a translation, you get a different result than applying a translation before a rotation. For additional information about the affect of changing the order of transformations, see Hour 10, "Introduction to 3D Concepts."

Another thing to note about the code in Listing 24.6 is that because the smart pointer classes return objects instead of HRESULTs, it allows us to use the result of one method call as an argument to another. In Listing 24.6, we use the XVector3, YVector3, and ZVector3 properties of the IDAStatics interface, which are really return values from get_ method calls on the interface. Without the smart pointer support, you would have to break each call out into a separate line, instead of chaining the calls the way we do here. The result from `IDAStatics::Translate2Rate()` is also used as an argument for the `IDAImage::Transform()` method.

You should also be aware that you can apply 2D transformations to 3D objects and vice versa in `DirectAnimation`.

Creating the Camera and Lighting

When creating a 3D scene, you also need a camera and lighting. The camera is the mechanism that you use to render the 3D objects into a 2D plane for projection on the screen. Listing 24.7 shows how to create a camera and lighting, project the scene into 2D, and then overlay the images into a final image that will be passed to the DirectAnimation model.

LISTING 24.7   Rendering the Scene

```
1: // Create a camera and light
2: IDACameraPtr camera = pS->PerspectiveCamera(.4,.1);
3: IDAGeometryPtr light = pS->PointLight;
4: light = light->Transform(pS->Translate3(100, 100, 1000));
5: IDAGeometryPtr geo= pS->UnionGeometry(dxGeo,light);
6:
7: // Render the 3D into the 2D
8: IDAImagePtr dxGeoImg = geo->Render(camera);
9:
10: // Overlay the dxGeoImg on  the background
11: IDAImagePtr finalImg = pS->Overlay(dxGeoImg,stars);
```

The perspective camera works much like a camera in Direct3D. The arguments include projection and clipping plane distances. Several types of lights can be created. Here we specify a point light and offset it a great distance over our right shoulder using the `IDAStatics::Translate3()` method. Note that the z-axis is coming out of the screen, as evidenced by the positive third argument to this method. We then use the `IDAStatics::UnionGeometry()` method to create a single geometry out of the 3D object and the light, and render them into a 2D image with the `IDAGeometry::Render()` method and the camera object. Finally, we merge the image of the 3D object with the background image to complete the scene.

Adding Sound

We will add one last behavior to our sample: sound. Just like with images and 3D objects, you can import sound in a variety of formats with a single method call. Listing

24.8 shows how to pull in a sound, slow it down to 60 percent of its normal speed, and set it to loop continuously.

LISTING 24.8   Importing Sound

```
1: // Import a sound, and send it looping
2: IDASoundPtr sound = pS->ImportSound(mediaBase +
   ➥_bstr_t("Sound\\copter2.mp2"))->Sound;
3: sound = sound->Rate(.6);
4: sound = sound->Loop();
```

One difference from the image and geometry import methods is you must specify that it is the sound you want from the import operation because the function is capable of reading sound from formats that include other media (that is, MP2 as in the example). `IDAStatics::ImportSound()` actually returns a result of type `IDAImportationResult`, on which you must retrieve the Sound property. The `Rate()` method allows you to speed up or slow down the playback of the sound. The `Loop()` method just makes the sound repeat endlessly. Other methods are available to change the phase or gain of the sound or to apply other effects to the sound through the underlying DirectSound libraries that DirectAnimation is using.

Animating the Scene

All that is left to do now is to hand off the behaviors we have created to the DirectAnimation control and set it running. Listing 24.9 shows how straightforward this step is.

LISTING 24.9   Running the Model

```
// Set the image and sound on the control and let it run
pVC->Image = finalImg;
pVC->Sound = sound;
pVC->Start();
```

Basically, you can pass a single `DAImage` and a single `DASound` object to the control. Those behaviors can be compound behaviors, as they are in our example. If you are using the windowed version of the control (`DAViewerControlWindowed`), a `BackgroundImage` property of the control can be set to fill the background by tiling the foreground image. The final call, the `IDAViewerControl::Start()`, sets the model running and starts the internal clock that DirectAnimation uses to perform timing calculations for the model.

If you get the following output in your Debug window within Visual Studio while running a DirectAnimation application in the debugger: "First-chance exception in DASample.exe (DANIM.DLL): 0xE0000001: (no name)." and the control does not run, it means that one of the behaviors you added to the control did not initialize correctly, and it might keep the control from running. The only way to isolate the problem sometimes is to add behaviors one at a time and make sure that they work correctly before adding more. This is often caused by a media file not being found when trying to import it.

Cleanup

By using the smart pointer classes, there is no cleanup remaining to worry about. When all the interface pointers we created go out of scope at the end of the try block in the WM_CREATE handler, Release() will be called automatically for each one by their smart pointer class. If you had gone the pure COM interface route, you would have had to call Release() on all those pointers yourself.

The DirectAnimation control will be cleaned up by the MFC hierarchy because we set it as a child window of the View window. When MFC destroys the View, it will destroy the child control as well with no further effort required on our part.

Doing it the DirectDraw Way

Now that you have seen how to do it the easy way, you might be wondering about the other way we mentioned: using a DirectDrawSurface and the DAView class. The main differences between the two approaches from a coding perspective all focus on the initialization and how the scene gets updated on the screen. When it comes down to creating the behaviors that compose the scene, it is the same approach of creating the behaviors one by one and then passing them off to the DAView object.

First you have to initialize DirectDraw and obtain a primary surface and an offscreen surface, which will be used by DirectAnimation. DirectAnimation uses DirectDraw in a primitive fashion, and it is not compatible with the DirectDraw7 versions of the interfaces. So you have to deal with COM a lot more directly than you have in the previous DirectDraw parts of the book. You have to create the DirectDraw object using a DirectDrawFactory object, and then use IDirectDraw and IDirectDrawSurface interfaces versus the IDirectDraw7 and IDirectDrawSurface7 versions seen earlier in the book.

To initialize `DirectAnimation`, you create an instance of the `DAView` object and get an interface to it. You will also need an instance of a `DAStatics` object, which you create directly. You create both of these through calls to the COM function `CoCreateInstance()`, which also requires that you call `CoInitialize()` at the beginning of your program and `CoUninitialize()` at the end of your program to invoke the needed COM services.

After you have obtained the `IDAView` and `IDAStatics` interfaces, you can start creating behaviors from the `IDAStatics` interface as seen earlier in our example. After you have all your behaviors created, you pass them and the secondary DirectDraw surface to the `DAView` interface, similar to what was done at the end of the example with the `DAViewerControl`. You set the `DAView` running with a call to its `StartModel()` method, similar to calling `IDAViewerControl::Start()`.

Finally, you have to manage all updating of the scene by calling the `IDAView::Tick()` and `IDAView::Render()` methods to get DirectAnimation to update the scene on the surface passed to it, and then you have to `Blt()` the DirectAnimation surface to the primary surface to update the screen.

If this sounds like a lot of work, it is compared to the DAViewerControl route we have already covered. But if you want to obtain the benefits of coding at a higher level by using DirectAnimation, but want to wring every ounce of performance out of it that you can, this is the route you need to go. A sample project called DADDSample is included with the source code on this book's CD-ROM that shows this approach, as well as how much extra work is required to handle all the interface creation and cleanup required by the DirectAnimation model without the assistance of smart interface pointer classes.

Sample Web Page Using DirectAnimation

So now you have seen how the DirectAnimation model works in C++ code. But one of the other big advantages of DirectAnimation is that you can create these kinds of animations from scripting languages embedded on a Web page. So we will now briefly cover how to go about this. We will use JScript because its syntax is very similar to what we have seen so far. But VBScript works equally well. We will not go into detail about each line of code because we will code the exact same scene we did in C++. In fact, the script code in Listing 24.10, and contained in the DASample.html file, was created by cutting and pasting the C++ code into a text editor, adding the HTML code at the top and bottom, doing a find and replace on "->" with ".", and removing a few other unnecessary C++ type declarations. Otherwise, it is the exact same code. This is why the #import style of DirectAnimation programming is so powerful. Besides being a lot easier to code than raw C++ COM programming, it allows rapid porting to script if desired. It is actually easier to code complex animations in C++ in this fashion because of the debugger support in Visual Studio. After you get them running in C++, you can then port the code to script quickly as done in Listing 24.10.

LISTING 24.10   DirectAnimation JScript Example

```
 1: <HTML>
 2: <HEAD>
 3: <TITLE>DirectAnimation JScript sample</TITLE>
 4: </HEAD>
 5:
 6: <OBJECT ID="pVC"
 7:   STYLE="position:relative; left:0; top:0;width:400;height:300"
 8:   CLASSID="CLSID:B6FFC24C-7E13-11D0-9B47-00C04FC2F51D"
     ➥ width="400" height="300">
 9: </OBJECT>
10:
11: <SCRIPT LANGUAGE="JScript">
12: <!—
13: // Get a DAStatics object and meter coordinates
14: pS = pVC.MeterLibrary;
15:
16: // Set media base
17: mediaBase = "C:\\Visual Studio\\DXMedia\\samples\\multimedia\\media\\";
18:
19: // Import image
20: stars = pS.ImportImage(mediaBase + "Image\\stars.jpg");
21: // Tile for a continuous background
22: stars = stars.Tile();
23:
24: // Import a geometry and scale to fit window
25: dxGeo = pS.ImportGeometry(mediaBase + "Geometry\\dx.x");
26: scale = pS.Scale3Uniform(.01);
27: dxGeo = dxGeo.Transform(scale);
28:
29: // Create a two rotation behaviors and apply to cube
30: PI = 3.14159;
31: rotx = pS.Rotate3Rate(pS.XVector3, 2);
32: rotz = pS.Rotate3(pS.ZVector3,5*PI/8);
33: roty = pS.Rotate3Rate(pS.YVector3,.3);
34: // Apply rotations - order is important!!!
35: dxGeo = dxGeo.Transform(rotx);
36: dxGeo = dxGeo.Transform(rotz);
37: dxGeo = dxGeo.Transform(roty);
38:
39: // Create a translation behavior and apply to clouds
```

continues

LISTING 24.10   continued

```
40: stars = stars.Transform(pS.Translate2Rate(.01,0));
41:
42: // Create a camera and light
43: camera = pS.PerspectiveCamera(.4,.1);
44: light = pS.PointLight;
45: light = light.Transform(pS.Translate3(100, 100, 1000));
46: geo= pS.UnionGeometry(dxGeo,light);
47:
48: // Render the 3D into the 2D
49: dxGeoImg = geo.Render(camera);
50:
51: // Overlay the dxGeoImg on  the background
52: finalImg = pS.Overlay(dxGeoImg,stars);
53:
54:
55: // Import a sound, and send it looping
56: sound = pS.ImportSound(mediaBase + "Sound\\copter2.mp2").Sound;
57: sound = sound.Rate(.6);
58: sound = sound.Loop();
59:
60: // Set the image and sound on the control and let it run
61: pVC.Image = finalImg;
62: pVC.Sound = sound;
63: pVC.Start();
64:
65: //—>
66: </SCRIPT>
67: </HTML>
```

The only differences here have to do with creating the object, declaring the script code, and the way JScript initializes variables and accesses automation objects. The <OBJECT> tag in HTML lets you embed an ActiveX object in your Web page and initialize some of the parameters for it (that is, size and position) in that declaration. The tags for declaring the script are pretty straightforward. The final thing to note here is that in JScript, you access the methods and properties on an interface with the dot (.) qualifier, versus ->.

Note that in the script, the path to the DirectX Media SDK sample media files is hard coded. You will need to change this to represent the path on your machine.

Summary

In this hour, we have covered the architecture of DirectAnimation, and how to code a sample application with a variety of media and behavior types using C++ and JScript. To dig deeper, you should look into the documentation and samples included in the DirectX Media SDK. A lot of good examples and information are there to let you develop much more complex animations than what we have done here.

Q&A

Q When should I use DirectAnimation to code animations, and when should I code at a lower level using other DirectX libraries?

A DirectAnimation is very good for creating animations that do not contain too many objects or behaviors. The main drawback you will find is that as the complexity and number of contained behaviors of your animation grows, the performance can get pretty poor. There is no clear-cut, break-even point or way to decide when to go to lower-level code. If performance is a problem, the first thing to try is to use the DirectDrawSurface/DAView approach described earlier. If this does not help, you might have to recode everything using the underlying DirectX libraries. This is again where you have to make a decision between speedy development and coding things at a lower level with the DirectX libraries to maintain full control over the performance and priorities in your application.

Q If I use DirectAnimation code in my application, what libraries will I have to redistribute to make it work?

A All the end user needs for the DirectAnimation portion of your application to work is to have Internet Explorer 4 or later installed. The `DirectAnimation` controls ship as part of this installation package, so you should not have to redistribute any additional libraries if they have IE4 or later installed.

Workshop

The Workshop is designed to help you anticipate possible questions, review what you've learned, and begin thinking ahead to put your knowledge into practice. The answers to the quiz are in Appendix A, "Answers."

Quiz

1. In what languages can you program DirectAnimation using both normal COM interfaces and automation interfaces?

2. Which two scripting languages are most commonly used to code DirectAnimation on Web pages?

3. What interface is used to create and modify other behaviors in DirectAnimation?

4. What is the base interface from which all `DirectAnimation` behavior objects derive their functionality?

5. How do you assign a background image for a `DAViewerControl` based animation? For a `DAViewerControlWindowed` animation?

6. What are the two units of measurement available for `DirectAnimation`?

7. At what point does the internal timer used by DirectAnimation start running?

8. If you use a DirectDraw surface with a `DAView` object, what version of the DirectDraw interfaces must you use?

Exercises

1. Change the sample application to use a `DANumber` created with `ModifiableBehavior()` for the rotation speed around the x-axis. Add a keyboard handler for the up and down arrow keys, and increase or decrease the speed of rotation based on keyboard input by using the `SwitchTo()` method in these handlers.

2. Change the sample application to make the object rotate around a different axis, offset from the center of the scene. Experiment with other translation, scaling, and rotation transformations.

3. Import a movie file and run it in a `DirectAnimation` control.

4. Apply a DXTransform behavior to the object by using the `IDAStatics::ApplyDXTransform()` method (see the JScript sample explode.html for an example).

PART IX
Appendixes

APPENDIX A

Answers

Hour 1, "About DirectX—The Pieces That Make It Happen"

Quiz

1. What does the acronym COM stand for?

   Component Object Model

2. What macro can be used to test the result of `QueryInterface()`?

   `FAILED()`

3. Which DirectX interface supports game controllers?

   `DirectInput`

4. What is the base class from which all COM objects are constructed?

   `IUnknown`

Hour 2, "Our First Step—DirectDraw in a Windows Application"

Quiz

1. Which window handle should be passed to a DirectDraw clipper object?

   That of the topmost window of the applications.

2. What type of DirectDraw surface is created to represent the screen surface?

   The primary surface.

3. What type of surface is used to store images for later use?

   Offscreen surfaces.

4. What is the definition of blitting?

   The transfer of blocks of image data from one surface to another.

Hour 3, "Moving On—Grabbing Control of the System"

Quiz

1. What window handle must be used when setting the cooperative level?

   The top-level window for the application.

2. What function can be used to determine the display modes available?

   `EnumerateDisplayModes()`

3. When using double buffering, which surface receives blits when you redraw the screen?

   The back buffer

4. What is a complex surface?

   A surface with one or more attached surfaces.

Hour 4, "Creating the Game Loop"

Quiz

1. What is the standard frequency for the performance counter?

   3.19 MHz

2. What is the resolution of the `timeGetTime()` function?

1 millisecond

3. True or false: The performance counter is available on all systems.

False

4. True or false: The WM_TIMER message has a higher priority than other messages in the message queue.

False

Hour 5, "Make It Move—DirectDraw Animation Techniques"

Quiz

1. What are the two most common 16-bit pixel formats?

C. 5,6,5 5,5,5

2. What are the two types of color keying?

Destination and Source

3. Which function is used to set the color of a surface in DirectDraw?

`SetColorKey()`

4. Using Z-Ordering, the first image drawn is:

B. In the background

5. True or false: During cleanup you should release DirectDraw surfaces before releasing DirectDraw object interfaces.

True

Hour 6, "DirectSound—Adding Ambience and Sound Effects to Your Game"

Quiz

1. What is the purpose of the DirectSound HAL?

The HAL (Hardware Abstraction Layer) is a layer of software implemented by the DirectSound device driver that provides a uniform interface to the sound hardware.

2. How is the DirectSound HAL implemented?

   The HAL is implemented as an extension to the standard audio device driver, which means that a DirectSound driver is really just a Windows device driver with HAL extensions.

3. What is the most important feature of DirectSound?

   The most important feature of DirectSound is low-latency audio mixing.

4. To what does the term *latency* refer?

   Latency refers to the delay between when a sound is played programmatically and when the user actually hears it.

5. What happens if the user doesn't have a DirectSound driver?

   If a user doesn't have a DirectSound driver, there will more than likely be noticeable latency delays.

6. What DirectSound COM object represents a physical hardware sound device?

   The `DirectSound` object represents a physical hardware sound device.

7. How do you initially create a `DirectSound` object?

   You initially create a `DirectSound` object by calling the global `DirectSoundCreate()` function.

8. What priority level provides the safest sharing of sound resources with other applications?

   The `DSSCL_NORMAL` flag specifies the lowest priority level, which provides the safest sharing of sound resources with other applications.

9. What happens to any associated `DirectSoundBuffer` objects when a `DirectSound` object is released?

   When a `DirectSound` object is released, all associated `DirectSoundBuffer` objects are released too.

10. What happens to the playback of a sound if you set the panning value to 10,000?

    The entire left channel is attenuated, which means the sound is heard only through the right channel.

Hour 7, "Applying DirectSound"

Quiz

1. What do you do to give a sound buffer a better chance of being mixed in hardware?

The first sound buffers that are created and initialized have a better chance of being mixed in hardware because there is a limited amount of memory available on sound devices.

2. What Win32 API structure do you use to contain format information about a wave?

   The Win32 API structure used to contain format information about a wave is WAVE-FORMATEX.

3. What method in the CWave class is used to obtain raw wave data?

   The CWave::GetData() method is used to obtain raw wave data.

4. What file format serves as the basis for Windows waves?

   The RIFF (Resource Interchange File Format) file format serves as the basis for Windows waves.

5. What is the purpose of the lSirenPan variable in the cityscape application?

   The lSirenPan variable in the cityscape application keeps track of the panning value for the siren sound effect; this allows you to gradually alter the panning so that the sound moves from one channel (speaker) to the other.

6. What value do you pass to the SetVolume() method to completely silence a sound?

   To completely silence a sound, you must pass -10000 to the SetVolume() method; a value of 0 sets a sound to its original recorded volume level, whereas a value of 10000 amplifies a sound by 100 decibels.

7. Why do you not need to call the Release() method on DirectSound buffers?

   You do not need to call the Release() method on DirectSound buffers because they are automatically released when their associated DirectSound object is released.

8. What should you do if the memory associated with a sound buffer is freed?

   If the memory associated with a sound buffer is freed, you should call the Restore() method on each buffer and then reinitialize the sound data.

9. How does the move_rate variable impact the footstep sound in the cityscape application?

   The move_rate variable is used as the basis for calculating the frequency of the footstep sound; a higher value for move_rate results in a higher frequency, which makes the footsteps appear to be faster.

10. What method do you call on a sound buffer to see if the buffer memory has been lost?

    The GetStatus() method is called on a sound buffer to see if the buffer memory has been lost.

A

Hour 8, "DirectMusic—Interactive Music"

Quiz

1. What is the purpose of a synthesizer?

   The purpose of a synthesizer is to take MIDI data, or non-waveform data, and convert it into waveform output for playback.

2. What are two of the primary features of the Microsoft Synthesizer?

   The Microsoft Synthesizer has two main purposes. The first is to provide a software synthesizer that can adapt itself to any hardware available. This shields the DirectMusic programmer from having to deal directly with the hardware itself. The second major purpose is that by allowing the capability of loading DLS instruments, the waveforms that are played by virtually every sound card will sound identical.

3. How does DLS architecture allow the Microsoft Synthesizer to produce exact music sounds on different audio cards?

   The DLS architecture allows you to include any of the sampled sounds you want to use with your game. For any musical piece that is played, the DLS samples are loaded and played, thereby recreating the exact sounds you recorded.

4. What is meant by the phrase interactive music?

   Simply that the music can be changed in response to some kind of user event.

5. What is the purpose of the `IDirectMusicPerformance` object?

   The performance object manages the playback of musical data at runtime. It handles the ports, downloads wave files, manages segments and segment event notifications, and plays the segments.

6. What kind of instruments can DirectMusic use?

   Any of the included Roland GM/GS instruments, or virtually any wave file, can be used as instruments.

7. What is the difference between a segment object and a template object?

   A segment object is a collection of patterns that will be played using a default chord. A template object is a specialized segment that actually chooses a chord from a list of available chords. When a signpost occurs within the segment, a new chord is chosen and the notes following the signpost are transposed to the new chord.

8. What is an advantage of multi-track music synthesis?

Multi-track music synthesis allows creating the different parts of the music all at once. The composer can create the rhythm component in one track and follow with the melody in another.

9. What is the difference between interactive music and dynamic music?

Interactive music and dynamic music differ in their intended purpose. Interactive music is simply music that changes—in whatever way, big or small—to the actions of the user. These changes can be controlled through methods available through the IDirectMusicPerformance object. Dynamic music is created programmatically during runtime, using random selections of predetermined musical components. It is possible to combine the two concepts. For example, you could be playing dynamic music that you then modify during runtime based on a user event.

Hour 9, "Applying DirectMusic"

Quiz

1. How can I change the instruments that are playing the current segment to a different set of instruments?

You can change the instruments that are playing the current segment by creating a secondary segment from a band object that contains the instruments to which you want to change. The newly created segment object can then be played, which will cause the instruments to change to those within the new band object.

2. What are the differences between pan and volume, and where can these values be changed within the Producer application?

The pan of a note refers to whether the note is being played more to the left speaker or to the right. The volume of a note refers to the overall loudness of the volume, sometimes called velocity. These values are set in the PChannel Properties window or by relocating the instrument number on the grid on the Band Editor window.

3. What different methods can I use to change my music as it is playing?

There are several different ways to change your music. First, cue a new band for the currently playing segment object. Second, you could create several different segment or template objects, and just change between them. Third, you can add motifs or other secondary segments to enhance the currently playing segment. These can even occur in response to user events. Finally, you can change the parameters of some of the tracks of the currently playing segment. We used this in our game to change the tempo of the music.

A

Hour 10, "Introduction to 3D Concepts"

Quiz

1. The world transform converts coordinates

   b. From model coordinates to world coordinates

2. Name the three transformation matrixes that are used in the transformation pipeline.

   World, View, and Perspective

3. Name the three kinds of matrix transformation.

   Scaling, Translation, and Rotation

4. What type of transform is used to move an object in a straight line?

   Translation

5. True or false: Multiplication of matrices is commutative, meaning that it is the same in either order.

   False

Hour 11, "Rendering the 3D Scene"

Quiz

1. Back-face culling in Direct3D by default removes which faces?

   Those with a counterclockwise winding order.

2. A viewport is set on which interface?

   The `IDirect3D7` interface.

3. How many radians represent a complete revolution?

   2π radians

4. An angle of 45 degrees is equal to what angle in radians?

   Pi/4, approximately .7854.

5. What value determines how far the view can see?

   The far clipping plane.

Exercises

1. By keeping track of the objects in your scene, you can use sphere visibility as a basis to avoid rendering objects outside the viewport.

2. The best example is when you turn on alpha blending and render, for example, a projectile image using D3DBLEND_SRCCOLOR. Black areas should blend into whatever is in the destination (back) buffer; if nothing is there, a black pixel is written, making the z-buffer think something is there. A subsequent render of something behind the projectile shows a black square outline. Turning the z-buffer off helps some, but now you lose the benefit of the z-buffer, that is, obscuring the blended object where it is behind something solid. The answer is, compute the distance to each visible object, and then render far to near with the z-buffer on. You might still have occasion to render; for example, if you have a cockpit panel at the end of the cycle where you always want to see it, in which case it is usually best to disable the z-buffer.

Hour 12, "Creating Our First Direct3D Application"

Quiz

1. Which mesh type is based on a central vertex to which all other vertices connect?

   A triangle fan connects a single vertex to two or more vertices.

2. In which vertex format does the coordinates match the pixel coordinates of the screen?

   The DIRECT3DTLVERTEX contains coordinates that match those of the screen.

3. Which mesh type requires the most vertices to create?

   A triangle list uses the most triangles, containing three vertices per triangle.

4. What is the advantage of indexing a primitive?

   It allows vertices that are shared between multiple triangles to be listed only once, so less vertex storage is required.

5. What is the purpose of applying a specular color to a vertex?

   A specular color is used to create a glossy highlight on an object.

Hour 13, "Adding Textures and Z-Buffers to the Scene"

Quiz

1. What is the purpose of the z-buffer?

    The z-buffer provides pixel-level depth sorting so more distant pixels will not overwrite closer ones.

2. When would you want to use a larger bit depth z-buffer?

    Z-buffers consume video memory but are worthwhile. Perhaps the question should be, "When would you use a shallow one?" If you use shallow viewport depths, use a shallow z-buffer to keep that much more video memory free, but if you need a deep viewport, you should look for a greater z-buffer bit depth.

3. How do you define the domain of the z-buffer?

    You set the domain of the z-buffer when you set the projection matrix via the near and far clipping planes.

4. Are there occasions when you would want to disable the z-buffer?

    Yes, especially when rendering objects with alpha blending enabled.

5. If so, how do you control whether the z-buffer is enabled?

    You can enable and disable the z-buffer with the device `SetRenderState()` function.

6. What are uv coordinates?

    Uv coordinates define how a 2D texture will be positioned on rendered geometry.

7. Identify the minimum preparation required in Direct3D to render a texture mapped object.

    Assuming the device is in place, you must load a texture, provide mapping coordinates in the geometry's vertex data, and then set the device's proper texture, state, and texture stage state settings.

Hour 14, "Adding Realism Through Lighting"

Quiz

1. What are the three types of lights implemented by the Direct3D lighting pipeline?

    Point Lights, Directional Lights, and Spotlights.

2. How do you enable/disable the Direct3D lighting pipeline?

To enable lighting, call IDirect3DDevice7::SetRenderState(D3DRENDER-STATE_LIGHTING, TRUE). To disable lighting, call IDirect3DDevice7::SetRenderState(D3DRENDERSTATE_LIGHTING, FALSE).

3. How do you enable/disable a specific light in Direct3D?

To enable a specific light, call
`IDirect3DVertexBuffer7::LightEnable(lightIndex, TRUE)`, where `lightIndex` is the index of the light you want to enable. To disable a specific light, call `IDirect3DVertexBuffer7::LightEnable(lightIndex, FALSE)`.

4. How do you create a light in Direct3D?

To create a light, you call `IDirect3DVertextBuffer7::SetLight(dwIndex, lpD3DLight7)` where `dwIndex` is the index of the light you are creating, and `lpD3DLight7` is a pointer to a `D3DLIGHT7` structure.

5. What is ambient light?

Ambient light is light that has been reflected so many times that it is impossible to tell what direction it is coming from. In other words, ambient light is the general level of light in a scene.

6. What is diffuse light?

Diffuse light is light that has a certain direction. It is brightest when it hits a surface directly on.

7. What is specular light?

Specular light is the light that is responsible for making objects look shiny.

8. What is a vertex normal, and what is it used for?

A vertex normal is a vector that is specified for each vertex of an object. The Direct3D lighting pipeline uses vertex normals during lighting calculations.

9. What do the theta and phi elements of the D3DLIGHT7 structure specify, and what are their valid ranges?

They specify the angle of the inner and outer cones of a spotlight. Phi should be between 0.0 and pi, and theta should be between 0.0 and phi.

10. What are the three different attenuation factors?

Constant attenuation, linear attenuation, and quadratic attenuation.

Hour 15, "Importing 3D Objects and Animations Into the Scene"

Quiz

1. What is the name of the "special" template that can contain application-specific information?

   The "special" template that can contain application-specific information is the Header template.

2. What are the three different types of template restrictions?

   The three different types of template restrictions are open, closed, and restricted.

3. What utility can you use to convert 3D Studio files into the Direct3D X file format?

   CONV3DS can be used to convert 3D Studio files into the Direct3D X file format. CONV3DS is included with the DirectX 7 SDK.

4. Which type of Direct3D X file format is better: text or binary?

   There are tradeoffs to each file format. Text files are easy to read and edit, however they are larger and will usually take longer to load. Binary files are smaller in size, and load quickly, but they cannot be edited as easily.

5. What is the name of the template that is used to store vertices?

   The name of the template used to store vertices is the Mesh template. In addition to vertices, the Mesh template can also hold materials, vertex normals, and texture coordinates.

Hour 16, "Modeling a Complex World—Applying Physics and Object Hierarchies"

Quiz

1. Given that vector **a** = [7 3 9] and vector **b** = [8 2 4], calculate the dot product and cross product for the two vectors.

   The dot product for a·b is the scalar value 98. The vector product for aXb is the vector [-6 44 -10].

2. What are the difference between kinematics, kinetics, and inverse kinematics?

   Kinematics deals with calculating object position and orientation without regard to force. Kinetics deals with calculating the forces acting on objects. Inverse kinematics deals with calculating object orientation and position from an end-node object back to the root object.

3. What is the difference between an AABB and an OBB?

   An AABB is an axis-aligned bounding box that completely surrounds an object with the box's edges aligned with the world axis. An OBB is an oriented bounding box whose edges are aligned with the object's axis.

Hour 17, "Introducing DirectInput—Getting User Input"

Quiz

1. With respect to DirectInput, what does the term "low latency" mean?

   Low latency refers to the delay between interacting with an input device (moving the joystick left) and the game responding to the interaction (moving your character left).

2. How does DirectInput offer improved performance over the Win32 API approach to handling device input?

   DirectInput offers improved performance over the Win32 API by skirting the Win32 layered approach and communicating directly with input device drivers.

3. What COM object acts as an input device manager that allows you to enumerate and access devices for use with DirectInput?

   The DirectInput COM object acts as an input device manager that allows you to enumerate and access devices for use with DirectInput.

4. What global function must you call to create a `DirectInput` object?

   You must call the `DirectInputCreate()` global function to create a DirectInput object.

5. Why do you typically never need to call the `Initialize()` method to initialize a `DirectInput` object?

   You typically never need to call the `Initialize()` method to initialize a DirectInput object because it is called by the `DirectInputCreate()` function when you first create a DirectInput object.

A

6. What is an attached device?

An attached device is a device that is installed and physically connected to the system.

7. Why can't you just call CreateDevice() to create joystick device objects as you do keyboard and mouse devices objects?

You can't just call CreateDevice() to create joystick device objects as you do keyboard and mouse devices objects because joysticks are optional devices, and therefore can't be assumed to be available. Instead, you must first call EnumDevices() to determine what joystick devices are attached to the system.

8. What method do you call to determine to what degree an application allows an input device to be shared with other applications?

The SetCooperativeLevel() method is called to determine to what degree an application allows an input device to be shared with other applications.

9. What method must you call to obtain unbuffered input data from a device?

You must call the GetDeviceState() method to obtain unbuffered input data from a device.

10. What must you do to properly clean up a DirectInput session?

To properly clean up a DirectInput session, you must unacquire all previously acquired devices by calling the Unacquire() method on each, release the devices by calling the Release() method on each, and then release the DirectInput object by calling the Release() method on it.

11. Does reading the keyboard with DirectInput inhibit normal Windows keystroke messages?

No, and there might be times when you use DirectInput to read motion control, and then rely on WM_KEYDOWN for less time-critical commands, such as to activate a gadget. This avoids the occasion when the user strikes and releases a key between (keyboard) polling events, preventing the application from seeing the event. If you monitor WM_KEYDOWN, you're guaranteed to get the leading edge of the keystroke.

Hour 18, "Getting Through to the User— Force Feedback"

Quiz

1. What is the force of a force feedback effect?

The force of a force feedback effect is the push or resistance associated with the effect.

2. What is the magnitude of a force?

   The magnitude of a force is the strength of the force.

3. How does gain impact an effect?

   Gain serves to weaken the magnitude of an effect's force.

4. What specific direction does the direction of a force indicate?

   The direction of a force indicates the direction from which the force is acting.

5. What is a periodic effect?

   A periodic effect is an effect that repeats according to a certain pattern, or cycle.

6. What is an envelope?

   An envelope is a set of values that are used to alter the shape of an effect.

7. What is the sustain of an effect?

   The sustain of an effect is the period in the effect when the basic force magnitude is attained (after the attack and before the fade); applies only to effects with envelopes.

8. What is the attack of an effect?

   The attack of an effect is the period at the beginning of the effect when the force magnitude is approaching its sustain level; applies only to effects with envelopes.

9. What is the fade of an effect?

   The fade of an effect is the period at the end of the effect when the force magnitude is moving away from its sustain level; applies only to effects with envelopes.

10. What are the four basic types of force feedback effects?

    The four basic types of force feedback effects are constant force, ramp force, periodic, and condition.

Hour 19, "3D Sound—From Panning to Doppler Effects"

Quiz

1. How is sound created?

   An object vibrates, which causes the air around it to vibrate. The resulting pressure waves are what we perceive as sound.

2. What five factors influence our perception of sound?

   Rolloff, intensity difference, intensity delay, muffling, and visual-to-aural spatial location.

3. Which of the five factors you listed is most critical?

   Visual-to-aural spatial location is most important because your users' eyes will help convince them the sound came from the direction of the visual object.

4. Why process DirectSound3D parameter changes in a batch (if possible)?

   It reduces the overhead of parameter processing during low-latency (time-critical) processing. Your game will be more responsive.

5. True or false: Setting the sound buffer's velocity changes its spatial location.

   False. The buffer's velocity, and the listener's for that matter, are used only for Doppler effect calculations.

6. True or false: You create the listener object using a secondary sound buffer object.

   False. You obtain a listener from the primary sound buffer. The effect of this is you can have only a single listener.

7. What is rolloff?

   The sound pressure attenuation that occurs over distance. The farther away from the sound's source you are, the lower in volume the sound will be when it reaches your ears.

8. What is Doppler shift?

   The frequency shift involved when an object making a sound is also in motion. The object's motion is added (or subtracted) from the frequency of the sound pressure waves.

9. Must the orientation vectors be at 90 degrees to each other?

   Absolutely. If they're not, DirectSound3D will make them so (and probably not to your liking).

10. Can you request DirectSound3D to manage the relative velocities between the sound buffer and the listener?

    Yes, and it's a good idea to do so. Simply pass `DS3DMODE_HEADRELATIVE` to `IDirectSound3DBuffer::SetMode()` and you're set.

Hour 20, "Putting Your Game on the Net— Writing Multiplayer Titles"

Quiz

1. What is a DirectPlay Service Provider? What is an example of one?

A DirectPlay Service Provider is a specific network transport that handles actual network transfers, the details of which are hidden by the DirectPlay interface. TCP/IP (sockets) is an example of a service provider.

2. What two main models of communication are used by DirectPlay?

Peer-to-peer and client/server are the two main communication models used by DirectPlay.

3. What is a callback function and how is it used?

A callback function is a function passed as a parameter to various IDirectPlay4 functions. The callback function is called by the IDirectPlay4 function many times, usually once for each item in a list.

4. What is meant by deterministic data?

Deterministic data is data that can be calculated based on previous values. Non-deterministic data cannot be calculated and must be transmitted over a communications link.

5. How do you create a secure session?

You can create a secure session by using the `SecureOpen()` function, and setting the dwFlags parameter to `DPOPEN_CREATE`.

6. How are DirectPlay players and groups identified?

DirectPlay players and groups are identified by a `DPID` type. They are initially created using the `CreatePlayer()` and `CreateGroup()` functions.

7. What is meant by guaranteed messaging? How do you use it?

Guaranteed messaging means that DirectPlay provides a guarantee that a message will be delivered to its destination. This is not done by default, and you must use the `DPMSG_GUARANTEED` flag when using the `Send()` function to send the message.

8. What is the `DPSESSION_MIGRATEHOST` flag used for in the `DPSESSIONDESC2` structure?

The `DPSESSION_MIGRATEHOST` flag is used to indicate that if the session host in a peer-to-peer game exits, the duties of session host will automatically migrate to another computer participating in the session.

9. How might you send a message to all players in a session?

By setting the `idTo` parameter in a call to `Send()` to `DPMSG_ALLPLAYERS`, you will—in effect—send a broadcast message to all the players in a session.

A

10. Can an `IDirectPlay4` object be used for more than one session?

    Actually, no. An `IDirectPlay4` object cannot be used for more than one session. To create or join multiple sessions, you must create instances of multiple `IDirectPlay4` objects. One for each session. All the `DPID` values representing players and groups are specific to each session, and thus, to each `IDirectPlay4` object.

Hour 21, "Game Central—Creating Lobbies"

Quiz

1. How does the game client relay information back to the lobby?

    By using the functions `SendLobbyMessage()` and `ReceiveLobbyMessage()`, a game client is able to relay information to a lobby client.

2. How does the lobby pass the connection information needed to a game client?

    The lobby uses the function `SetConnectionSettings()` to inform the game application of the connection parameters needed to connect to the other computers in the session. It can also pass this information in the call to `RunApplication()`.

3. When does the lobby begin running a lobby-aware game, and how does it start it?

    The lobby begins running the game client when it receives the `DPMSG_STARTSES-SION`. It launches the game by calling the `RunApplication()` method.

4. How does the lobby obtain a list of games that are lobby-aware and that can be launched by a lobby?

    By calling the `EnumLocalApplications()` method, and providing a pointer to a `LPDPENUMLOCALAPPLICATIONSCALLBACK` function.

5. How do you create an address representing an Internet based server for a game to connect to?

    You can use the function `CreateAddress()` to create an address for a game client to connect to using a DirectPlay service provider. Alternatively, you can use the `CreateCompoundAddress()` function to create a complex address composed of many elements.

6. What is meant by a "lobby-aware" game?

    A lobby-aware game is a game that contains code to check whether it was launched by a lobby. If the application determines that it was, it gets the connection settings for the game via a call to `GetConnectionSettings()`.

7. Which client can change information about a session?

Only the game client (or server) which first called Open() to create a session, and set the DPOPEN_CREATE flag can change any session data.

Hour 22, "Adding Video with DirectShow"

Quiz

1. What is a DirectShow filter?

A DirectShow filter is a module that processes some part of the media stream.

2. What is a DirectShow pin?

A DirectShow pin is used so that filters can communicate data in a unified way.

3. What happens if the destination rectangle of a DirectShow stream is larger than that of the stream itself?

The video will be stretched to fit the destination rectangle, just like a regular DirectDraw surface.

4. Mention a few streaming and nonstreaming DirectShow supported media formats.

Streaming formats: MPEG-1, MPEG-2, MPEG-3, ASF (Advanced Streaming Format), VOD (Video On Demand), RA (Real Audio) version 4, and RV (Real Video) version 4.

Nonstreaming formats: AVI, MOV, MIDI, WAV, SND, and Indeo 5.

5. What would happen if you put a 20MB nonstreaming video on your homepage?

The browser would load all 20MB before showing anything, angering a lot of users visiting your Web site.

Hour 23, "Bring Surfaces to Life with DirectX Transform"

Quiz

1. What is the difference between the PMARGB32 and ARGB32 pixel formats?

The PMARGB32 is premultiplied to increase performs during alpha blending.

2. What kind of objects do 2D transforms operate on?

DXSurfaces.

A

3. What kind of objects do 3D transforms operate on?

   `Direct3DRMMeshBuilder3`.

4. Why is reading pixels from a procedural surface usually slower than reading pixels from a normal surface?

   Reading pixels from a procedural surface is usually slower than reading pixels from a normal surface because procedural surfaces must use a mathematical function to create the pixel value.

5. Why are procedural surfaces smaller than normal surfaces?

   Procedural surfaces are generally smaller than normal surfaces because they do not have to store a large two-dimensional array of pixel data.

6. What function must you call before you create your `DXTransformFactory` object?

   `CoInitialize()`.

7. What type of string (ANSI or Unicode) does the `DXTransformFactory::LoadImage()` function take?

   Unicode.

8. In what order should you release DirectX Transform objects?

   You should release objects in the opposite order that they were created.

9. What type of transform is most likely to take advantage of the `DXEffect` interface?

   Transition-type transforms are most likely to take advantage of the `DXEffect` interface.

10. What does the progress variable in the `DXEffect` object stand for?

    The progress variable in the `DXEffect` interface is a value between `0.0` and `1.0` that stands for the percentage-complete of a transition-type transform.

Hour 24, "Integrating Media Into Web Pages and Applications with DirectAnimation"

Quiz

1. In what languages can you program DirectAnimation using both normal COM interfaces and through automation interfaces?

   C++, Visual Basic, and Java.

2. Which two scripting languages are most commonly used to code DirectAnimation on Web pages?

   JScript and VBScript.

3. What interface is used to create and modify other behaviors in DirectAnimation?

   `IDAStatics`

4. What is the base interface from which all DirectAnimation behavior objects derive their functionality?

   `IDABehavior`

5. How do you assign a background image for a `DAViewerControl` based animation? For a `DAViewerControlWindowed` animation?

   For a `DAViewerControl`, you set the background by overlaying the foreground image on the background image with `IDAStatics::Overlay()` and assigning it to the `IDAViewerControl::Image` property. For `DAViewerControlWindowed`, you can simply assign it to the `IDAViewerControlWindowed::BackgroundImage` property.

6. What are the two units of measurement available for DirectAnimation?

   Meters and pixels.

7. At what point does the internal timer used by DirectAnimation start running?

   When `IDAViewerControl::Start()` is called.

8. If you use a DirectDraw surface with a `DAView` object, what version of the DirectDraw interfaces must you use?

   You must use `IDirectDraw` and `IDirectDrawSurface` (the first version).

Exercise

The basic process to make the rotation behavior modifiable at runtime is to follow these steps:

- Add two member variables to the `CDASampleView` class: a double for the speed value called `m_spd`, and an `IDANumberPtr` for the variable speed rotation behavior called `m_rotnbr`.

- Add an `IDAStaticsPtr` member variable to the `CDASampleView` class called `pS` and initialize it in the WM_CREATE handler instead of the local variable used before (remove the declaration of `pS` in the WM_CREATE handler).

- Add a handler for the WM_DESTROY message, and set the `IDAStaticsPtr` member `pS` to NULL (ps = NULL;) in this handler before the call to the base class `OnDestroy()` handler so that it is released before the window is destroyed.

- Add a message handler for the WM_KEYDOWN message. In it, add a switch statement with handlers for VK_UP and VK_DOWN key codes.

- Create the modifiable X rotation behavior with the following code by replacing the call to Rotate3Rate() for the x-axis with the following. Note that you change from Rotate3Rate() to Rotate3Anim() with a call to IDAStaticsPtr::Integral() to turn the modifiable rotation value into a rate.

```
m_spd = 2;
m_rotnbr = pS->ModifiableBehavior(pS->DANumber(m_spd));
IDATransform3Ptr rotx = pS->Rotate3Anim(pS->XVector3,
➥pS->Integral(m_rotnbr));
```

- In the handler for the VK_UP key, add the following code:

```
m_spd += .5;
m_rotnbr->SwitchTo(pS->DANumber(m_spd));
```

- In the handler for the VK_DOWN key, add the following code:

```
m_spd -= .5;
m_rotnbr->SwitchTo(pS->DANumber(m_spd));
```

- You can now recompile and run the sample. When you hit the up or down arrow keys, the rotation of the object will speed up or slow down accordingly.

APPENDIX B

Prepare Your Application for Distribution with DirectSetup

Programming a Windows application can be a complex task. But few tasks in Windows programming can be as difficult (and as scary) as installation pro-gramming. After all, even though Windows provides a hardware-independent platform for general programming purposes, installation program-ming requires you to be cognizant of various and subtle version differences for *each* and *every* thing you install. That means every DLL, every COM object, every data file, every driver, every application—*everything*. That includes things you *didn't* write yourself. And not just any version of any given thing you want to install will work with every version of every Windows component in the field. If installations don't scare you, you haven't been doing this long enough.

That's what makes DirectSetup so interesting. It's a very different installation architecture from any other Microsoft installation support tool. This is likely because of the fact that Microsoft wants developers to use the DirectX technology, and DirectX affects hardware and driver installation like few other application-level technologies. Rarely will you otherwise install a video driver, for example, unless you're completely reloading a copy of Windows itself. Installing traditional applications is hard enough, but installing new hardware drivers can easily toast a user's system in microseconds. And your customer support will have to pick up the pieces. Over the phone. Guess who pays for that. Scared yet?

In fact, DirectX installation is so complicated that Microsoft advises against any attempt to install DirectX components yourself. Just don't do it. Don't even consider it. Use DirectSetup.

Now that I have your attention, I'll begin a high-level overview of DirectSetup. DirectSetup's goal is to relieve you of the burden of installing the myriad of components and registry changes DirectX will require on any given user's system. This is a wonderful boon for you, the installation developer, because much of the installation code has already been written for you. And unlike most other Microsoft redistributable packages, DirectSetup is completely customizable. Microsoft provides the core functionality and allows you to tailor the user interface. Most other Microsoft redistributables come as pre-compiled executables that you can, at best, install silently. You get an overall error code from the installation process, if you're lucky. And in most cases, you won't be so lucky. So your own installation application will install some required Microsoft technology and have no clue whether the installation was successful or not! (Can you say Microsoft Data Access Components 2.1?)

NEW TERM DirectSetup, on the other hand, allows you to provide a callback function. If you're not familiar with the term, a *callback function* is code you provide that some other routine will execute at some time in the other routine's lifetime. Callbacks, as they are known, are typically used for notification. And so it is with DirectSetup. This is what is so different about DirectSetup—you have the ability of providing your own user interface to the installation process while still using DirectSetup's expertise to actually do all the work. This is very cool.

DirectSetup is used not just for DirectX installation and upgrade in an application-installation sense. It is also used to set up a networked computer for DirectPlayLobby interaction. If you're interested in DirectPlayLobby and establishing remote users, be sure to review the online DirectSetup documentation. See especially the `DirectXRegisterApplication()` and `DirectXUnRegisterApplication()` API calls.

I'll leave the design of the user interface to you. If you've just completed a hot 3D first-person shooter game, you have plenty of artwork lying about. Use it! Instead, I'll concentrate on a high-level look at how you use DirectSetup. I can't cover all the details here, so consider this an introduction. For the details, see the DirectX online documentation and the DirectSetup sample provided with the DirectX SDK.

To begin, everything you'll require to install DirectX on an end-user's system is contained in the `Dxf\Redist\DirectX7` directory on your DirectX SDK CD-ROM. The information in this directory is not installed on your development system when you install the SDK, so you'll have to go back to the CD-ROM and copy the entire contents of the redistributable directory to your media in a folder named DirectX (case-insensitive). The data in this directory does have localized installation items, so you can reduce the size of the directory by removing products for languages you don't intend to support. In any case, when you begin the DirectSetup process, you will have to provide DirectSetup with a path to this information contained on your installation media. Obviously, DirectSetup will copy the appropriate information from this directory to the user's system.

You will also need to copy the DSetup.dll and DSetup32.dll DLLs to your setup program's root directory. DirectSetup uses these DLLs to provide the installation support you're looking for.

After you have this preliminary work complete, you can turn your attention to developing your part of the installation—the user interface. Your user interface could consist of multiple message boxes or be much more complex. However, DirectSetup will provide you with message box-like information through the callback function that I mentioned earlier.

You begin the installation by calling the DirectX `DirectXSetup()` API method, which looks like this:

```
int WINAPI DirectXSetup(HWND  hWnd,
                        LPSTR lpszRootPath,
                        DWORD dwFlags);
```

It's fairly simple to use—simply provide the Window handle for the controlling user interface window, the path where DirectX will find the redistributable information, and a flag from this set:

- `DSETUP_DDRAWDRV`
- `DSETUP_DIRECTX`
- `DSETUP_DSOUNDDRV`
- `DSETUP_DXCORE`
- `DSETUP_TESTINSTALL`

Normally, you'll install everything DirectX requires, so Microsoft recommends that you use the DSETUP_DIRECTX flag. The DSETUP_TESTINSTALL flag is special, in that it's used only during the installation program's development (that's you). If this flag is set, the installation proceeds as if it were a true installation without actually installing anything. Note that you won't receive some installation errors, such as when the user's disk becomes too full to continue.

If successful, DirectXSetup() will return one of two values:

- DSETUPERR_SUCCESS
- DSETUPERR_SUCCESS_RESTART

If you are returned DSETUPERR_SUCCESS, you're done. If you see DSETUPERR_SUCCESS_RESTART, restart the system. If you receive any other value, it's an error value, and you'll need to take some appropriate action (crashing is not an appropriate response!).

If you intend to customize the installation by providing a callback function, you must register it with DirectSetup prior to calling DirectXSetup(). There is no requirement that you implement a callback function, and if you elect *not* to, simply *don't* register any callback function with DirectX. However, if you do want to tailor the installation, you do so through a callback function you register using the DirectXSetupSetCallback() API call:

```
INT WINAPI DirectXSetupSetCallback(DSETUP_CALLBACK Callback);
```

Remember that you must register your callback function *before* you make the DirectXSetup() call.

The callback function, known to DirectSetup as DirectXSetupCallbackFunction(), has this signature:

```
DWORD DirectXSetupCallbackFunction(DWORD Reason,
                                   DWORD MsgType,
                                   char *szMessage,
                                   char *szName,
                                   void *pInfo);
```

The Reason parameter will be an item from this list:

- DSETUP_CB_MSG_BEGIN_INSTALL
- DSETUP_CB_MSG_BEGIN_INSTALL_DRIVERS
- DSETUP_CB_MSG_BEGIN_INSTALL_RUNTIME

- DSETUP_CB_MSG_BEGIN_RESTORE_DRIVERS
- DSETUP_CB_MSG_CANTINSTALL_BETA
- DSETUP_CB_MSG_CANTINSTALL_NOTWIN32
- DSETUP_CB_MSG_CANTINSTALL_NT
- DSETUP_CB_MSG_CANTINSTALL_UNKNOWNOS
- DSETUP_CB_MSG_CANTINSTALL_WRONGLANGUAGE
- DSETUP_CB_MSG_CANTINSTALL_WRONGPLATFORM
- DSETUP_CB_MSG_CHECK_DRIVER_UPGRADE
- DSETUP_CB_MSG_INTERNAL_ERROR
- DSETUP_CB_MSG_NOMESSAGE
- DSETUP_CB_MSG_NOTPREINSTALLEDONNT
- DSETUP_CB_MSG_PREINSTALL_NT
- DSETUP_CB_MSG_SETUP_INIT_FAILED

I won't belabor each item here because you'll find the meaning behind each listed in the online documentation. From this list, though, you can see many are errors, whereas some are status. Check the result in your callback and manage the situation as required.

MsgType will contain bits appropriate for the MessageBox() API call (an exception is when MsgType is zero, in which case no action is required from the user, and status can merely be displayed). For example, if DirectX wanted to ask the user if it was okay to overwrite a given file, the callback would be executed, and MsgType would be set to MB_YESNO ¦ MB_DEFBUTTON2.

szMessage is simply a localized status string you can use to display information to the user regarding the installation or error condition.

If DirectX is installing or upgrading a driver, szName contains a string representation of the driver. Note this parameter will usually be NULL. The exception is if Reason is DSETUP_CB_MSG_CHECK_DRIVER_UPGRADE. In this case, the pointer will indicate a valid string.

pInfo is a pointer to a DSETUP_CB_UPGRADEINFO structure and is only valid if Reason is SETUP_CB_MSG_CHECK_DRIVER_UPGRADE. The DSETUP_CB_UPGRADEINFO structure is quite simple:

```
typedef struct _DSETUP_CB_UPGRADEINFO {
    DWORD UpgradeFlags;
} DSETUP_CB_UPGRADEINFO;
```

B

UpgradeFlags tells DirectSetup how to proceed with the upgrade of a given driver:

- DSETUP_CB_UPGRADE_CANTBACKUP
- DSETUP_CB_UPGRADE_DEVICE_ACTIVE
- DSETUP_CB_UPGRADE_DEVICE_DISPLAY
- DSETUP_CB_UPGRADE_DEVICE_MEDIA
- DSETUP_CB_UPGRADE_FORCE
- DSETUP_CB_UPGRADE_HASWARNINGS
- DSETUP_CB_UPGRADE_KEEP
- DSETUP_CB_UPGRADE_SAFE
- DSETUP_CB_UPGRADE_UNKNOWN

The flags are fairly self-explanatory, but for additional details, again refer to the online documentation.

If you're using a callback to customize the installation, you can expect the callback to be executed many times during the execution. Simply examine the Reason parameter and take some action based upon its contents. If you're being asked to request information from the user, you might find the MsgType parameter useful. If there is something to display to the user, use the szMessage information. And if DirectX is installing a driver, you might need to manage the szName and pInfo data.

Be sure to take a look at the sample DirectSetup installation program supplied with the SDK, DInstall.exe. Not only should that help address any questions you might have regarding using the DirectSetup API, but it should also provide you with a hefty amount of source code you can easily swipe and make your own. That's always an added benefit!

INDEX

Get **FREE** books and more...when you register this book online for our Personal Bookshelf Program

http://register.samspublishing.com/

SAMS

Register online and you can sign up for our *FREE Personal Bookshelf Program*...unlimited access to the electronic version of more than 200 complete computer books—immediately! That means you'll have 100,000 pages of valuable information onscreen, at your fingertips!

Plus, you can access product support, including complimentary downloads, technical support files, book-focused links, companion Web sites, author sites, and more!

And you'll be automatically registered to receive a *FREE subscription to a weekly email newsletter* to help you stay current with news, announcements, sample book chapters, and special events, including sweepstakes, contests, and various product giveaways!

We value your comments! Best of all, the entire registration process takes only a few minutes to complete, so go online and get the greatest value going—absolutely FREE!

Don't Miss Out On This Great Opportunity!

Sams is a brand of Macmillan Computer Publishing USA.

For more information, please visit *www.mcp.com*

Other Related Titles

What's on the Disc?

The companion CD-ROM contains all the authors' source code, samples from the book, and some third-party software products.

Windows 95, Windows 98, and Windows NT 4 Installation Instructions

1. Insert the CD-ROM disc into your CD-ROM drive.

2. From the desktop, double-click the My Computer icon.

3. Double-click the icon representing your CD-ROM drive.

4. Double-click the icon titled START.EXE to run the installation program.

5. Follow the onscreen instructions to finish the installation.

If Windows 95, Windows 98, or Windows NT 4 is installed on your computer and you have the AutoPlay feature enabled, the START.EXE program starts automatically whenever you insert the disc into your CD-ROM drive.

Read This Before Opening the Software